ALSO BY PAGE SMITH

Rediscovering Christianity
Killing the Spirit
Redeeming the Time
America Enters the World
Dissenting Opinions
The Rise of Industrial America
Trial by Fire
The Nation Comes of Age
The Shaping of America
The Constitution
Jefferson, A Revealing Biography
Religious Origins of the American Revolution
A Letter from My Father
The Chicken Book
A New Age Now Begins
Daughters of the Promised Land
As a City Upon a Hill
The Historian and History
John Adams
James Wilson

DEMOCRACY ON TRIAL

THE JAPANESE AMERICAN

EVACUATION AND RELOCATION IN

WORLD WAR II

PAGE SMITH

SIMON & SCHUSTER
New York London Toronto Sydney Tokyo Singapore

SIMON & SCHUSTER
Rockefeller Center
1230 Avenue of the Americas
New York, NY 10020

Copyright © 1995 by Page Smith
All rights reserved,
including the right of reproduction
in whole or in part in any form.

SIMON & SCHUSTER and colophon are registered trademarks
of Simon & Schuster Inc.

Designed by Hyun Joo Kim

Manufactured in the United States of America

10 9 8 7 6 5 4 3 2 1

Library of Congress Cataloging-in-Publication Data

Smith, Page
    Democracy on trial : the Japanese American evacuation and
relocation in World War II / Page Smith.
        p.   cm.
    Includes bibliographical references and index.
    1. Japanese Americans—Evacuation and relocation, 1942–1945.
2. World War, 1939–1945—Japanese Americans.
3. Japanese Americans—Civil rights.   I. Title.
D769.8.A6S64   1995
940.53′15039556073—dc20

95-17957
CIP

ISBN 0-684-80354-2

Acknowledgments

I would like to gratefully acknowledge the assistance of Father John Yamazaki, the Reverends Sumio Koga and Heihachiro Takarabe, Jeanne Wakatsuki Houston, and Ruth Asawa. And, of course, to Frances Rydell, dear friend and typist *par excellence*. Needless to say, my interpretations and conclusions are entirely my own.

In memory of Mei Higashiura, who, with

her colleague Akio Akagi opened for me the

soul of Japan.

And for Ruth Asawa, who has borne witness

through her art to the evacuation and relocation.

Contents

PART 4: THE RETURN

Introduction

Pearl Harbor

ON THE MORNING OF DECEMBER 7 (DECEMBER 8 IN JAPAN) JAPANESE war planes, flying from carriers, bombed Pearl Harbor, the base of the United States Pacific Fleet. Although the full extent of the damage inflicted by the Japanese bombers was initially suppressed to avoid giving information to the enemy, enough was known to make clear that it was the most horrendous defeat in the nation's history. Indeed it was soon clear that it was the most brilliantly conceived and executed surprise attack in the annals of modern (or ancient) warfare. Over 2,400 American sailors, soldiers, marines, and civilians were killed, 1,178 more wounded, and 149 planes destroyed on the ground or in the water. The battleships *Arizona, Tennessee, West Virginia,* and *California* were sunk, the *Oklahoma* capsized, and the *Nevada* run aground to prevent its sinking. All this had been accomplished, it turned out, at the cost of thirty Japanese planes and pilots.

The evident intention of the Japanese Imperial Command was to destroy, or at least neutralize, the U.S. Pacific Fleet, an undertaking of unimaginable audacity.

American shock and indignation was accentuated, if possible, by the fact that the U.S. government believed it was involved in negotiations with the Japanese over the terms of a U.S. embargo on shipments of oil to Japan. Up until December 7 Americans had been engaged in a heated and often acrimonious debate over the role of the United States in what was called the "European war," a conflict that had begun September 1, 1939, with the invasion of Poland by Hitler's armies. England had immediately declared war on Germany. Four weeks later the world was startled by the announcement that communist Russia and her bitterest rival, Nazi Germany, had agreed to divide Poland between them in what may have been history's most cynical deal. What followed was a seven-month interval referred to as "the phony war," in which little military action took place. (The Russians, to be sure, invaded Finland, and, after suffering several humiliating defeats, forced the Finns to surrender on March 12, 1940.)

In the United States the struggle took place between those political leaders who pointed to the defeat of American hopes for a peaceful world order by the Versailles Treaty as an excuse for staying out of the conflict between the Allies (France and England primarily) and Nazi Germany, and those Americans who, like President Franklin D. Roosevelt, were convinced that the United States must eventually become involved.

Those opposed to the U.S. involvement, the so-called isolationists, rallied under the banner of an organization called "America First." Prominent among the Firsters was the American aviation hero Charles A. Lindbergh.

In the spring of 1940, the phony war turned deadly serious when Germany invaded Denmark (April 9) and struck with startling speed against Norway. The Germans were aided and abetted by pro-German Norwegians, called Quislings after the accommodating Norwegian prime minister, Vidkun Quisling.

A month later, the German armies swept into Holland and through Belgium. Belgium surrendered on May 28 and two weeks later, Italian leader Benito Mussolini, like a vulture anxious to share in the spoils, declared war on France and Great Britain (June 10). Three days later the Germans rolled into Paris in an eerie reprise of World War I.

In the United States President Roosevelt's compromise with the isolationists was to insist that he had no intention of initiating the entry of the United States into the European war while insisting that we must give all assistance short of war to Great Britain in its struggle for survival against the Nazis, meanwhile arming for the defense of the United States against what were now known as the Axis Powers, Germany and Italy (and, at this point, a prospective ally—Russia), soon to be joined by Japan.

At the end of 1941, the European war took another startling turn when

Germany tore up the Russo-German Non-Aggression Pact (the basis of the dismemberment of Poland) and attacked its presumed ally along a two-thousand-mile front. The Japanese took advantage of the occasion to move into Indochina and Thailand, and the United States reacted by shutting off oil exports to Japan. When the prime minister, Prince Fuminaro Konoye, resigned he was succeeded by General Hideki Tojo.

One immediate consequence of the Japanese aggression in the Far East was a rising level of anxiety on the West Coast of the United States and an increasing hostility toward Japanese Americans in that region. By the fall of 1941, the public attitude toward the Japanese in California had grown so negative that Robert Gordon Sproul, president of the University of California, called together a number of prominent California liberals to form an organization whose specific purpose would be to combat such hostile attitudes. The group called itself the Northern California Committee for Fair Play for Citizens and Aliens of Japanese Ancestry. A weightier group could hardly have been assembled. In addition to Sproul, Ray Lyman Wilbur, president of Stanford, and Robert Millikan of the California Institute of Technology were on the committee, as were representatives of the American Friends Service Committee and the American Civil Liberties Union. The main reason that the lead was taken by the presidents of the three most prestigious universities in the state was that all three institutions had a number of Nisei (second-generation Japanese Americans) enrolled in undergraduate and graduate programs.

Another important voice speaking out against anti-Japanese attitudes was that of the Federated Council of Churches of Christ in America. Justice for Japanese Americans was not a new concern of the council. It had been an outspoken opponent of the Immigration Act of 1924 excluding Japanese immigrants as "aliens ineligible to citizenship." Alarmed by the anti-Japanese sentiment that accompanied the passage of the act, the Pacific Coast Christian churches had sent delegations to a conference in San Francisco to discuss ways of combating prejudice toward the Japanese. A series of joint Caucasian-Japanese meetings and conferences had followed. By 1940 interracial conferences and gatherings were commonplace. In Los Angeles a citywide worship service was held on February 10, 1940, at the Union Church to mark the 2600th anniversary of the founding of Japan. The well-known church leader E. Stanley Jones, whose special concern had been the Japanese mission churches in the U.S. declared that the best way to stop Japanese aggression would be to give that nation free access to oil and other raw materials embargoed by the United States *because* of Japanese aggression. He wrote to President

Roosevelt urging him to open U.S. trade with Japan. If the President were to do so, Jones argued, Japan would not only "doubly reciprocate but might also possibly end up as an ally."

All such efforts were, of course, simply whistling in the wind. The die had been cast many months, indeed perhaps several years, before at the point when the Japanese high command had decided to launch surprise attacks on Allied (and especially American) military bases in the Pacific. Such intricate military forays require long lead times of staff planning. The coordinated assaults on western colonies and bases constituted, like the attack on Pearl Harbor, an overall operation of such an extent and complexity as to be literally without precedent. The Japanese high command combined the most up-to-date military technology of the West with its own ancient tradition of stealth and cunning.

In November, Prime Minister Hideki Tojo threw down the gauntlet to the Western powers by announcing, under the banner of the Greater East Asia Co-Prosperity Sphere, that the influence of Great Britain and the United States must be eliminated from the Far East. President Roosevelt's response was to appeal on December 2 to Emperor Hirohito to help in preserving peace between Japan and the United States by defining more specifically the legitimate aims of Japan in the area. The Japanese response was the attack on Pearl Harbor. The next day it took thirty-four minutes for the House and Senate to declare war. The only dissenting vote was that of Jeannette Rankin of Montana. Rankin, oddly enough, had been in Congress when it declared war against Germany in 1917. A dedicated pacifist, she had voted against the declaration of that war as well.

Traumatic as the attack on Pearl Harbor was, in the days that followed that unparalleled disaster the news of the progress of Japanese arms throughout the Pacific area was, if possible, even more alarming. The day after Pearl Harbor, Japanese naval and air forces attacked Guam and Wake Island, strategic U.S. protectorates. Resistance on Guam ended five days later and Wake Island's garrison surrendered the following week.

On December 10, the British battleships *Prince of Wales* and *Repulse* were sunk by Japanese aircraft. British forces in Hong Kong surrendered to the Japanese on Christmas Day. By January 2, Manila, the capital of the Philippines, had been occupied by the Japanese, and U.S. and Filipino National Guard troops had taken refuge in the fortress of Corregidor on the Bataan Peninsula.

Eight weeks after Pearl Harbor, Lieutenant General John Lesesne De-

Witt, head of the Western Defense Command, was authorized by President Roosevelt in Executive Order 9066 to require, at his discretion, the evacuation from the area under his command all persons who, in his judgment, might pose a threat to the security of the United States. At DeWitt's request, the order comprehended all "alien enemies," Germans, Italians and Japanese, who might aid an enemy in the event of an invasion of the West Coast. The invaders, it was assumed, would be the Imperial forces of Japan.

Under the authority ceded to him by Executive Order 9066, General DeWitt on March 2 ordered "all persons of Japanese ancestry," "alien enemies" and American citizens alike, to "voluntarily" evacuate Military Area No. 1 of the Western Defense Command. That order, which was soon changed from "voluntary" to "controlled" evacuation, affected drastically and permanently the lives of some 120,000 "persons of Japanese ancestry" living in the defense command area. Of these 41,089 were Issei (alien enemies who were barred from becoming American citizens). Among the Issei some 25,000 were men and 15,000 were women. The disparity in the number of men and women—10,000 or so—represented, in the main, the so-called Issei bachelors, a class or group quite distinct in themselves. The roughly 71,896 Nisei were men and women who were American citizens by virtue of having been born in the United States. Many, as we shall see, enjoyed dual citizenship; they were citizens of both Japan and the United States. Among the American-born Nisei were a large number of young men and women who had visited Japan. In addition some 9,000 of the so-called Kibei had been sent back to Japan for part or all of their education. Many of the Kibei spoke little English and were strongly oriented toward what they considered their homeland.

To account for the events that took place between December 7 and General DeWitt's decision to order the evacuation of "all persons of Japanese ancestry," I believe that it is necessary to review the relationship between Japan and the United States, a relationship that began, for all practical purposes, with Commodore Matthew Perry's famous voyage to Japan in 1853 which opened up that exclusive, essentially feudal society to the modern industrial world.

Part 1

A DIVIDED
PEOPLE

Chapter 1

THE UNITED STATES "OPENS" JAPAN

Perry, given the assignment of establishing diplomatic and commercial relations with Japan, had taken some pains to collect all the information he could about the land and its people. The principal, reasonably current source, was the archive of Dutch trade with Japan.

What Perry learned at third hand, largely through the United States ambassador to Holland, stood him in good stead when his little fleet anchored in the harbor of Shimoda. There he had (among other things) to contend with an Imperial edict "which proclaimed that anyone who carries a letter from abroad will be put to death with his entire family." His arrival, not surprisingly, produced consternation. It appeared at first to the alarmed Japanese, who had never seen a steam vessel before, that the harbor was filled with burning ships. More careful inspection revealed that the clouds of smoke apparently came from engines that drove the odd-looking vessels. The governor of the province where Perry made his landfall was in a quandary as to how to respond to the arrival of the unwelcome foreigners. The *bakufu* was informed but no one dared tell the Emperor. He overheard discussion of Perry's arrival at a Noh play and promptly took to his bed.

Perry, for his part, showed a remarkable instinct for the convoluted formalities of Japanese diplomacy. Combining tact and firmness with an understanding of the importance of "face," he announced his determination to negotiate some kind of agreement with the Japanese government and then sailed away to China for six months or so to allow the *bakufu* time to decide how best to respond.

The president of the *bakufu* decided to poll the daimyo and found them sharply split on the question of whether to enter into any negotiations with the foreign devils. Indeed, Perry's appearance served to polarize the daimyo into pro- and anti-shogun factions in a conflict that would not be fully resolved for some fourteen years.

The *bakufu* majority, recognizing the military weakness of the country, argued that Japan should make a "show of commerce and intercourse, and thus gain time to equip the country with a knowledge of naval architecture and war," adding that the most essential thing was "that Christianity should not be admitted in the train of foreign trade."

Afraid that a flat rejection of Perry's overtures might mean war with the United States and dismayed at the depleted condition of the nation's treasury and the lack of a trained army, the *bakufu* finally agreed to meet with Perry. A pavilion was built and thousands of armored soldiers lined up to receive the admiral and his staff. Nine armed samurai were concealed beneath the floor of the pavilion in case of treachery on the part of the Americans. The agreement between Perry and Japanese officials (it hardly deserved the name of a treaty) provided for the safety of American sailors and the possibility of consulates if either nation desired to establish them.

The agreement concluded, Perry lingered on in Japan for some four months. A short telegraph line was strung to demonstrate the marvel of modern communication and a miniature railroad erected with cars large enough to carry a person. Telescopes, which proved to be especially prized treasures, were distributed to important officials. Perry was, in turn, presented with gifts, among them a series of erotic paintings that he noted were proof "of the lewdness of this exclusive people." In lieu of photographers, Japanese printmakers were assigned to make a record of the Americans' visit. An American tourist who wants to know how he and his countrymen look to the Japanese can hardly do better than consult the voluminous record of Perry's visit compiled by the Japanese artists. The Americans appear as large, untidy men with outsized noses (Western noses are especially amusing to Japanese).

Before his little fleet left Japanese waters, Perry wrote in his diary that he was "inclined to believe that, by just and honorable relations with the educated classes, they will in time listen with patience and respectful attention to the teachings of our missionaries. They are in most respects a refined and rational people. . . . *Indeed, I have never met in any part of the world, even in Europe, with a people of more unaffected grace and dignity* [emphasis in original]. . . . In the practical and mechanical arts the Japanese show great dexterity, and when the rudeness of their tools and their imperfect knowledge of machinery are considered, the perfection of their manual skills appear marvelous. Their handi-craftsmen are as expert as any in the world, and, with a freer development of the inventive powers of the people, and their readiness in adapting them to their own uses, the Japanese would not long remain behind the most successful manufacturing nations. Their curiosity to learn the results of the material progress of other people, and their readiness in adapting them to their own uses, would soon, under a less exclusive policy of government which isolates them from national communion, raise them to a level with the most favored nations." Perry went on to predict: "Once possessed of the acquisitions of the past and present of a civilized world, the Japanese would enter as powerful competitors in the race for mechanical success in the future."

The Japanese were also impressed. It was reported that a Japanese official said to the court physician: "These Americans are certainly different from the British and others. They seem to be sincere and honest; I hear that their military order is strict and they know the rules of politeness. From now on the Japanese had better stand on friendly relations with them."

The "opening up" of Japan was still not easy. Townsend Harris, who appeared with his young German-American interpreter, Henry Heusken, at Shimoda as the first U.S. consul in 1856, had every possible impediment placed in his path by Japanese officials. Harris, for his part, was determined to wrest a commercial treaty from the *bakufu*. That body was acutely aware of the hazards to its own survival in such a treaty. What followed was a strange comedy of procrastination and delay. Harris, established at Shimoda, his every move reported to the *bakufu*, insisted upon an audience with the shogun at Edo (now Tokyo). Finally, after months of negotiations, the audience was agreed to.

When Harris and Heusken made their way to Edo to be received by the shogun, they discovered that bridges had been built over intervening streams, the roads repaired and, in many places, swept. All travel along the Tokaido, the great road between northern and southern Japan, was forbidden during the journey and an official proceeded them shouting, *"Shita ni iro,"* "Kneel down, kneel down." "And all the common people," Heusken wrote, "knelt down and remained in an attitude of deepest respect until we had passed. . . . The sight of all these human beings, as good as I am or even better, on their knees began to disgust me. Here a white-haired old man bent his trembling knees and lowered his venerable brow; there a young girl turned her lovely face toward the ground and remained in a humiliating posture . . . if I had been allowed at least to kneel with her, the thing would have had a different complexion."

On his arrival in Edo, Harris received a gift of seventy pounds of bonbons from the shogun, "enough," Henry Heusken wrote, "to fill the shop of a confectioner and make ill an infinite number of children."

When Harris realized that his Edo hotel was swarming with spies he insisted that they be removed. He was told that they were simply there to honor him by serving him. To this Harris replied that he considered himself and the President of the United States both dishonored at the refusal of the officials to remove the servant-spies and that such obduracy on the part of the officials was "sufficient reason for the United States to declare war on Japan." Harris's strenuous objections to being spied on by the retainers assigned to him prompted the *bakufu* to pursue the gentler course of assigning him a spy-mistress, a gift he apparently accepted without demur.

On December 7, 1857, Townsend Harris and Henry Heusken proceeded to the audience with the shogun in considerable pomp. Harris's *norimon,* or palanquin, was carried by twelve men and guarded by ten samurai. After him came his umbrella-bearer, his shoe-bearer, and his horse. Heusken had much the same arrangement but with only three guards. A million people lined the streets by Heusken's estimate. "Among these thousands of faces, of men, women, boys, and young girls, not one showed signs of antipathy, anger, or even of indifference . . ." he wrote. "I was . . . swept with admiration in viewing the order which reigned over this vast multitude. If people pressed too far forward, thereby preventing the free passage of our procession, an officer shaking his paper fan sufficed to cause hundreds of persons to step back." Heusken could not refrain from imagining such a scene in the United States: "How much profanity seasoned by a liberal use of spirituous beverages! What a tumult; how many hurrahs and shrill cries!"

At the shogun's palace the Americans found the members of the *bakufu* lying prostrate on their faces before the shogun. Harris conveyed the good wishes of President James Buchanan (Japanese accounts say that the

American envoy "shouted," apparently a reference to the fact that he spoke in a normal tone of voice, whereas it was customary to whisper).

Heusken was deeply impressed by "the simplicity of the Court of Edo, the noble and dignified bearing of the courtiers, [and] their polished manners, which would do honor to the most illustrious court. . . ." But he could not avoid certain gloomy reflections about the future of a country "which has become so dear to me." "Is the progress really progress," he asked himself, "this civilization really civilization for you? I, who have admired the artlessness of your inhabitants as well as their simple customs, who has seen the abundance of your fertile fields, who has heard everywhere the happy laughter of your children, and never been able to discern misery, I fear, Oh, my God, that this scene of happiness is coming to an end and that the Occidental people will bring here their fatal vices."

The courteous reception of Harris by the shogun was, it turned out, misleading. It was the *bakufu* that wielded the real power and the members of that body were caught on the horns of a dilemma. The subsequent negotiations between Harris and the "Great Commissioners," as Heusken called them, were prolonged and, certainly, from the Japanese point of view, excruciating. As the principal officer of the *bakufu* put it, on the one hand Japan "is threatened with war and conquest if she does not grant certain privileges. On the other her people will revolt if she does grant these privileges." There was a special problem with Article VII of the treaty proposed by Harris, which provided for the right of free travel around Japan; this, the *bakufu* insisted, was simply impossible. The power of the government rested on its following "faithfully the ancient laws and customs of the Empire," as Heusken reported the discussion. "If it suddenly deviated from these laws and opened the Empire to foreigners, there would be a mass uprising. . . ." On February 20, 1858, Heusken noted impatiently in his diary: "Today one of the most alarming, boring, tiring, erratic, ignorant, and childish conferences we have had so far with the sages of Japan."

The lesson taught by a China pillaged and exploited by the West was not lost on the Japanese. Finally, Harris got his treaty, which provided that five Japanese ports should be opened to trade with U.S. vessels. In those towns Americans might legally reside, and "they shall have the right to lease ground, and purchase the buildings thereon, and may erect buildings and warehouses."

By 1862 further treaty negotiations allowed Americans to live in Edo and Osaka. "Americans residing in Japan shall have the right to employ Japanese as servants or in any other capacity." Americans who committed "offences against Japanese" were to be tried in American consular courts and were to be punished by American law. Most important of all in terms of this work, Article VIII stated: "Americans in Japan shall be allowed the free exercise of their religion, and for this purpose shall have the right to erect suitable places of worship. No injury shall be done to such buildings, nor any insult offered to the religious worship of the Americans. . . . The Americans and Japanese shall not do anything that may be calculated to excite religious animosity. The government of Japan has already abolished the practice of trampling on religious emblems. . . ." Article VIII turned out to be all the opening that American missionaries needed to begin their labors.

The treaty did not, however, end the resistance to the intrusion of Western powers. Townsend Harris's own situation remained precarious in the extreme. An attempt on his life was thwarted, but his interpreter, young Henry Heusken, was murdered, although the motive was apparently less political than material. Europeans who tried to travel about without protection were murdered and the slogan *Sonno joi*—"Revere the Emperor, drive out the barbarians"—was often heard. The daimyo of Satsuma and Choshu took aggressive actions against foreigners, and the British in turn shelled the seaport town of Kagoshima.

Although officials of the *bakufu* traveled to the United States and certain pro-shogun samurai were likewise favored, many daimyo and samurai remained bitterly opposed to such contacts. The enemies of an open Japan were primarily the *goshi,* who called themselves *shishi,* "men of high purpose." It was they who assassinated Ii Naosuke, a member of the *bakufu,* for allegedly supporting foreign trade. Indeed, the *goshi* began a reign of terror, using the weapon of assassination to remove officials who supported trade with the West.

In the struggle between the *bakufu* of the shogunate and the *shishi,* whose initial intentions were purely reactionary—to rally around the puppet Emperor at Kyoto in order to thwart opening Japan to foreign trade— the *shishi,* in effect, did two things: they destroyed the credibility, as we would say today, of their own samurai class by their incessant warfare and by their program of assassinations; also, paradoxically, many of them became converted to a policy of foreign trade. With the capitulation of the shogun, the ablest of them stepped forward as officials of the Imperial restoration.

Yet to describe the *shishi* simply as reactionaries would be misleading.

While it was true that they glorified sword fighting and the ancient Shinto ideals and were violently anti-foreign, they were also in revolt against the decadence and mismanagement of the late Tokugawa shogunate and the *bakufu.* A typical *shishi* pamphlet entitled *Hanron,* "Discussion of the Fiefs," attacked the corruption of the shogunate and charged that the daimyo had become indolent and selfish, taking no care for the poor, who often died of starvation. "Offices are constantly filled by unqualified men, and corruption is so rife as to defy all attempts to suppress it," the writer declared.

In their final acceptance of Western influence, the *shishi* justified their actions on the grounds that only by so doing could Japan become a modern military power able to hold her own against European interlopers and exploiters. At the same time, from the earliest contacts, American ideas and ideals, as well as practical American achievements, exercised a particular fascination for those Japanese exposed to them.

The result was a profound ambivalence. The Japanese historian Kamei Sunsuke describes the two dominant attitudes as *hai-Bei* (revere America) and *sai-Bei* (revile America) and writes of the pendulum-like swings of admiration and hostility that are reflected in the writings of the Japanese who have visited America. Sunsuke groups the reactions of Japanese visitors to America as the affirmative *Sasuga ni America* (Ah, that is the America I know!), and *Kore demo America ka* (Can this be America?). Sometimes the same individual, of course, expresses both attitudes alternatively. One of the first Japanese visitors, Yukichi Fukuzawa, came to the United States in 1860. In his autobiography he wrote of his experiences: "Before I left Japan I was a brash and boastful chap, full of self-confidence and afraid of nothing. Then when I arrived in America I suddenly found myself bashful and tonguetied. . . . ." At parties "the ladies and gentlemen showed us this thing called 'dancing,' but I could not understand it at all. The men and women seemed to hop around the room in the strangest manner, something one could only describe as comical." Fukuzawa was astonished to find that the descendants of George Washington were not held in the highest regard like the descendants of the famous Tokugawa Ieyasu. "In the areas of science and technology nothing really surprised me," he wrote, "but I was at quite a loss to understand even the simplest aspects of American life and society."

Because of his interest in the United States, Yukichi Fukuzawa lived in constant fear of assassination. In his autobiography he wrote: "Nothing can be worse, more unsettling, more generally fearful, than this shadow of assassination. No one without the actual experience can really imagine it. It is something indescribable by word or by any artifice of the writing brush.'' Marked for death, he had a secret trap door built into one of the closets of his house. This was to be his means of escape if ''ruffians'' came to kill him. Reflecting on assassination as a political tool, Fukuzawa wrote: ''To recount the history of assassination since the beginning of our foreign intercourse—in the beginning, people simply hated all foreigners because all foreigners were 'impure' men who should not be permitted to tread the sacred soil of Japan.'' Two prominent politicians were attacked by Choshu clansmen simply because they were ''scholars of foreign affairs.'' Jiro Hanawa ''had his head cut off by an unknown man because of his sympathy for foreign culture.'' When Fukuzawa's friends and colleagues Tojo and Tezuka were assassinated, ''I knew,'' he wrote, ''that the hands of the assassins were not far from my door.'' Fukuzawa had a number of narrow escapes but none so harrowing as an attempt on his life by a young cousin, Masuda Sotaro, who professed a warm friendship while secretly planning to kill Fukuzawa. One evening while Fukuzawa was entertaining a friend, Sotaro hid in his yard, hoping to kill him, but Fukuzawa and his friend spent the night drinking and Sotaro crept away at dawn. In his autobiography, Fukuzawa noted, ''all students and interpreters of Western languages constantly risked their lives.''

When the heir to the Tokugawa shogunate assumed the office in 1867, a group of the most powerful daimyo and samurai insisted that he give way to the Emperor Mutsuhito, who was then fourteen. The shogun acquiesced, and the leadership of the country passed into the hands of the rebellious samurai.

The Meiji (Enlightened Rule) Restoration marked the beginning of the modern era for Japan. The samurai who had constituted the Tokugawa bureaucracy were swept aside by the samurai who had opposed the shogunate. Their motto was *Fukoku kyohei,* or ''rich country, strong arms''; they proclaimed *Shin Nippon,* the New Japan. In 1869 the daimyo of Choshu, Satsuma, and Tosa offered their lands to the Emperor as a step toward the abandonment of feudalism. In August 1871 an Imperial decree abolished the feudal fiefs and substituted seventy ''prefectures,'' which were, in effect, the successors to the fiefdoms of the daimyo, while most of the daimyo were appointed governors of newly created prefectures. The transition from fiefdoms to prefectures did not seriously disrupt the identification of the inhabitants of the prefectures with their feudal past. Since the subjects of the daimyo had owed absolute loyalty to their lords and had fought for centuries under their banners against rival lords, their basic identification was with their *shoen,* or manor, rather than with the nation. Different fiefdoms observed different customs and spoke dialects that often could not be understood by the members of other fiefs. In this case the Emperor became an even more important figure since he alone represented the history and unity of the nation. In a deep sense the *Emperor was the nation:* amid the chaos of shifting alliances and rival ideologies, the only fixed point was the Divine Emperor.

In addition to making the Emperor the unifying symbol of the nation, the reformers undertook to adapt to Japanese use the best aspects of every Western power. Precisely how that happened is almost impossible to say. China was experiencing the outside world in a wholly different and quite devastating manner. The world was imposing on China its ideas of what China should be (primarily a source of wealth to the Western world). Yet when we think of the enormous power of tradition in Japan and the profoundly conservative nature of its culture the fact that it should have almost instantly undertaken to adapt from the thoroughly alien Occidental world everything it considered usable is one of the puzzles of history. In the end it seems to come down to the inspiration of a handful of remarkable men, individuals imbued with the tradition of scholarship. There was, after all, a precedent. More than a thousand years earlier, the Japanese had taken a great part of their culture, their language, their art, and their religion from China. Perhaps buried in some residual gene, was a disposition, long neglected, to adapt the forms of another culture. Still, who could imagine that it would prove equally susceptible to a culture as wildly different as that of the United States or, more generally, of the West. The United States was, to be sure, the most seductive. In the first six years of the restoration, 209 Japanese students, one third of all those who went abroad, went to the United States.

Perhaps the most notable event of the Meiji Restoration was the Iwakura, or Imperial, mission, made up of leaders of the new government, who toured the world with the explicit purpose of surveying all the social and political institutions of Western industrial nations in order to determine those best suited to the needs of the New Japan. In San Francisco on the first leg of their famous journey, Okubo and Kido, members of the Imperial embassy, were astonished to discover that the bellboys and waiters in the hotel were avidly following a local election. It seemed evident to them that some form of general education must be instituted in the New Japan. Okubo is said to have declared: ''We must first educate the leaders, and the rest will follow,'' to which Kido purportedly replied: ''We must educate the masses; for unless the people are trained, they cannot follow their leaders.''

When the delegation reached New York, the lawyer-diarist George Templeton Strong noted: ''From early morning . . . the town was agog about the Japanese ambassadors. Streets were already swarming when I went downtown. . . . Every other person, at least, was manifestly a rustic or a stranger. Flags everywhere.'' The Japanese finally appeared, sitting in their carriages ''like bronze statues, aristocratically calm and indifferent. . . . Broadway was densely filled . . . for many blocks.''

When the mission arrived in Washington, Kume Kunitake, one of the members, was impressed by the fact that President Ulysses Grant lived simply in the White House without guards or companies of soldiers to protect him and visitors roamed freely about the White House lawns. The members of the mission were received with ''the epitome of warmth and cordiality,'' and given a ''big send-off'' that ''caused us to recall with some embarrassment,'' a member of the mission wrote, ''the traditional Asian opinion of Westerners as barbarians. As a new age dawns it is imperative that we not forget we are emerging from the bad dreams of centuries of isolation and beginning to bask in the warmth of world intercourse.'' It was the spirit of individual ''independence and self-reliance'' in the United States that most impressed the members of the mission. There were no princes and nobles, no aristocracy to monopolize the wealth and the land, ''therefore it is a new creation with newly discovered land . . . the people are immigrants . . . it was actually the result of the arrival of a group of the most self-reliant and capable people in Europe. In addition the land was vast, the soil fertile, and the people productive. . . . That is how America came to be what it is.''

Not all reactions were so favorable. When the visitors were taken to the Smithsonian Museum they were shocked to see mummies displayed among stuffed birds and animals. ''These foreigners,'' one member of the mission wrote, ''are not nicknamed barbarians for nothing.''

Nitobe Inazo, a young samurai who spent three years in the United States, recalled with embarrassment how, on his arrival, he had claimed that all progress was the work of ''the upper class, the nobility . . . the common people are like fertilizer, nourishing the soil of a growing nation.'' ''There are no common people in the U.S.,'' his American acquaintances replied. ''We are all aristocrats; everyone is king.'' The notion seemed to Nitobe ''truly magnificent,'' and he contrasted it with the doctrine of the *Tso Chuan:* ''There are ten classes of people. Each

pays homage to the one above, and the one at the top serves the god."
The American attitude seemed to Nitobe far more humane.

Back in Japan the members of the mission set about remodeling Japanese society on a grand scale. The daimyo were dealt with by bestowing on them titles ranging from prince to baron, by giving them military commands, and by involving the ablest of them as officers of the government. The roughly two million samurai were more of a problem. Idle, restless, and disgruntled with the turn of the historical tide, they were the major obstacle in the program of modernization. Some were absorbed into the army as officers but there were far too many. They were first put on pensions and then the pensions were withdrawn as they became too great a drain on the nation's finances. Gradually, their privileges were whittled away. They were forbidden to carry two swords and wear their traditional hairdo; commoners were also allowed two names. Finally, in 1877, the discontent of the samurai broke out in an open rebellion in Satsuma province. The new conscripted army of commoners quickly suppressed it and with that defeat the power of the samurai as a class was broken, although individual samurai continued to play a central role in Japanese life both as leaders in the war clique and as liberal opponents of that clique.

If Japan was to be taken seriously as a modern nation it clearly had to have a written constitution, that essential badge of political modernity. Prussia was the model and Bismarck the counselor. After six years of labor the more conservative Japanese leaders produced a document that, under the guise of parliamentary government, kept power firmly in the hands of a small ruling class. A few hundred thousand tax-paying males were allowed to vote. The principal power rested with an upper House of Peers, appointed by the Emperor and made up of nobles and certain rich merchants with close ties to the nobility. The lower house had virtually no power. It was little more than political window dressing.

One of the most important social reforms was the abolition of the caste system of farmer, craftsman, and merchant. All of these traditional classes were lumped together as "commoners." The lowest class, a class comparable to the Untouchables of Hindu Indians, was the *burakumin* (literally "people of the village"). The *buraku* were divided into the *hinin* and the *eta*. They were the people who slaughtered animals for meat butchers and preparers of meat and those who worked with leather, tanners and shoemakers. The rationale were that these people were irredeemably inferior because they broke the Buddhist edict against killing animals and were thus unclean.

Restrictions on travel were abolished and the Japanese were set free to discover their own country.

Equally important was the Imperial Rescript on Education establishing a system of compulsory public education. The members of the Imperial Mission had been profoundly impressed by the capacity of the industrial West, especially the United States, to utilize the energies of ordinary people, of the "masses." This seemed to them—the *genro* as the ruling class came to be called—to be the consequence, primarily, of public education. What was perhaps most striking of all to the members of the mission was the relationship in the West between learning and daily life. In China and Japan learning was a monopoly of the aristocratic class and it was valued for its very uselessness. It was an adornment, prized to the degree that it was esoteric. The Iwakura Mission discovered that there was another kind of education that produced engineers, doctors, chemists, and teachers. The Imperial edict, establishing a system of compulsory education, declared: "Although learning is essential to success in life for all classes of men, yet for farmers, artisans and merchants, and for women, it has been regarded as beyond their sphere; and even among the upper classes, aimless discussions and vain styles of composition only were cultivated, from which no practical use could ever be deduced. Much poverty and failure in life are owing to these mistaken views. It is intended that henceforth education shall be so diffused that there may not be a village with an ignorant family, nor a family with an ignorant member."

The rescript, thoroughly Confucian in spirit, covered much more than education and is worth quoting at some length: "Ye, Our subjects be filial to your parents, affectionate to your brothers and sisters; as husbands and wives be harmonious, as friends, true; bear yourselves in modesty and moderation; extend your benevolence to all; pursue learning and cultivate the arts, and thereby develop intellectual faculties and perfect moral powers; furthermore advance public good and promote common interests; always respect the Constitution and observe the laws; should an emergency arise, offer yourselves courageously to the State; and thus guard and maintain the prosperity of our Imperial Throne coeval with heaven and earth. . . . The Way set forth is indeed the teaching bequeathed by Our Imperial Ancestors, to be observed alike by Their Descendants and subjects, infallible for all ages and true in all places."

In the state-prescribed curriculum of the public schools every student took six hours of English a week in addition to music, manual training, gymnastics, law, and economics. The graduates, in the early years, were required to take positions as schoolteachers themselves.

The Imperial rescript became a "sacred" document. One of the four major Japanese holidays, Meiji-setsu was celebrated every year on November 3 and marked by the reading of the rescript by Japanese dignitaries wearing white gloves as a mark of respect for the Emperor.

The issuing of the Imperial Rescript on Education was clouded by the assassination of Yurei Mori, a well-known advocate of "liberal" or "progressive" education. Shigenobu Okuma, president of Waseda University, was also assassinated for having pro-Western sentiments.

The officials of the Meiji government were obviously not attracted to republican government. Japanese journalist-intellectuals came to the United States and, in many instances, returned home champions of democracy, but those in whose hands the power of government rested had no notion of creating a democratic Japan. They simply wished to appropriate as much as they could of the industrial and, especially, military technology of the West while establishing a military dictatorship under the aegis of the Emperor as the symbol of a unified Japan. They therefore undertook to use such "democratic" institutions as free public education not to encourage democracy, but conversely to impose an ever greater uniformity, discipline, and respect for authority on the mass of the Japanese people. The specific and inescapable manifestation of this intention was dressing male students in German naval uniforms and the girls in the middy blouses of British sailors. The whole educational apparatus thus became an adjunct of the military ambitions of the state. The student who had spent a substantial portion of his youth in a uniform, donned one to go off and fight for the glory of Nippon when he graduated. The Japanese educational system, ostensibly adopted from the West where it was considered the essential adjunct of democracy, was made into the first totalitarian education system in the world. It thereby revealed something about the nature of education that Western idealists were reluctant to face. Education could be a both liberating influence, opening up the possibilities for the individual, or a repressive and inhibiting system that imposed rigid doctrines on a mass of passive students, making them willing servants of the state.

The receptivity of the Iwakura Mission to Western know-how brought with it a great fad for American and European styles. In the words of an American missionary: "A regular foreign fever set in. Everything domestic came to be looked upon as inferior; everything from abroad was accepted as superior. . . . Chairs, tables, and other foreign furniture became common. All officials were required to dress in European style. Soldiers, policemen, postmen, and railway employees, were put into foreign uniforms.'' Japanese women abandoned kimonos for French fashions. "Food cooked, or supposed to be cooked, in foreign style, became the rage."

WHILE THE RULING-CLASS *GENRO* WERE BUILDING THE FIRST MODERN authoritarian military regime, Christian missionaries were busy creating, in a manner that seemed at the time harmless enough, quite a different spirit. The missionaries had found it uphill going initially. Even after the treaty of 1858, Christianity was discriminated against and indeed forbidden by government edict. Japanese who professed Christianity were subjected to persecution. One prominent Japanese Christian was assassinated and Western missionaries, although allowed to reside in Yokohama, were forbidden to evangelize. The missionaries took the opportunity to learn Japanese so that they could carry out their mission when official sanction was received. With the beginning of the Meiji Restoration, missionaries encountered a surprisingly receptive atmosphere. The reasons were various. In the enthusiasm of the New Japan movement when everything Western had an enormous attraction, the missionaries were one of the principal means by which Japanese might learn English; moreover the long coexistence of Shintoism and Buddhism bred both a tolerance of diverse religious views and a degree of skepticism about the claims of any; science, which seemed to many Japanese the magic talisman of modernization, bore hard on many of the basic beliefs of Shintoism and Buddhism; moreover, religious feeling of any sort was at a low ebb in the late Tokugawa period. While Buddhism and Shintoism preserved rituals and ceremonies that were important in the life of the people, they did not have regular services in the manner of Christian churches, did not preach, and were only slightly involved in the daily life of most Japanese. The missionaries with their schools, and soon their colleges, seemed to hold the key to the new learning that, it was assumed, must underlie the New Japan.

Finally, the leaders of the New Japan suspected that there might be a link between railroad trains and Christianity. The West, after all, presented itself as a "Christian civilization" and most Americans and Europeans did not hesitate to say that the technological marvels that they had achieved were due, more than anything else, to superiority of "Christian civilization.'' Prince Bismarck, in addition to advising the Japanese emissaries, who so admired the efficiency of the Prussian state and the Prussian army, that they must have colonies to guarantee them supplies of raw materials, also declared that they must become a Christian nation if they were to enjoy the rewards of capitalist technology. The German philosopher-historian Max Weber was soon to argue that Protestant Christianity was the essential precondition to capitalism; the notion had already occurred to the leaders of New Japan.

One of the first acts of the Meiji government had been to send a dozen young samurai to Yokohama to be taught English by a missionary teacher, and half of the members of the Imperial Mission of 1872 had been his students. A language school was also started in Edo and missionaries were soon teaching in the Imperial University.

In addition to these favorable auspices there was the fact that the Christian missionaries put a great emphasis on the doctrines of human brotherhood and equality. Far more than other Westerners, they avoided acts and gestures that implied they thought the Caucasian race superior to the Oriental. They also preached a seductive doctrine of redemption and salvation.

In part because of the language barrier, the missionaries concentrated on developing an independent Japanese Christian church and in doing so they showed an ecumenical spirit that would have been impossible at home, joining interdenominational missionary associations and working together with a surprising degree of unanimity. In the words of one missionary: "It may be questioned whether so many distinct bodies [over twenty], engaged in the same occupation, ever before worked together so harmoniously." At a ministerial convention in 1872, the members unanimously declared: "Whereas the church of Christ is one in Him, and the diversities of denominations among Protestants are but accidents . . . [they] do obscure the oneness of the church in Christendom . . . we, as Protestant missionaries, desire to secure uniformity in our modes and methods of evangelization, so as to avoid as far as possible the evil arising from marked differences."

The first Japanese Christian church, consisting of nine young men, was organized in Yokohama in March 1872. Fifteen years later there were 344 churches with an adult membership of 34,000, 164 native Christian ministers, 209 male missionaries and 178 females. Soon after the establishment of the missionary schools, promising scholars were sent to American colleges like Amherst and Williams. Katayama Sen, traveling to the United States from a missionary school to attend Grinnell College, found

that "being a student at an American college was one of the most carefree, enjoyable existences one could imagine." His fellow students were
from wealthy families. "Naive, inexperienced, still too young to know
the hardships of life, they came together in search of knowledge. They
shared their daily lives like one big happy family. . . . The relationship
between the students and the faculty was quite close. The faculty entertained the students in their homes and the townspeople did likewise. . . .
Yes, life at college was . . . footloose and fancy free. We were content
as long as we passed, even if only barely. The rest of the time we enjoyed
ourselves. . . . At that time the United States was a free country, and the
mood of imperialism was not as strong as it is to-day," Katayama added,
in a sentence that spoke volumes of the changing relationship between
Japan and the United States by the end of the century.

Doshisha (One-Purpose) University was founded in 1876 to meet the
"rapidly opening demands for a thoroughly scientific yet Christian education." The samurai Yamamoto, a man high in the councils of the
government, had urged its establishment at Kyoto. Prince Ito, Barons
Kido and Tanaka, successive prime ministers, and Count Inouye, the
minister for foreign affairs, were all supporters of the enterprise. The
argument often used in the United States to raise money for the support
of the university was that "a representative government could be stable
and salutary in its influence only if founded upon a pure morality. For that
morality Christianity furnished the only basis." It thus followed, in the
words of I. H. Neejima, a Japanese Christian, that the university should
have a department "in which men could receive under Christian influences the legal and economic instruction necessary to make them intelligent voters and legislators." The purpose of the school was not merely
to "train up . . . men of science and learning, but men of conscientious-
ness and sincerity. . . . We believe it is our special work to nourish the
spirit of self-reliance in our students' bosoms, and to train up a self-
governing people."

A number of graduates of Doshisha University went on to do graduate
work in the United States at Harvard, MIT, Johns Hopkins, Worcester
Polytechnic Institute, and similar institutions. The graduates of the wom-
en's schools favored Mount Holyoke, Wellesley, and Smith, all of whom
had produced a number of missionary women. When Isobel Anderson
visited a girls' school in Tokyo, she discovered that the headmistress,
Miss Tsuda, had graduated from Bryn Mawr. The students sat at desks
rather than on traditional Japanese pillows on the floor and when Anderson visited the girls' rooms she found Christian precepts hanging on the

shoji; photographs of relatives, and such items as might well adorn the walls of an American girl's dormitory room. European as well as Japanese food was served and the girls played baseball, which to older Japanese was "very unladylike." In the evening the pupils played games in both English and Japanese.

In the early years of mission work, meetings were commonly held in theaters and public halls. At a Noh theater in Kyoto in 1881 a dramatic meeting took place attended by over three thousand people that lasted nine hours. Many of the phenomena of revival meetings were evident at such gatherings—extreme expressions of emotion, tears of repentance or joy, and ecstatic cries, strange for such a reserved people as the Japanese.

One of the principal stumbling blocks to conversion of the young, otherwise the most likely material for the missionaries' work, was the frequent opposition of their parents and the strong tradition of filial obedience. On more than one occasion mothers threatened suicide if their sons or daughters persisted in the determination to become Christians and at least one instance is recorded where a mother carried out her threat.

A notable aspect of the conversion of Japanese to Christianity was the discovery of the sermon. There had been no public speaking in Japan prior to the Meiji Restoration for the simple reason that there had been no politics. Now when the word was set free as it had been in the early days of the European Reformation, there was a kind of intoxication with its power. Japanese preachers, to the surprise and pleasure of their missionary sponsors, turned out to be remarkably gifted speakers, using humor, eloquence, and homely illustrations to make theological points. Although the Kyoto meeting was exceptionally long, many of the new converts listened to four hours of sermonizing at a time. Services were often interrupted and Japanese Christians were abused, stoned, and occasionally killed. Stonings indeed were so frequent that some Christian groups saved the stones to use in the foundations of their churches.

The mode of conversion adopted by the missionaries came to be known as "evangelistic touring." This touring took them to Japanese homes in many parts of the country and made them thoroughly familiar with Japanese inns, where they were not infrequently disturbed by fellow guests "who called in *geishas* (low women who sing, play, and dance) and make the night hideous with their revelry," in the Reverend Gordon's words. They also provided a chance for common baths, which were "sure to lead to a frank discussion of national peculiarities, elements of strength and weaknesses, with the need and methods of reform, both in America and Japan; they also tempt to a mutual relation of personal experiences, and so lead on to earnest words from the depths of hearts light and warm with Christian love." It might be an interesting topic for a dissertation writer to pursue—the role of the Japanese hot tub in the spread of Christianity.

There were, in fact, two classes of Christian schools; those run by missionaries and those run by Christianized Japanese. By 1890 there were at least ten of the latter with six hundred pupils.

An important category of missionaries were the medical missionaries. Their mission was healing, not conversion, but they undoubtedly extended the influence of the denominations that sent and supported them.

It was in the matter of the changed status of women that the missionaries took the greatest pride. A classic Confucian text on the role of women entitled *The Great Learning for Women* declared "that it is a girl's destiny . . . to go to a new home and live in submission to her father-in-law and mother-in-law." She must be above everything else entirely submissive to her husband's and her in-laws' will. Women were not supposed "to sit in the same room, to keep their wearing apparel in the same place, or to transmit to each other anything directly from hand to hand. . . . The five worst maladies that afflict the female mind are: Indocility, discontent, slander, jealousy, and wiliness. Without any doubt, these five maladies infest seven or eight out of every ten women, and it is from these that arises the inferiority of women to men. . . . Such is the stupidity of her character that it is incumbent on her in every particular to distrust herself, and to obey her husband." Only men could enter Nirvana or become Buddhas and even Amida, the merciful Buddha, could only take women to paradise by changing them first to men. A wife had to receive her husband's concubine in her home and could be divorced for any one of seven reasons or sold into a house of ill-repute by parents, husband, or brother. Besides cooking and cleaning, tea making, flower arranging, music, and verse were considered the only appropriate feminine activities. It was not only that Christian missionaries insisted that women were equal with men in the eyes of God, it was also that in the relationships between missionaries and their wives and in the persons of female missionaries, Japanese men and women saw models of the "new" relationship of men and women. "The character of our missionary ladies," the Reverend Gordon wrote, "has made a profound impression. Their intelligence, their interest in affairs, their independent, self-sacrificing lives, their teaching abilities, their executive powers, have had an incalculable influence."

Gordon told of four samurai girls who vowed to commit seppuku—

ritual suicide—if their parents would not allow them to attend a mission school. Two of them, denied the opportunity, did kill themselves, one was saved by her uncle, himself a Christian, and one was allowed to attend the mission school. By 1890 there were fifty-one mission schools for girls for a total enrollment of 4,249, and the graduates, many of whom married influential men of liberal persuasion, represented an influential network of Christian women. *Joqaku Zasshi,* the *Magazine of Female Education,* was one product of the conversion of Japanese women.

The missionaries also prided themselves on developing the new field of comparative religion. "It should not be forgotten," one of them wrote, "that this is a *Christian* science . . . nowhere else than among Christian peoples have the inductive sciences found a hospitable home." Japan provided an ideal field of study in comparative religion because the attentive scholar could observe the relationship between the teachings of three great religions—Shintoism, Buddhism, and Confucianism—and the daily lives of believers.

One of the most notable missionary reforms was in establishing Sunday as a day of rest for all public officials and for the teachers and pupils in public schools. In addition, by 1885 seventeen thousand pupils were enrolled in Christian Sunday schools.

When the first Imperial Parliament met in 1890 there were twelve professed Christians among its three hundred members, and the speaker of the House of Commons, appointed by the Emperor, was a Christian. Much the same was true of the prefectural assemblies.

By the mid-1890s a strong reaction against Westernization set in—political, social, and religious. In religion, biblical criticism questioned the authenticity of the Scriptures and Unitarians announced their devotion to the Buddha. Young Japanese who visited the United States often came back disillusioned by the rawness and crudity of American life and deeply offended by racial prejudices that they encountered. One such was Uchimurka Kanzo, who visited in 1884, writing "My idea of the Christian America was lofty, religious, Puritanic. I dreamed of its templed hills and rocks which rang with hymns and praises . . . how *could* it be a land of mammon-worship and race-distinction! . . . The image of America as pictured in my mind was that of a *Holy Land.*" Uchimura was especially dismayed at the treatment of the Indians: "After a 'century of dishonor,' the copper-colored children of the forest, from whom the land was wrested by many a cruel and inhuman means, are still looked upon by the commonality as no better than buffaloes or Rocky Mountain sheep, to be trapped and hunted like wild beasts." Whatever "sympathy and Christian brotherhood" had been shown to blacks at the time of the Civil War "to atone for the iniquity of merchandizing upon God's images" had long since been forgotten and the grossest forms of discrimination were experienced by them daily. "Time fails me to speak of other unchristian features of Christendom," Uchimura wrote. Gambling, drinking, cock fighting, football matches, and prizefights "more inhuman than Spanish bull-fights," oppressed him, along with lynchings, "demagoguism in politics . . . denominational jealousies in religion . . . capitalists' tyranny and laborers' insolence . . . of millionaires' fooleries . . . men's hypocritical love toward their wives; etc., etc., etc. Is this the civilization," he asked, "we were taught by missionaries to accept as an evidence of the superiority of the Christian religion over other religions? . . . If it was Christianity that made the so-called Christendom of to-day, let Heaven's eternal curse rest upon it! Peace is the last thing we can find in Christendom. Turmoils, complexities, insane asylums, penitentaries, poor-houses! . . . O heaven, I am undone! I was deceived!" Uchimura gave up his newfound Christian faith only to come back to it years later.

When Isobel Anderson traveled in Japan in 1910, there were some 140,000 Christians and, so she was told, 29,420,000 Buddhists, of whom 18,000,000 were described as "Believing Buddhists." There were 19,390,000 Shintoists, but only 710,000 "Believing Shintoists," or substantially less than five percent.

The fact that the officials of the restoration were deeply concerned about the role of religion in New Japan was indicated at a conference of Buddhists, Shintoists, and Christians called by the minister of education in 1910. "What Japan needs is more vital religion," he told the delegates, "and I ask you to become more in earnest in bringing your faith to bear upon the lives of our people."

Chapter 2

IMPERIAL JAPAN

As BEFITTED A WARLIKE NATION, JAPAN'S GREATEST EFFORTS WERE directed at military and naval technology, most significantly for a previously nonseafaring nation, ironclad battleships and naval gunnery. By the end of the century the Japanese were ready to challenge Russia for hegemony in the Far East. War broke out in 1904, largely as a result of Russian arrogance, and that nation suffered a series of disastrous defeats. The chaotic condition of Russia's economy and the decline of its power had been recognized throughout Europe but the notion that a European power, however decadent and corrupt, could be seriously challenged by an upstart Asian nation that had telescoped a hundred years of industrial development into a few decades was quite inconceivable.

The startling military setbacks of the Imperial Russian army spread dismay throughout Europe and revolutionary zeal among the Russian people. The American philosopher William James declared that the defeat of Russia constituted one of the "great modern turning points of history." Henry Adams, a shrewd observer of international politics, wrote to a friend, "Russia is dropping to pieces. . . . Revolution is inevitable."

Of all American political figures, Theodore Roosevelt was the one most preoccupied with Japan and Japanese culture. The code of the samurai warrior fascinated him; he clearly considered himself a kind of American equivalent. Roosevelt prevailed on a Japanese naval cadet, studying at the Naval Academy at Annapolis, to teach him jujitsu and tried to arrange for a match between an American amateur wrestling champion and a Japanese master of jujitsu to determine which was the superior art. In his respect for the fighting qualities of the Japanese and his well-founded apprehension about their imperial designs, he showed his sure instinct for realpolitik. The Japanese victories against Russia pointed up an awkward and possibly dangerous development on the western coast of the United States. State legislatures were busy passing discriminatory legislation against the Japanese, as they had done earlier against the Chinese. "I am utterly disgusted," Roosevelt wrote to Henry Cabot Lodge in May 1905, "at the manifestations which have begun to appear on the Pacific slope in favor of excluding the Japanese exactly as the Chinese are excluded. The California State Legislature and various other bodies have acted in the worst possible taste in the offensive manner to Japan."

Roosevelt's indignation at the behavior of the Californians in regard to the Japanese—he called it "as foolish as if conceived by the mind of a Hottentot"—was based less on distaste of racist attitudes than on his concern that the Japanese might be moved to take military action against the United States, such as seizing the Philippines and/or Hawaii. "These Pacific Coast people," he wrote, rather as though he were writing of a foreign land, "wish grossly to insult the Japanese and to keep out Japanese immigrants on the ground that they are an immoral, degraded and worthless race . . . and at the same time . . . they expect to be given advantages in Oriental markets. . . . The Japanese soldiers and sailors have shown themselves to be terrible foes. There can be none more dangerous in the world . . . [and] if, as Brooks Adams says, we show ourselves 'opulent, aggressive and unarmed,' the Japanese may some time work us an injury."

Roosevelt was so concerned about Japanese military might that when the San Francisco school board barred Asian children from the city's public schools, Roosevelt summoned the board to Washington and, warning that their action might bring on war with the race-proud Nipponese, prevailed on them to reverse their ruling. When a group of California congressmen waited on Roosevelt in 1905 to urge the passage of anti-Asian legislation, Roosevelt gave them a stern lecture, adding, "Why I would veto it [such a bill] if it passed unanimously!" The chastened Congressmen dropped the plan, at least for the moment.

It was, indeed, Roosevelt's apprehension about Japanese ambitions in the Pacific that guided much of his foreign policy. He undertook to mediate the war between Russia and Japan at least in part in hopes of checking the growing power and arrogance of the Japanese in the Pacific Basin. He also built up the U.S. fleet, demonstrated the power of newly developed U.S. naval gunnery in a display that he made sure Japanese naval officers witnessed, and, in the face of considerable opposition from Congress, sent the White Fleet around the world in an awesome parade of naval might. His principal motive was to make the Japanese think twice before considering an attack on any of the U.S. naval bases in the Pacific.

One of Roosevelt's rationales for building the Panama Canal was to enable the Atlantic Fleet to join forces with the Pacific Fleet in event of a war with Japan. Roosevelt feared that the Japanese would destroy the Pacific Fleet piecemeal. His strategy, in the event of war, was to withdraw the Pacific Fleet before it could be engaged by the Japanese and then combine it with the Atlantic, confident that the combined fleets could defeat the Japanese navy.

In 1908 a young Stanford Law School graduate, Homer Lea, wrote a best-selling book entitled *The Valor of Ignorance*. Lea took the line that war between the United States and Japan (and probably Germany) was inevitable. Americans exaggerated "not Japan's capacity to make war, but our capacity to defend ourselves." Lea believed that the Japanese would attack the Philippines with overwhelming force at Luzon, seize the main island (which Lea believed was indefensible) in some three weeks, and then capture Hawaii, Alaska, and California. The novel, with its prophetic tone, contributed substantially to the anxiety about Japanese plans to attack American installations in the Pacific, culminating in a landing on the California coast.

When Lea's book was translated and published in Japan it sold 84,000 copies in the first few months and became, subsequently, a text for the Imperial general staff.

In 1908 when eight West Coast Chambers of Commerce visited Japan in a party of fifty, the Baron Ei-ichi Shibusawa told his visitors how sensitive the Japanese were about slights experienced by Japanese Americans in the United States. It was difficult, the baron declared, to believe that "the Americans would do anything of the kind, because it would be against the original principles upon which America was founded. It was America that introduced Japan to the world, and we Japanese have kept up friendly relations with the Americans on the strength of this memory. Now, if the Americans, out of the race prejudices and religious differ-

ences, are to treat the Japanese with discrimination, that is something
which they should not do. If they persist they may not escape the criticism
that they were reasonable at first and then became unreasonable in the
end.''

The officers of the chambers quite agreed and the next year when their
Japanese counterparts visited the United States they got the royal treatment, whisked about in private railroad cars visiting "fifty-four or fifty-
five places," until they were all in a daze; they had lunch with President
William Howard Taft in Minneapolis and returned home encouraged
about the relations between the two countries. A program of exchange
professors was also instituted, and David Starr Jordan, president-to-be of
Stanford University, visited Japan along with other academic notables.

It was to try to counteract the growing hostility between Japan and the
United States that Naoichi Masaoka edited a volume designed to "explain" Japan to Americans. Masaoka was one of the journalists who
accompanied the Japanese foreign minister, Baron Komura, to Ports-
mouth, New Hampshire, in 1905 where Theodore Roosevelt mediated
peace between Japan and the United States. Masaoka was dismayed at
what seemed to him the misconceptions of Americans about Japan. In
1914, he published a collection of essays by leading Japanese politicians
and intellectuals entitled *Japan's Message to America: A Symposium by
Representative Japanese on Japan and American-Japanese Relations*.
"What the average American knows about Japan," Masaoka noted, "is
far less than what the average Japanese knows about America."

The first essay in Masaoka's book was by Count Shigenubo Okuma,
one of the founders of the Progressive Party and the champion of representative government (he was assassinated for his pains). The count
described Japan's mission as that of harmonizing "Eastern and Western
civilizations in order to help bring about the unification of the world."
The Japanese could well be described, the count noted, as "eclectics . . .
free from any racial or religious prejudices; we have collected, or are
trying to collect, what is good, what is true, and what is beautiful from
all quarters of the earth. . . . The true difference of mankind is neither in
the color of his skin nor in the frame of his body, but is, if any, in the
degree of culture itself. . . . To brand us Japanese as inferior because we
are a colored race is a bigotry that we must combat and destroy through
the fulfillment of our national mission."

Throughout the essays there runs, like a refrain, the sensitivity of the
contributors to any notion of Japanese inferiority. Sometimes this takes
the form of claims that qualities admired in the Western world had been

present in Japanese culture from the nation's earliest days. Viscount Kentaro Kancho had attended Harvard and received a degree from Harvard Law School in 1878. He was president of the American Friends Society and "an intimate friend" of "Col. Roosevelt." Kancho quoted Roosevelt as "eulogizing" Japan in a message to Congress as a nation "who is ready to learn [and] fit to teach. I may add that he [Roosevelt] clearly saw through the mind of our nation." Japan was not content to be "a mere importer of Western civilization," it had much to teach the world.

The Baron Shimpei Goto, a graduate of the University of Berlin with a degree in medicine and former head of the Formosan government, made the point that the ancient Japanese principle of *Yamato Damashii*, which, to Goto, meant that "the learned are only vassals of the Creator; the simple are his immediate attendants," had guided Japan long before the West developed the notion of "humanitarianism." "We are, of course," the baron concluded, in a sentence that perfectly revealed the ambivalence of Japan toward the Western world and the United States in particular, "great admirers of Western civilization. In a sense, however, we can charge it with the destruction of the beauties of our culture."

Baron Ei-ichi Shibusawa told of his lifelong interest in the United States that began when Commodore Perry's fleet arrived in Japanese waters during his childhood. Yet when, in fulfillment of his dearest dreams, he visited America, one of the first sights he saw was a sign in Golden Gate Park in San Francisco that said: "Japanese Are Not Admitted." The baron was indignant. In light of the fact that there was "already such antipathy between the Orientals and the Occidentals," such an insult "might bring serious trouble between the two nations." In Washington, the baron, like a number of high Japanese officials before him, had met with President Roosevelt, who "praised to me the Japanese army, the art, and other things of Japan. He said: 'The Japanese soldiers are not only full of valor and of knowledge of military science, but also they are very humane, have self-restraint, and are honest.' " Roosevelt had learned these things, he told the baron, when Japanese and American soldiers stood shoulder to shoulder in China at the time of the Boxer Rebellion. "I have great admiration and respect for them," Roosevelt concluded.

Much of the same ambivalence was expressed by a Japanese visitor, Hakuson Kuriyagawa. Kuriyagawa, repelled by the materialistic spirit of the United States, reflected that there were ways in which Japan, "governed by a rigid bureaucracy, dominated by stubbornly persistent, outmoded ideas, and inhibited by the conventions of statism, is a far easier and freer place to live.'' America was ruled by two tyrants—public opinion and materialism. To Kuriyagawa the United States seemed hypocritical in proclaiming its devotion to freedom while denying its benefits to many of its citizens. It was to him "a nation of mobs and curiosity-seekers" where "majority public opinion reigns supreme. . . . No matter what is said or done, as long as it accords with the will of the masses, even blindly, it will be acclaimed as right and proper." The United States, at the same time, was "made up of men and women from every corner of the earth" and they were "the builders of a new civilization for a new world. . . . Even in its finest hour, the Roman Empire did not begin to amass the range of things, good and bad, from all over the world that the United States has. The influence of this new civilization is already enormous, and it will continue to extend itself in the future. . . . We Japanese deprecate the U.S. for many things, and yet the pace of Americanization here is just astounding."

Working against all such efforts was the growing Imperial ambition of Japan. The Japanese were pleased to find an ally on the United States's southern border, as Mexico shared with Japan a common hostility toward the United States. The theory that Mexicans had, centuries earlier, made their way to America from Japan suggested to military leaders of both countries that the Japanese and the Mexicans were of common racial stock, thus brothers under the skin, so to speak. Both countries deeply resented the slights that their nationals experienced in the United States. It was reported that the grand admiral of the Japanese fleet was cheered at a Mexican state banquet when he spoke of the fraternal ties between Japan and Mexico. There were cries of "Viva Japón! Abajo los gringos!"

In the process of flexing her muscles, Japan learned a lesson on her account. Even as she was preparing to enter the race for empire, reaction was setting in the Western world against imperialism, the often brutal subjugation of pre-industrial peoples for the purpose of acquiring colonies rich in raw materials to increase the wealth and improve the strategic position of the acquirer. Having swallowed up most of the non-Western peoples of the globe and, in some cases, experiencing severe indigestion as a consequence, the Western powers began proclaiming piously that such behavior was immoral and unchristian and must stop. Conversely, the military leaders of Japan did not hesitate to evoke *Hakko Ichiu*—"to bring the eight corners of the world together under one roof," the reputed declaration of a 600 B.C. Japanese Emperor, as a goal for modern Japan.

Such domination must begin with the conquest of Asian and South Pacific nations, or colonies as the case might be.

Another fisher in troubled waters was Kaiser Wilhelm of Germany, who startled an American newspaper editor, interviewing him in 1908 for the *New York Times,* by telling him that the Americans would have to fight the Japanese within a year or two. To counter the Japanese threat, the Kaiser declared, he intended to form an alliance with China, Germany, and the United States. Britain was the enemy because Britain had betrayed the white race by making a treaty with Japan. The Kaiser, who was probably mad, also was obsessed with Japanese naval power.

The whole issue surfaced again in 1914 and once more the Kaiser was the culprit, but this time he was entitled to share the blame with the California state legislature, which passed anti-Japanese legislation. When the Japanese ambassador issued an angry protest, the Joint Army and Navy Board ordered five U.S. warships to Manila and recommended that the Pacific Fleet be dispatched to Hawaii. For a time talk of war was once again in the air. Josephus Daniels, President Woodrow Wilson's secretary of the navy, wrote caustically that "the admirals sat up nights thinking how Japan was planning to make war on America and steal a march on us by taking the Philippine Islands and going on to Hawaii." Wilson was so indignant at what he considered the board's usurpation of executive powers that he dissolved it forthwith.

With the outbreak of World War I, there were fresh anxieties about the course that Japan might follow. Rumors circulated that Germany hoped to prevail on Mexico to become a staging area for German units to attack the American Southwest. Certainly German agents swarmed through Mexico. There was talk in the German general staff of trying to persuade the Japanese to join in an attack through Texas and up the Mississippi River. The so-called Carranza Plan was said to envision stirring up Mexicans, Indians, and blacks in New Mexico, Arizona, Nevada, and California to join forces with invading German, Mexican, and, it was hoped, Japanese armies.

The famous Zimmerman telegram dispatched in 1917 instructed the German ambassador to Mexico to offer the Mexican government a "definitive alliance" with Germany if it would declare war on the United States and succeed "in drawing Japan into the alliance."

All this was fodder for the Hearst newspapers, whose stock-in-trade for years had been the "yellow peril." Hearst's papers harped tirelessly on the threat of a German-Mexican-Japanese invasion. A Hearst film company made a serial starring Irene Castle, the theme of which was just such an invasion led by fierce samurai warriors. Japan was pleased by the rumors, believing they would have the effect of making its soldiers and sailors seem more formidable than ever. Convinced that Germany would win the war, the Japanese military was eager to remain on good terms with the Germans. After threatening to join forces with Germany and encouraging rumors of a joint German-Japanese invasion of the American Southwest, the Japanese reached an accommodation with Great Britain that entitled Japan to a share of the spoils parceled out to the Allied nations by the Treaty of Versailles ending the war. Japan thus seized the German-occupied islands—the Marianas, the Marshalls, and the Carolines—and moved once more against China. The Twenty-one Demands were made on China, the most important of which was the cession of Shantung Province.

At the peace conference the Japanese were also determined to use the occasion to fight racial discrimination wherever it might affect Japanese interests and, more important, Japanese pride. They pushed to have a clause inserted in the Versailles treaty renouncing racial discrimination. The American delegation agreed to go along with the clause if the Japanese, in turn, would not make an issue of the curtailment of Japanese immigration into the United States, but the "yellow perilists" in the United States and Australia made such a to-do that the United States and Great Britain backed off. Japan failed to get the anti-discrimination clause.

China now became the principal bone of contention. Having pillaged that helpless people for a half-century, the West, and especially the United States, which, again through its missionary connections and generations of trade, had close emotional ties with China and relatively clean hands in terms of its exploitation, came to see itself as China's protector against an aggressive and "imperialistic" Japan. For the West, China suddenly appeared, not as part of the "yellow peril" that had haunted the dreams and inflamed the rhetoric of William Randolph Hearst, but as an ancient civilization from which the upstart Japanese had purloined the better part of their culture. In the minds of many modern moralists, the Chinese influence on Japan made the modern Japanese aggression against China far more horrendous than, let us say, the British conquest of India or the American operations in the Philippines. There was a considerable degree of hypocrisy in the international tongue-clucking that went on over Japan's aggression, as well, one suspects, as a substantial measure of outright racism. The Japanese, after all, did not belong to the Caucasian

Club. They were "yellow" and "yellow" was, not entirely incidentally, an American word for cowardly (in any discussion of Japanese imperialism and militarism it is important to keep in mind that Japan had its own liberal and radical reformers and its own enemies of these practices).

In the 1920s a conflict developed between the Diet and the military clique. For a brief time it seemed as though a genuine party system might emerge. Takaaki Kato led a movement designed to establish civilian control over the military through parliamentary democracy. All males over twenty-five were given the franchise without property qualification, adding some 10 million voters to the rolls. At the same time a kind of FBI was set up to ferret out and suppress "dangerous thought," and severe penalties were provided for "agitators," which was to say any radical critics of the government.

Although Kato was far from a liberal democrat, he exerted great power and made important reforms. When he died in 1927, the new prime minister, General Giichi Tanaka, pushed Japan ahead on a reckless program of imperialist expansion. Tanaka sent Japanese troops into China without consulting the Diet, and once there, the generals began operating as virtually independent agents, pursuing their own objectives with little regard for the Diet or cabinet. They arranged the assassination of an uncooperative Chinese warlord and did their best to precipitate a conclusive conflict with the Chinese. Their efforts were abetted by the effects of the Great Depression, which had begun officially with the collapse of the American stock market in 1929. Junior officers, many of them members of the former samurai class, led a profoundly reactionary movement that called for the abandonment of any pretense of parliamentary government and the establishment of a military dictatorship to carry out plans for Imperial Expansion, the Greater East Asia Co-Prosperity Sphere, as it was euphemistically called. Secret right-wing terrorist organizations, such as the Cherry Blossom Association and the Amur River Society, did not scruple to murder liberal opponents.

Japan was, in the same period, party to a series of international agreements designed to prevent an armaments race in the aftermath of World War I. Under the terms of the Washington Treaty of 1921, and subsequent treaties, the United States scrapped fifteen new capital ships on which over $300 million had already been spent. The United States, Britain, and, reluctantly, Japan, agreed to the so-called 5-5-3 battleship and carrier ratio, the 5s being United States and Britain, the 3 Japan. In order to secure the agreement of Japan, the United States and Great Britain pledged not to strengthen any of their naval bases in the Pacific between Hawaii and Singapore. Even this very considerable concession failed to satisfy the Japanese. The liberal government that had negotiated the agreement was replaced by a conservative one with close ties to the military. Under a government dominated by generals and admirals, the Japanese denounced the 5-5-3 ratio and began an ambitious program of warship building. By the time of Pearl Harbor, the Japanese had more warships in every category than the U.S. and British Pacific and Asiatic fleets combined.

Despite the series of agreements intended to limit Japanese aggression, in September 1931 the Japanese army moved into Manchuria. The Japanese government had not authorized the action but under the threat of assassination the ministry ratified it. A year later Manchuria was declared the independent kingdom of Manchukuo under a puppet of Japanese choosing.

When the Japanese invasion of Manchuria was presented to the League of Nations, that body testified to its own weakness by waffling on the issue. The United States, not a member of the league, tried to bring pressure on Japan to mend its ways by invoking an embargo on American goods to Japan. The action only increased the obduracy of the Japanese military clique and its terrorist supporters. Two prime ministers were assassinated in a period of two years and a number of liberal politicians were murdered or driven into hiding.

AGAINST THIS BACKGROUND OF INCREASINGLY TENSE RELATIONS BE-tween Japan and the United States, we must consider one of the principal causes of that tension—the immigration of Japanese to the United States, primarily Washington, Oregon, and California.

By 1890 the pressures of population in Japan led that country, inherently hostile to foreigners, to permit emigration. Brazil, Peru, Canada, and the United States were the countries most favored by the Japanese emigrants. A trickle at first, by 1900 there were over 24,000 Japanese in a California population of 1,485,053. Ten years later the number in the United States had swelled to 72,157, of whom 41,356 were in California. In 1910 Japanese farmers in California grew more than $12 million worth of crops, some twenty percent of the entire agricultural output of the state. Millions of dollars more was produced by Japanese labor on land owned by others. The *Los Angeles Times,* editorializing in a generally laudable tone, noted: "The Japanese have become an important factor in the agricultural and commercial life of the southwest. Their thrift is remarkable, their patience inexhaustible, and they are natural gardeners, seeming to read the secrets of the very soil. . . . The result of this close study of soil condition, close observation of crop and weather conditions, enables the Japanese to control to a great degree the vegetable-raising industry of Southern California.''

In 1907 President Theodore Roosevelt, who as we have seen was determined to check any congressional legislation limiting Japan (or Asian) immigration, compromised to the extent of negotiating a "Gentleman's Agreement" in which the Japanese government would deny emigrant passports to Japanese "laborers" except those who, "in coming to the continent, seek to resume a formerly acquired domicile, to join a parent, wife or child residing there, or to assume control of an already possessed interest in a farming enterprise in this country."

The generally negative effect of the Gentleman's Agreement was heightened by California legislation in 1913 denying the right of Japanese immigrants—noncitizens—to hold certain kinds of property. Although this stipulation was evaded in a variety of ways, it added to the sense of grievance by Japanese immigrants against California Caucasians.

The Gentlemen's Agreement slowed but did not stop immigration. By 1920 there were 111,010 Japanese in the United States, 71,952 of them in California. Much of the increase in the Japanese population of the West Coast was the result of a high birth rate among Japanese immigrants who, like most farm people, prized children as a labor force.

At this point resistance to further Japanese immigration began to grow. Instead of being perceived, as they had been in the *Los Angeles Times* editorial in 1910, as exemplars of the Protestant ethic of thrift and hard work, the Japanese immigrants were increasingly depicted as people of alien ways whose tireless labors depressed the wages of Caucasian farm-workers and gathered more and more of the region's agricultural wealth into their own hands. U.S. Webb, the California attorney general, spoke for many embattled West Coast farmers when he told a congressional committee in 1924 that the Japanese were "different in color; different in ideals; different in race; different in ambitions; different in their theory of political economy and government. They speak a different language; they worship a different God. They had not in common with the Caucasian a single trait."

James D. Phelan, mayor of San Francisco, took much the same line, declaring, "The Japanese are starting the same tide of immigration which we thought we had checked [by the Gentleman's Agreement] twenty years ago. . . . The Chinese and Japanese are not bona fide citizens.

They are not the stuff of which American citizens are made.'' That was clearly the opinion of an increasing number of Americans living on the West Coast of the United States.

Congress responded by imposing further restrictions in the Immigration Act of 1924. Two years earlier the courts in the case of *Ozawa v. United States* had ruled that Japanese immigrants could not become U.S. citizens under the terms of the Constitution, which limited naturalization to ''free white persons.''

Not surprisingly the Exclusionary Act, as the Immigration Act of 1924 was also called, added fuel to the anti-American feeling in Japan. Harold and Alice Foght, travel writers from Wichita, Kansas, and champions of Japanese American friendship, experienced Japanese resentment over the Exclusionary Act at first hand. The two writers divided all Caucasian books on Japan into two major categories: those that described the Japanese as a new race of supermen, and those depicting them as ''a nation of knaves—dishonest, crafty, and untrustworthy.'' They were committed, they assured their readers, to the not-so-simple truth. As guests of the National Association for the Encouragement of Learning and one of Japan's principal newspapers, *Kokumin Shimbun,* at a banquet at the Pan-Pacific Club, Mrs. Foght committed the unforgivable faux pas of mentioning to one of her hosts the Japanese Exclusionary Act. There was a moment of terrible silence; it was clearly a taboo subject. Then her luncheon partner, very tactful, replied: ''You Americans are entirely within your rights in determining who may and who may not become citizens of the United States.''

''But,'' poor Mrs. Foght persisted, ''how is the action in Congress received in Japan?''

There was another pause. ''That,'' her host replied, ''is quite another matter. The Japanese are an exceedingly proud and sensitive people and are convinced in their own minds that their civilization of twenty-five or more centuries with its training in the arts, in literature and philosophy, is at least the equal of your Western industrial civilization. Since the Restoration we have looked to America as our friend and schoolmaster. We have been proud of your friendship. When America expressed the fear that continued influx of Japanese laborers might bring about an embarrassing problem and cause international misunderstanding, we readily entered into a treaty agreement to settle the vexing problem. This, we thought, had ended the matter definitely. For, from the time that the gentlemen's agreement was signed, the Imperial Government has refused to issue passports to a single Japanese laboring man. But it was not to be.

When the Johnson Immigration Bill was enacted it came as a terrible blow to Japan. As I have said, we are a people both proud and sensitive . . . and now you, our friends and schoolmasters, have spurned us as a people inferior and unfit! But, as I have said, you are entirely within your rights.''

When a touring journalist, Tokutomu Kenji, visited New York not long after the Immigration Act had passed, talk of an ''inevitable'' war between Japan and the United States was much in the air. He wrote bitterly: ''What of the oppression and abuse meted out to Negroes'' and toward ''resident Japanese nationals, whose own country is America's equal? Exclusion and more exclusion. . . . Japan continues to be insulted in an unforgivable manner. . . . That is not all. America is filled with gangs, roving bands of murderers, and plagued by the politics of the dollar, boundless eroticism, grotesquerie and scandalous decadence . . . who can prevent it from meeting with a hundred years of grief?''

One of Tokutomu's countrymen, Hachiro Shishimoto, expressed similar sentiments. Writing in 1932, when the effects of the Great Depression were being severely felt in Japan, Shishimoto mocked ''such high-sounding phrases'' as ''justice and humanity, freedom and equality.'' The pretension that the United States actually embodied ''such ideals was offensive.'' How, Shishimoto asked, could the United States justify its armed intervention in Nicaragua, or the shady deal that resulted in the Panama Canal, ''the ceaseless pressure . . . on Mexico'' and the seizure of the Philippines, Guam, and Puerto Rico. ''But America ignores all this while continuing to condemn Japan as a disturber of the peace and aggressor.'' Japan's policy in China was simply a ''policy of self-defense.''

So it was that a relationship that had begun so promisingly became increasingly embittered. A popular Japanese song went: ''Gone is the old America where once the tower of liberty soared.''

Chapter 3

JAPANESE IN AMERICA

T HE REASONS JAPANESE MEN (AND A LESSER NUMBER OF WOMEN) poured into the United States in a thirty-five-year period were as various as the people who came, but, as with other nineteenth- and early-twentieth-century emigrations, most immigrants were driven by poverty in their homeland. The population pressures in Japan that grew alarmingly with every passing decade have already been mentioned. The initial group of Japanese immigrants were the desperately poor farmers and laborers who were considered the nation's surplus. They were, in general, the least literate, those whose emigration the motherland was most anxious to encourage; they were, at the same time, the least Westernized, the most tradition-bound, and, in consequence, the most unlikely to be readily assimilated into American society. It was this segment—to borrow a phrase from the Statue of Liberty—"the wretched refuse of [Japan's] teeming shore," that aroused the resistance of those West Coast farmers and laborers with whom they were soon in competition.

Those Japanese—the Issei of first-generation immigrants who have testified about their motives in coming to the United States—have, not surprisingly, given a wide variety of reasons for emigrating. The most common, as noted, was economic. We like to believe that immigrants came (and come) to the United States in search of "freedom" and "democracy" but clearly the overwhelming motivation throughout our history has been material advancement and in this respect the Japanese immigrants were no different from any others.

Most Japanese came in hope of making enough money in a few years of desperately hard labor in the United States to return to Japan and live there in relative prosperity for the rest of their lives; the rate of exchange, dollar to yen, was such that that was a practical goal. It was estimated that by the time of Pearl Harbor some 20,000 Japanese had followed this course and returned home. The fact that, despite a very high birth rate, the number of Japanese in the United States had been dropping in the decade before the war gives further indication of how widespread this practice was. Between 1930 and 1940, the Japanese population in the United States declined from 138,834 to 126,947, a decrease of 11,887, or 8.6 percent (the Chinese showed a modest increase to 74,954). Of the 126,947, 111,887 lived on the West Coast (roughly 93,000 in California, 14,000 in Washington, and 4,071 in Oregon). Annoying as it might be to those patriotic Americans who, like the Japanese, thought their country the greatest nation on earth, there was nothing reprehensible (or unusual) in the ties that Japanese felt to their homeland or in their desire to return to it with as much money in their pockets as possible.

Re-migration home is a major theme in the history of immigration. Of 430,624 Poles who came to the United States in the last decade of the nineteenth century and the first decade of this, 152,617 returned to Poland and many more would have if they could. Of the Magyars 123,000 came and 87,000 returned. The same was true of Croatians, Serbs, Slavs, and Slovaks. Of Slovaks 117,868 came and 70,000 returned. Of all immigrant groups of the period, some 4,300,000 came and 1,452,239 returned to their homelands.

A study conducted in the mid-1930s indicated that 76 percent of Japanese farm laborers and 53 percent of city wage earners intended to return to Japan, whereas, not surprisingly, only 40 percent of farm owners or leasers and 38 percent of businessmen planned to return. Additionally, the more successful a Japanese farmer or businessman had been, the less likely he was to wish to return to Japan.

For many Japanese Japan was "home" and the United States was primarily a place to make money in order to return home to a comfortable and prosperous old age among friends and relatives in a familiar prefecture.

One young Nisei noted that his father's aim in coming to America was "to find some work where he could make a fortune very quickly and then return to Japan." Like many of those who came to California, the father came from the Hiroshima prefecture. After some twelve years in the U.S. his father had returned to Japan where a marriage had been arranged for him.

Katsusaburo Kawahara was "called" by his parents to come to the United States in 1911. "The people in my village," he recalled, "didn't know much about freedom or anything like that, but I think in a way they respected America and its tremendous resources and wealth." Young Kawahara was bitterly disappointed at the America he found and begged his parents to let him return to Japan. In the Santa Clara Valley he found work picking fruit and, finally, reconciled to staying at least for a time, he set about learning English. It was a wise decision that contributed directly to his success as a farmer, eventually owning over 250 acres and employing fifteen farmhands. But he, too, cherished the dream of returning to Japan.

Riici Satow told Heihachiro Takarabe —a Presbyterian minister who interviewed many Issei—that in Japan he was one of five children of a dissolute father who had trouble feeding his brood. "One day, at last, my father came to his senses and realized he was a complete failure. Then, he came to the United States to recover from it." His father went first to Hawaii on a three-year labor contract and then made his way, with a friend, to the Napa Valley of California. There he prospered as the manager of a large "fruit ranch" and sent for Riici as a *yobiyose* (one who is summoned). In those days (circa 1912), Satow recalled, "the amount of $2,000 or $3,000 meant quite a lot to a Japanese person and anybody coming back to Japan with that much money could do whatever he wanted to do, say build a new house, or buy farm lands, for instance. This sort of dream was what most of the Japanese immigrants had in mind in those days. Three years of hard work could bring them a fortune, and they wanted to use it back in Japan." Responding to his father's call, Riici Satow landed in San Francisco. Although he intended to return to Japan as soon as he had accumulated some money, Satow decided to get married. The marriage was arranged by his parents and the parents of his prospective bride. "Children," he noted, "didn't have the right to decide for themselves; instead parents would arrange their children's partners.

The children obeyed their decision. My case was just like that, and that's how I married.''

Masuo Akizuki came to the United States to help his father make enough money to return to Japan and live there comfortably. He promised his mother that he would do his best to insure that his father returned in five years. Akizuki worked as a field hand and slept in the horse stable of the ranch where he worked ten hours a day for ten cents an hour.

Some Japanese who came to the United States solely with the intention of making enough money to live in Japan changed their minds. In Raymond Katagi's words: "When they came to America at first they were trying to make money. But as they lived long in this country, they found out it is a good place to live, and their descendants have so much more opportunity in this country so they want their descendants to want to stay in this country, and they have the same ideas as those pilgrim fathers.''

Haruko Niwa was born in Japan and came to the United States when she was seventeen to visit her father and brother, who lived in San Francisco. "But I stayed instead,'' she recalled. "I liked it very much. I liked San Francisco and the United States. It's very attractive. And I stayed here and went to a girls school in San Francisco.'' Her father and brother returned to Japan but Haruko married and, at the time of the evacuation, had two teenage children, Nobu fifteen and Aki thirteen.

Like Riici Satow, James Sakoda described the prewar Issei as individuals, men primarily, since women were hardly considered apart from their husbands and fathers, whose long-term goal was "to earn enough money to return to Japan to live in comfort.'' "In the meantime,'' Sakoda wrote, "they generally withdrew into the protection of the [Japanese] community. . . . The Issei identified with Japan. Japan was their country, and most expected to return to the homeland. But because of their connection with their Nisei, the Issei often suppressed their overt identification with Japan.''

Those who planned to return to Japan obviously had no incentive to adopt American ways, learn the American language, or make any substantial effort to become assimilated with the dominant culture. They came deeply imbued with the ways of a two-thousand-year-old culture, and in the main they remained as they came, thoroughly Japanese in their manners, customs, and loyalties.

Those loyalties were first and foremost to the Emperor, whose birthdays they dutifully celebrated, and then to their *ken* or prefecture. Ordinarily they came by *ken* or clan, going to those areas where other members of the *ken* had preceded them, and then promptly joined the *kenjinkai* or prefectural association in their area.

As noted, the *ken* was, typically, the residue of a feudal fief hundreds of years old. It had its own traditions and customs, its own emblems, and even to a degree its own language, since the accent of people from one *ken* might be so different as to sound like a foreign language to members of another. Nisuke Mitsumori recalled that on the boat to the United States the dialects of Japanese from other prefectures were so different from his (Yamanashi) that he could not understand them and thought at first that they were speaking some language other than Japanese.

A number of young Japanese emigrated to the United States (and Brazil) in the early years of the century to avoid the draft, which became especially onerous with the beginning of hostilities with Russia. Such was the case with Francis Hayashi. Hayashi's father had come to California in 1901 and his mother a year later, leaving Francis and his brother with grandparents. Francis left high school in Japan before graduation to avoid the draft. He joined his parents in San Francisco, where friends advised him to learn English as his first step. The best place to learn, he was told, was at the Reformed Church. He studied there and was baptized there, going on to Lowell High School and then to Stanford, where he majored in engineering. When Hayashi graduated, he, like many of his Japanese friends at Stanford, found that he could not get a job. A number of his friends returned to Japan, where their Stanford degrees were a great asset. "All the Nisei" who remained, Hayashi recalled, "were working for fruit stands of farmers." Discouraged, Hayashi decided to try his luck in Los Angeles but the minister of his church persuaded him to undertake youth work with the young Nisei in the congregation. In this manner, Hayashi found his calling. He attended a theological seminary in Dayton, Ohio, and began his career as a Methodist minister.

In the village in which Yoshisada Kawai grew up as a farmer's son, only ten boys and girls were able to go on from elementary to middle school, and only one or two could advance to high school. "If you were able to graduate from high school," he recalled to Heihachiro Takarabe, "you would be able to work as a salesman, or a clerk of the city government, village government, or as policeman or a mailman." Kawai's father was "a very serious Buddhist" of the Jodo-shinshu sect. "In the morning he would face the east and clap his hands to thank God and in the evening he would light the lantern and offer a bowl of hot rice as an offering, and recite okyo . . . as he rang a chime." He remembered his mother telling him: "If you disrespect rice grains, then you will become blind.'' That seemed a strange admonition to the child but he was careful to say, '' 'Itadakimasu,' I receive this food in gratitude.' . . . and [was] very careful not to drop my rice.''

With few opportunities in his native village, Kawai was encouraged by his teacher, Heitaro Wakabayashi, who had already come to the United States (and who wrote a guidebook for ''upwardly mobile'' immigrants called *Rafu Shogyokaigisho no Shoki* [*Memoirs from the Chamber of Commerce in Los Angeles*]), to make the long, arduous journey to California. He thought of the classic Chinese poem:

> *A young man leaves his native town to achieve his goal.*
> *If he is not successful in*
> *his learning even if he dies*
> *he shall not return.*

> *Ancestors' land is not the only*
> *place where you should bury your bones,*
> *Man can be buried in any mountain of the world.*

The owner of the hotel where Kawai stayed helped him find a job with an apple-canning factory in Watsonville.

One substantial group of immigrants most of whom came with the intention of remaining were Japanese Christians. Scorned and persecuted in their homeland, they came to the United States to an at least ostensibly (and frequently and piously announced) ''Christian nation,'' and indeed found help and encouragement from the Caucasians in the denominations to which they belonged.

As noted, Christian missionary labors bore at least modest fruit in Japan. Although the Japanese government officially granted religious freedom (in large part as a result of U.S. and, to a lesser degree, Western pressure), it considered Christianity a religion of weaklings and cowards. In striking contrast to the warriors' ethic of Shintoism and the code of *bushido* that penetrated all levels of Japanese society, Christianity preached (if it did not always practice) peace and love even for those ''who despitefully use you''; the turning of the other cheek; meekness and humility—all anathema to non-Christian Japanese.

The hardships, the confusion, and demoralization inevitably attendant on immigration to a strange, a very strange land by Japanese standards, were ameliorated by missionaries, Caucasian as well as Japanese in Japan, who referred emigrants to Americans of their denominations in the

United States, or, more specifically, on the West Coast, where they soon formed mission churches of their particular denomination. Such churches were supported initially by the denominations to which they belonged. By the late 1930s a hundred Japanese "mission churches" of various denominations had been established in Canada, the United States, and Hawaii.

Igarashi Toshiko was the daughter of one of the first Western-trained doctors in Japan, a graduate of Chiba Medical School. Western medicine was still viewed with great suspicion and her father found it difficult to establish a practice. This difficultly was compounded when he became a Christian as a consequence of reading John Bunyan's *Pilgrim's Progress* and the Bible in Japanese. Toshiko attended *Meijingakuin,* a private missionary school, and had stones and, on one memorable occasion, a snake, thrown at her by other children because she was a Christian. She told Heihachiro Takarabe: "The reason why I came to the U.S. was, of course, because of my faith. This is a Christian country; I have the same Christian faith, so did my parents." Once in California, Toshiko recalled, "white people came to help our church. Those from the First Baptist Church, that's a white church, opened up English classes, cooking classes, and sewing classes."

Young Nisei Christians went to Christian Endeavor meetings with the *hakujin* (white people), visited *hakujin* homes, and joined in such social activities as folk dancing and choral singing.

John Yamazaki was converted to Christianity in Japan by an Episcopalian Canadian heiress named Louise Pederson. She encouraged young Yamazaki to emigrate to the Episcopal diocese of Los Angeles, where he found a friend and patron in John Gooden, bishop of the diocese. Impressed by Yamazaki's intelligence and piety, Bishop Gooden presented him to the Women's Auxiliary of the diocese and solicited their support to send him to an Episcopal theological seminary. They raised enough money on the spot to underwrite three years at the Berkeley Seminary in Connecticut. John Yamazaki became an Episcopal priest and founded St. Mary's Japanese Episcopal Church in Los Angeles, over which his son, also John, subsequently presided. The senior John Yamazaki named his daughter Louise after his benefactor.

Isamu Nakamura was another Japanese Christian who emigrated with the encouragement of Christian missionaries. Nakamura's impression of the United States was that "everything was so huge." At Pacific Union College, Nakamura chopped wood to help pay for his room and board and tuition. Nakamura's aunt and uncle had offered to pay for his university education in business or medicine but when he told them that he had decided to be a Christian minister, they denounced him as a fool and withdrew their offer of support.

Minori Kimura, the daughter of Christian parents, attended a missionary school in Korea and completed her schooling in Kobe. There, through an aunt and uncle in California, she began to correspond with a young Japanese man who had graduated from Monterey High School and, because he spoke good English, had been able to get a job working for the New York Life Insurance Company. Their correspondence resulted in marriage. She and her husband were active in the San Jose Methodist Church, among whose members were the Mineta family, also in the insurance business.

Kazuko Hayashi's husband, who, like Kazuko was a Christian, was the head of a utopian Japanese Christian community near Livingston, California, famous in its day as the Yamato Colony. Kazuko recalled that when she left Japan her father-in-law gave her a sword and told the young couple that "in case things did not go well for them, they should commit hari-kari with it."

One rough distinction between those Japanese immigrants who planned to stay in the United States and those who intended to return to their homeland might be found in the personal names they adopted. Jeanne Wakatsuki's father took as his American personal name George, after George Washington, and named one daughter Martha after Martha Washington. A son was named Woodrow after Woodrow Wilson and Jeanne was named after Jean Harlow.

Japanese Christians often gave the names of Christ's apostles—James, Peter, John, Paul—to their sons. Frank and Charlie were also common, as were Jane and Ellen.

There was, of course, a practical reason as well. Those Japanese who had frequent contact with *hakujin* found that their Japanese names were extremely difficult for *hakujin* to master. Minori was simple enough but Yoshisada was much more of a challenge and Katsusabaro was impossible.

A small but significant group of emigrants were political refugees. In the words of Katsusabura Kawahara: "Funny thing, they [the Japanese] thought all you need is 'AMATO DAMASHII'—love for the Emperor. I think that's how most of the educated Japanese were brought up. If you said any principle negating this idea of worshipping the Emperor in Japan, they said you were a Communist. Japanese had no use for you and sent you out of the country. They point you out and you cannot have a job. . . . A lot of them got chased out of the country and settled in America. It's famous; they were called Communist, or 'Kyosan-to.' "

IN MOST OF THE ACCOUNTS BY ISSEI AND NISEI OF THEIR LIVES ON THE West Coast prior to Pearl Harbor, the major theme is the financial precariousness of their lives. Due in large part to the Depression, the failures of farms and small businesses were endemic. Equally evident was the resilience of the Japanese. Time after time they suffered severe reverses and made dogged new starts. To be sure, part of the problem could be attributed to racist attitudes on the part of the general public but much was simply due to the effects of the Depression itself, which so grievously affected all Americans. Since many Japanese, especially in California, were farmers, they were, like farmers everywhere, also extremely susceptible to climatic conditions and the fluctuations in the markets for farm produce. Moreover, there is little doubt that the Depression contributed to the hostility of the *hakujin* toward the *Nihonjin*. When agriculture had been in a depressed state for almost a decade before the Great Depression, the Japanese practice of having the whole family working, often from sunup to sundown, seemed to the *hakujin* farmers unfair competition. No white man was willing to work such hours, nor were his parents, his wife, or his children. Work was work; the average American farmer was habituated to it. But the labors of the Nippons smacked of self-imposed slavery to their white rivals. Riici Satow and his brother worked with their father in Napa, who, Riici recalled, "kept all our money, and gave me and my brother some pocket-money, enough for us to buy shoes, or shirts, or things of that sort. With three people working in one family, it wasn't that difficult to make good money."

One thing that impresses anyone reading the autobiographical accounts of Issei and Nisei is the frequency of serious illness and, often, early death. Americans, especially those who don't engage in gross physical labor, tend to glorify "hard work." But hard work kills and hard work killed many Japanese-Americans long before their time. The men seemed to have died most often of heart attacks, the women of cancer.

ONE OF THE PARADOXES IN THE LIVES OF MANY NISEI WAS THAT THEY held both U.S. *and* Japanese citizenship. When Japan first permitted emigration it was with the stipulation that the emigrant should "never lose allegiance to the Mikado." Down to 1924 the Japanese government considered that any child of Japanese parents wherever born was a Japanese citizen. In 1924 the Japanese Diet changed the law to stipulate that children of Japanese parents born in another country could have Japanese citizenship *if* the parents applied for it within fourteen days of the date of birth (which many did). So they were citizens both of the United States *and* of Japan.

Chapter 4

AND WHAT DID
THEY DO?

HOW DID THE JAPANESE ON THE WEST COAST OF THE UNITED states make their living (besides working very hard)? At the time of the evacuation they were given lengthy questionnaires to fill in, including questions about their occupation. These are the best index we have to the work performed by the 89,000 adult Japanese living on the West Coast.

A total of 1,852 Japanese were in "professional occupations." Of these 570 were Nisei men and 436 Nisei women. Among the Issei the figures were surprisingly similar, 502 men and 335 women. With the Nisei, 64 men and 143 women were listed as "teachers"; with the Issei it was 64 men and 235 women. Of a total of 192 Nisei doctors and dentists, 96 were men and 11 women. Among the Issei, the figures were 81 and 4 respectively, again suggesting that Japanese women in America enjoyed far greater opportunities than in Japan. There were 65 engineers and 24 judges and lawyers, 2 of whom were women. Of 176 Nisei "clergy persons," 28 were men and 2 were women. Among the Issei, 143 were men and 3 were women. Of 172 pharmacists there were 77 Nisei men an 23 Nisei women. The category "semiprofessional occupations" included retail and wholesale managers, managers of hotels and restaurants, buyers, and store managers. Of the 6,333 evacuees listed under this heading, by far the largest division was "retail managers" (3,271). Here Issei men were predominant, 1,774 to 1,094 Nisei.

Under the heading "technical, managerial," 878 Nisei were listed and, in one of the most suggestive statistics, these were divided 406 males and 385 females. In other words, in the second highest occupational category almost half were women.

There were 46 commercial artists (most of whom worked for the Disney Studios as animators and 8 of whom were women) and then (an intriguing category) 22 dancers and chorus girls; 76 photographers (indicating, presumably, the Japanese infatuation with the camera); 31 ship captains, pilots, mates, and engineers; 16 Post Office clerks (10 men and 6 women); and 113 midwives, 2 of whom were men.

"Clerical operations" included bookkeepers, secretaries, stenographers, typists to the number of some 3,000, and here, as one might have expected, both Nisei and Issei women had a 3 to 1 edge. Of the 5,661 in "sales occupations," women slightly outnumbered men. In the category of "domestic service," women predominated but with this interesting distinction—among Nisei, including "housemen and yardmen," there were only 372 men as opposed to 2,450 women; with the Issei, however, there were 864 men engaged in such work against only 608 women. Much the same ratio prevailed with janitors and custodians, suggesting that Nisei sons had been conspicuously more successful in avoiding lower-level jobs than their fathers. The "personal service" category (cooks, waiters and waitresses, barbers and beauticians) included somewhat over 4,000, and again it is clear that proportionately far fewer Nisei sons were involved in such tasks than their fathers, pointing up the classic American dream of the son bettering the social and material condition of the father.

In the Seattle area over 200 hotels were owned and operated by Japanese. Hotels, markets, and dry-cleaning establishments were heavily represented in Portland, dry-cleaning businesses and nurseries in the San Francisco area. In the Los Angeles area residential property, hotels, apartments, and markets predominated.

Finally, it is worth noting that of the 89,000 Japanese whose occupations were recorded, only some 4,500 were listed as engaged in "semi-skilled" or "unskilled" labor (1,500 in the latter category).

Agriculture, as one might have expected, was the largest single occupational category. It included slightly over 25,000 men and women and was broken down into thirteen subdivisions. In 1913 the California legislature had passed the Alien Land Law intended to deny the right of *any* alien to hold land, the exceptions being pre-existing provisions of "any treaty." In the case of the Japanese the relevant treaty, signed in 1911, gave Japanese "the right to own and lease certain sorts of buildings and to lease land for residential and commercial purposes only." Ways were soon found around the act. Most common was the vesting of land in a Nisei child called, for this purpose, a "citizen child." The father was then appointed guardian of the minor. Other ruses were employed such as having Nisei listed as owners of record. Masuo Akizuki recalled that some Nisei became "very wealthy" simply by letting Issei use their names as owners of farmland.

Ichiro Yamaguchi recounted: "After I was 21, being one of the older nisei, I had to buy land for other people. The Kizukas were one of them. I bought a parcel under my name and the other parcel was bought in his son's name and I was the trustee. . . . When people asked me to help them this way, I never refused. I would sign all the papers and they made all the payments."

Shig Doi was born in Auburn, north of Sacramento, in 1920. The Doi family worked an eighty-five-acre orchard with peaches, pears, and grapes. When Doi's older brother reached the age of twenty-one, the farm was bought in his name. "So in 1939 and 1940, we worked it within our family. I guess all the Nihonjin, that's how they did it—a family deal, so a lot of money didn't go out of the family."

Henry Kazato's father had bought the house the family was living in at the time of Pearl Harbor in his son's name. In addition they bought five acres of land to farm also in the name of the minor son.

By such legal expedients, Issei farmers effectively owned or controlled (by lease) most of the land they farmed.

Since the use of citizen children to deed land seemed to many Californians a legal dodge, efforts were made to divest the children of ownership by escheat proceedings. These cases enjoyed some success but in 1928 the Superior Court of Sonoma County ruled: "Children born in California of Japanese parentage are citizens of the United States and of California, and are entitled to the same rights of property, real and personal, as other citizens, irrespective of their racial descent: a Japanese father though incompetent himself to acquire real property may furnish money in good faith for the purchase of real property for his minor children, who are citizens of the United States; minor children have the same right to acquire real property as adults, and if a gift of real property is made by deed to minors, delivery and acceptance will be presumed: Japanese aliens are entitled to the possession of real property for residential and commercial purposes under Article I of the Treaty of 1911 between the United States and Japan: a Japanese alien parent otherwise competent is entitled to be appointed guardian of the person and estate of his citizen child and the citizen child has the right to have his alien Japanese parent appointed as such guardian.'' There were other court decisions to the same effect. By the Fujita case the expedient of citizen children ownership of land became legal. Through various legal loopholes the number of Japanese ''manager-operated'' farms increased from 113 in 1920 to 1,816 in 1930. The number of ''tenant-operated'' farms increased from 1,580 in 1930 to 3,596 ten years later.

In the various agricultural subdivisions, there were 1,671 fruit farmers; 4,336 farmhands in wheat and grain farms, and 4,483 farmhands on fruit farms; 5,524 farmhands on vegetable farms; 2,067 farm managers and foremen; 1,805 evacuees listed their occupation as ''drivers,'' chauffeurs, taxi, bus, and tractor drivers. Some 4,000 were truck farmers. There were 2,365 gardeners and groundskeepers (''parks and cemeteries, etc.''), of whom 1,550 were Issei men and 815 Nisei. Indeed, in virtually all agricultural areas, Issei men substantially outnumbered Nisei, suggesting that many Nisei sons of farmers were drawn to other than agricultural pursuits.

By 1939, 149 Japanese wholesale businesses were located in Los Angeles operating fleets of trucks that picked up produce at Japanese farms and carried it to the city for distribution. It was estimated that by 1941 they did 60 percent of the wholesale fruit and vegetable business of the city and grossed some $26 million.

The number of farms operated by Japanese owners or lessees constituted only 2 percent of all farms and involved only .3 percent of total farm acreage. But due to the intensive methods of Japanese cultivation the output of their farms was positively awesome by American standards. One result was that Japanese farmland was far more valuable than the land of American farmers. The average per acre value of West Coast farmland in 1940 was $37.94, whereas that of Japanese farms was $279.96, a startling discrepancy. The Florin area near Sacramento was a classic example of marginal land made fruitful by the skill of the Japanese farmers who raised strawberries and grapes there. Individual farms varied in size from fifteen to fifty acres depending in part on the size of the farmer's family, since the members of the family provided the labor force.

The average size of Japanese farms was forty-two acres and 85 percent of the Japanese farms contained less than fifty acres. As contrasted with native farmers, the Japanese had three out of four acres in productive crops while the native American farmers had one out of four. In addition, most Japanese farmers harvested several crops a year. Strawberries, tomatoes, lettuce, onions, celery, nursery stock, peas, beans, fruit, melons, and sugar beets were all favored by the Japanese. The estimated value of their crops was $32,317,700 in 1940 (a present-day equivalent would be at least ten times more). The value of the lettuce crop was estimated at $5,942,100, celery at $4,667,250, cantaloupe $2,720,000.

The agricultural story was not just a matter of income dollars, certain crops were, as has been noted, a virtual monopoly of the Japanese. Ninety percent of all strawberries grown in California were grown by the Japanese, 73 percent of snap beans, 75 percent of celery, 50 percent of tomatoes. On .3 percent of the land. Other farmers were only human to resent the superior skills of their Japanese rivals and the greater productivity of their land. In the words of Raymond Katagi, "the Japanese always came from behind, but they always get ahead of them."

A preponderance of farmworkers were the so-called Issei bachelors. They were, for the most part, lower-caste Japanese who had come to the United States prior to the Immigration Act of 1924, which, by cutting off immigration, prevented the Issei bachelors from returning to Japan to find wives to bring back to the United States or from importing "picture brides" from Japan. Wives were missed as sexual partners and mothers, of course, but almost equally for their economic value. Deprived of wives the bachelor Issei found themselves at a great disadvantage as far as prospering in the United States; they were condemned, in large part, to being agricultural field hands. Perhaps most important of all they had no children to draw them into contact with the Caucasian world. Riici Satow told Heihachiro Takarabe that the "magic-three" was the ruination of many Issei bachelors. The "magic-three" were "gambling, drinking and prostitution." Of the three, gambling, in Satow's opinion, was the most destructive.

Chapter 5

YAMATO DAMASHII

IT MIGHT BE WELL AT THIS POINT TO GIVE SOME FURTHER ATTENTION to the character of those Japanese who came to the United States. It was in essence the character of the Japanese of the homeland, much of which has already been described—what the Japanese call *Yamato Damashii*, the Japanese spirit.

The key to the character of a people is to be found not in their genes but in their history. The character of the Japanese had been shaped by several thousand years of tumultuous history and was full of paradoxes that puzzle the Western mind to this day. The Japanese were secretive, conspiratorial, and suicidally courageous, ready to make any sacrifice, including that of their lives, for their daimyo, or feudal lord, for the shogun, and later for the Emperor (who was believed to be divine). A famous Noh play tells the story of a samurai who misreads a message suspended from a cherry tree. He interprets it as an instruction to kill his youngest son in order to prove his loyalty to his daimyo. He does so in the approved Japanese fashion by cutting off the child's head and presenting it to his lord in one of those baskets made for the purpose of holding severed heads, only to find out that it was all a mistake. The proper interpretation of the message was to the effect that "he who cuts a limb from the tree would lose one of his own limbs in punishment," a bloody enough retribution. Besides suggesting the ambiguity of the Japanese written language, the story illustrates the Japanese notion of loyalty to one's superiors, a hierarchy that reached to the Emperor. One of the most important Japanese holidays, Suishingura, celebrates the ideal of loyalty. December 14 is observed as the anniversary of the raid on Lord Kira's residence in 1705 by the forty-seven ronin. The ronin were the former samurai, now unemployed, of Lord Asano. Asano had applied to Lord Kira, chief of protocol, for instructions as to how to perform the proper offices in the presence of the Emperor. Lord Kira deliberately gave Asano the wrong instructions. Asano disgraced himself in the presence of the Emperor and had to commit seppuku. His followers thereupon resolved to have vengeance on Lord Kira. They waited for two years until Kira let his guard down and then attacked his palace and killed him. They all were then condemned to commit seppuku themselves and became national heroes. The anniversary of their collective deaths is celebrated as the ultimate example of fidelity; they were the "Faithful Ones" who did their duty to their lord. A classic Japanese history notes: "This bold deed aroused universal admiration."

In the words of the historian Marius Jansen: "Duty, above all to a higher political calling, was superior to family considerations and responsibilities. Loyalty was the mark of the good warrior, and, since Japanese feudalism was strongly familistic and [stressed] filial piety, they reinforced the demands of duty. . . . In particular, it was the phrase of Chu Hsi, *taigi meibun*, 'the highest duty of all.' " Loyalty to the superior.

Next to loyalty to the daimyo and later the Emperor, the Japanese sons and daughters vowed loyalty to their parents—*Oyakoko*, "filial obligation." When Charles Kikuchi's father returned to Japan to find a wife some thirty years after he had fled his father's wrath, he built a $3,000 shrine in memory of his father, who had been mayor of the town when Kikuchi's father ran away.

Jack Nishida recalled that he was brought up "as a real Japanese." There was never any open show of affection between various members of the family. He had never kissed or been kissed or hugged by his mother. "You just don't have physical contact. When my father was dying, we couldn't say anything. I should have hugged him but I didn't. We just didn't do that. Now that we are married, [my wife] Takeko lets me hug her, but with my mother I still don't do that. Not that I don't love her, but it is not done in our culture. . . . My father and mother never held hands . . . they never touched my hands."

Romantic love as a basis of marriage was virtually unknown in Japan and indeed in the United States. Arranged marriages or marriages with picture brides were the rule. The advantage of picture brides was that the whole procedure was far less expensive than marriages arranged in Japan since the picture bride involved only one steamship fare while a marriage in Japan required three—the husband's fare back to Japan and the fare of husband and wife to the United States. Riici Satow did not know of any Japanese among his friends who were not married to a picture bride, primarily for economic reasons.

Honor, especially "family honor," was another deeply ingrained concept. Charles Kikuchi recalled that when as an eight-year-old he did badly in school and his teacher called in his father to ask for his assistance in improving the child's work, his father was enraged. He had been so "dishonored" by his son that he beat and kicked him unmercifully. His father declared that he was "a disgrace to the race of Nippon . . . [and] had not any Japanese virtue of any sort!" In an attempt to remedy that lack, Kikuchi recounted, his father "hung me by the feet to the two-by-six rafters that cut the ceiling of the room in half, and whipped me with an old razor strop. I hung there, head down, for five or ten minutes."

Then there was Japanese fatalism. An old Japanese saying noted that everyone had to face five disasters—fire, flood, earthquake, tornado, and father. Jack Tono's parents were Nisei. "When anything went against them," Tono told John Tateishki, "they had this last word, which they said all the time, *Shikataganai* (Can't be helped)."

One characteristic shared by all Japanese Americans was their devotion to *kai,* or associations and clubs, of various kinds. Among more than 160 Japanese organizations in San Francisco alone, twenty-seven were prefectural organizations, associations of immigrants from a particular prefecture who shared a strong regional feeling. Included in the 160-plus were associations or clubs for calligraphy, tea ceremony, kendo, sumo and judo, golf, tennis and baseball.

For many Westerners the most seductive aspect of *Yamato Damashii* was the disposition (one might almost call it the obsession) to turn everything into art—the box a gift was presented in, the wrapping of the gift, the placing of flowers in relationship to one another, the preparation of tea, the placing of items of food on a plate—all such matters were governed by rules as strict as those that governed the relationship between parents and children and between classes or castes.

When the anthropologist Ruth Benedict tried to explain the "Japanese spirit," she used the images of the sword and the chrysanthemum. The Japanese were people who had lived for centuries by the sword, the

beautiful and deadly weapon of the samurai, and who adored chrysanthemums, lavishing infinite care and attention upon that flower (and, of
course, others as well). Every year there were national competitions for
the most beautiful chrysanthemums and prints of the winners were faithfully rendered by artists.

The Japanese critic Soetsu Yanagi wrote of the *Yamato Damashii* as
it respected art: "To me the greatest thing is to live with things of
beauty. . . . As long as beauty abides only in a few articles created by a
few geniuses, the Kingdom of Beauty is nowhere near realization."
M. Anesaki wrote in the same vein: "To a remarkable degree, Japanese
art enters the daily life of the people, whether they are educated or
ignorant, trained or not. It influences their homes and the utensils of their
domestic life."

So there it was, the beautiful, murderous sword and the flower; the
severed head, the eviscerated body in what must be the most cruel ritual
of self-immolation that the human imagination has devised.

Such was the character of Japanese culture and that was the culture that
Japanese immigrants brought with them and the culture that they tried to
preserve in their new homes. Of all the various nations and races of man
and woman who have come to these shores since the Norsemen or those
Asians who presumably passed over the Alaskan land bridge centuries
ago, no more exotic people made that ocean journey than the Japanese.

It is hard to imagine two more incompatible cultures than that of the
United States and Japan. Actually, though, the United States did not (and
does not) have a *culture* in the proper sense of that word. The United
States is a *society* held together by a few basic ideas, the most prominent
being those of freedom and equality. Democracy and individualism are
also important. Where America was "free," full of improvisation and
innovation, Japan was formed and formal in the highest degree. Where
"society" encounters "culture" culture always wins because it is far
denser and more comprehensive. We can usually adapt quite readily to a
new "society"; the forms and orders of a culture are much more difficult
to comprehend and often impossible to master. Inscrutable, in other
words. And that, of course, is what the Japanese Americans were to the
hakujin—inscrutable. To the Nippons the *hakujin* seemed like large, ugly
"hairy" precocious children, absurdly rich in technologies, but poor in
the things that counted most—the intricate arts of living, the *Yamato
Damashii,* the spiritual life of the Japanese people.

Dense and persuasive as was traditional Japanese culture, it was powerless against the classic American agent of assimilation—the American high school—and, indeed, the educational system in general.

As they had for previous generations of immigrant children, the schools (and increasingly the colleges) turned young Japanese into Americans. Education (*Kyoiku*), which the Japanese so revered, was also an instrument of alienation as Nisei children learned English while their Issei parents, in most instances, could speak or understand only Japanese.

For those who attended elementary or secondary school on the West Coast, the fact that they excelled in their studies and, perhaps more important, in that ultimate measure of juvenile approval, athletics, did much to smooth their way. Over a ten-year period in one Seattle high school one fourth of graduation day valedictorians and salutatorians were Nisei, who made up only 10 percent of the student population.

Frances Kirihara was typical. She became the first Nisei president of the California Scholarship Association of the Livingston high school. As the "pet" of the orchestra teacher she was often featured in the orchestra. "We went to the class dances and things like that," she recalled, "but we always had our own group within the big group at school." Kirihara remembered that "Nisei students really did not make many friends among *hakujins*. I sort of think that . . . our parents brought us up with the idea that we were better than the *'hakujins.'* " Kirihara was not sure, looking back, that this was not a kind of defense mechanism "to try to bolster their morale," but she recalled feeling that "I was equal or even better."

Yoshiye Togasaki was born in San Francisco, the fifth of eight children. She and her sister were sent to Japan to live with their maternal grandmother in Tokyo because her grandmother was all alone and because caring for eight children and helping her husband run his store were too much for Togasaki's mother. When the grandmother died Togasaki and her sister returned to the United States. After finishing high school, she did her undergraduate work at the University of California at Berkeley and then went on to Johns Hopkins Medical School, where she got her degree in 1935, the first Japanese woman to graduate from that famous institution.

There were, of course, numerous cases of discrimination, especially in rural communities. When Mary Tsukamoto's family moved from Turlock to Florin they found that the Florin elementary school was segregated. Some years later, when she and her husband joined the Florin chapter of the Japanese American Citizens League, one of their first causes was to get the elementary school desegregated. When they proposed it to the superintendent of schools, rather to their surprise he acquiesced "and the trustees and principal were agreeable." Mary Tsukamoto herself had attended an unsegregated high school. There, the Japanese American boys who were outstanding athletes were popular while those who were less athletically inclined were often bullied by their Caucasian class-mates. Mary Tsukamoto recalled that such bullying became more common with word of the Japanese conquest of Manchuria. Tsukamoto herself experienced prejudice when, having been chosen as a finalist in the school oratorical contest, she was told by the principal that she could not compete because she was Japanese. On the more positive side, one of her Caucasian teachers, impressed by her scholastic promise, persuaded her father to relieve her of her strawberry-picking chores so that she could go on to college and paid her initial tuition fee to attend the College of the Pacific. As Tsukamoto told the story, her father suffered losses in his strawberry-growing business because he couldn't write or read contracts and was, in consequence, often cheated in verbal agreements. "All of this," she recalled, "was part of what he remembered, but he also re-membered this wonderful teacher who got me to college. That's how I ended up being a schoolteacher."

With each passing year more and more Nisei went on from high school to college. The first Japanese college graduate in the United States was apparently Manroku Matsumoto, who got an A.B. degree from the University of California in 1914. He was soon followed by hundreds more.

Raymond Katagi had been born in Osaka in 1903. He came to the United States in 1921 to join his father in Seattle. After a year in high school, Katagi went on to the University of Washington to study journalism. There was relatively little evidence of anti-Japanese feeling in Seattle so it was somewhat of a shock to move to Los Angeles, where anti-Japanese feeling was much more evident.

William Hosokawa was born in Seattle in 1915 and educated in the city's public schools. He graduated from the University of Washington in 1937 at the depths of the Depression; the only job he could find was working as an "English secretary" at the Japanese consulate in Seattle. When evacuation came, the fact Hosokawa had worked in the Japanese consulate put him under a cloud.

Eddie Sakamoto was born in Japan. When he came to the United States in 1921 he was seventeen years old. He attended an American high school and then UCLA for two years but the Depression cut short his hopes for a degree and he went to work for his father at a fruit stand in Brentwood.

As was the case in high school, the status of Japanese American college students was much enhanced by their athletic skills. Hito Okada earned letters in five varsity sports at the University of Washington, and Harry Yanagimachi was chosen for the conference all-star team for two years in a row; Roy Yamaguchi starred on the Oregon State Rose Bowl team in 1940.

Most of the Nisei who went to colleges and universities on the West Coast found helpful and encouraging teachers and mentors. The autobiographical accounts of college-educated Nisei stress the importance of such sponsorship. For Frank Miyamoto it was, first, Jesse Steiner, a sociologist who had taught for several years at a mission school in Sendai, Japan. Later, at the University of Chicago, his mentor was Herbert Blumer, a well-known sociologist.

Miyamoto had two years of engineering at the University of Washington before he dropped out. While at the university he did a study of Japanese Americans in Seattle and was struck by the "seemingly endless etiquette and formalities" and emphasis on such concepts as *on*, "obligations," in that community.

Engineering was a favorite field of undergraduate and graduate study for Nisei. Hundreds of them enrolled in such programs but few of them found jobs. In part the problem was the Depression; Caucasian engineers went unemployed, too, but it was the case that the Nisei had to deal with the Depression *plus* prejudice.

At this point we might introduce a young Nisei who will be our ingratiating guide through the early stages of the evacuation, Charles Kikuchi; we have already encountered Kikuchi as the victim of his father's rage at being dishonored by the son's poor record at school. After a year of his father's drunken rages, his mother persuaded Kikuchi's father to place Charles in a Salvation Army home. For the next decade Kikuchi's life was centered in the orphanage with a heterogeneous group of boys. An outstanding student in high school, Kikuchi traveled to Vallejo for a reunion with his family, now consisting of four girls and two other boys. The reunion was a touching one. His father had stopped drinking and was making his living as a barber. "My mother recognized me at once, with a little gasp," Kikuchi wrote. "She was still a few seconds, looking at me. Then she closed her eyes and smiled as though she had been expecting me. Three months before, through the lawyer, she had received a notice from the institution that I had left for San Francisco.

"There were several youngsters in the room, my brothers and sisters. At first I barely saw them. They all stared at me, and whispered excitedly.

"My father shuffled into the backroom from the shop. He said something in Japanese, perhaps inquiring what was going on, who I was, and what I wanted. He did not recognize me, partly because his eyes did not immediately become adjusted to the darkness of the room. I saw him clearly. He wore Japanese slippers over bare feet. He was only a shadow of the figure he had been ten years before. He was much smaller than I. Like a gnome.

"When informed who I was, he folded his arms and his head dropped on his sunken chest, and he began to talk in a jumble of Japanese and English. I gathered that he thought I hated him. Finally he sat on the edge of one of the three beds that crowded the room, and clutching a brass nob, asked me to forgive him for his treatment of me. . . . I felt dreadful over this, but managed to pat him on the shoulder and take his hand, which was weak and small and cold. Then he folded up on the bed and cried."

Although he declined the offer to move into the family's crowded quarters, Kikuchi visited frequently and slowly wove himself into the lives of his brothers and sisters as well as the lives of his parents. He reluctantly took a job as a houseboy, one of the few jobs open to young Japanese Americans in San Francisco, and attended San Francisco State College, where he became a student leader and president of the International Relations Club. His plan was to major in history and become a high school teacher but he soon realized that no Caucasian school board would appoint a Japanese American to teach in a public high school. Houseboy and farmworker seemed to be all that his education had qualified him for. He and his friends followed the crops in classic migrant worker fashion. After several years of hand-to-mouth existence, Kikuchi decided to enroll at the Berkeley campus of the University of California to get a certificate in social work. While still in graduate school, Kikuchi wrote a paper on the paradoxical situation of those Nisei who wished wholeheartedly to become Americanized but found the way blocked at every turn. "Adopting the American symbols of status," he wrote, "the Nisei are now faced with the question that perhaps this pattern of opportunity he has learned in school is not for him. . . . It is hard for them to reconcile democracy with prejudice and the fact that they can't go to certain bowling alleys, barber shops, swimming pools, and hotels. . . . Torn between two cultures, the Nisei finds no place or security in either."

Chapter 6

A DIVIDED PEOPLE

THOSE ISSEI WHO THOUGHT OF THEMSELVES AS JAPANESE WERE DIS-
mayed to see their children turning into "Americans" and in evident
danger of losing their "Japanese-ness." Unlike other immigrant groups,
the Issei found a powerful ally in their efforts to check or reverse the
process of Americanization that threatened to alienate them from their
children and their children from their parents' homeland. As an element
of their Greater East Asia Co-Prosperity Sphere campaign, the Japanese
Imperial government undertook to bring the children of Japanese immigrants back to Japan for their elementary and secondary school education.
Those Japanese who expected to return to Japan after they had acquired
sufficient capital to assure them of a prosperous life in their homeland
were naturally alarmed at the prospect of having their children seduced by
American life and American ways (and thus perhaps resist returning to
Japan) and they welcomed the opportunity to, they hoped, inoculate their
offspring against assimilation.

While the Japanese consuls in West Coast cities were tireless facilita-
tors of such educational "returns" the fact that Issei parents were willing
to part with their children for periods of time ranging up to ten years was
eloquent testimony of their *Yamato Damashii* as well as their devotion to
the Emperor.

Those Nisei who were sent to Japan for a portion (or all) of their primary and secondary school education were called Kibei. Enjoying both U.S. and Japanese citizenship, most were bilingual (as most of their American-educated peers were not) and were often as ardent Japanese nationalists as their parents. As U.S. citizens, they were due all the rights of U.S. citizenship, while considering themselves in many instances subject to the obligations of Japanese citizenship. By the time of Pearl Harbor some nine thousand Nisei had had all or a substantial part of their elementary and secondary school education in Japan and had thereby become Kibei.

Ruth Asawa grew up in the farming community of Norwalk, California, where her father, a worshipper of the Emperor, raised tomatoes on eighty-five acres. He was determined to have his children educated in Japan. Two of Ruth Asawa's sisters were sent to live with relatives and Ruth herself at the age of eight was scheduled to go to Japan with a cousin but the cousin had a stroke on the eve of their departure and Ruth was sent to the local elementary school. Her older sister returned to the United States a few months before Pearl Harbor but the other sister decided to cast her lot with the Japanese homeland.

The strange limbo that many Kibei lived in is suggested by the story of Harry Ueno. Ueno had had a few years of elementary school when his father sent him back to Japan with an uncle. For the next eight years Ueno went to school in Japan. His father returned to Japan and in 1923 Harry Ueno sailed for the United States. His older brother, who had finished high school in Hawaii, had gone on to Milwaukee. But Harry had no way to communicate with his brother. He could not speak or read English and his brother could not speak or write Japanese. When Harry finally made his way to Milwaukee they could do no more than embrace.

A significant group of Nisei were those who had simply visited Japan and then returned to the United States. Anxious to woo Nisei college students, the Japanese government encouraged such visits and offered special privileges to the visitors, hoping that they would stay in Japan or at least return to the United States as advocates of Japan. But such visits were seldom successful. The head of the Tokyo YWCA told a group of American educators visiting Japan, "We strongly advise against the coming of great numbers of second-generation Japanese Americans to Japan where opportunities for work or success are rare. All [Nisei] meet with great difficulty in finding work, entering schools, or in adjusting themselves to conditions here."

A Nisei faculty member from the University of California, Berkeley, went to Japan for a visit in 1937 and returned to the United States disillusioned. He wrote: "My wife's habit of walking beside me instead of behind me brought the family criticism and wrath. It did not look well. The relatives said that she had no respect for her husband. . . . A scandal could arise from such a situation."

Another Nisei professor, this one from the University of Washington, wrote: "I was a member of what is usually termed the underprivileged class . . . during most of my youth and early manhood. This country [America] is the only one in which an individual of my background could have been permitted to become a university professor. Our stay in Japan, where most personal liberties as we know them are denied, made us realize even more the importance of the democratic way of life."

By the time of Pearl Harbor 19,908 Nisei had spent some time in Japan, and as noted earlier more than 9,000 (the Kibei) had spent three years or more.

For those parents unwilling or unable to send their children to Japan, the Japanese government sponsored so-called Japanese language schools. During the Showa era (1926–1941) the language schools grew abundantly. Innocuous-sounding, the schools were in practical fact agencies of Japanese nationalism. The teachers were, in the main, Japanese nationals, some of them former army officers. Ostensibly committed to teaching, after regular school hours, the Japanese language to children attending public elementary and secondary schools, the language schools stressed *komi*, or "customs of Japan," and their basic purpose was plainly to try to counteract the influence of the American schools by a strong emphasis on *Yamato Damashii*, the principal element of which was the revived code of *bushido* with its message of Emperor worship. The textbooks that were used were sent by the Department of Education of the Imperial Government and were, in consequence, strongly nationalistic.

The teachers usually began their instruction by having the students line up in ranks at stiff attention like miniature soldiers. The teacher would then hold up a picture of the Emperor or a famous Japanese general or admiral and the students would raise their hands in a salute and shout *Banzai* (praise to the emperor) in unison.

The schools stressed the classic martial arts—judo, sumo, and kendo, or fencing. In the words of one historian of Japan, Marius Jansen, kendo was closely tied to the notion of undying loyalty to the Emperor: "The romantic overtones of the cult of the swordsman—the wise and courageous samurai, eye ever fixed on the ultimate objective with a heart as pure as his shining blade, trained to set aside all personal considerations, cultivating self-perfection in order to be a more perfect instrument of justice. There was cruelty as well as courage in the conduct of the *ronin* swordsmen. . . . Since they took for themselves the highest of morality and duty, their enemies could be dismissed with hatred and contempt.''

By 1940 there were 261 Japanese language schools in California alone with a faculty of 454 and 17,800 pupils. Many, although not all, Nisei who attended the language schools found them burdensome and resented being forced to attend, the public schools being far more congenial. If one were to judge only by the number of Nisei fluent in Japanese, one must declare the schools a failure.

In addition to the Kibei program and the Japanese language schools there were two other important agencies of ''re-Japanization,'' or of holding the loyalty of Japanese expatriates in other countries. They were the *kai*, or patriotic associations, and the Japanese language press.

The *kai* were formed under the commodious umbrella of the *Nihonjin Kai*, the Japanese Association, which, in California, was under the direction of the Japanese consul in San Francisco. Like many immigrant organizations the Japanese Association performed a number of important services for Japanese immigrants, helping the sick and indigent, rewarding and publicizing the accomplishments of Japanese immigrants, assisting those who wanted to return to Japan, arranging for Nisei tours to Japan, and assisting Kibei to go to Japan for their education. The Nihonjin Kai ''did mainly political things,'' Nisuke Mitsumori recalled. ''They celebrated the Emperor's birthday, showed Japanese movies, did some campaigns for fund raising, etc.''

The Heimisha Kai was founded in San Francisco in 1937 and by 1940 it claimed more than ten thousand members. It was made up primarily of men of military age liable to be called as conscripts. One of the main functions was the collection of funds to be sent to the Japanese War Ministry. The prospectus for Heimisha Kai declared: ''The world should realize that our military action in China is based upon the significant fact that we are forced to fight under realistic circumstances. As a matter of fact, whenever the Japanese government begins a military campaign we, Japanese, must be united and everyone must do his part.

''As far as patriotism is concerned, the world knows that we are superior to any other nation. However, as long as we are staying on foreign soil, what can we do for our mother country? All our courageous fighters are fighting at the front today, forgetting their parents, wives and children in their homes: It is beyond our imagination, the manner in which our imperial soldiers are sacrificing their lives at the front lines. . . . Therefore, we, the Japanese in the United States, have been contributing a huge amount of money for war relief funds and numerous comforting bags for our imperial soldiers.

"Today, we Japanese in the United States, who are not able to sacrifice our lives for our National cause are now firmly resolved to stand by to settle the present war as early as possible. We are proud to say that our daily happy life in America is dependent upon the protective power of Great Japan. We are facing a critical emergency and we will take strong action as planned. We do hope and beg you all to cooperate with us for our National cause."

The Hokubei Butoku Kai, the Military Virtue Society of North America, was organized in 1931 to instill the ideals of *bushido*. One of its principal duties was to train Japanese boys in kendo, judo, and sumo.

Another Japanese patriotic society was the Kanjo Kai (Society for Defending the Country by Swords, the Sword Society for short), whose leadership came from former Japanese officers and whose members were former Japanese soldiers. The Togo Kai was named after Admiral Togo, the hero of the Russo-Japanese war, and its purpose was to raise money for the Japanese navy.

When Charles Kikuchi was picking pears on the Sacramento River delta during summer vacation, one of his fellow-pickers was a former Japanese army officer who was a member of the Black Dragon Society, another fiercely patriotic *kai*.

Among the numerous other *kai* were Aikoku Fujin Kai (Patriotic Women's Society), Jugo Sekisei Kai (Behind the Gun Society), Hokoku Kai (Society for Service to the Country), Aikokui Kenno Kisei Domei Kai (Patriotic League for Contribution to the Airplane Fund), Josho Kai (Ever-Victorious Society), Sokoku Kai (Fatherland Society), Zaibei Ikuei Kai (Society of Educating the Second Generation in America). It was this latter *kai* that sponsored the Japanese language schools.

Although the FBI had identified only a dozen or so Japanese American associations that it felt confident were made up of individuals devoted to the Emperor, over a hundred others were identified that, with their branches, came to more than three hundred whose purposes were, on the whole, quite obscure to the various intelligence services, but the mere existence of which made them nervous.

The Japanese press was extensive and ubiquitous. Newspapers were printed almost exclusively in Japanese and contained primarily news of the homeland and of Japanese social and cultural events. They gave relatively little attention to "American" news, although by the time of Pearl Harbor a number of Japanese newspapers had sections in English for Nisei who could not read Japanese.

In Los Angeles three dailies were published in Little Tokyo in 1941; all were unabashedly supportive of Japan and its Greater East Asia Co-Prosperity Sphere policy. A typical news item in one such paper on March 13, 1941, noted that thirty-two bales of tinfoil collected by Japanese in Fresno, Kern, and San Bernardino counties had been sent to Japan. On July 6, another paper reported that the Central California Japanese Association had collected $3,502.45, which had been sent to the War Ministry. Another news story dated March 20, 1941, noted that the war veterans associations in Japan, Germany, and Italy "in keeping with the spirit of the Axis Treaty have formed joint and advisory committees to aid and establish the New World Order. There are 3½ million veterans and reservists, headed by General Imei who have pledged their cooperation to the Axis aims."

Japanese language papers also reported numerous celebrations of "Emperor worship" intended to stimulate "burning patriotism" and "all-out support of the Japanese Asiatic Co-Prosperity Program."

On February 11, 1940, the Nippon-jin Japanese Association of San Francisco sponsored a ceremony involving the worship of the Emperor that was attended by some three hundred Japanese Americans. A celebration of the 2601st year of the founding of the Japanese empire was held in Lindsay, California, in January 1941. Those attending bowed their heads toward Japan to indicate that they were "ready to respond to the call of the mother country with one mind. . . . Our fellow Japanese countrymen must be of one spirit and should endeavor to unite our Japanese societies in this country," an editorial in the paper observed.

As reported in the *New World Sun* of January 7, 1941, the ceremonies of the Lindsay group included the singing of the Japanese national anthem, the opening of the Emperor's portrait, the reading of the Emperor's Rescripts and of the Message of Reverence, and the shouting in unison of *Banzai,* and "long live the Emperor."

The potency of baseball was not overlooked in trying to tie young Nisei to the mother country. For Masuo Akizuki his fondest memory of prewar San Jose, California, was organizing a baseball team in Japantown that went on a fifteen-day tour of Japan, playing with Japanese teams. In addition, he organized a sumo wrestling league that included teams from Fresno, San Francisco, and Sacramento.

Through its various propaganda channels, the Japanese government played tirelessly upon two themes that had more than a modicum of fact beneath them: one was the desperate need for land to accommodate the nation's rapidly growing population. The other closely related argument was that Japan was a nation poor in the natural resources, most notably oil and iron ore, needed by a modern industrial nation to maintain a respectable place on the international stage. In the Pacific area, greedy Western nations had gobbled up all such resources in the form of colonies and now were determined to slam the door in Japan's face. Moreover, they slammed the door (or did their best to slam it) in a particularly arrogant and condescending way, taking the high moral ground that Japan's ambitions were lawless and illegitimate, while their pillaging had been conducted, in the main, for the good of backward Asiatic people.

Those Japanese who had cast their lot with the United States, men and women who had done their best to assimilate—businessmen, professional men and women, doctors, lawyers, engineers, prosperous farmers, hotel owners, successful nurserymen, all such—were dismayed at the activities of the various patriotic *kai*. They might belong to certain *kai* to retain credibility within the Japanese community but they felt that the activities of the more zealous Japanese nationalists compromised their own positions in the Caucasian world, positions they had fought so hard to achieve, positions they highly valued. Some of the men were veterans of World War I, members of American Legion Posts (Charles Kikuchi's father was a World War I veteran), members of Chambers of Commerce and Kiwanis Clubs.

Each new Japanese act of aggression that increased the fervor of the Japanese nationalists increased the alarm of those Japanese determined to protect their American status. To all these individuals the nationalists posed an agonizing dilemma. They feared the nationalists would simply reinforce the public image of all Japanese as enemies. Their response to the activities of the Nihonjin-kai, or Japanese Association, was the Japanese American Citizens League, whose very name expressed its defiance of nationalists.

The historian of the Japanese American Citizens League, T. Tanaka, discovered several antecedent organizations, but it was not until the Sino-Japanese hostilities in July 1937 that the league began to grow rapidly.

One of the league's appeals, in addition to its emphasis on the loyalty of the Nisei to the U.S., had been its strenuous lobbying efforts to prevent state legislation unfavorable to the interests of the Japanese. It was even alleged that certain anti-Japanese bills were routinely introduced into the California legislature in order to stimulate contributions from JACL lobbyists to kill the bills. The core of the California JACL was the Japanese farmers' and fishermen's associations, especially the Seine and Line Fishermen's Union of San Pedro, which, conscious of its vulnerability, made its own declaration of loyalty in June 1940.

In its early years, the JACL did its best to carry water on both shoulders, taking the line that loyalty to Japan was not necessarily incompatible with loyalty to the United States, but with the Sino-Japanese War the position of the JACL began to shift. Dual citizenship seemed no longer possible as Americans in general identified more and more strongly with China.

Prominent in the California JACL was Tokutaro Nishimura Slocum, a veteran of World War I. A close ally of Slocum was Ken Matsumoto, president of the Los Angeles chapter of the JACL. Matsumoto had a successful jewelry store that catered primarily to Caucasians. As the conflict between the nationalistic Japanese and the leaders of the JACL grew more bitter, some JACL leaders turned for support to the various U.S. intelligence agencies—primarily the FBI and Military and Naval Intelligence. In the words of the most comprehensive study of the JACL: "Close personal relationships characterized most of these top contacts." Ken Matsumoto, for example, was a friend of Lieutenant Commander Kenneth Ringle, a Naval Intelligence officer.

Inevitably, members of the Japanese American Citizens League began to provide information to the FBI and to Naval Intelligence about the leaders of the patriotic organizations. In their view they were doing no more than fighting to maintain their own status as loyal Americans. True to the ancient Japanese practice of conspiratorial activity, once they had transferred their allegiance from one lord (Japan and the Emperor) to another (the United States), virtually any action was justified to sustain their cause.

What appeared to Japanese nationalists as the basest treachery—the alliance between the leaders of the JACL and the FBI—seemed to the JACL merely the duty of loyal Americans. In Japan, the informer, the *inu*, or dog, was the most feared and despised individual (and one of the most common). The history of Japan is a nightmarish kaleidoscope of conspiracies. Such betrayals are the stuff of numerous Kurosawa films and Japanese historical dramas. It was thus as natural for the leaders of the Japanese American Citizens League to inform the FBI about the pro-Japan sentiments and activities of the nationalists as it was for the nationalists to seek vengeance against those they believed had betrayed them to the enemy.

As we approach the denouement of Pearl Harbor, we thus find the West Coast Japanese deeply divided among themselves. There were at least three identifiable groups, or factions. Those Issei who intended to return to Japan to live out their later years were overwhelmingly loyal to the Emperor. That fact was both natural and inevitable. Unable, for the most part, to even speak English (or be American citizens), they had no knowledge of or interest in American principles and ideals. To many of them, Caucasian Americans appeared hardly better than barbarians. Among their American-born children—citizen children, the Nisei—were many who had been sent to Japan for their education and who there had imbibed the tenets of *Yamato Damashii*, which included among its principles unquestioning devotion to the Emperor.

Contrasted sharply with them were the Americanized or assimilated Nisei, most of whom had attended the Americanizing institution the high school and, with increasing frequency, a college or university. Indeed, we can even speak of a category of "college Nisei." From their ranks came the founders and members of the Japanese American Citizens League.

Finally, there was what was in many ways the deepest division, that between Japanese Christians and Japanese Buddhists. It was from the Japanese Christian community that the majority of the pro-U.S. Japanese came although it must be noted that some Japanese Christians were fervent nationalists. While the line could not be clearly or simply drawn, it was nonetheless true that Japanese Christians constituted the core of those who, with whatever inevitable reservations and misgivings, cast their lot with the United States. Although Christians were outnumbered more than two to one by Buddhists, a disproportionate number of Christians were to be found in urban areas and among the college Nisei. In California the largest proportions of Buddhists lived, not surprisingly, in the rural areas, where 80 percent of the men and 84 percent of the women were Buddhists as opposed to 11 and 12 percent Christian. In urban areas 32 and 36 percent of the Issei were Christians while the number rose to 59 percent for Nisei women and 53 percent for Nisei men living in urban areas. The figures were even more striking in relation to college Nisei. At the University of Washington, 69 percent of the graduate and undergraduate students were Protestant Christians, while 17 percent were Buddhists; 11 percent gave no religious affiliation.

*   *   *

AN IMPORTANT POINT TO EMPHASIZE IS THE RAPIDLY CHANGING POLIT-
ical scene in Japan itself. An elderly Issei, looking back over his years
in the United States, saw the period from 1924 to 1931 as a time of
Americanization in Japan when the ideals of democracy penetrated the
Japanese community reflecting a period of democracy and general lib-
eralization. In 1931, this same Issei wrote, "a vitally significant event
occurred, changing the tide and trend of immigrant Japanese development. This was the year of the Manchurian incident, where the Japanese military, breaking the bonds of liberal government, invaded
Manchuria. This was the start of the aggression that was to eventually
lead to Pearl Harbor. From 1931 on, the Japanese government launched
a very active and pronounced campaign to indoctrinate colonists
abroad. The military was again on the march. . . . The differences in
Japanese national attitudes soon expressed themselves in magazines and
publications which reached overseas.

"Immigrant Japanese in America, ruled by law as ineligible to American citizenship, began to feel, 'Well, perhaps there is something to
Japanese nationalism. Maybe Japanese destiny is written as the Tokyo
government spokesmen, the extreme rightist military men, say.

"There was also a revival of the emphasis upon ritual in connection
with ancient Japanese sports—jiu jitsu, kendo, sumo, yumi. The Japanese virtues were endowed with halos."

The Nisei college students perhaps suffered most from the Sino-
Japanese conflict. Some undertook to picket the Oakland shipping lines as
protest against the shipment of American scrap iron to Japan. Others
sponsored films or speakers that presented the "Japanese side" of the
conflict. Many had to confront for the first time the issue of their com-
mitment to the United States *or* Japan. Many Nisei in college, surrounded
by Caucasian friends who were highly critical of Japan, came down on
the side of the United States, thereby often finding themselves in direct
opposition to their Issei parents. On the other hand, at the University of
Washington, the pro-Japanese students persuaded the student newspaper
editor not to publish articles by Chinese students.

A Nisei student expressed the feelings of many of his peers:

> *Behold*
> *We are clay pigeons traveling swiftly and aimlessly*
> *On the electric wire of international hate,*

Helpless targets in the shooting gallery of political dis-
  cord
Dulled by the chattering shells
That rip toward us from both sides.
Perhaps we are merely incidental in the gunplay,
Irrevocably set in the dizzy pace of whining bullets,
Forced to travel up and down an uncertain line
The hesitating border of two countries.

Part 2

THE DECISION
NOBODY MADE

Chapter 7

THE AFTERMATH OF
PEARL HARBOR

ALL OF WHICH BRINGS US AGAIN TO THE MORNING OF DECEMBER 7, 1941. Francis Biddle, the newly appointed attorney general of the United States, who as head of the Department of Justice and the FBI, was to be active in the events that followed the bombing of Pearl Harbor, was giving a fund-raising talk for Detroit Democrats when his aide, Ugo Carusi, handed him a note that read, "Japanese today attacked Pearl Harbor, great U.S. Naval Base in the Hawaiian Island, and they are also bombing Manila from planes probably released by aircraft carriers. . . . The raids are still in progress."

Biddle flew back to Washington for an emergency cabinet meeting. He found the President "deeply shaken, graver than I had ever seen him." After a somber review of the military situation, the leading senators and congressmen were called into the Oval Office. There was little to say and it was quickly said. Tom Connally, senator from Texas and recently head of the Foreign Relations Committee, jumped up, banged on the President's desk with his fist, and shouted: "How did they catch us with our pants down, Mr. President?" "And the President," Biddle wrote, "with his head bowed, his assurance at a low ebb, muttered, 'I don't know, Tom, I just don't know.'"

The afternoon of December 8 Biddle took Roosevelt a proclamation to sign authorizing the attorney general to intern Japanese enemy aliens. "Most of the first group scheduled for detention," Biddle noted, "had already been arrested." Biddle asked about the detention of Italian aliens. "I don't care much about the Italians," Roosevelt replied. "They are a lot of opera singers, but the Germans are different, they may be danger- ous." Biddle took the President's frivolous response as a sign that he was recovering his spirits.

In the days following Pearl Harbor there was near panic; a Japanese invasion on the West Coast, feared for so many years, now seemed imminent. The dire warnings of decades appeared to be coming true. Were the Japanese? German? Mexican armies poised for a thrust into the heart of the Southwest, or a naval landing planned for somewhere on the long unprotected West Coast reaching from Canada to Mexico? There were rumors and alarms almost nightly. West Coast cities were blacked out. Anti-aircraft guns opened fire sporadically. Dean and Jane McHenry, who had just moved into their new Westwood home, took cabinet panels off each night and used them to cover the windows to prevent any ray of light escaping. Some people moved (and many more contemplated mov- ing) inland away from the anticipated raids or landings.

For the Japanese, the bombing of Pearl Harbor brought emotions too deep and complex to be easily sorted out. In 1929 a Japanese journalist, Murobuse Koshin, visiting the United States wrote: "Know America! We must study that nation before any other, not for its own sake but in order to better understand the world, and the end result will be knowledge of our own nation. . . . America is the world, America alone. As American capital began its unrival ascendancy, so too did the culture, spirit and way of life of America. In the twentieth century, particularly after the World War, the world is coeval with America. . . . Know America first, whether you worship or despise it, are capitalist or socialist, Westernizer or Pan- Asian. The world presents us with only one overriding issue: we worship the United States or we overcome it."

In the light of Pearl Harbor one reads the concluding sentence with a feeling of its prophetic nature. Koshin was a liberal reformer, yet he felt, as his countrymen did, the oppressive weight of the United States as the dominant power in the world, the nation with which every other nation must perforce come to terms or be trampled into the dust of history. Inevitably we place Koshin's outburst beside the fact of Pearl Harbor. Pearl Harbor was irrevocable. By its brilliant conclusiveness (in the sense that virtually destroyed the U.S. Pacific Fleet) it was assured of its place in history, and the Japanese soul was, in the most decisive way, freed from the incubus of American might. "Yes," the Japanese could always say (and will always be able to say), "in the end with your vastly superior wealth, far larger population, your allies, and your ultimately irresistible technology you defeated us but REMEMBER PEARL HARBOR!" If there was a Japanese man or woman in Japan or in the United States, anyone, liberal, radical, socialist, friend, or enemy of the Imperial system who did not feel somehow *freed* by Pearl Harbor, whatever other emotions or sentiments they might have entertained, it has not been recorded and it would indeed have been against human nature.

It was as though centuries of the Japanese military ethos were somehow concentrated in this spectacular, inconceivable event. All the remarkable ingenuity of an ingenious people was focused on this one episode. The pilots chosen for the mission were subjected to a process of selection and training more rigorous than the preparations of U.S. astronauts many years later. They were from the samurai class and we have seen the unforgettable Japanese films of the samurai pilots climbing into the cockpits of their planes with their swords clutched at their sides. The story of the planning and execution of the raid has been often and well told, so it is only necessary here to recall its dramatic impact on the world.

The emotions that Japanese felt after the initial euphoria depended, in large part, on their political orientation. Charles Kikuchi wrote in his diary: "Pearl Harbor. We are at war! Jesus Christ, the Japs bombed Hawaii and the entire fleet has been sunk. I just can't believe it. I don't know what in the hell is going to happen to us, but we will all be called into the army right away. Wang [a Chinese friend] says he has to do a report, but is so stunned that he does not know what he is doing. He is worried about his relatives as the radio says there are riots in Los Angeles, and they think it is sabotage. I can't believe that any Nisei would do anything like that, but it could be some of the Kibei spies. I don't know what is going to happen to us, but I just can't think of it.

"I think the Japs are coming to bomb us, but I will go and fight even if I think I am a coward and I don't believe in wars but this time it has to be. I am selfish about it. I think not of California and America, but I wonder what is going to happen to the Nisei and to our parents. They may lock up the aliens. How can one think of the future? We are behind the eightball."

Many Japanese American families were at church when word first came of the attack on Pearl Harbor. Frank Chuman and his family had just returned from the morning worship service at St. Mary's Episcopal Church in Los Angeles and were sitting down to lunch when the word came. "I was tremendously shocked," Chuman recalled, "and my immediate reaction was that Japan had done a very foolish thing. This was my very first objective, cold reaction, to Japan's bombing of Pearl Harbor. My parents' reactions were quite different. Their reaction was, Now that we are at war and we are of Japanese ancestry, we don't know what is going to happen to us; and in order to protect ourselves we should dispose of everything that has to do with any affiliations or associations with Japan." Chuman's father had many letters and pictures from Japan including awards that he received when he lived in Japan. These were destroyed or buried, including two ceremonial samurai swords that his father owned. The hilts were dismounted and the swords driven deep into the ground.

Like the Chumans many Issei destroyed or otherwise disposed of personal belongings that might suggest pro-Japanese sympathies. Osamu Doi, who was born in Salinas in 1925, was one of seven children in a Japanese Christian family. Like so many other Japanese families in the aftermath of Pearl Harbor, her mother tried to dispose of any possessions that seemed "Japanese," among them a sword that had been given to her husband by his father in Japan, a symbol of family status.

Unsure of what the FBI would consider incriminating evidence, the Satow family buried Japanese artifacts, from books in Japanese to precious inherited samurai swords: "anything that would sound nationalistic, even a bit, that I burned." Thinking back, he couldn't remember anything that really could have been considered subversive but in a panic he burned almost everything "Japanese."

One Issei remembered that on hearing the news of Pearl Harbor he hurried to his church where several members of the congregation were repairing the roof of the parsonage. When he called out "*Oi, Sensohda, Sensohda,* Hey, it's a war! It's a war!" adding, "It's going to be very bad," the workers on the roof called down, "Where? Where?" "Between Japan and America!" One worker cried out, "My knee is shaking very badly and I can't get off the roof. Help me!" His friend, Yamamoto, took his hand to help him down. "They were crying. They said, 'Well, they had to do it, ha?' "

Kimi Sugiyama recalled that when she told her husband that she had heard on the radio that the Japanese had bombed Pearl Harbor he replied,

"*Sonna baka na koto wanai,* Such a preposterous thing could never be. . . . It must be some kind of drama on [the radio]."

Emi Somekawa was a supervising nurse at Emmanuel Hospital in Portland, Oregon, at the time of Pearl Harbor. She and her family had just come back from church when the news of the bombing of Pearl Harbor came over the radio. "Of course everything goes through your mind. Now what? We're Japanese; I wonder how the neighbors feel toward us?" The neighbors it turned out were very friendly. They went to church with Caucasian friends and their next-door neighbors were Germans, who, recalling the hostility that German Americans had encountered in World War I, went out of their way to be helpful and reassuring. The customers at her father's fish store were solicitous. Some advised them to close the store for their own safety but Somekawa's husband said: "No, there's no need to do that. We're American citizens."

Raymond Katagi was having lunch with the radical San Francisco lawyer Vincent Hallinan, also Katagi's employer. They discussed the possible consequences for Katagi and other Japanese Americans, and Hallinan advised Katagi to organize his farmer friends and "go some other place . . . and start a new farm." If Katagi could round up his friends, Hallinan would "furnish some money." But it seemed to Katagi too formidable an undertaking.

Tom Kawaguchi's father and mother were from Kochi, Japan. His father was a watch repairer and photographer and Tom had grown up in a Jewish neighborhood in San Francisco. His playmates were Russian and German Jews and he learned to curse in Yiddish before he knew how to swear in Japanese. Kawaguchi was at the public library when the news of Pearl Harbor broke. He came out of that quiet sanctuary to hear newsboys screaming "Extra, Extra, Japs Bombed Pearl Harbor!" He didn't know where Pearl Harbor was. He had "funny feelings going home. I thought everybody and his uncle was staring at me, ready to pounce on me or something. I came back to Japantown and the place was just stone quiet. You didn't see anyone around. You felt very apprehensive and thought that something big was going to happen. You began to notice extra police cars and extra patrols coming into the area. . . . I guess they were there to provide some security against reprisals. There were some Filipinos who lived in the area who would want to start a fight with you. We avoided being out in the street. And like everybody else we listened to what was happening on the radio."

Charles Kikuchi went into San Francisco from Berkeley on December 10 and found everyone "in a daze in Jap Town." There were rumors circulating that all the Issei were going to be locked up. "If they are spies," Kikuchi wrote, "I don't see anything wrong with that. That's war." Kikuchi was reluctant to leave the Berkeley campus; he was anxious to complete the academic work required for his certificate in social work but beyond that the campus was a haven from the "mess" outside. He had a number of Caucasian as well as Chinese friends. A Chinese friend, Henry Lee, gave him his identification card to use in case a policeman stopped him.

Kikuchi noted his anxieties in his diary: "I think that the Nisei should forget all the things Japanese and not attract . . . attention to ourselves. We must wave the old flag like the very first patriot. I think the Nisei are loyal, but we may be too short for the Army, and I refuse to be a messboy. There is a lot of hysteria going on," he added. Kikuchi's sister Mariko talked of going East. "She says," Kikuchi noted, "that the Japs are going to raid California; and she is convinced of it."

The following day, Charles Kikuchi's diary revealed his confusion and uncertainty. "I should have confidence in the democratic procedures," he wrote, "but I'm worried that we might take a page from Hitler's methods and do something drastic toward the Issei. I hope not. I don't give a damn what happens to me, but I would be very disillusioned if the democratic process broke down. . . . I just feel we will win the war and I will survive nicely as things do turn out for the best. . . . We shall see. Maybe I'll go to San Francisco tonight and chase girls. Wang says chase the girls for tomorrow we die, and he tries to act like a man about town, but he is virgin."

The foray into downtown San Francisco was an unnerving one. "Holy Christ!" Kikuchi wrote the next day, "San Francisco last night was like nothing I ever saw before and everybody was saying that the Japs are going to get it in the ass. I ran into Jimmy Hong up on Grant Avenue and he says I'm not allowed to screw Chinese girls anymore." Kikuchi felt that although his father had served in the United States Navy during World War I he was vulnerable because of his membership in Japanese patriotic associations.

Still uncertain what the future held, Kikuchi, armed with his Chinese Student Club card, prowled the deserted streets of San Francisco's Japan Town again. The windows, he noted, "were bare except for a mass of 'evacuation sale' signs. The junk dealers are having a roman holiday, since they can have their cake and eat it too. It works like that! They buy cheap from the Japanese leaving and sell dearly to the Okies coming in for defense work. Result, good profit.''

A curfew had been imposed on all Japanese Americans but Kikuchi was equal to the occasion. He carried his Chinese Student Club card with the name Shar Lee and when a cop stopped him, he displayed the card and the cop "apologized for taking me for a Jap, and I said it was okay since we all had to sacrifice.''

Kikuchi suspected that his father was loyal to the Emperor. He wrote in his diary: "Pop would praise Japan, but he is not going to blow up anything.'' Kikuchi told his sister to have their father's honorable discharge framed and placed on the wall of his barber shop "and to take that Buddha statue the hell out of there.''

What was most striking (and infuriating) to many Japanese Americans was the speed and assurance with which the FBI and Naval Intelligence moved to arrest and incarcerate leaders of the various Japanese patriotic associations. In the five days following Pearl Harbor, the FBI rounded up 1,370 Japanese on the West Coast. Japanese aliens or nationals were, of course, not the only ones picked up; some sixteen thousand suspected subversives were arrested in the initial round-up, of whom 1,200 were German and Italian seamen. Only a third were interned, nearly half of them Germans. The rest were paroled, released, or repatriated.

Donald Nakahata was twelve at the time of the evacuation. His father had been secretary of the Japanese Association, manager of a farmers' co-op ruined by the Depression, and a part-time newspaper man. He was thus doubly suspect by the FBI, who arrested him a few days after Pearl Harbor and carried him off to an internment camp as a dangerous alien. It was the last time his family saw him. He died of a heart attack in an internment camp in Bismarck, North Dakota.

George Wakatsuki was a fisherman, a member of the Terminal Island fishing fleet. On the morning of December 7, his seven-year-old daughter, Jeanne, watched as her father and the other members of the fleet put out to fish for sardines. Suddenly the boats turned and started back for the harbor. The crews had heard on their radios that Pearl Harbor had been attacked. That night her father burned the Japanese flag that he had brought with him from Japan more than thirty years earlier. He also burned papers and documents that he thought might incriminate him, but two weeks later the FBI picked him up as a prospective spy and shipped him off, with hundreds of others, to an internment camp near Lincoln Nebraska. It was almost a year before the Wakatsuki family saw him again.

At this point it is important to make a distinction between "evacuation," "relocation," and "internment." It is often said that all persons of Japanese ancestry were "interned" during World War II. Technically, at least, that is an incorrect statement as we shall see. The facts are that all persons "of Japanese ancestry" living in the Western Defense Command—California, Oregon, Washington and Arizona—were required to evacuate the area of the command. Those who had been previously identified as strongly "pro-Japan" by U.S. intelligence agencies and were thus considered a threat to national security were "interned" at camps in Bismarck, North Dakota, Lincoln, Nebraska, and later, Crystal City, Texas. All others were first sent to Assembly Centers and then to Relocation Centers. At the internment camps procedures were established to attempt to determine whether the internees were in fact threats to the security of the United States. Those who were judged not to be were sent to relocation centers, commonly to the center where members of their family had gone.

Ruth Asawa's father was carried off in such a fashion and it was a month before his family knew of his whereabouts.

Ichiro Yamaguchi recalled that the FBI began taking away "people who were leaders of the church and community. . . . They took most of the Japanese Association leaders."

Isamu Nakamura noted that the day after Pearl Harbor the FBI picked up three Issei who were the backbone of the Japanese community and of the local Japanese Methodist Church.

The Caucasian college group at St. James Episcopal Church in Los Angeles had planned a meeting with the college group at the Japanese St. Mary's Church for Sunday evening, December 7, 1941. When the news of the bombing of Pearl Harbor reached Los Angeles on that Sunday morning, the suggestion was made that the meeting should be called off. The St. James group rejected the notion. After a Vesper service and dinner in the St. James parish hall, the Episcopal bishop of the Los Angeles diocese, the speaker of the evening, apologized to his young listeners for his generation's failure to achieve a peaceful order in the world and expressed his hope that "out of the horror some good would come." When the St. Mary's contingent returned home that night some of them found that in their absence their fathers had been taken away for detention by the FBI as suspicious aliens.

Attorney General Biddle, solicitous for the rights of all Americans, put Edward J. Ennis in charge of the alien enemy control program. Ennis,

Biddle noted, shared Biddle's and Biddle's assistant James Rowe's determination that "everyone in our country, whatever his racial or national origin, should be treated with fairness. We did not want people pushed around."

Almost as soon as aliens suspected of subversive activities had been rounded up, Ennis began setting up parole boards, made up of local citizens, to review each case. When the program was fully in operation there were ninety boards made up of citizen volunteers who reviewed the case of every alien and recommended release of all those who seemed to the members of the board to pose no threat to national security. Meantime, the internees were in camps run in conformity with international agreements on the treatment of prisoners of war. Biddle recalled visiting one camp to hear any complaints of the internees. A German ex-naval officer complained bitterly that he was not getting enough butter, to which Biddle replied that he was getting the same ration as Americans.

MENTION HAS ALREADY BEEN MADE OF THE EFFORTS OF THE JAPANESE American Citizens League to counter the growth of nationalist sentiment in the Japanese population. Inevitably, the outbreak of war intensified the conflict between the *Nihon-jin* and the JACL. The resentment of the Japanese nationalists was exacerbated when the leaders of the JACL stepped forward as spokesmen for the Japanese American community and urged cooperation and accommodation with the policies of the U.S. government.

Mike Masaoka, national secretary of the JACL, warned his fellow league members in the January 9, 1942, issue of the *Japanese American Courier:* "We must gird our loins, tighten our belts and prepare for the hardest fight of our generation, a fight to maintain our status as exemplary Americans, who, realizing that modern war demands great sacrifices, will not become bitter or lose faith in the heritage which is ours as Americans, in spite of what may come." Masaoka called on his fellow Japanese "to make heroic sacrifices equal to those made on the battle field, but also a fight in which we will be subjected to suspicions, persecutions, and possibly downright injustices.

"Ours is a difficult task, and yet the very tragedy of our position becomes a great challenge to win in such a manner that no one can ever dislodge us, or question our loyalty, or doubt our sincerity."

The five-point program of the Japanese American Citizens League called for "(1) volunteering for service in the U.S. military; (2) working to eradicate subversive activities within the Japanese communities; (3) serving in the Civilian Defense Program; (4) purchasing National Defense Bonds and Stamps; (5) volunteering for service in the American Red Cross."

The touchiest point of course was number 2—"working to eradicate subversive activities within the Japanese communities." It was, in effect, a declaration of war on the pro-Japanese Issei, Nisei, and Kibei and it was followed by memorials to President Roosevelt and Congress to "disenfranchise by due processes of law those citizens who have violated their obligations by such acts as publicly advocating the principles of a foreign government with which the United States is at war, by rendering aid, comfort, or advice to such governments or their representatives." The memorial was not directed specifically at the Japanese, of course. It applied to all "American citizens" whether of Italian, German, or Japanese ancestry who had given aid or comfort to the enemies of the United States. Nonetheless, it was taken by the pro-Japanese Nisei and Kibei as a direct attack upon them.

Mary Tukamoto recalled that after Pearl Harbor she and her friends "frantically wanted to do what was American. We were Americans and loyal citizens. . . . So we were wrapping Red Cross bandages and trying to do what we could to help our country." Tukamoto also opened an office of the Japanese American Citizens League to help people who were being evacuated but she soon found that her efforts were resented by those she was trying to help; she was accused of arranging for her friends to go to the more desirable assembly centers.

A late 1942 study reported that along with the deep distrust of the Japanese American Citizens League, the leaders among the Issei were reluctant to come forward since their prominence in various Japanese patriotic associations (like that of the reserve officers association) made them especially vulnerable to action by the FBI. A number had already been arrested and detained by the Department of Justice and they had no wish to attract further attention to themselves. At the same time they were the individuals most respected by the majority of the evacuees because of their superior caste and, often, military experience. Were there to have been a Japanese invasion of the West Coast, for example, they were the individuals who would have provided the leadership for any Japanese fifth column.

The resistance of many Issei to the JACL complicated things for the Japanese generally. There was, in effect, no clear and authoritative voice to speak for Japanese Americans as a whole; and that was primarily because they were so deeply divided in their loyalties.

In the weeks immediately following Pearl Harbor, relatively little anti-Japanese feeling was evident. Various influential politicians and rights advocates urged the public to refrain from any hostile actions toward the Japanese, who were generally described as "loyal Americans." Biddle, hearing that a number of Germans and Japanese had been discharged by their employers, took to the airwaves to deplore such actions. "I reminded employers," he noted in his autobiography, "that many of the 'foreigners' whom they were discharging had sons who were serving in the American Army and Navy." Biddle also appealed to state governors to vigorously oppose any "molestation of peaceful and law-abiding aliens, whether Japanese, German, or Italian."

Three days after Pearl Harbor the Federal Council of Churches of Christ in America in conjunction with the Foreign Missions Conference and the Home Missions Council issued a statement urging tolerance: "Under the emotional strain of the moment, Americans will be tempted to express their resentment against the action of the Japanese government by recriminations against the Japanese people who are in our midst. We are gratified to observe that the agents of our government are treating them with consideration.

"Let us remember that many of these people are loyal patriotic American citizens. . . . We therefore call upon the church people of this country to maintain a Christian composure and charity in their dealings with the Japanese among us."

A few weeks later, Biddle reinforced his plea for the protection of civil rights of all Americans: "War threatens all civil rights," he wrote, "and although we have fought wars before, and our personal freedoms have survived, there have been periods of gross abuse, when hysteria and hate and fear ran high, and when minorities were unlawfully and cruelly abused. Every man who cares about freedom, about a government by law—all freedom is based on a fair administration of the law—must fight for it for the other man with whom he disagrees. For the right of the minority, for the chance for the underprivileged with the same passion of insistence as he claims for his own rights. If we care about democracy, we must care about it as a reality for others, for Germans, for Italians, for Japanese, for those who are with us as those who are against us. For the

Bill of Rights protects not only American Citizens but all human beings who live on our American soil, under our American flag. The rights of Anglo-Saxons, of Jews, of Catholics, of Negroes, of Slavs, Indians—all are alike before the law. And this we must remember and sustain—that is if we really love justice, and really hate the bayonet and the whip and the gun, and the whole Gestapo method as a way of handling human beings.''

Biddle was pleased when Roger Baldwin, the director of the American Civil Liberties Union, wrote praising his statement ''as the most eloquent and practical words of any public man about civil rights in wartime.''

To Biddle's high-minded words, President Roosevelt added his own admonitions: ''It is one thing to safeguard American industry, and particularly the defense industry, against sabotage; but it is very much another to throw out of work honest and loyal people who, except for the accident of birth, are sincerely patriotic. . . . Remember the Nazi technique: 'Pit race against race, religion against religion, prejudice against prejudice. Divide and conquer.' We must not let that happen here. We must not forget what we are defending: Liberty, decency, justice.''

The Northern California Committee for Fair Play for Citizens and Aliens of Japanese Ancestry, under the chairmanship of the governor, C. L. Olson, reported proudly if not entirely accurately: ''Californians have kept their heads. . . . There have been few if any serious denials of civil rights to either aliens or citizens of Japanese race, on account of the war. The American tradition of fair play has been observed . . . all the organs of public influence and information—press, pulpit, school welfare agencies, radio and cinema—have discouraged mob violence and have pleaded for tolerance and justice for all law-abiding residents of whatever race.''

The attorney general of California, Earl Warren, cautioned his fellow-Californians against any actions directed at ''persons of Japanese ancestry'' who had given no evidence of disloyalty. In Hawaii, Lieutenant General Delos Emmons, commanding general, sounded the same note in a radio address on December 21, declaring: ''There is no intention or desire on the part of the federal authorities to operate mass concentration camps. No person, be he citizen or alien, need worry, provided he is not connected with subversive elements. . . .

''While we have been subjected to a serious attack by a ruthless and treacherous enemy, we must remember that this is America and we must do things the American way. We must distinguish between loyalty and disloyalty among her people.''

In the words of Edward Spicer, the first historian of the evacuation, ''The tense 2 months after Pearl Harbor marked a high point in American respect for the civil rights of enemy aliens and their citizen children.''

Chapter 8

THE DECISION
NOBODY MADE

IF THE INITIAL REACTION TO PEARL HARBOR HAD BEEN TO STRESS THE importance of protecting the civil rights of all Americans, citizens and alien enemies alike, what happened in the following weeks that resulted in the uprooting of some 110,000 men, women, and children from their homes on the West Coast and their relocation in ten centers, hastily constructed to accommodate them? The question obviously lies at the heart of this work. The bombing of Pearl Harbor and America's entry into the war began a strange process that within a few months acquired a kind of momentum of its own so that even from the present perspective, fifty years later, it is difficult to unravel cause and effect. One thing seems clear. At the heart of the matter lies a contest between two strong-willed individuals: Francis Biddle, United States attorney general, and Lieutenant General John Lesesne DeWitt, commanding general of the Western Defense Command, embracing California, Washington, Oregon, Arizona, Nevada, Idaho, Montana, and Utah.

Francis Biddle was almost fanatical in his determination to resist any infringement of the civil rights of U.S. citizens, and, indeed, of Americans in general, whether citizens or alien enemies. General DeWitt was equally determined to leave nothing undone to prepare to repel an imminent enemy attack upon the West Coast of the United States, the defense of which was his direct responsibility.

General DeWitt, at the age of sixty-one, was near the end of a long and undistinguished career. Born in Fort Sidney, Nebraska, he had gone to Princeton University. After two years there, he left to enlist in the army at the beginning of the Spanish-American War. After the war he was commissioned in the regular army and served from 1899 to 1902 in the Philippines, where he was involved in campaigns against the insurgents who were protesting U.S. rule as they had the rule of the Spanish. After a year in the United States, DeWitt served two more years in the Philippines. Returning to the United States, he attended the Infantry and Calvary School in Leavenworth, Kansas, and four years later returned to the Philippines for another tour of duty. In World War I he served as a quartermaster and supply officer of the general staff and, after the war, four years (1930–1934) as quartermaster general of the army. After a stint as commandant of the War College (1937) he was given command of the Fourth Army, stationed on the West Coast, and it was in this role that the war discovered him.

Several observations might be made about his military career. It was the thoroughly pedestrian ascent of a career officer who climbed patiently through the various ranks of the military bureaucracy, who was skilled at paperwork, rather fussy and demanding, a stickler for military minutiae.

DeWitt's three tours of duty in the Philippines suggest several lines of thought. There were relatively few U.S. Army posts in the first three decades of the twentieth century, when the army was a poor and neglected second cousin to the navy. But DeWitt's overseas tours raise the thought that his attitude toward the Japanese may well have been influenced by the time he spent in the Philippines. For one thing, Filipinos were very anti-Japanese; the Philippines were generally thought to be a tempting target for Japan's imperialist ambitions. The reader will recall Homer Lea's *Valor of Ignorance,* a best-selling novel featuring an invasion of the Philippines by the Japanese, an invasion that landed on Luzon, as indeed the Japanese did a few days after Pearl Harbor.

As noted, war with Japan had been widely anticipated and endlessly discussed since the early years of the century, and the general staff (and Theodore Roosevelt) believed that in all likelihood it would begin with an attack on the Philippines. (It was this assumption that, in large part, made possible the surprise attack on Pearl Harbor. It wasn't supposed to happen there.) Any officer serving in the Philippines must have been acutely aware of the Japanese menace and imbibed some of the anti-Japanese feeling that was so strong among the general populace. Without pressing this argument too far, it is at least reasonable to conjecture that what we might call the Filipino mind-set influenced DeWitt to the point of making him rather more apprehensive about a Japanese assault on the West Coast than he might otherwise have been had his military background been a different one. It may also have given him a somewhat more jaundiced view of the Japanese people in general than he would otherwise have had. In any event, it was the case that a less suitable individual to have been saddled with this particular command would have been hard to find. A competent bureaucrat, rather suggestable, in love with memos, and paranoid about shortwave radio transmitters was hardly the person that one would wish to have making decisions that would affect the lives of over a hundred thousand people.

Francis Biddle, DeWitt's adversary, was an Eastern upper-class snob in the grand style. In his autobiography, Biddle traced his ancestry back to Colonel William Randolph of Turkey Island, a colonial grandee and plantation owner who came to Virginia in 1673 and married Catherine Isham of Bermuda Plantation. They had ten children, one of whom was distinguished for marrying a granddaughter of Pocahontas. Biddle counted among his ancestors Edmund Jennings Randolph, the first attorney general of the United States. And that was just his mother's side. William Biddle came to the United States in 1681, lagging along eight years after the first Randolph, and settled in Philadelphia. One of his paternal forebears was burned as a wizard in Salem in 1692, a rare distinction. Francis Biddle's great-grandfather had been a friend and aide to Washington in the American Revolution and he had named his eldest son George Washington Biddle. A great-great-uncle was Nicholas Biddle, who edited Lewis and Clark's account of their famous expedition and became president of the Bank of the United States in 1823. In that capacity, he found himself the bitter opponent of Andrew Jackson, who set out to bend the bank to his will. To Nicholas Biddle, Jackson was simply a low-class frontier bully.

Six generations of Biddles had been leaders in the social and political life of Pennsylvania and a clue can be found to their tradition of liberalism in Francis Biddle's father, Algernon Sydney Biddle, named after the republican hero of England's Great Rebellion.

In the United States, blood does not get any bluer than the Biddle blood. But along with the blue blood and the splendid upper-class snobbery went a profound sense of *noblesse oblige*, the obligation to serve the public good in acknowledgment of one's social standing and financial prosperity. Biddle belonged to the clan of "goo-goos," as the reform-minded upper-class progressive champions of good government were called.

Two other important figures in the cast of characters were Henry Stimson and John McCloy. Minor but influential players were Provost Marshal General Allen Gullion and Major Karl Bendetsen, a graduate of Stanford Law School.

Secretary of War Henry Stimson was, like Biddle, a gentleman-politician, another blue-blooded member of the old boys club of Yale as an undergraduate, Harvard Law School, and a lifetime of public service. A Republican, respected by the leaders of both parties, he symbolized the bipartisan nature of the war effort. In addition, he was something of a student of Japanese culture. He had already served as secretary of war in William Howard Taft's administration and was considered a man whose integrity was matched by his intelligence. The list of his accomplishments was remarkable. As an emissary for Coolidge, he had negotiated a cease-fire between warring actions in Cuba, served as governor-general of the Philippines, and in a dozen other important and responsible posts.

John McCloy, assistant secretary of war, was the War Department official with whom Biddle (and DeWitt) had the most direct dealings.

An obvious ground for tension between Biddle and DeWitt was the fact that Biddle, in his office in the Department of Justice in Washington, was some three thousand miles from the vulnerable West Coast. It was thus doubtlessly inevitable that he should feel far less urgency than the belea-guered DeWitt surrounded by alarmed and often hysterical citizens living in daily fear of attack by Japanese super-soldiers and sailors and clam-oring for action.

A few days after Pearl Harbor a "federal intelligence agent" told DeWitt that some twenty thousand Japanese in the San Francisco area were "ready for organized action," presumably in support of a Japanese assault. Plans began to be drawn up for the immediate evacuation of the area but when the story was checked out with the FBI they dismissed it out of hand. For one thing, there were only thirteen thousand Japanese men, women, and children in the greater San Francisco area. The report, it turned out, was the work of a discharged FBI agent, but its effect was to increase DeWitt's already high level of anxiety. We might well judge the general's frame of mind from his remarks to a hastily called meeting of San Francisco civic leaders that included Mayor Angelo Rossi. There, as a *Life* reporter noted, the general "almost spit with rage." San Franciscans, a fearless and sophisticated lot, had been slow to respond to DeWitt's order for a citywide blackout. Planes had been heard flying over the city and the rumor spread that they were U.S. rather than Japanese planes and that their purpose had been to frighten San Franciscans into observing DeWitt's blackout orders.

"You people," he told the assembled gathering, "do not seem to realize we are at war. So get this: Last night there were planes over this community. They were enemy planes. I mean Japanese planes. And they were tracked out to sea. You think it was a hoax? It is a damned nonsense for sensible people to think that the Army and Navy would practice such a hoax on San Francisco."

A reporter for the *New York Times* noted that General DeWitt's voice rose several decibels as he denounced the group for "criminal, shameful apathy" in failing to blackout the city: "Remember that we're fighting the Japanese, who don't respect the laws of war [which was certainly true]. They're gangsters, and they must be treated as such." If the planes had dropped a bomb or two, "It might have awakened some of the fools in this community who refuse to realize that this is a war," he shouted.

Los Angeles, where anti-Japanese feeling was far stronger than in San Francisco and where fears of an invasion were acute, was scrupulous in observing the blackout instructions.

The anxieties of West Coast residents were considerably elevated by a report from Secretary of Navy Frank Knox. After a hasty trip to Hawaii, Knox told newspaper reporters, "I think the most effective fifth column of the entire war was done in Hawaii with the possible exception of Norway." Subsequently, Supreme Court Justice Owen Roberts made a more thorough investigation and although he denied that there was any verifiable link between the attackers and the pro-Japanese Hawaiians, he found that many Japanese living in the island were strongly pro-Japan and it was this aspect of his report that drew most attention on the West Coast.

Meanwhile, like any intelligence system, that of the Fourth Army provided General DeWitt with the intelligence it knew he wished for. Much was made by G-2 staff of the fact that "whether by design or accident virtually always the Japanese communities were adjacent to very vital shore installations, war plants, etc." In Seattle a Boeing aircraft plant was located near Green Valley where there was a large Japanese population. The same was true at the Bremerton Navy Yard near Seattle. One of the most vulnerable areas was thought to be L.A.'s Terminal Island, which contained an important naval air base and was, at the same time, the home of a colony of Japanese fishermen. In both the north and south of Santa Barbara County, an intelligence report noted "is a stretch of open beach ideally suited for landing purposes, extending for 15 or 21 miles, on which almost the only inhabitants were Japanese. Such a distribution of the Japanese population appeared to manifest something more than coincidence." In the opinion of DeWitt's staff, whether by conspiracy or coincidence, "the Japanese population . . . was . . . ideally situated . . . to carry into execution a tremendous program of sabotage on a mass scale." The same report noted that in the coastal plain south of Gaviota there were no Japanese but a number were living "immediately adjacent" to oil fields as well as "near the Santa Barbara airport and lighthouse."

In the towns of Santa Maria and Guadalupe "every utility, air field, bridge, telephone and power line or other facility of importance was flanked by Japanese." A few miles away in the fertile Santa Inez Valley, the report noted, there were no Japanese. And so it went all down the coast. In southern California it was noted that Japanese "truck farms are contiguous to the vital aircraft industry concentration in and around Los Angeles."

It must be said, I think, in defense of both Army and Naval Intelligence that intelligence agencies have a responsibility to consider worst-case scenarios. It is certainly better policy to overestimate than to underestimate enemy capabilities. Pearl Harbor is a vivid reminder of the principle.

Despite such alarming reports from his G-2 section, reinforced by the reports of Naval Intelligence, DeWitt resisted the growing chorus calling for the mass evacuation of all "persons of Japanese ancestry," as the phrase went, a phrase that included citizen Nisei as well as alien Issei. In DeWitt's words: "An American citizen, after all, is an American citizen. And while they all may not be loyal, I think we can weed the disloyal out of the loyal and lock them up if necessary." In another statement, accompanying an order for all aliens to register with Social Security boards, he wrote: "The proclamations directing the Department of Justice to apprehend, and where necessary to evacuate alien enemies, do not, of course, include American citizens of the Japanese race. If they have to be evacuated, I believe that this would have to be done as a military necessity in these particular areas." Such action should, in DeWitt's view, be carried out by the War Department.

According to Biddle, DeWitt told James Rowe (Biddle's assistant) that talk of a mass evacuation of all Japanese from the coast was "damn nonsense." At the same time, DeWitt was determined to press ahead with mass raids designed to unearth caches of contraband consisting of "firearms, bombs, explosives, short-wave receiving and transmitting sets, signal devices, codes or ciphers and photographs, and maps of any military installations." Most important, from DeWitt's perspective, were shortwave radio transmitters, which could be used to contact Japanese submarines and naval vessels in the event of a Japanese attack; DeWitt's intelligence officers assured him that illegal shortwave transmissions were being picked up.

If mass raids were conducted, they would be the responsibility of the Department of Justice, or, more specifically, the FBI. This was Biddle's jurisdiction and J. Edgar Hoover, as head of the FBI, assured Biddle that his agents had things well in hand. Thus Biddle, to DeWitt's indignation, insisted that all raids must be accompanied by search warrants and that no "mass raids" would be approved by his department. An angry DeWitt offered an example of the necessity for mass raids: Assume that a fix is established on unlawful transmissions "but the location is determined only within a defined area such as a city block." Under such circumstances the operator's name and address and "a description of the equipment could not be furnished." Therefore the agents making the search would need a John Doe search warrant. The search of a specific premise armed with a standard warrant would simply serve, in most instances, to alert other alien enemies who could move *their* transmitters "without a trace."

Starting with vagrant radio transmitters, DeWitt went on to underline, in a memo to Biddle, a whole series of often rather far-fetched situations on which, presumably, the security of the West Coast and, by extension, the fate of the nation might rest. Consider the case of a "known alien enemy [that is to say someone who looks Japanese] who is observed in transit, in the possession of contraband or in the possession of articles believed for good cause to be contraband [like a suitcase?] the enforcement officer on the ground" has no warrant or time to get one. If he follows prescribed procedure and goes to get one from a judge "the quarry will be lost." "What action can be taken?" the memorandum asked. Biddle remained obdurate. No search warrants, no raids, no random arrests.

Things seemed at an impasse. In an effort to resolve the growing differences, a three-day conference was held early in January in San Francisco. It included representatives of the various federal agencies involved, the Departments of Justice and War, the provost marshal's office, and of course DeWitt himself; Biddle's assistant, James Row, represented the Department of Justice.

In responding, through Rowe, to DeWitt's urgent request that the FBI extend the range of its search for contraband, Biddle's memo stated: "The Attorney General requested Mr. Rowe to make clear to the Commanding General that under no circumstances will the Department of Justice conduct mass raids on alien enemies. It is understood that the term 'mass raid' means eventually a raid on every alien enemy within the Western Theatre of Operations. The Attorney General will oppose such raids and, if overruled by the President, will request the Army to supersede the Department of Justice in the Western Theatre of Operations." In other words, declare martial law.

DeWitt produced a memorandum headed "Alien Enemy Control Requirements." In it he disavowed any desire (or capability) on the part of the Western Defense Command to carry out mass evacuation should it be judged necessary. He stated quite emphatically that it was his recommendation and desire that the Department of Justice act with "expedition and effectiveness" in carrying out the presidential proclamations of December 7 and 8. The difficulties that he was experiencing in providing for the security of the West Coast and preparing for the anticipated Japanese invasion or, what was more likely, "raids" against naval installations, were, he declared, the result of "the almost complete absence of action on the part of the Department of Justice over a period of nearly four weeks." That stated DeWitt's cases plainly enough. In reply Rowe had a few concessions to offer. The most important was designed to meet DeWitt's argument that spot raids would simply alert other aliens in the same area who possessed contraband. Biddle conceded that a number of spot raids might be made in the same area. "That is to say," the Justice Department memo read, "if lists of known alien enemies with the addresses of each are prepared by the F.B.I. and warrants are requested to cover such lists, a search of all the premises may be undertaken simultaneously."

The Department of Justice, for its part, agreed to conduct an enemy alien registration "with the least practicable delay." In addition, the FBI was authorized to "entertain Army requests for apprehensions submitted in writing, or, if time does not permit, oral requests which shall be confirmed later in writing." For example: "A known enemy alien found within a restricted area without authority is subject to apprehension without a warrant." Once agreement had been reached on the issue of searches supported by warrants as opposed to more general fishing expeditions, a new point of contention arose. Individual raids and spot raids on premises thought to contain contraband could only be conducted on premises occupied by alien enemies where there was no "mixed occupancy," that is to say, no U.S. citizens, which was also to say, no children, since all children were citizens. This seemed to DeWitt a ridiculous distinction, a legal nicety that made no sense and simply served to hamstring the FBI and the Army and Navy Intelligence officers.

There was, by this time, growing support in DeWitt's staff for a program of evacuation of alien enemies from certain "spots" thought to be particularly vulnerable in the event of any enemy attack, spots DeWitt's officers had begun to identify. DeWitt raised the issue with Rowe, strongly urging that the Department of Justice "undertake to establish immediate liaison and coordination with all appropriate relief agencies prepared to alleviate hardships resulting from compulsory change of residence." It was increasingly evident that the War Department, or at least DeWitt himself, wished to place the responsibility for any problems that might arise in the evacuation process squarely on Biddle's shoulders, while Biddle, for his part, was determined to avoid such responsibility. If DeWitt wished, with the assistance of the Justice Department, to evacuate from such sensitive spots all alien enemies, he would have to justify such steps explicitly. "What further requirement [the Attorney General] will make," Biddle's memo read, "will depend in large measure upon the nature of the area involved and the extent of enemy alien population in such area. If the designated areas or zones turned out to be so large as to require evacuation of a large number of enemy aliens, the Attorney General would require from the Army commander a detailed plan for such an evacuation to assure that it would be carried out in an efficient and humane manner."

DeWitt's indignation over what appeared to him to be Biddle's overscrupulosity was considerably increased by an FBI raid near Monterey that uncovered a cache of sixty thousand rounds of ammunition and a number of rifles, shotguns, and maps. The argument that the ammunition was simply part of the stock of a Japanese-owned sporting goods store was not especially reassuring to residents of the area. An angry and frustrated DeWitt reported to Biddle that his headquarters had been flooded by reports of signal lights, presumably from submarines. He noted that lights had been observed on premises that could not be entered without a warrant because of mixed occupancy. In DeWitt's view the problem "required immediate solution. It called for the application of measures not then in being."

"Further," the report read, "the situation was fraught with danger to the Japanese population itself." The combination of "spot raids revealing hidden caches of contraband, the attacks on coastwise shipping, the interception of illegal radio transmissions, the nightly observation of visual signal lamps from constantly changing locations and the success of the enemy offensive in the Pacific, had so aroused the public along the West Coast against the Japanese that it was prepared to take matters into its own hands.''

Stalemated in large measure by Biddle's constraints on raids, DeWitt and his staff, after the January meeting, turned their attention to the designation of spots considered especially vulnerable to sabotage in the event of enemy attack. These spots, they believed, should be promptly evacuated. DeWitt's staff officers, under the direction of Major Bendetsen and Provost Marshal General Gullion, drew up a list of what were called "exclusionary zones," areas of special sensitivity. These were termed Category A Zones, areas from which alien enemies were to be excluded and to which access was to be controlled by a pass and permit system. By the middle of January some eighty-six such zones had been identified. With the inclusion of Washington, Oregon, and Arizona, it was estimated that some 9,500 aliens were involved. DeWitt was firm on the point that *all* alien enemies—Italians (including presumably opera singers), Germans, and Japanese—be included in the evacuations.

When recommendations for the exclusionary zones were forwarded to Biddle on January 21, the attorney general was dismayed and notified DeWitt (and Stimson) that he could not accept the recommendation for the establishment of zones prohibited to enemy aliens in the states of Washington and Oregon. "Your recommendations of prohibited areas for Oregon and Washington," he wrote DeWitt, "include the cities of Portland, Seattle and Tacoma and therefore contemplate a mass evacuation of many thousands. . . . No reasons were given for this mass evacuation." Biddle notified Stimson that DeWitt had been asked to provide convincing evidence that an evacuation of such "very great magnitude" was necessary. Moreover, Biddle stated, the evacuation of American citizens, that is to say "citizen children," could not be carried out constitutionally. Therefore, if such a policy was to be pursued it must be under the color of military necessity and must be carried out by the military.

DeWitt replied with reasons that Biddle clearly did not believe adequate, and he once more refused the participation or cooperation of the Department of Justice. Not only was the Justice Department without the resources to carry out such an evacuation, it was unwilling to administer "such general civil control measures," in the words of DeWitt's official report of the evacuation.

When California Congressman Leland Ford wrote to Biddle, making it clear he wanted all those of Japanese ancestry, alien citizens and aliens alike, evacuated, Biddle sternly reminded him that there was no way to do this unless the writ of habeas corpus was suspended, a measure that he, Biddle, would certainly resist. In short, he would not undertake any "enforced migrations." Biddle insisted that such action "should be predicated on convincing evidence of the military necessity," which, at that point, he clearly felt had not been demonstrated.

Within the President's cabinet there were serious misgivings over the growing talk of evacuation. Henry Morgenthau, secretary of the treasury, was urged by some of the staff of the Foreign Funds Control Office to take over thousands of small businesses owned by Issei and Nisei in the region thought to be most susceptible to enemy attack, but when Morgenthau asked J. Edgar Hoover if he thought such extreme action was necessary, Hoover replied that the FBI had things under control. When the general counsel of the Treasury Department, Edward Foley, pressed Morgenthau for action, Morgenthau wrote in his diary: "Listen, when it comes to suddenly mopping up 150,000 Japanese and putting them behind barbed wire, irrespective of their status, and consider doing the same thing with the Germans, I want at some time to have caught my breath. . . . Anybody that wants to hurt this country or injure us, put him where he can't do it, but . . . indiscriminately, no."

Increasingly, Biddle had the feeling that things were getting out of control. There was an air verging on desperation that hung over the numerous discussions of what was to be done. Various alternatives to "mass evacuation" were debated endlessly. James Rowe, and Edward Ennis, head of the Justice Department's Alien Enemy Control Division, suggested that the Kibei be expatriated to Japan on the grounds that having been educated in Japan and having, in most instances, that troublesome dual citizenship, it was reasonable to assume that most of them were loyal to the Emperor. But the principal obstacle to such a far-reaching and expensive plan was constitutional rather than practical. They were, after all, U.S. citizens and there would doubtlessly be unsurmountable legal problems in any plan for expatriation. To ship some nine thousand Nisei back to Japan under wartime conditions would present staggering logistical problems. Bendetsen and Gullion discussed the notion of repatriating the Issei, who numbered some forty thousand, but that seemed even more impractical. An alternative that was debated by Bendetsen and Gullion (and doubtlessly many others) was simply evacuating the Issei. But that would mean, inevitably, breaking up families. Where were the Issei to go in any event? Bendetsen wrote to Gullion arguing that the evacuation of the Issei alone would be of little use since many of them were elderly and posed little threat in the event of a Japanese invasion, while the younger and more vigorous Kibei constituted a far graver danger.

In the continuing discussion, the *Los Angeles Times* noted: "Possibilities of detaining alien and other dangerous Japanese in the County's string of mountain road camps and the jail honor farms at Castaic were explored yesterday by Supervisor Roger Jessup and Sheriff Biscailus."

In California, DeWitt met with Governor Olson. Olson favored moving the Issei to the eastern part of the state but Bendetsen ridiculed the suggestion. It was much too "weak" and "too much in the spirit of Rotary," which apparently had made a similar suggestion; it was "not sufficiently 'cold-blooded' " and it was "dangerous" as well. Gullion, for his part, pressed on DeWitt his plan for the evacuation of all Issei east of the Sierra with as many Nisei and their families as would voluntarily accompany them. Those Nisei remaining would be barred from the restricted zones and assisted by the government in resettling elsewhere.

On January 30, Bendetsen, now a colonel, appeared before the California congressional delegation, where he stated that "military judgment on the West Coast on whether or not this evacuation of citizens and aliens should take place was positively in the affirmative." The California delegation thereupon approved the evacuation from "critical areas" of aliens and "dual citizens," the latter being a category that might well include Nisei in addition to the Kibei, since many Nisei who had not been educated in Japan had, at least in the eyes of the Japanese government, dual citizenship. Provost Marshal General Gullion, who attended the congressional caucus, reported to DeWitt that the real sentiment of the congressmen was "that all Japanese, including citizens, be removed from the West Coast."

One of the persistently troublesome issues had to do with the evacuation of Italian and German alien enemies. While there was clearly no threat of a naval foray against the West Coast by German or Italian warships, it was well known that pro-Hitler Germans and pro-Mussolini Italians, especially the latter, were to be found in significant numbers on the West Coast. Moreover, DeWitt was adamant that alien enemies of whatever extraction be evacuated from the exclusionary spots. His determination clearly made government officials, and congressmen and senators with large numbers of Italian and/or German constituents, uneasy. Among other things the mayors of two of the nation's largest cities—San

Francisco and New York—were Italian Americans. What of their parents? And, most troubling of all, what about Joe DiMaggio's father, a resident of Oakland, California, and thus subject to removal in any mass evacuation of the West Coast. The average American not of Italian ancestry might be indifferent to the fate of Mayor Angelo Rossi's parents or Mayor Fiorello La Guardia's, but if anything rude or uncivil were done to Joe DiMaggio's father, the popular reaction was bound to be highly unfavorable. To offend America's greatest hero since Babe Ruth would be impolitic to say the least. Colonel Bendetsen was directed to call DeWitt and make a plea for the exemption of Italian aliens. He called at 1:15 P.M. on February 1 to express the Department of Justice's and the War Department's reservations about including Italians in any general evacuation order.

Bendetsen: "There has been a great deal said in the papers about people like Joe DiMaggio's father, that is Italians who have never become citizens but concerning whom, it seems at least in the press, I don't know what their backgrounds are, there is no doubt as to loyalty. He [James Rowe] wonders whether all of them need to be excluded."

DeWitt's response was emphatic: "No, you can't make an exception. If you start that you're just in an awful mess. You establish procedure, and it would just upset everything that's been done. . . . I had one man speak to me about it the other day. He happened to be the editor, Mr. Patterson, I think of the *New York Sun*. He was in here and asked me about Joe DiMaggio's father, and I said, yes he's got to go. You can't make a single exception because if you do that you're lost."

Bendetsen did his best; perhaps it would be better, after all, to establish categories. To put it in a more positive light, to say "all persons of such-and-such a class are permitted" in the exclusionary zones; all others are excluded. In this way a troublesome union leader such as Harry Bridges and any number of suspected reds could be excluded as well.

But DeWitt remained adamant. "These people," he told Bendetsen, referring to the Japanese, "are beginning to move, and the public reaction has been so good, and it's going to be so helpful to me from the military standpoint, I wouldn't want anything to enter into it that would . . ."

Bendetsen: "Very well, sir."

Although no one knew exactly what it meant, or, perhaps even more important, how it was to be done, the phrase "mass evacuation" gradually developed a life of its own. To the apparently hopeless complexity of who was a danger to the republic—Issei, Kibei, Nisei—who was loyal to the Stars and Stripes and who was loyal to the Emperor—it seemed to offer a clear, if not a simple, solution.

So the evacuation juggernaut rolled on of its own momentum. The drift of things alarmed Biddle, apprehensive about the mounting clamor for general evacuation. He called a meeting on February 1 attended by Rowe, Gullion, Bendetsen, and McCloy. Biddle had a press release ready to be issued jointly by the Justice Department and the War Department reviewing the steps taken so far. It included the sentence: "The Department of War and the Department of Justice are in agreement that the present military situation does not at this time require the removal of American citizens of Japanese race." Gullion and Bendetsen were dismayed. Biddle's proposed press release was directly contrary to their convictions and repeated recommendations. It was throwing down the gauntlet to DeWitt and his allies in the provost marshal general's office. In his diary, Biddle noted that he wished to make it unequivocally clear that the Justice Department would not condone interfering with the rights of citizens or with the suspension of the writ of habeas corpus.

Gullion and Bendetsen, fearing the game was lost, insisted that DeWitt must be consulted before the sentence in question was approved. There was to be a meeting the next day in Sacramento with Governor Olson, State Attorney General Earl Warren, DeWitt, Tom Clark, representing the Justice Department, and "various state and federal officials." To issue such a statement prior to that meeting must create widespread confusion. At the very least, DeWitt and, even more important, Stimson should be consulted.

The Sacramento meeting the next day was inconclusive, although the general sentiment clearly favored some form of evacuation in the exclusionary zones.

In his autobiography, Biddle rather unfairly blames Clark for not upholding the position of the Justice Department with sufficient vigor. Clark, Biddle wrote, who was "a wary but amiable Texan, with a predilection to please those with whom he was immediately associated, construed his assignment as a direction to imply that the Justice Department would patriotically follow the military." It was rather ungracious of Biddle to indict Clark. If Clark's instructions were as definite and clear as Biddle implied, he would have been acting outside his orders by suggesting that the Department of Justice was prepared to go along with whatever the military suggested. Biddle, a bit disingenuously, quotes a remark of Earl Warren about Clark as though to imply that Clark was "soft" on the evacuation issue. Warren had written the California Joint Immigration Committee that they should get in touch with Tom Clark—"he is the man whose recommendations are taken. You will find him a very approachable fellow, and I think it would be a very good plan for you to talk to him."

AT THIS POINT, IT IS NECESSARY TO REMIND THE READER OF FARAWAY military events that directly affected the increasingly fevered debate over the fate of the "coastal Japanese." Each day the news was more alarming. The apparently invincible forces of Imperial Japan were everywhere triumphant. In early February, Admiral Chuichi Nagumo's carrier planes bombed Port Darwin in Australia, inflicting severe damage on Allied supply ships in the port and forcing its abandonment as a supply base. Yielding to the demands of the Dutch that a Dutch admiral command the Allied fleet off the Dutch East Indies, the American admiral, Thomas Hart, was replaced by a Dutch admiral who took command of a substantial force that included two heavy cruisers, one American and one British, and three light cruisers of the British, Dutch, and Australian navies with four American, three British, and three Dutch destroyers. Two Japanese fleets convoying a total of ninety-seven transports were approaching Java from opposite directions. The confused and confusing Battle of the Java Sea lasted some seven hours and when it was over half of the Allied ships had been destroyed without the loss of a single vessel by the Japanese.

While the Battle of the Java Sea was taking place, the USS *Langley,* a seaplane carrier, was sunk by aerial bombing south of Tjilatjap. A few days later two ships that survived the Battle of the Java Sea, HMS *Perth* and U.S. heavy cruiser *Houston,* were sunk by torpedoes. On the same day the British cruiser *Exeter* tried to lead the U.S. destroyer *Pope* and HMS *Encounter* through the Surabaya Strait and all three were sunk by enemy gunfire and carrier-based bombers.

In the face of such a series of disasters, the West Coast felt more vulnerable than ever to a Japanese invasion and the pressures mounted to do something. There were indications everywhere of demoralization and disarray. Signs blossomed along highways reading: "This Way to Air Raid Shelter." Dirty piles of sand were placed around cities for use in putting out fires from incendiary bombs; thousands of citizens tried to sign up for civil defense but no one seemed to know what to tell them to do.

The national press took up the demand for action. The sports writer

Damon Runyon, one of the most widely read columnists in America, wrote: "It would be extremely foolish to doubt the continued existence of enemy agents among the large alien Japanese population. Only recently, city health inspectors looking over a Japanese rooming house came upon a powerful transmitter, and it is reasonable to assume that menace of a similar character must be constantly guarded against throughout the war."

Westbrook Pegler, who could be counted on to be on the wrong side of virtually every public issue and was therefore much admired by millions of conservative readers, wrote in his syndicated column: "The Japanese in California should be under guard to the last man and woman right now and to hell with *habeas corpus* until the danger is over."

Henry McLemore, another popular columnist, wrote: "Let us have no patience with the enemy or anyone whose veins carry his blood. . . . Personally, I hate the Japanese. And that goes for all of them." In another column, McLemore wrote: "Everywhere that the Japanese have attacked to date, the Japanese population has risen to aid the attackers. . . . What is there to make the Government believe that the same wouldn't be true in California. . . . I am for the immediate removal of every Japanese on the West Coast in a point deep in the interior. Herd 'em up, pack 'em off and give 'em the inside room in the Badlands. Let 'em be pinched, hurt, hungry and dead up against it."

Walter Lippmann, generally acknowledged to be the most influential American journalist and long associated with liberal causes, traveled to California and informed his readers that the whole Pacific Coast was "in imminent danger of a combined attack from within and without." In a column headed "The Fifth Column on the Coast," Lippmann argued that the enemy could inflict "irreparable damage" through an attack supported by "organized sabotage." It was Lippmann's considered opinion that the whole coast should be treated as a war zone under special rules. As on the deck of a warship "everyone should be compelled to prove he has a good reason for being there." Those who could not offer bona fides should be removed, since "nobody's constitutional rights included the right to business on a battlefield." Tom Clark took Lippmann to task for stirring up popular antagonism to the Japanese in California and Attorney General Biddle showed Lippmann a telegram from a southern California newspaper editor stating: "Alien Japanese situation deteriorating rapidly. Lippmann's column and new newspaper attacks have started local citizens organizing some kind of irresponsible drive."

When Francis Biddle once more urged respect for the rights of all "persons of Japanese ancestry" the same issue of the *Los Angeles Times* that reported Biddle's speech carried a very different editorial message and one that undoubtedly reflected the opinion of most Californians. After quoting from the attorney general's talk, the writer of the editorial, entitled "The Questions of Japanese-Americans," aimed his fire specifically at the Nisei. "A viper is nonetheless a viper wherever the egg is hatched. A leopard's spots are the same and its disposition is the same wherever it is whelped.

"So a Japanese-American, born of Japanese parents, nurtured upon Japanese traditions, living in a transplanted Japanese atmosphere and thoroughly inoculated with Japanese thoughts, Japanese ideas and Japanese ideals, notwithstanding his nominal brand of accidental citizenship, almost inevitably and with the rarest of exceptions grows up to be a Japanese, not an American in his thoughts, in his ideas, and in his ideals, and himself is a potential and menacing, if not an actual, danger to our country unless properly supervised, controlled and, as it were hamstrung."

The *Times* noted that the Los Angeles Defense Council was urging internment of "all dual citizens," and the paper's Washington correspondent reported that the West Coast congressmen were pressing for mass evacuation. California law enforcement officers had petitioned State Attorney General Warren for the removal of "all alien Japanese within 200 miles of the Pacific Coast for the duration of the war." Governor Olson announced, after a meeting with district attorneys and the sheriffs, that he still hoped to "avoid the extreme action of removing all adult Japanese to and concentrating them in the interior of the United States for the duration of the war."

While most public discussion centered on the threat to the security of the United States posed by the West Coast Japanese, the precarious situation of the Japanese themselves also received increasing attention. There were numerous reports (and many more rumors) of attacks on Japanese by angry Caucasians. State and, above all, local agencies, police and sheriffs, and law enforcement officials most vulnerable to popular pressures were, not surprisingly, reluctant or, in many cases, simply unwilling to take strong action to protect "enemy" property. They had, after all, to answer to their constituents; in the case of sheriffs they had to run for office. They were thus disinclined to irritate the voters. The police likewise were subject to the wishes or whims of city councils, who in turn had to answer to the electorate. The consequence was that the federal government was constantly at odds with state and local officials, trying, as best it could, to protect "the enemy" from "the people," the people being U.S. citizens in a country at war.

The sheriff of Merced County wrote to Warren: "To avoid disaster, I believe that action must be taken to protect both the State and enemy aliens, as there are already 'rumblings' of vigilante activity which has been caused in the main, by the influx of Japanese."

In early February the California State Personnel Board put out an order barring Japanese Americans from state civil service positions. Attorney General Warren entered a strong dissent, writing apropos of the decision: "A substantial portion of the population of California consists of naturalized citizens and citizens born of parents who migrated to this country from foreign lands. They have in the past and do now represent the highest standards of American citizenship. . . . To question that loyalty or put them in a category different from other citizens is not only cruel in its effect upon them but is also disruptive of the national unity which is so essential in these times." The principal effect of Warren's dissent was to bring public criticism down on his head.

Francis Biddle, well aware of the way the wind was blowing, had asked three New Deal attorneys who were not members of the Justice Department—Benjamin Cohen, Oscar Cox, and Joseph Rauh—for an opinion on the constitutionality of the exclusion or evacuation of groups considered a threat to national security. Benjamin Cohen was one of Roosevelt's closest and most trusted advisers, a member of the New Deal inner circle, and Cox and Rauh were golden boys of the administration. On February 10, the three announced their opinion: "So long as a classification of persons is reasonably related to a genuine war need and does not under the guise of national defense discriminate against any class of citizens for a purpose unrelated to the national defense, no constitutional guarantee is infringed."

The combination of the war news from the Pacific Theater and the barrage of hostile journalistic commentary helped to swing the tide of public opinion toward some form of evacuation. In addition to the drumbeat of radio and newspaper criticism of the government's indecision, more and more public figures spoke out in favor of evacuation. On February 11, Fletcher Bowron, mayor of Los Angeles, gave a Lincoln Day address in which he declared: "If Lincoln were alive today, what would he do . . . to defend the nation against the Japanese horde . . . the people born on American soil who have a secret loyalty to the Japanese Emperor?" Bowron then confidentially answered his own question:

"There isn't a shadow of a doubt but that Lincoln, the mild-mannered man whose memory we regard with almost saint-like reverence, would make short work of rounding up the Japanese and putting them where they could do no harm."

In Congress, Southern congressmen, always ready to agitate the race issue, pressed for evacuation. Mississippi Congressman John Rankin rose to declare: "This a race war. . . . The white man's civilization has come into conflict with Japanese barbarism. . . . I say it is of vital importance that we get rid of every Japanese, whether in Hawaii or on the mainland. . . . Damn them; Let's get rid of them now."

In the Senate Tom Stewart of Tennessee took a similar line. The Japanese were "cowardly and immoral. They are different from Americans in every conceivable way, and no Japanese should ever have the right to claim American citizenship. . . . A Jap is a Jap anywhere you find him, and his taking the oath of allegiance to this country would not help, even if he should be permitted to do so."

Hiram Johnson, Progressive Party vice-presidential candidate in the stormy election of 1912, liberal California governor, and now senior senator, appointed a committee chaired by Senator Mon Wallgren of Washington to examine the issue of sabotage and the dangers posed by "aliens." General Mark Clark and Admiral Harold Stark, chief of naval operations, who were called to testify, ridiculed the notion that the Japanese could mount any serious attack on the West Coast, but their testimony was played down in press reports.

Congressman Ford of Los Angeles reported that he had called Biddle's office "and told them to stop fucking around. I gave them twenty-four hours notice that unless they would issue a mass evacuation notice I would drag the whole matter out on the floor of the House and of the Senate and give the bastards everything we could with both barrels. I told them they had given us the runaround long enough . . . and that if they would not take immediate action, we would clean the god-damned office out in one sweep. I cussed the Attorney General himself and his staff just like I'm cussing you now and he knew damn well I meant business." Which is, of course, the way legislators like to talk.

Far more serious, California Congressman Jerry Voorhis, the liberal idol of the West, came to believe that the evacuation order was "a wise and proper move." And finally, Earl Warren, who had held out so long against the idea of mass evacuation, capitulated. Warren wrote: "I have come to the conclusion that the Japanese situation as it exists today in this state may well be the Achilles heel of the entire civilian defense effort. Unless something is done it may bring about another Pearl Harbor.''

In his autobiography, Francis Biddle pointed out that there were two notable exceptions to the political chorus calling for mass evacuation (and incarceration). Senator Sheridan Downey of California was a clear voice of reason and he had a strong ally in Harry Cain, mayor of Tacoma, Washington, who declared: ''America has always been interested in selection, and I feel it would be preferable to make careful selection of those who are to be evacuated than just say: 'Let's get rid of our problem by the easiest, most obvious way, by moving everybody out.' ''

In the face of all the clamor, Biddle continued to hold out against general, or ''mass,'' evacuation. On February 9 he wrote Stimson ''and made it clear that the Department of Justice would not under any circumstances evacuate American citizens.'' When the navy asked the Justice Department to approve the evacuation of citizens from the Seattle area's Bainbridge Island, Biddle replied that he would do so only if the navy declared it a military zone and then excluded all citizens except those to whom passes had been issued. Three days later Biddle wrote again to Stimson to the effect that ''the Army could legally evacuate all persons in a specific territory if such action was deemed essential from a military point of view,'' but that American citizens of Japanese origin could not be ''singled out of an area and evacuated with other Japanese.''

When discussions between Stimson and Biddle failed to produce any clear agreement on the proper course to follow with regard to ''Americans of Japanese ancestry,'' Stimson sent one of his deputies ''to survey the situation on the West Coast.'' In the words of DeWitt's final report, ''The War Department representative carried back to the Secretary the recommendation of the Commanding General that some method be developed empowering the Federal Government to provide for the evacuation from sensitive areas of all persons of Japanese ancestry, and any other persons individually or collectively regarded as potentially dangerous.''

In a memorandum dated February 11, Stimson posed the following questions for the President:

''(1) Is the President willing to authorize us [the War Department] to move Japanese citizens as well as aliens from restricted areas?

''(2) Should we undertake withdrawal from the entire strip DeWitt originally recommended, which involves over 100,000 people, if we include both aliens and Japanese citizens?

''(3) Should we undertake the immediate step involving, say, 70,000 which includes large communities such as Los Angeles, San Diego, and Seattle?

"(4) Should we take any lesser steps such as the establishment of restricted areas around airplane plants and critical installations even though General DeWitt states that at several, at least, of the largest communities, this would be wasteful, involve difficult administrative problems, and might be a source of more trouble than 100 percent withdrawal from the area?"

After his meeting with General Mark Clark and Assistant Secretary of War McCloy, Stimson tried to arrange an appointment with the President but Roosevelt was too busy to see him. When Stimson finally reached him by phone, he reported that the President was "very vigorous" in response to Stimson's questions and "told me to go ahead in the line I thought best." Stimson's reaction was that it was best to begin the immediate evacuation of both citizen Japanese and alien Japanese from the most vulnerable areas of army and navy production. McCloy then called DeWitt to report: "We have carte blanche to do what we want as far as the President's concerned." Military necessity had been the overriding consideration for the President. If those most directly responsible and presumably most knowledgeable recommended that course of action as essential, the President gave his approval. "Be as reasonable as you can," the President had instructed Stimson.

The evening of the day they had received the President's approval for a policy of removal, McCloy, Gullion, and Bendetsen met at Biddle's home. Ennis and Rowe were also present. Biddle decided that further opposition was pointless, the President had made up his mind. DeWitt had won. It was not surprising. He held, after all, the winning cards. He had only to persist in his tireless litany that military necessity required the evacuation of his "spots," which had now become "zones" (and were about to become "military areas"), to prevail. Biddle accepted his defeat with good grace, doubtlessly glad to see the whole issue shifted from the Justice Department to the War Department. Heaven knows he had fought a good fight; he had protected, as well as he could and as long as he could, the constitutional rights of all Americans, aliens as well as citizens. He had been true to the spirit of his ancestor, Edmund Jennings Randolph, the first attorney general of the United States, and to his grandfather, Algeron Sydney Biddle. His conscience was clear.

Yet certain speculations are irresistible. Was Biddle *too* scrupulous, too rigid and doctrinaire? Was pride and arrogance and a touch of self-righteousness mixed in with a splendid solicitude for constitutional rights?

What, one wonders, would have been the outcome if Biddle had been more sympathetic with DeWitt's dilemma and more cooperative. Would mass raids have relieved the pressure, reassured DeWitt, given the impression of swift and decisive action? Even if some rights had been abrogated, would not mass raids have been far preferable to mass evacuations? Such questions are impossible of definitive answers but at least they serve to remind us of how strange the whole process was.

AT STIMSON'S REQUEST, DEWITT SUMMARIZED HIS RECOMMENDATIONS IN a memorandum dated February 14, 1942.

The mission of the Western Defense Command was:

"(1) Defense of the Pacific Coast of the Western Defense Command, as extended, against attacks by sea, land or air.

(2) Local protection of establishments and communications vital to the National Defense for which adequate defense cannot be provided by local civilian authorities."

Then followed a "Brief Estimate of the Situation," the final, fateful step that made virtually inevitable Presidential Order 9066:

(1) Any estimate of the situation indicates that the following are possible and probable activities:

    (a) Naval attack on shipping in coastal waters.
    (b) Naval attack on coastal cities and vital installations.
    (c) Air raids on vital installations, particularly within two hundred
        miles of the coast.
    (d) Sabotage of vital installations throughout the Western Defense
        Command.

"Hostile Naval and air raids will be assisted by enemy agents signaling from the coastline and the vicinity thereof, and by supplying and otherwise assisting enemy vessels and by sabotage." The most significant phrase in the above sentence is undoubtedly "will be assisted." It had a kind of assertiveness that was hard to resist.

There followed a hair-raising scenario of the kind of sabotage that might be expected if all alien enemies were not evacuated from the vulnerable coastal areas of the three states: "Sabotage [for example, of airplane factories] may be effected not only by destruction from within plants and establishments, but by destroying power, light, water, sewer and other utilities . . . in the immediate vicinity thereof or at a distance.

Serious damage or destruction in congested areas may readily be caused by incendiarism.''

The ''Estimate of the Situation'' was followed by an analysis of Japanese culture and character. ''The Japanese race is an enemy race,'' the memorandum declared, ''and while many second and third generation Japanese born in the United States soil, possessed of United States citizenship, have become 'Americanized,' the racial strains are undiluted. To conclude otherwise is to expect that children born of white parents on Japanese soil sever all racial affinity and become loyal Japanese subjects, ready to fight and, if necessary, to die for Japan against the nation of their parents. That Japan is allied with Germany and Italy in this struggle is no ground for assuming that any Japanese, barred from assimilation by convention as he is, though born and raised in the United States, will not turn against this nation when the final test of loyalty comes. It, therefore, follows that along the vital Pacific Coast over 112,000 potential enemies, of Japanese extraction, are at large today. There are indications that these are organized and ready for concerted action at a favorable opportunity. The very fact that no sabotage has taken place to date,'' the memorandum declared, ''is a disturbing and confirming indication that such action will be taken.''

It is hard to quarrel with the logic behind the major thesis of the above paragraph. We know that a number of Japanese patriotic organizations existed, a complex and intricate network of associations dedicated to advancing the interests of the Emperor. The most far-fetched notion, however, is that the fact that ''no sabotage has taken place'' was a ''confirming indication that such action will be taken.''

If no one could say that such activities as the memorandum described *would* take place, it was equally true that, under the circumstances described in the memorandum (Japanese raids and attacks on vital naval and military installations), it was equally the case that no one could guarantee that they *wouldn't,* and that proved enough to carry the day.

DeWitt's memorandum of February 14 took particular note of the ''large numbers of Italians and Germans, foreign and native born, among whom are many individuals who constitute an actual or potential menace to the safety of the nation.'' The action recommended in such cases was ''the exclusion of all such individuals from Category A areas, considered to be those most vulnerable,'' including ''all alien enemies, and all other persons suspected for any reason by the administering military authorities of being actual or potential saboteurs, espionage agents, or fifth columnists.''

DeWitt set up four categories of persons to be excluded from sensitive areas. They were:

"(1) Japanese aliens
(2) Japanese American citizens
(3) Enemy aliens other than Japanese aliens
(4) Any and all other persons who are suspected for any reason."

Finally, the evacuation of "classes (a), (b), and (c)," DeWitt recommended, "from such military areas be initiated on a designated evacuation day and carried to completion as rapidly as practicable."

Such a program necessitated the establishment of "initial concentration points, reception centers, registration, rationing, guarding, transportation to internment points and the selection and establishment of internment facilities." It should be noted that the words "concentration" and "internment" were promptly banished from the official vocabulary to be replaced by "assembly centers" and "relocation centers." It was DeWitt's notion that classes (a) Japanese aliens and (c) other "alien enemies" be "evacuated and interned at such selected places of internment . . ." (b) Japanese American citizens be offered an opportunity to accept voluntary internment. . . ." Those who refused should be "excluded from all military areas, and left to their own resources, or, in the alternative, to be encouraged to accept resettlement outside of such military areas with such assistance as the State government concerned or the Federal Security Agency may be by that time prepared to offer." This was all to be done with "the utmost secrecy."

That DeWitt was at least to a degree aware of the difficulties involved in distinguishing among alien enemies—virtually all the Issei and Nisei citizens, their children and grandchildren—is indicated by his recommendation that "adult males (above the age of 14 years) be interned separately from all women and children until the establishment of family units can be accomplished." It is hard to know exactly what DeWitt meant to accomplish by this odd proposal. DeWitt and the army would take the responsibility for setting up the "internment points" or, later, "assembly centers." DeWitt went on to recommend that "mass interment be considered largely as a temporary expedient pending selective resettlement to be accomplished by the various Security Agencies of the Federal and State Governments."

It is not clear what DeWitt meant by referring to "internment points" as a "temporary expedient pending selective resettlement." It seems reasonable to assume that he saw the internment points as places where evacuated Issei and Nisei would be kept while those considered to be no risk to national security ("the selectives") were resettled outside the restricted areas. What does seem clear at this point is that no one had thought of the establishment of long-term relocation centers to which evacuees would be moved from the internment points.

DeWitt estimated the number to be evacuated from the designated military areas as 133,000 (the actual number was nearer 120,000, with no more than 110,000 in the centers of any one time).

The final paragraph in DeWitt's memorandum read:

"Pending further and detailed study of the problem, it is further recommended: (1) That the Commanding General Western Defense Command [DeWitt himself] . . . coordinate with the local and state authorities, in order to facilitate the temporary physical protection by them of the property of evacuees not taken with them; (2) That the Commanding General . . . determine the quantity and character of property which the adult males . . . may be permitted to take with them; and (3) That the Treasury Department or other proper Federal agency be responsible for the conservation, liquidation, and proper distribution of the property of evacuees if it cannot be cared for through the usual and normal channels."

On February 17 Provost Marshal General Gullion telegraphed corps area commanders on the West Coast: "Probable that orders for very large evacuation of enemy aliens of all nationalities predominately Japanese from Pacific Coast will be issued within 48 hours. Internment facilities will be taxed to utmost. Report at once maximum you can care for, including housing, feeding, medical care, and supply. Your breakdown should include number of men, women, and children. Very important to keep this a closely guarded secret." The same day, Stimson, McCloy, Gullion, General Clark, and Bendetsen had another meeting to make further plans. General Clark protested the mass evacuation vigorously on the grounds that it would involve too many soldiers desperately needed elsewhere.

DeWitt's memorandum reached the desk of the secretary of war two days later and, as the official language has it: "After consultation between War and Justice Department representatives it was determined that a Presidential executive order should be sought authorizing the Secretary of War to institute civil control measures." The War Department drafted the order and the Justice Department "concurred," although "acquiesced" would probably have been a more accurate term.

What followed was Executive Order 9066, issued on February 19. It read: "WHEREAS, The successful prosecution of the war requires every possible protection against espionage and against sabotage to national-defense material, national-defense premises and national defense utilities. . . .

"NOW THEREFORE, by virtue of the authority vested in me as President of the United States, and Commander in Chief of the Army and Navy, I hereby authorize and direct the Secretary of War, and the military Commanders whom he may from time to time designate, whenever he or any designated Commander deems such action necessary or desirable, to prescribe military areas in such places and of such extent as he or the appropriate Military Commander may determine, from which any or all persons may be excluded, and with respect to which, the right of any person to enter, remain in, or leave shall be subject to whatever restriction the Secretary of War or the appropriate Military Commander may impose in his discretion. The Secretary of War is hereby authorized to provide for the residents of any such area who are excluded therefrom, such transportation, food, shelter, and other accommodations as may be necessary in the judgment of the Secretary of War, or the said Military Commander, and until other arrangements are made, to accomplish the purpose of this order."

Looking back on Executive Order 9066 in later years, Biddle wrote: "I do not think [Roosevelt] was much concerned with the gravity or implications of his step. He was never theoretical about things. What must be done to defend the country must be done. The decision was for the Secretary of War, not for the Attorney General, not even for J. Edgar Hoover, whose judgment as to the appropriateness of the defense measures he greatly respected. The military might be wrong. But they were fighting the war. Public opinion was on their side, so that there was no question of any substantial opposition, which might tend to the disunity that all costs he must avoid. Nor do I think that constitutional difficulty plagued him—the Constitution has never greatly bothered any wartime President. . . . Once, he emphasized to me, when I was expressing my belief that the evacuation was unnecessary, that this must be a military decision."

The following day a letter was sent to DeWitt over Stimson's signature designating him "military commander," a title that gave him virtually complete control over the Western Defense Command area. The letter confirming his authority was dated February 20. Among other things, DeWitt was authorized to make "such changes in the prohibited and restricted areas heretofore designated by the Attorney General as you may deem proper to prescribe."

One of the more significant sentences in the letter read: "In carrying out your duties under this delegation, I desire, so far as military requirements permit, that you do not disturb, for the time being at least, Italian aliens and persons of Italian lineage except where they are, in your judgment, undesirables or constitute a definite danger to the performance of your mission." The reasons given by Stimson were that he considered "such persons to be potentially less dangerous as a whole, than those of other enemy nationalities." Stimson also added that there were so many Italians on the West Coast that "their inclusion in the general plan would greatly overtax our strength." Moreover, although Stimson did not mention it as being perhaps too crass, the Italians were the only serious rivals to the Japanese as farmers in California. To incarcerate large numbers of Italian Americans would not only infuriate Italian voters but probably create a food crisis. As it developed, in many instances Italians took over by lease or purchase the farms of Japanese who were evacuated and did so with the encouragement of officials who were anxious to maintain agricultural production.

DeWitt was admonished to carry out his plan "gradually so as to avoid, so far as it is consistent with national safety and the performance of your mission, unnecessary hardship and dislocation of business and industry. In order to permit the War Department to make plans for the proper disposition of individuals whom you contemplate moving outside of your jurisdiction, it is desired that you make known to me your detailed plans for evacuation. Individuals will not be entrained until such plans are furnished and you have been informed that accommodations have been prepared at the point of detraining." Stimson also directed DeWitt to take the "fullest advantage of voluntary exodus of individuals and of the facilities afforded by other Government and private agencies in assisting evacuees to resettle. Where evacuees are unable to effect resettlement of their own volition, or with the assistance of other agencies, proper provision for housing, feeding, transportation and medical care must be provided."

The next day Assistant Secretary of War John McCloy dispatched a memorandum to DeWitt amplifying the instructions from Stimson. McCloy directed DeWitt to proceed "by stages, evacuating first those categories of persons considered potentially the most dangerous." He renewed Stimson's demand for "detailed plans" for any displacement of people in any category. In the most "critical areas" DeWitt might feel it necessary to order "an almost immediate evacuation" but in order to take "full advantage of voluntary exodus and of re-settlement facilities arranged by other agencies, both public and private, the timing of your program ought to be most carefully conceived and coordinated.'' The Departments of Justice and Agriculture had urged that as much time as possible be given to evacuees to make arrangements for the effective use of their property as well as to make their own arrangements for resettling outside the restricted or prohibited zones, thereby reducing the pressure on already overextended army forces. In moving evacuees ''appropriate'' exceptions ''will be made in favor of the aged, infirm, and the sick.'' Persons above the age of seventy years should not be disturbed unless for sufficient reason, you consider them suspect.'' Whereas Stimson had directed DeWitt to treat Italian Americans gently, McCloy urged him to go easy on German aliens (he did not mention that Americans of Germany ancestry made up the largest single bloc of voters in the country).

''It will of course be necessary,'' McCloy wrote DeWitt, ''that your plans include provision for protection of the property, particularly the physical property, of evacuees. All reasonable measures should be taken through publicity and other means, to encourage evacuees to take steps to protect their own property. When evacuees are unable to do this prior to the time when it is necessary for them to comply with the exclusion orders, there is always danger that unscrupulous persons will take undue advantage or that physical property unavoidably left behind will be pillaged by lawless elements. The protection of physical property from theft or other harm is primarily the responsibility of state and local law-enforcement agencies, and you will doubtless call upon them for the maximum assistance in this connection. *Where they are unable to protect physical property left behind in military areas, the responsibility will be yours, to provide reasonable protection, either through the use of troops or through other appropriate measures* [italics added].''

The suggestion of using federal troops, however well intentioned, was impossible on the face of it. If we assume that from a half to two thirds (or more) of the evacuated persons could not depend on local or state officials to protect their physical property, homes and their furnishings, businesses, farms and farm implements, and so forth, it would have taken perhaps twenty thousand or more soldiers (assuming ten thousand properties were in need of such protection, two soldiers each on a twelve-hour shift) to provide adequate protection, not of course to mention the problems of housing, feeding, and supervising the soldiers themselves. And what McCloy had in mind by the phrase ''other appropriate measures'' is hard to imagine. McCloy did suggest to DeWitt that the general appoint a ''property custodian'' with authority ''to create an organization to deal with such property in military areas. . . . The provisions of the Executive Order and the necessity in each given instance are such that you have authority to take such action, either directly or through another federal agency. In the development of your program, it is desired that you accomplish it with the minimum of individual hardship and dislocation of business and industries consistent with safety.''

Neither Stimson's nor McCloy's letters suggested, or directed, that whole areas as large as what came to be called Military Area No. 1 and, subsequently, Military Area No. 2, be evacuated by *all* Japanese American citizens and Japanese aliens. Indeed, a careful reading of the letters suggests rather that both men assumed that a kind of partial and piecemeal evacuation would be carried out in specific zones or areas. Even the distinction between a "zone" and an "area" was vague. A "zone" implied a limited area, while an "area" might be, and as it turned out was, vast. The words were often used interchangeably and the general tenor of the letters is one of caution, moderation, and an evident concern for the persons of the evacuees—adequate food, housing, medical care, concern for the elderly, etc., and, even more specifically, for their property.

At a cabinet meeting on February 27, Stimson confessed to the President that many issues having to do with the evacuation were still alarmingly vague. He noted in his diary that night: "There was general confusion around the table arising from the fact that nobody realized how big it was, nobody wanted to take care of the evacuees, and the general weight and complication of the project." It was Biddle's suggestion that one man be chosen to direct the resettlements and bring the various agencies into some kind of common effort, "and the President seemed to accept this," Stimson added, "the single person to be, of course, a civilian and not the Army. . . ."

At last DeWitt had the authority he had desired and fought for over some nine long weeks; he no longer had to contend with the scruples of the Attorney General. But armed as he was with the authority he had sought it was by no means clear to him, or indeed anyone else, how he intended to use it.

Chapter 9

TERMINAL ISLAND AND THE
TOLAN COMMITTEE

TERMINAL ISLAND HAD BEEN A BONE OF CONTENTION BETWEEN DE-
witt and Biddle from the beginning. There were two shipyards on the
island, the Todd Shipyard and the Kaiser, as well as an airfield, Reeves
field, where P-38 fighter planes were stationed. It was, of all the spots
along the West Coast, perhaps the most sensitive from the point of view
of security. It was also the location of a colony of Japanese fishermen. A
number of the fishermen, well aware of their vulnerability, had signed
statements attesting to their loyalty but DeWitt persisted in calling for the
evacuation of the island (which Biddle resisted). When the island was
declared a critical area by the War Department, the Justice Department
complied. A notice was posted around the island on Tuesday, February
10, warning all aliens that the deadline for their departure from the island
was the following Monday, February 16. The next day a presidential
order was issued transferring jurisdiction of the island to the navy, and
Secretary Knox instructed Rear Admiral R. S. Holmes, commander of
the Eleventh Naval District in San Diego, that Japanese dwellings were
condemned and that all Japanese must evacuate within thirty days. This
order superseded the Justice Department order, which had allowed only
six days for evacuation, but it included all Japanese residents of the
island. Within a week the thirty days were shortened to forty-eight hours.

The confusing and contradictory orders demonstrated the confusing and contradictory policies that lay behind them. All of which focused public attention, media attention, on the fate of the island's inhabitants. The efforts of junkmen and secondhand dealers to exploit the plight of those forced to flee their homes and dispose of their possessions within a few hours, invariably at a fraction of their true value, were vividly chronicled in the daily press and aroused widespread criticism.

The *Los Angeles Times* reported that Japanese were being victimized by "junkmen and second-hand furniture dealers" who were preying upon "the confused and panicky families of alien Japanese seized by the Federal Bureau of Investigation at Fish Harbor." A detail of officers had been assigned to protect the vacated property of the fishermen under arrest.

When junkmen, roaming like vultures through the areas of Japanese homes, came to Fred Fujiawa's home, his mother, rather than sell the family furniture for a pittance, made a bonfire and "burned everything up, kitchen table and chairs and so forth." Their neighbor Mrs. Shigekawa ran the Ishi Pharmacy. Without time to clear her shelves she locked the shop and left for Pasadena. When she got back a few days later, the store had been ransacked.

Jeanne Wakatsuki's mother was outraged when an antiques dealer offered her $17 for a set of prized china that she knew to be worth $300 to $400. Like Mrs. Fujiawa, she preferred to destroy it than be so victimized. In front of the dismayed dealer she smashed the china, piece by piece.

A Terminal Island Nisei woman wrote later: "Everybody took advantage of us. Some people took things when we were not watching. While we were packing inside the house, these people would go around the back and take everything they saw. . . . It was difficult to keep our tempers. For seventeen years, Dad and Mother had struggled to build up their business. Every profit they made was put into the store for remodeling and improving it little by little. At the same time they were raising four little kids. When they finally reached the peak of their business success and had nothing to worry about, when they finally succeeded in raising four children and sending them through high school and even had one attending college—BOOM came evacuation and our prosperity crumbled to pieces. . . . The precious 48 hours notice we had in which to pack passed like a nightmare."

K. Higashi, president of the Japanese American Citizens League, complained that junkmen and used-furniture dealers were "telling the wives of arrested aliens that the federal government intended to seize their household belongings. ''Through this technique they were buying refrigerators, radios, stoves and other furniture costing from $50 to $200 for from $4 to $5, loading their purchases on their trucks and driving away.'' The police were instructed to aid Higashi in warning his people not to sacrifice their belongings.

Numerous Japanese organizations did their best to help their fellow nationals. The Japanese American Citizens League was in the forefront of this effort, as was the Southern California Japanese Fishermen's Association. Y. Sakamoto, the president of the fishermen's association, undertook to get the power of attorney from arrested boat owners to permit the sale of their fishing boats in order to provide funds ''to support the fishermen's families pending receipt of Federal aid.'' Some forty-five boats were involved.

Since the number of families displaced at Terminal Island was relatively small, churches and neighborhood social centers were able to provide shelter and food. At Compton, Saratoga, Norwalk, Blue Hills, and El Monte, all outside designated ''spots,'' centers received Japanese families and provided them with whatever comforts they could muster. In the words of the official report of the evacuation: ''The friendly groups worked at high speed, begging, borrowing and renting delivery and farm trucks to carry families and such of their possessions as had not fallen into the hands of junk dealers to the hostels or to relatives or friends with room to accommodate the homeless outside the prohibited area.'' Even with the best efforts by sympathetic Caucasians, much property had to be abandoned because it could not be loaded within the forty-eight-hour period.

The Terminal Island fishermen (and shopkeepers) who ''voluntarily'' evacuated under orders to areas outside the military area were, five weeks later, forced to move again when Military Area No. 2 was proclaimed.

Close on the heels of the notorious Terminal Island episode came the hearing of the Tolan Committee, a subcommittee of the Congressional Committee on National Defense headed by John Tolan, a California congressman. Its hearings, which began February 22, three days after Executive Order 9066 had been issued, were clearly after the fact. ''Voluntary'' evacuation from Military Area No. 1 had already begun. Nonetheless the testimony before the committee does cast additional light on the general state of public opinion on the West Coast and, on the positive side, by taking testimony on the Terminal Island fiasco and giving it wide publicity, the committee undoubtedly helped to draw attention to the issue of protecting evacuee property.

Tolan opened the hearings on a somber note by telling the San Francisco newspapers: "It is possible that the entire Pacific Coast may be evacuated. They tell me back in Washington that it is not only possible but probable that the Pacific Coast will be bombed. That has come to me from men who are supposed to know." To the various witnesses who appeared before the committee, the chairman repeated like a mantra: "We can lose this war. They tell me in Washington we can lose this war."

At the beginning of the hearings, the chairman stated their purpose: "To many citizens of alien parentage in this country it has come as a profound shock that almost overnight thousands of persons have discovered that their citizenship no longer stands between them and the treatment accorded by any enemy alien within our borders in time of war. . . . The Nation must decide and Congress must gravely consider, as a matter of national policy, the extent to which citizenship, in and of itself, is a guaranty of equal rights and privileges during time of war. Unless a clarification is forthcoming, the evacuation of the Japanese population will serve as an incident sufficiently disturbing to lower seriously the morale of vast numbers of foreign-born among our people."

The witnesses who appeared before the Tolan Committee were a varied group. Ministers and lawyers predominated, the ministers speaking from a Christian perspective as to the morality of the operation, the lawyers, many of whom represented evacuees, on the legal aspects. California Attorney General Earl Warren addressed the committee, urging strong action by Congress to protect the property rights of evacuees. The regional director of the Social Security Board spoke, in addition to welfare workers, educators, and representatives of benevolent societies.

The evacuees did not want for advocates. An ardent young reformer, Carey McWilliams, chief of the Division of Immigration and Housing of the California Department of Industrial Relations, took the stand to make an eloquent plea for justice. "There is ample evidence," McWilliams declared, "that social and economic vultures are already preying upon the unfortunate aliens who expect to be evacuated. They are told to dispose of their property and are frequently offered ridiculous sums which in panic and desperation the evacuees are inclined to accept. Stories are also being circulated which indicate that unless great care is exercised, and that immediately, we shall have a repetition here of what transpired in Germany and other countries as a result of large-scale evacuation. People have been threatened that unless they dispose of their property to those who are eager for it, they will be reported to the Federal Bureau of Investigation and their property will be confiscated. In the absence of a statement from high government authorities to the contrary, the aliens who are at the mercy of rumors and rumor mongers have no choice but to accept what they are told at the moment. The immediate creation of an Alien Property Conservator . . . with an immediate announcement that transactions under duress will not be recognized and that the interests and property of aliens will be protected in every way, would not only give the unfortunate victims a sense of needed relief, but make them feel that they are living in a country were human dignity and human values are more than mere phrases mouthed by politicians.''

McWilliams ended his testimony by stressing the urgency of prompt action on behalf of the evacuees, specifically to address ''the problem of welfare, maintenance [presumably of the property of the evacuees], property conservation, preservations of morale, etc.'' The establishment of such an agency, McWilliams concluded, would ''above all demonstrate that democracy can work efficiently, effectively, and with that consideration for the welfare of the people who brought it into being, which differentiates from autocracy and makes it worthy of any sacrifice.''

Implicit in McWilliams's closing comments was the notion that the evacuation, if handled intelligently and humanely, could serve as a lesson in democracy for a people who, at least in their native land, had only known autocracy. Japanese immigrants, in the main, he believed, had shown little interest in American values, political practices, or ideals. If they were to experience such values in a time of traumatic dislocation and severe stress, that might make a lasting impression despite (or perhaps because of) the unhappy circumstances under which they took place.

An Oakland attorney testifying before the committee declared: ''I find no popular demand for the efforts to drive the so-called alien enemies from California. [Chester Howell, an influential San Francisco columnist had also stated this as his impression.] The clamor seems to come from the chamber of commerce, Associated Farmers, and the newspapers notorious as spokesmen for reactionary interests. In view of this fact, effort should be made to determine whether there is any connection between the clamor for the dispossession of the Japanese farmers and the desire of these clamoring interests to get possession of the Japanese farms and the elimination of the Japanese competition. . . . So far the Attorney General has resisted the mad pressure; but the mad pressure mounts. Even now we hear the rumble of the threats of martial law for all of California—a State of 'nonlaw' which would, abolish the rights of all of us and make many wonder whether totalitarianism is to be fought with the same and so reduce the struggle to an abstraction.''

So persistent was the testimony concerning the importance of protecting evacuee property that on February 23, at the conclusion of the first
phase of the hearings, Tolan sent telegrams to House Speaker Sam Ray-
burn, to the President, the secretary of the treasury, the attorney general,
and the secretary of war. The telegrams read: "We urge immediate establishment of a regional alien-property custodian office for the Pacific
Coast area. We have learned of numerous sacrifice sales by aliens; this
office should have existed before the evacuation of February 15. It must
be functioning before additional prohibited areas are evacuated." In addition to the alien Japanese, the citizen Japanese were in need of similar
protections.

Three days after the telegram was dispatched the committee received
a reply from the Treasury Department: "Your telegram . . . has been
carefully studied by this Department. We are in agreement that there is a
general need for careful planning with respect to the resettlement of
persons, both aliens and citizens, evacuated from strategic areas and that
the problem is one in which the Federal Government should assume a
major responsibility." The problem recalled the government's role in the
Dust Bowl migration. Rather than create a new agency, the "social
problems" created by removing people from their homes and property
had best be dealt with by agencies already concerned with various "social
problems" in the larger society.

Secretary of the Treasury Morgenthau clearly had second thoughts, for
a few days later he dispatched another telegram, this one to the Federal
Reserve Bank of San Francisco, reviewing the problems involved. As
though struck by a sudden illumination, the telegram acknowledged that
"the evacuation on short notice of tens of thousands of persons from
military areas on the Pacific Coast raises serious problems in connection
with the liquidation of their property holdings and the protection of the
property of such persons against fraud, forced sales, and unscrupulous
creditors. Obviously the emergency will cause financial loss to the group
involved. However, the following program is intended to accord to this
group reasonable protection of their property interests consistent with the
war effort."

The nature of the problem dictated that a West Coast agency be given
the authority to act "without reference to Washington." The direct responsibility for "the execution of the property aspects of the program"
was placed in the Federal Reserve Banks of San Francisco, Los Angeles,
Seattle, and Portland. The prestige of the Federal Reserve Banks as
agencies of the government should be a guarantee of fair treatment. All

other federal, as well as state and local agencies, were expected to co-ordinate their activities and cooperate with the bank. "These agencies will undoubtedly be called upon by the military authorities to handle other aspects of the evacuation problem, such as the transportation and reset-tlement of the evacuees, and their re-employment in new areas."

The wording of the Treasury Department's communiqué indicated some confusion on its part as to the nature and extent of the evacuation. The words "re-settlement" and "re-employment" seemed to suggest that the drafters of the telegram had rather a different notion of the fate of the evacuees than the Western Defense Command.

There were other oddities in the telegram. It announced that the Trea-sury Department would "furnish the San Francisco Bank by airplane" with "trained experts" to the number of one hundred or more. "The keynote of this program is speed," the telegram concluded. "It is be-lieved that it can be put in operation by Monday, March 9, 1942." Four days hence! That was speed with a vengeance.

The fact was, of course, that the problems were such that no directive however well intentioned (and however naive) could readily mend them, but at least the telegram of March 5 acknowledged the scope of the problem and made a start at addressing it.

In Seattle, an officer of the Japanese American Citizens League used the opportunity afforded by the Tolan hearings to express the league's unhappiness at the policy of "voluntary" evacuation. "A large number of people have remarked that they will go where the Government orders them to go, willingly, if it will help the mutual defense effort. But the biggest problem in their minds is where to go," the witness testified. The first unofficial evacuation announcement pointed out that the government did not concern itself with where evacuees went, just so long as they left the prohibited areas. Obviously, this was no solution to the question, for immediately, from Washington, Idaho, Montana, Colorado, and else-where authoritative voices shouted: "No Japs Wanted Here!"

A Seattle banker, testifying before the Tolan Committee about "his many and he hoped [but he was not sure] loyal, old friends of Japanese descent," confessed he found it "exceedingly difficult to divine the ori-ental . . . their mental processes may not be identical with our own." His views were echoed by the mayor of Tacoma, who felt he could make a shrewd guess about the country to which his Japanese acquaintances were loyal because "a man's background, regardless of who he is, very gen-erally has much to do with what he is going to do. If born in this country; if a Christian; if employed side by side with others who fill the same classification; . . . if educated in our schools; if a producer now and in the past; if maintained in a position of production—I should think that person to be construed to be a loyal American citizen." Certainly he would not group Japanese Americans as a whole as disloyal. The mayor's studied analysis of what he considered grounds for believing a particular Japanese American loyal to the United States suggested the complexity of the problem.

The Los Angeles police chief, speaking of the Nisei, said that they presented "as difficult, if not a more difficult, problem than the enemy alien. They are cognizant of the American language and inference; and subject to small limitations, are allowed to associate and mingle with the general American public. . . . In addition to the family traits and the patriotism for the native country of Japan, you have the racial character-istics of being a Mongolian, which cannot be obliterated from these persons, regardless of how many generations are born in the United States."

Mike Masaoka, secretary of the Japanese American Citizens League, also testified before the Tolan Committee: "If in the judgment of military and Federal authorities," Masaoka declared, "evacuation of Japanese residents from the West Coast is a primary step toward assuring the safety of this nation, we will have no hesitation in complying with the neces-sities implicit in that judgement. But if, on the other hand, such an evacuation is primarily a measure whose surface urgency cloaks the de-sires of political or other pressure groups who want us to leave merely from motives of self-interest, we feel we have every right to protest and to demand equitable judgment of our merits as American citizens." Masaoka also was highly critical of "voluntary" evacuation.

The Japanese feared that, forced to evacuate their homes, unable to find a place to stay, they would be kicked from town to town in the interior like the Okies of John Steinbeck's novel. Other witnesses went further, and envisioned a day when inhabitants of inland states, aroused by the steady influx of Japanese, would refuse to sell gasoline and food to them. They foresaw, too, the possibility of mob action against them as, "exhausted, impoverished, and unable to travel further, they stopped in some town or village where they were not wanted."

In its Fourth Interim Report, entitled "Findings and Recommendations on Evacuation of Enemy Aliens and Others from Prohibited Military Zones," the Tolan Committee severely criticized the failure of the de-fense command to protect the property of the evacuees. "Witness after witness," the report noted, ". . . deplored the fact that no provision was being made for protecting the property of the persons who had already been, or were about to be, evacuated. Evidence that there were numerous instances of sales of personal property at great sacrifice appear throughout the record. In addition to the unanimous demand for appointment of some agency with authority to take custody of property, both personal and agricultural, suggestions were made that other minor but important details, such as tax deferments and mortgage moratoriums should be given serious consideration."

The committee report pointed out that "there are few, if any, precedents for dealing with the endless number of problems raised by the enforced evacuation of aliens and citizens from strategic military areas in this country. . . . However, a farsighted policy of resettlement demands that future negotiations point more in the direction of salvaging useful household items and other property effects consistent with future activities of the War Relocation Authority, rather than toward undue encouragement of liquidation." As the report emphasized to the point of repetition, not only would the evacuees need the personal belongings and household appliances when they were eventually resettled, they would need them in the relocation sites themselves.

The sale or storage of personal household goods and appliances was discouraged in the report of the Tolan Committee on the grounds that with the shortages caused by the war such items, needed by the evacuees in whatever place they were to be relocated, would be difficult or impossible to replace. "It is impracticable," the report of the committee noted, ". . . to urge the evacuees the hurried sale of these articles, when they will undoubtedly be needed badly at a later date." There should thus be a plan "for the storage of all generally recognized useful household articles . . . rather than the present system of making such storage optional to the evacuees. Storage should be insisted upon."

The Farm Security Administration was urged by the Tolan Committee to act as agent "for returns due evacuees for crops planted and growing prior to evacuation; it could also receive and forward property payments to the Japanese, since the new operators may find it difficult to keep in touch with the various resettlement projects. This must be done to assure the property rights of the evacuees."

The committee added a sobering reflection: "Having in mind that the majority of the present evacuees are American citizens, it is not inconceivable that law suits may be instituted at the close of the war in the event negligence or damage to the property is suffered by individuals affected by the evacuation.''

Henry Morgenthau, secretary of the treasury, reacted promptly to Congressman Tolan's appeal for action to protect evacuee property. He wired General DeWitt to give a high priority ''to protect the equity of an evacuee from grasping creditors.''

The Federal Reserve Bank through its branches was enjoined to do all in its power ''to assist evacuees with the problem of liquidating their property and protecting them against those seeking to take unfair advantage of their plight.'' The Federal Reserve should put the evacuees ''in a position to obtain buyers, lessees, and other users of their property on fair terms.'' In cases where the evacuee was ''unable to select his own agent to dispose of his property, the Federal Reserve will be prepared to act as agent for the evacuee under a power of attorney.''

Evacuees threatened by creditors were to be encouraged ''to come to the representatives of the Federal Reserve for advice and guidance. . . . By and large the mere existence of this program will eliminate or forestall most of the sharp practices that are now feared.'' In addition, the bank was to assist the evacuees in storing property that could not be disposed of by sale.

The telegram stressed the importance of finding solutions to the problem involving property that were ''satisfactory to the evacuee.'' If such a solution could not be found through negotiations between the owner and possible purchasers or lessees, it might be necessary ''for the bank's representatives to step in and take the property over for the purpose of obtaining a fair and reasonable liquidation.''

The response of the Federal Reserve was to establish the Evacuee Property Department. By May 1942, 184 persons were employed in five branch Evacuee Property Department offices to assist evacuees. On March 18 the president of the Federal Reserve Bank of San Francisco issued Special Regulation No. 1, which provided for freezing an evacuee's property if it appeared that he was in danger of being victimized by a creditor. Accompanying the freeze order was a public announcement: ''We want any Japanese or other evacuee who finds that he has difficulty in reaching an equitable settlement with his creditors to come to the nearest office of the Evacuee Property Department of the Federal Bank'' so that ''the bank can discuss his case and take the necessary steps to protect the evacuee from unjust losses.''

If the evacuee and his creditor could still not reach agreement, a sign would be posted at the property in question stating that it was "Special Blocked Property." After the property had been classified as Special Blocked Property, "any acquisition, disposition, or transfer" was subject to a license issued by the Federal Reserve Bank.

In practice, freezing a property and designating it as Special Blocked Property was never employed. Apparently, the threat of such action was enough to prevent the more egregious frauds.

The most important function of the Federal Reserve Bank was undoubtedly that of providing storage space for the personal belongings of evacuees, including cars and trucks. Despite an instruction that stated: "Evacuees will not be permitted to take their motor vehicles to reception centers," some evacuees were allowed to drive themselves and their families to assembly centers and/or relocation camps. An edict of the Evacuee Property Department stipulated: "Prior to evacuation, motor vehicles may be stored, sold or otherwise disposed of by the owner privately, without government interference or assistance." An alternative was to deliver the motor vehicle to the Federal Reserve Bank "for storage at the owner's risk, without insurance" and in most cases in the open air. Since vehicles stored under such circumstance would deteriorate rapidly, resulting "in a loss to the evacuee," the evacuee was given the option of selling the vehicle to the Federal Reserve Bank. Of the 1,905 vehicles received into custody by the bank, 1,469 were sold to the army and 319 "released in accordance with the directions of the evacuees," most commonly to friends or purchasers.

One conspicuous advantage of using the bank's storage facilities was that the bank agreed to ship the evacuees' possessions free of charge to them once they were established in a particular relocation camp.

In the relocation centers a number of evacuees who had left their personal possessions in the charge of the Federal Reserve requested that they be sent to them without cost so that they could have the comfort of familiar objects as well as needed household appliances. Those who made private arrangements were not so fortunate. They were required to pay for the transportation of their belongings from whatever private storage they had arranged to the government warehouses from which they could receive them without charge. It was soon evident that some evacuees had so depleted their savings that they could not afford to pay to have personal belongings moved to a government warehouse.

When the functions of the Wartime Civil Control Administration were turned over to the War Relocation Authority, the Federal Reserve Bank had in its warehouses "2,983 family units of property, made up of 38,694 individual parcels." Confused by the mass of red tape, the forms, affidavits, and declarations that they were required to complete, often with a very imperfect knowledge of the English language and, perhaps even more important, having an instinctive reluctance to deal with agents of the government that was subjecting them to such a bitter fate, many evacuees turned to the government representatives only as a last resort and those, ironically, were often the fortunate ones. The evacuees' natural inclination to avoid dealing with government representatives had been reinforced by advice to make their own private arrangements for storing their possessions in "vacant stores, churches, vacant houses, garages or other outbuildings on their own land." It was also the case that much personal property was transported to the centers at the request of the owners for use or storage in the centers themselves and that this transporting of property was at government expense.

At the bottom of "the personal property inventory" list supplied by the Federal Reserve Bank to evacuees there were the following at least mildly encouraging words: "If the property herein claimed to have been delivered, and which actually was delivered, is lost, damaged, or destroyed as the result of negligence while it is in the possession or custody of the United States, or of an agency acting for it, the Congress of the United States will be asked to take appropriate action for the benefit of the owners."

By April 20, 1942, of 2,506 heads of families processed through control stations only 679 had discussed movable property problems and only 498 had at their request been provided with government storage in warehouses.

The Federal Reserve Bank, with a sigh of relief it must be presumed, turned over to the War Relocation Authority the responsibility for 1,325 Japanese American businesses in California, 185 in the Portland area, and 1,277 in Washington, the greater portion in Seattle.

The Tolan Committee, belated as it was, performed two valuable services. As noted, it focused the attention of Congress, the Treasury Department, and the general public on the issue of protecting evacuee property by whatever means might be devised. This was an issue to which property-conscious Americans were especially sensitive.

In addition it helped draw attention to the impracticality of "voluntary evacuation" and thereby doubtlessly hastened the abandonment of that hopeless policy.

The War Relocation Authority set up its Division of Evacuee Property in August 1942. Its obligations in dealing with evacuee property were "(1) to assist the evacuees to reestablish themselves outside of the prohibited area, first in some one of the War Relocation Authority centers and (2) to give evacuees all possible assistance in connection with their properties and holdings in the Pacific Coastal area from which they were excluded by military order."

Chapter 10

Voluntary Evacuation

ARMED WITH VIRTUALLY UNLIMITED POWER, AT LEAST AS FAR AS THE fate of "persons of Japanese ancestry" was concerned, on March 2 DeWitt issued Public Proclamation No. 1. The eight-six and then ninety-nine "spots" were transformed into Military Area No. 1, a line roughly bisecting the states of Washington, Oregon, and California (plus the southern half of Arizona). A series of north–south roads were designated as the eastern boundary of Military Area No. 1 and so marked at regular intervals. Every man, woman, and child of Japanese ancestry living to the west of the boundary was required to evacuate. Where they were to go and how they were to get there was left largely up to them. The entirely predictable result was the same chaos, confusion, and demoralization that had characterized the Terminal Island evacuation, many times compounded. Once more the harpies and exploiters descended on Japanese communities offering to buy household furnishings, appliances, and personal belongings at a fraction of their value. The Issei had had their bank accounts frozen immediately after Pearl Harbor and many were in want of food and the simplest necessities, dependent on Caucasian friends and Nisei relatives. Eleanor Roosevelt, visiting the West Coast and informed of this Issei plight, intervened to have Issei bank accounts unfrozen in instances where no charges of disloyalty had been brought; much hardship was thereby alleviated.

Between March 2 and March 10, uncertainty prevailed on all fronts. Some notion of the general state of affairs can be gained from the observation that "the General Staff of the Western Defense Command and Fourth Army had not engaged in any extensive planning or preparation for the program." On March 10, eight days after Public Proclamation No. 1, DeWitt established by General Order No. 34 a Civil Affairs Division as an addition to his general staff, and the following day, by Public Order 35 he created the Wartime Civil Control Administration, "as an operating agency of this command." Hereafter all matters having to do with the evacuation of persons of Japanese ancestry were handled by the Wartime Civil Control Administration, or WCCA as it was called. The offices of the Civil Affairs Division, general staff, and the Wartime Civil Control Administration were set up in the Whitcomb Hotel in San Francisco and they were given the assignment of carrying out the evacuation "of all persons of Japanese ancestry . . . with a minimum of economic and social dislocation, a minimum use of military personnel, and maximum speed, and initially to employ all appropriate means to encourage voluntary migration."

Added to the Wartime Civil Control Administration and the Civil Affairs Division of the general staff was the Division of Central Administrative Services of the Office for Emergency Management. The latter agency also moved into the Whitcomb Hotel to coordinate its activities with the WCCA.

In the effort to encourage voluntary emigration, forty-eight offices were established by the WCCA "one in each important center of Japanese population." The offices were staffed by representatives of the various agencies that had been designated to assist the WCCA in the evacuation (or emigration). The Federal Reserve Bank had been designated to assist, along with the Farm Security Administration, in protecting the property of those "emigrating." The Federal Reserve's responsibility was, in the main, for nonfarm property and equipment, for homes, businesses, and personal belongings. The Farm Security Administration had responsibility for farmers and farmhands in the military areas. "Through every available public information channel prospective evacuees were urged to prepare for evacuation," the WCCA report tells us, and to go to one of the offices set up to assist them "in the solution of their personal problems." They were assured that they would receive "aid in their . . . migration to the interior." The officers of the forty-eight offices were authorized, among other things, "to pay the cost of transportation of evacuees to points in the interior." (It is interesting to note that only a small portion of those who attempted to relocate voluntarily applied for the travel assistance and expense money available to them.) In addition, DeWitt ordered the establishment of two "reception centers," to expedite the voluntary movement. One reception center was to be located at Manzanar in the Owens Valley, Inyo County, on the eastern side of the Sierra. The other, the so-called Parker Center, was in Arizona near the California-Arizona border south of Parker Dam. Manzanar subsequently became a relocation center as did Parker, whose name was changed to Colorado River Relocation Center, and then to Poston Relocation Center. Each was designed to provide temporary housing for some ten thousand evacuees.

When plans for voluntary evacuation were first announced, the immediate response of the JACL was to urge all Japanese to comply promptly and cooperatively. The league declared: "You are not being accused of any crime. You are being removed only to protect you and because there might be one of you who would be dangerous to the United States. It is your contribution to the war effort. You should be glad to make the sacrifice to prove your loyalty."

Saburo Kido, president of the JACL, issued a widely publicized announcement: "We are going into exile as our duty to our country because the President and military commander of the area have deemed it a necessity. We are gladly cooperating because this is one way of showing . . . our loyalty." Both then and later (and especially later) there were Japanese who were highly critical of the advice of the JACL leaders. Jack Tono was born and grew up on a farm south of San Jose where his father grew strawberries. His reaction to the news of the evacuation was typical of that of many young Nisei. "I just couldn't understand the whole atmosphere of the whole thing, being a citizen. I could see it if I was an alien. You have no choice but to face things like that. But at the JACL meeting when they came out and nobody resisted—they're all for it in such a way to help the government out with this evacuation business—it was more shocking than the goddarn Pearl Harbor attack. It really frosted me. These people up front conducting that meeting—they're all professional people with college backgrounds, and none of them resisted."

Paul Shinoda was a Nisei who took advantage of voluntary evacuation. Shinoda's parents had been converted to Christianity in Japan by an English missionary. Like many other Japanese converts, they decided to come to the United States. Of their nine children, five had been born in Japan and four in the United States. They came, in Shinoda's words, "because they couldn't see raising five children under the predominant atmosphere of Buddhism." In the United States the senior Shinoda got seven of his nine children through college. "My father had a philosophy about when you're in America," Shinoda recalled: "this is your country, you're growing up here. Don't speak *Nihongo*. He was against Japanese schools. You go to the school your neighbor does, and what they play, you play." Shinoda went to the University of Illinois because of its superior horticulture major but, missing California, he finished his undergraduate work at UC Berkeley. Although Shinoda, a successful florist, was president of the Gardena Japanese American Citizens League, he felt that the league made a mistake in not resisting evacuation. "I kind of thought we were going too much like sheep," he recalled. "They hauled a lot of Issei away, but not the Germans and Italians." When news of the evacuation came, Paul Shinoda's first instinct was to round up some of his friends, get in a car, and head east. But his friends, enthusiastic at first, backed down and Shinoda became a volunteer evacuee, going to Grand Junction, Colorado, and working in the vicinity of the town as an agricultural laborer through much of the war.

Tom Watanabe's brother-in-law was a trucker and had five trucks he used for hauling tomatoes from Laguna Beach and Santa Ana to Los Angeles. Watanabe, twenty-three years old, urged his brother-in-law to round up his family and "Mom" and "get out of here" although it was not clear just where they would go. But his brother-in-law resisted, and when the family was evacuated it was to the Manzanar Assembly Center.

Charles Kikuchi's older sister, Mariko, "Americanized and independent," decided to borrow $55 for train fare and head for Chicago "without knowing a soul or having a job on the other end. That takes guts," her brother added. Few evacuees had so much courage; more important, few had such freedom from family obligations or were so Americanized.

The fact was "voluntary relocation" meant nothing to a farmer in Florin or a farmhand in the Imperial Valley. The attitude of most Japanese was if you want me to leave my home, my job, my farm or business, then you have to relocate me; you have to provide me and my family with a decent place to live, with adequate shelter, with food, transportation and medical care. And it is your responsibility to see that my property and personal belongings are stored safely against the day when the war is over (and you are called to account by the Emperor for your treatment of his loyal subjects). There was little or no incentive for voluntary relocation

and the host of problems and difficulties associated with it; the announcement of "voluntary relocation" served no real purpose except to create
several weeks of uncertainty and confusion.

Initially some 4,310 Japanese declared their intention of moving to
other places in California outside of Military Area No. 1; 2,134 moved to
Utah, 384 to Idaho, 121 to Montana, and 586 to all the other states. This
latter group was made up, in large part, of individuals, mostly Nisei, who
felt confident that they could make their way on their own; a number were
students referred by their professors in West Coast colleges and universities to the attention of colleagues in Midwestern and Eastern institutions.

Most voluntary evacuees moved in with friends and relatives living
somewhere beyond the eastern boundary of Military Area No. 1. For
example, 2,499 moved to Fresno, to that city's and county's alarm.
Tulare, an area where anti-Japanese feeling was strong, received 932 and
Placer County 495.

The largest number of those moving during the period of voluntary
migration came from Los Angeles (almost 2,000), Santa Clara was a
distant second with 443, and San Francisco counted only 207. Of the
3,000 or so leaving California, 69 percent were native born, or Nisei.
One factor was undoubtedly the relative fluency in English of the Nisei.
Many, if not most, of the Issei could speak very little English or none at
all and this was a virtually insurmountable handicap in undertaking the
complicated process of moving to some distant town or city. Evacuees
living in remote areas where police protection was scant or virtually
nonexistent were instructed by the WCCA to concentrate their belongings
"in depositories of their own choice" although it was not clear how this
was to be done. If evacuees decided to store their belongings in a church
or store, the Division of Evacuee Property could pay the cost of moving
an evacuee's property to such a depository. Some evacuees rented rooms
in office buildings to store their belongings, others used stores or found
accommodating churches.

With each passing day the impracticality, if not the imbecility, of
voluntary evacuation became more evident. Mike Masaoka joined in the
chorus of those protesting voluntary evacuation. He urged that "all plans
for voluntary evacuation be discouraged." "Tension is increasing all
around," he added, noting that he was fearful of "mob violence." When
an aged Issei couple named Hayakawa relocated in Santa Fe, New Mexico, they experienced so much hostility that they asked to be admitted to
a reception center. In the words of General DeWitt's final report: "Public

excitement in certain areas reached a high pitch." DeWitt should not have been surprised. He had been forewarned that he would encounter strong opposition to any plan that involved moving large numbers (or, indeed, small numbers) of Japanese to the eastern portion of the states in question. The director of the California State Department for Social Security had written on February 11: "Any uncontrolled evacuation of Japanese to this county [Fresno] would be a serious and grave mistake at this time as it would only tend to aggravate the present tense situation."

With mounting evidence that voluntary evacuation-migration-emigration-relocation, call it what you will, was failing of its purpose, the next step was announced. The assistant chief of staff for civil affairs recommended to the commanding general (DeWitt) on March 21 that the evacuation be placed "on the complete basis of Federal supervision and control." Public Proclamation No. 1 had announced the inauguration of voluntary emigration and after the voluntary departure "for the interior" of more than five thousand persons of Japanese ancestry, the program was abandoned. In the bland words of DeWitt's report, "The voluntary migration phase of evacuation was initiated by the promulgation of Public Proclamation No. 1, designating Military Area No. 1 as the zone from which persons of Japanese ancestry were to be required to leave during the first phase of evacuation. . . . The voluntary movement did not gain momentum because means had not been provided on the ground for aiding evacuees in the solution of personal problems incident to their voluntary exodus."

Voluntary evacuation was a mercifully brief delusion. It served primarily to dramatize the inadequacy of the whole planning process, if it could be dignified by that phrase.

The argument that voluntary evacuation (or migration) had from the first been considered simply the initial phase of evacuation and not the final step is rebutted by the admission in DeWitt's final report that no planning took place immediately after March 2 for a general or mass evacuation under government control. The establishment of the forty-eight offices to aid in voluntary migration would seem to indicate that the expectation was that voluntary migration would solve the problem. The result was that when it became evident that voluntary migration was creating far more problems than it could hope to solve, a period of frantic activity followed in the Wartime Civil Control Administration and its associated agencies.

With the collapse of the voluntary emigration program (now called, in an obvious attempt to save face, "Phase 1"), it became painfully evident that more or less permanent "temporary" living accommodations would have to be provided for virtually all evacuees, including many of those who had voluntarily evacuated. Site selection parties were promptly dispatched "to the interior states in the Western Defense Command to seek sites for the development of Relocation Centers." Now began a game at which Americans fortunately excel—the improvisation of heretofore unknown aggregations of people and material to effect some novel purpose. The director of the WCCA called together representatives of a half dozen bureaus and agencies—the Bureau of Reclamation, the Department of the Interior, the National Resources Planning Board, the Soil Conservation Service, the Farm Security Administration, the Works Projects Administration, and the Corps of Engineers, South Pacific Division. On March 16, site-selection parties were dispatched to identify appropriate locations. The Works Project Administration, the famous (or notorious) New Deal agency, was, at the beginning of the war, winding down its Depression-oriented activities. It had seasoned personnel who could be utilized in staffing the assembly centers through which, it was decided, the evacuees would be channeled to particular relocation centers (the word "camps" with its unhappy connotations was studiously avoided). There was, at the same time, general agreement that the WCCA would retain "complete responsibility" for "the establishment, administration, and operation of the Assembly Centers" (now spelled with capital letters). The "Relocation Centers" (now also caps) would, on the other hand, be planned, organized, and administered by an independent agency established for the specific and exclusive purpose to be called the War Relocation Authority. This agency would have a very different charter and, it was assumed, philosophy. It was soon thought of, although in no way officially, as a kind of extension of the New Deal. That is to say, it was seen as a kind of noble challenge to demonstrate the best principles of American democracy. Unfortunate as it may have been that more than a hundred thousand men, women, and children had, many felt at the time, been unjustly or at least unfairly singled out as prospective enemies of the United States, the centers must be conceived of as schools of democracy in dramatic and inescapable contrast to the concentration camps of our enemies.

THE DECISION FOR "CONTROLLED," OR MASS, EVACUATION CAME AS something of a relief to most Japanese. As "voluntary" had meant "forced" into a hostile and threatening world, "controlled" meant that the government was now committed to providing a safe haven with shelter, food, and other amenities of community life.

One of the relocatees that Charles Kikuchi talked to recalled the rumor that circulated persistently after Pearl Harbor that all of the Nisei were going to have their citizenship taken away and that they were going to be deported. "This," the man added, "was one of the biggest and most persistent rumors I heard and it certainly hurt our morale." Another was that the Japanese had invaded California "and the Japanese Army was running all over the state." From the coastal area, most Japanese were well aware that public sentiment was in favor of locking them all up in concentration camps, the sooner the better. In the meantime, the Japanese suffered numerous indignities, ranging from vituperation to physical assault, but perhaps most difficult of all was the almost three-month period of uncertainty. In addition to the freezing of Issei bank accounts, many Issei were forced to close their businesses. A number of Issei and Nisei employed by Caucasians were fired. Many Caucasians, hearing various interpretations of the Trading with the Enemy Act, were afraid to buy goods or farm produce from Japanese with whom they had done business for years. The consequence was that most Japanese faced a frighteningly uncertain financial future as one economic resource after another was cut off.

It was the continued uncertainty and the endless rumors that were most unnerving. One of Ricci Satow's first thoughts on hearing of the bombing of Pearl Harbor was how he could possibly make a living in the climate created by the attack. The news that "we were going to be put in a camp . . . in fact eased my mind, because I saw the possibility of getting our life stabilized. And at least the danger . . . was gone that the U.S. was going to leave us in starvation. You see, some people were actively stating that the government was going to make us all starve to death. There were thousands of wild rumors going around, you know, sounding as if they were all true and authentic stories."

One evacuee wrote, "I think some of us were a little relieved to be away from the minor irritations, the insults, slander, and the small humiliations unthinking people heaped upon us after Pearl Harbor. Many people may say, 'Well, that's to be expected,' but to be unable to go out in the streets, or just to the corner store, without the fear of being insulted, and being all tense inside with that same fear, was one of the most humiliating things. . . . What could we do? Nothing. Just endure in silence. Those are the things that are locked up in the hearts of many of us. Not big things, but many small things. We became 'sullen and morose' but can we help it? We were not sullen and morose, just leery of any kind [of] advance.''

June Toshiyuki had worried after Pearl Harbor ''that terrible things might happen to Japanese Americans. I really did. We were positive of that. At that time we had no idea that we would be put into camp and all that followed. But even when we got that order people were more or less resigned.'' She felt ''united with the rest of the Japanese community because even under these circumstances, being put into the camps and all, they were united and had pride in whatever they did.''

Those most angered, quite naturally, were those Nisei (and, of course, some Issei) who were assimilated, most Americanized. They felt betrayed, not only by a government that lumped them with the pro-Japanese, but by their pro-Japanese brothers and sisters whose loyalty to the Emperor had, in their view, contributed substantially to the drift into evacuation. This feeling was felt most strongly among certain Nisei college students, among veterans of World War I, and among many Christians of various Protestant denominations who, in sharing a common faith, were close to many Caucasian Christians. One Issei wrote: ''We . . . used to talk among ourselves and say that if war ever came with Japan, the Government might do something to us. We didn't think our children would be touched. My two sons were bitter when they heard that they had to go. One of them refused. He said the Government could put him in prison or shoot him. Almost all night I pleaded with him. The next day I went to see his teacher in college that he liked and respected most and asked the teacher to talk with him. They were together for several hours. After that he said that he would go. That was all he said. The look on his face made me afraid. He behaved strangely in the assembly center and in the relocation center. The other boy was not himself either.''

One of the cases of gross injustice concerned an Issei with the pseudonym of Nomura who lived in Elk Grove, California. At the time of Pearl Harbor, Nomura was manager of the State Farming Company and adviser to the Berry Growers Association of Elk Grove and the Sacramento Berry Exchange. He was also president of the State Ice Company of Sacramento and had loaned money to start these enterprises. In addition, he had an interest in the Garden City Investment Company and the San Jose Brewery. In the aftermath of Pearl Harbor his bank account had been blocked by governmental order. A few days later, Treasury officials entered his home and took all records and account books. A month afterward, four Treasury officials came to Nomura's home and searched it without a warrant and without explanation. For a week a Treasury official stayed in the Nomuras' house, apparently as a kind of guard. Neither of the Nomuras was allowed to leave the house even to purchase food. When the telephone rang it was answered by the guard. When they ran out of food the Nomuras requested that they be allowed to call a grocery store to have food delivered. The request was refused. Even after the guard was withdrawn, the Normuras were prohibited from leaving the house. They subsisted on a supply of rice and other food brought by friends. Twice during the period Nomura was taken by the FBI, questioned by as many as seven people. Finally, he heard from a Japanese friend who had arranged with two Treasury Department officials to pay them $250 a month "to handle his business." Nomura made the same offer and immediately things were straightened out. No more harassment, no more interrogations. The agent in question acted as Nomura's "attorney-in-fact." Even after the Nomuras had been sent to Tule Lake Relocation Center, the connection with the Treasury official was maintained and the officials took 20 percent of Nomura's business returns for "overseeing" his interests. It was almost two years before the activities of the Treasury official were investigated and exposed. It was clear that other Treasury officials were engaged in similar illegal or, at best, highly inappropriate arrangements.

Veterans of World War I were especially outraged. They seemed willing to accept the notion of the Issei being evacuated and even some of the more conspicuously pro-Japanese Nisei. But they were indignant at being swept up with all the other evacuees. One veteran, Joe Kurahara, who felt himself wholeheartedly American, was furious. Assigned to Manzanar, he became a leader of the Japanese nationalistic faction and eventually applied for repatriation to Japan.

Another veteran, given the fictitious name of Woodrow Higashi by the author of a War Relocation Authority report, owned a successful drugstore in Los Angeles. At the time of the evacuation, a Caucasian acquaintance who was a disabled veteran of World War I and an officer in the local chapter of the American Legion offered to assist him in selling his property. He assured Higashi that he could dispose of his drugstore equipment for $350, his neon sign for $75, his 1935 Oldsmobile for $100. In addition, he would undertake to sell his household furniture and any other possessions that Higashi wished to dispose of. After Higashi had been sent to the Santa Anita Assembly Center, the veteran visited him and told him that all his furniture had been stolen. He assured Higashi that he knew who the culprit was. If Higashi would give him power of attorney he would bring action in his behalf to recover the stolen property. Higashi complied and that was the last he saw or heard of the accommodating veteran. At the Granada Relocation Center he appealed to the center's legal counsel, who advised him to hire a lawyer. When that effort proved fruitless, Higashi applied to the War Relocation Authority for help. A WRA attorney made a thorough investigation and discovered that the disabled veteran had been made commander of the local American Legion post, had victimized a number of other evacuees and was "definitely guilty of misappropriation and misrepresentation." When the facts were presented by the WRA lawyer to the Los Angeles district attorney's office, that office proved to be not interested in filing charges against the commander of an American Legion post in behalf of a Japanese internee.

Ironically, those evacuees who "voluntarily" evacuated often suffered the severest property losses. Milton Eisenhower, the director of the WRA, wrote to Biddle's assistant, James Rowe: "The hardest battles so far are about the property of the evacuees. I am fearful that the voluntary system is going to bog down badly in spots." Eisenhower was determined to do his best; "on the whole," he added, "perhaps justice can be done to the Japanese. But there's no denying that there will be difficulties. . . . It may prove to be the darkest part of a pretty dark picture."

Chapter 11

TACHINOKI (EVACUATE)

WITH THE DECISION FOR "CONTROLLED EVACUATION," A VAST new set of problems presented themselves. There was, above all, the sobering realization of what controlled evacuation really meant—a staggeringly complex and expensive operation. A number of "cities" would have to be built *instantly* (it was decided to build ten) and, *in the meantime*, provision would have to be made for all those who were being evacuated.

As soon as the die had been cast for mass evacuation, Roosevelt had issued Executive Order 9102 establishing a civilian agency, the War Relocation Authority, to organize and run the relocation centers and appointed Milton Eisenhower, a younger brother of General Dwight Eisenhower, as its director.

It might be noted here that the anxiety level of West Coast Caucasians had been considerably elevated by the shelling of an oil refinery at Goleta, just north of Santa Barbara, by a Japanese submarine on February 23. Much was made of the fact that a U.S. coastal battery had just been withdrawn from the vicinity of the refinery; the conclusion was that a Japanese-operated radio had sent this information to the submarine. At Astoria, Oregon, a few weeks later a Japanese submarine surfaced and shelled shore batteries from a distance just out of range of American guns. Again the assumption was that information about the range of the shore batteries had been transmitted to the submarine in question.

Time, it thus seemed, was of the essence. With invasion, or at the least, bombing and shelling, of the West Coast expected daily, those being evacuated needed to be moved immediately. Three months had passed without substantial action. Each additional day weakened the argument that evacuation was an emergency measure. To wait for what it was decided to call "relocation centers" for over a hundred thousand people to be built would mean more months of "military emergency," of "danger, confusion, and general demoralization . . . among the public and evacuees alike," in DeWitt's words.

It was decided that the most practical solution was to ship evacuees to interim "assembly centers," hastily converted racetracks and fairgrounds in the main, while the sites for the relocation centers were selected and what would become, in effect, ten small towns were thrown together.

The decision to locate the assembly centers at fairgrounds and racetracks was made on the assumption that these sites would already have essential utilities available and sufficient space for the construction of temporary housing.

In addition to these, an abandoned Civilian Conservation Corps camp was chosen along with the Pacific International Livestock Exposition facilities outside Portland. At Pinedale, California, an abandoned saw mill was utilized. Since the Manzanar and Parker/Colorado River reception centers were largely completed, they were converted into relocation centers and 9,800 evacuees were sent directly to Manzanar while 11,711 were dispatched to Colorado River, without a stay in an assembly center. The Wartime Civil Control Administration had the responsibility for setting up the assembly centers, organizing and equipping them, and transporting the evacuees to them.

The task of evacuating, for the most part, whole families was a formidable one. All those Japanese who had not registered had to be registered. They then reported to "civil control stations," located in all centers of Japanese population. From these stations they were transported, with a maximum of five hundred pounds of personal belongings, to one of the assembly centers. As described, household belongings and personal possessions had to be stored in private or government warehouses, and for those families with cars, arrangements had to be made to store or sell the cars. A number of families drove to the assembly centers, where provision had to be made to store or sell their automobiles or, in a good many instances, trucks.

The Tanforan and the Santa Anita assembly centers most clearly fore-shadowed the relocation centers themselves—larger than the other as-sembly centers and located near the two largest cities in California, they were prototypes for the relocation centers.

Each day from mid-March to the first of June groups of evacuees, assigned to leave on a particular date, gathered at the control stations for transportation, typically by bus, to the nearest assembly center. At the control stations, evacuees were permitted to designate their extended families as families and request that all be sent to the same center (they were known as "evacuation families" and given the same identification number). Similarly, young unmarried men who were close friends could request to be sent to the same center as families. Evacuees from the same town, county, or city (as well, of course, as the same prefectures and church congregations) were generally able to go as a group to a particular assembly center. The trips were usually short, a few hours (unless the evacuees were going to Colorado River, soon called Poston), since most assembly centers were near Japanese communities.

At every control station church people were much in evidence, doing all they could to ameliorate the rigors of evacuation. Operating under a coordinating body known as the Protestant Church Commission for Jap-anese Service, a division of the Federal Home and Foreign Mission Councils, they had strongly opposed mass evacuation and, as soon as the evacuation began, rallied to assist the evacuees in whatever ways they could. *Forth*, the magazine of the Episcopal Church, reported in its June 1942 issue some of those ways. "The special work of all Christian forces has been to prevent any possible 'hysteria' on the part of white neigh-bors," it informed its readers, "to provide counsel and interpretation, help secure justice, and reduce tension all around. Neighboring churches and other groups of the white population have gone out of their way to express their friendly feeling toward the Japanese. All the upheaval and hardship involving the breakup of family ties and disruption of business and trades, and especially of agricultural work that has gone on for many years, the Japanese have taken in a spirit of complete cooperation."

Among the most active church denominations in assisting the evacuees was a United Brethren group, led by Ralph and Mary Smeltzer. The Smeltzers (he was, as a member of a "peace church," a conscientious objector) worked with the evacuees, as did thousands of other Caucasian Christians, trying to assist in the actual mechanics of evacuation, bringing food to control centers, arranging for storage of belongings, helping with transportation. In Tulare County, the Smeltzers undertook to monitor the dates and times of departure, destination, and whether the evacuees could count on receiving adequate meals in transit. On July 16, 1942, Ralph Smeltzer reported, "Six of our cars transported approximately 35 evacuees and most of their baggage to the depot. . . . Our activities were well organized and went smoothly. Our closest estimate is that 65 workers helped prepare and serve 45 gallons of punch, 1800 sandwiches, and 12 lugs of peaches and other fruit to 564 evacuees." Smeltzer went on to list the volunteers participating in the send-off. Besides thirteen "work campers" from the nearby Civilian Public Service Camp, there were "Methodist work campers from Porterville, F.O.R. [Fellowship of Reconciliation] members, and representatives from the following churches: Lindsay Church of the Brethren, Lindsay Presbyterian, Strathmore Baptist, and possibly others."

Josephine Whitney Duveneck was a Quaker who, with Caucasians of other denominations, came to one of the San Francisco control stations to give help and comfort to evacuees. She saw "little groups of people . . . laden with suitcases, bags, cartons and all manner of impediments. One carried a bird cage, another a hundred year old dwarf tree in a pot, blanket rolls, baby baskets, toy animals, dolls, packages of books, heavy coats, umbrellas." At the control center, the Quakers had organized a canteen with hot coffee, tea, chocolate, doughnuts, and sandwiches. They provided extra twine to tie up boxes, paper and stamps, bandages, and a small Primus stove to heat baby bottles, Kleenex to wipe away tears. One of the volunteers took an old man back to his house to retrieve the false teeth he had left in the bathroom. Duveneck drove three crippled old people to the Tanforan assembly area. Many other volunteers drove the elderly or handicapped to Tanforan or Santa Anita.

When Haruko Niwa and her husband and two children arrived at their control station, a Japanese school near the Santa Anita Assembly Center, the church federation of the area served coffee and doughnuts. All "the West Los Angeles church people and the friends and residents, all go together, all this area that we're familiar with," Niwa recalled.

In Pasadena, Esther Rhoades led the work of the churches in assisting evacuees. In Visalia, California, Elizabeth Evans organized the Visalia Committee to Aid the Japanese. Like the Smeltzers, Evans worked to collect and distribute food to those evacuees departing for assembly centers.

In Seattle the Caucasian Baptist churches established a Storage Committee to assist evacuees in storing furniture and personal belongings. Some worked with Japanese friends to help them sell or lease their homes and offices.

Isamu Nakamura remembered that a few days before the evacuation the minister and a number of members of the Westminster Church came to the Japanese American church "to bid us farewell by singing hymns and offering their prayers." Rhoda Akiko Iyoya recalled the wife of the Reverend Stanley Hunter, the minister at St. John's Presbyterian Church in Berkeley, coming to talk and knit as her family packed their belongings. The Hunters were active in the Fair Play Committee, which had opposed evacuation, and Mrs. Hunter tried, by her presence, to encourage the Iyoyas.

Hatsune Helen Kitaji, who lived on the R. C. Olsen ranch near Sunnyvale, California, recalled that her family packed and labeled things carefully so that they could later have them sent to their center. Among the belongings that they requested (and received) were golf clubs and a sewing machine.

Most of Kitaji's friends were Caucasians, many from her days as a student leader at San Jose State. When orders came for her family to report to the Salinas Assembly Center, one of her fellow teachers found a small trailer that she could use to bring belongings to the center. That was a real luxury. It carried a phonograph player, records, a teapot, a hotplate, "things other people couldn't take with them." One friend, hearing of the volunteer evacuation plan, called from Lake County inviting Kitaji and her family to come live with her but it was soon evident that the friend lived too near the coast.

After Pearl Harbor, Therea Takayoshi and her husband experienced the help and concern of her Caucasian neighbors. They gave her a surprise party in April 1942. "They gave me so many things I could use in camp," she noted, "like heavy pants and heavy nightgowns and things like that." The Takayoshis had a flourishing ice cream parlor that sold their own homemade brand. They calculated its value at $10,000 but they sold it for $1,000.

Yoshisada Kawai's wife had a similar experience. She owned a laundry business at the time of the evacuation that she had to sell to a "white man" for virtually nothing. Her husband took the money and hid it inside a bar of soap.

"When we left," Mary Tsukamoto recalled, "we swept our house and left it clean, because that's the way Japanese people feel like leaving a place. . . . I remember that sad morning when we realized suddenly that we wouldn't be free. It was such a clear, beautiful day and I remember as we were driving, our tears. We saw the beautiful snow-clad Sierra Nevada mountains that we had loved to see so often, and I thought about

God and about the prayer that we often prayed.'' Mary Tsukamoto's grandparents had to leave their lovingly tended flower garden and vineyard.

The Tsukamotos had "a very dear friend," Bob Fletcher, who agreed to stay at their house and run the three adjacent Japanese-owned farms. Since no pets could be taken to the assembly centers, the Tsukamotos had to leave their daughter's dog with Fletcher, an unhappy parting.

June Toshiyuki's parents had a drugstore that also sold art objects from Japan, mostly to *hakujin*. Her parents had insurance through a Caucasian insurance man who helped them pack their stock in sturdy crates and store them in a safe warehouse for the duration. The drug supplier took back most of the drugs and credited the Toshiyukis. When the relocation ended, the wholesaler helped them get back in business.

Emi Somekawa and her husband had been confident in the aftermath of Pearl Harbor that their status as American citizens would protect them from persecution. But as anti-Japanese feeling mounted, they realized they were in for difficult times. In Somekawa's words, their question was: "Why us? I felt like we were being punished for nothing. . . . I don't really know how to put it into words, but the day we left the house, the German lady came with a cake, and she said if there was anything they could do for us, to call. So twice they came to the assembly center. I think they felt like they were a little bit displaced too.''

When the evacuation was announced, Charles Kikuchi had decided to identify himself with his family and go with them to Tanforan, the racetrack near San Francisco where most of his college friends would also be sent. Kikuchi's brother Jack, several years younger, told Charles, "it's going to be bad." His ambition had been to go to the East and study medicine but Jack too decided that he couldn't "walk out on the family like that.''

At his control center, Charles Kikuchi noted, "The Nisei around here don't seem to be so sad. They look like they are going on a vacation. They are all gathered around the bulletin board to find out the exact date of their departure. 'When are you leaving?' they are saying to one another.'' A few days later Kikuchi wrote in his diary: "The Church people around here seem so nice and full of consideration saying, 'Can we store your things?' 'Do you need clothes?' 'Sank you,' the Issei smile even though they are leaving with hearts full of sorrow.'' The manners of some of the Nisei seemed "brazen" to Kikuchi. "They are demanding service. I guess they are taking advantage of their college educations.'' He had "a queer sensation and it doesn't seem real. There are smiling faces all around me and there are long and gloomy faces too. All kinds of Japanese and Caucasian faces around this place. Soon they will be neurotic cases.'' When Kikuchi's Chinese friend, Wang, who had accompanied him to the center, complained of an empty feeling in the pit of his stomach, Kikuchi recommended that he fill it with one of the hamburgers that the church people were passing around. He heard ''some little kids . . . yelling down the street 'the Japs are leaving, hurrah, hurrah!' '' And Kikuchi, who had done his best to avoid involvement in ''Japanesy'' groups, wrote in his diary that evening: ''God, what a prospect to look forward to living among all those Japs!''

Kikuchi wrote to his sister who had voluntarily relocated in Chicago that his professor at Berkeley had urged him to complete the work for his certificate. He was also ''quite frank in telling me my chances for getting a social work position were nil, but in the post-war period there would be a very good chance for me.''

A week later, Kikuchi wrote his sister: ''About 700 people have already gone to the Assembly Center in Santa Anita (move over Seabiscuit).'' The Kikuchi family had been alerted to be ready to leave for the Tanforan center. Kikuchi's youngest siblings, Tommy and Miyako, were, he reported to sister Mariko, ''all excited about the 'vacation'; Alice confused; Jack calm; Emiko still thinking about the boys and the clothes she has to take; and Mom and Pop not worrying too much as they think I have a special 'in' with the government.''

Kikuchi did not accompany his family to the Tanforan Assembly Center. He was given permission to remain behind to take a final examination in one of his Berkeley courses. When he went to the bank to close out his account, the teller, whom he had never seen before, ''solemnly shook my hand and he said, 'Goodbye, have a nice time.' I wonder if that isn't the attitude of the American people? They don't seem to be bitter against us, and I certainly don't think I am any different from them.''

A total of 117,116 persons were evacuated between March 2 and October 31, 1942. Of this number, 6,393 did not enter an assembly center. Six hundred forty-one entered centers as parolees from detention centers where they had been sent as suspected subversives. Some came as voluntary evacuees who had been unable to relocate successfully ''in the interior.'' Mixed-marriage families where one partner was not of Japanese ancestry number 465, of whom 206 entered a center and were later released and 259 were exempted from the evacuated area prior to mass evacuation and did not go to a center.

Of the 110,000 to 120,000 evacuated, some 72,000 were American-

born but of these only 22,400 were over twenty-one years of age and
these made up approximately one third of the adult population. The total
foreign-born—the Issei—numbered 38,500. By June 1942, removal from
Military Area No. 1 had been accomplished, and by August 7 from Area
No. 2.

The whole vast complex undertaking was accomplished with remarkable efficiency. Newspaper and army photographers covered the evacuation and hundreds of photographs from the time show evacuees boarding
trains and buses. In the photographs many of the young men and women
are smiling as though they were about to embark on a lark of some kind.
The disposition of the Japanese to obey authority, whatever the source, as
well as the expectation of many that the war would soon end in a Japanese
victory, doubtlessly contributed to the smoothness of the evacuation,
which was accomplished without any untoward incidents, without
violence and without resistance, organized or spontaneous. Indeed, so
cooperative were the evacuees that they won a commendation from Secretary of War Stimson, who stated: "Great credit is due our Japanese
population for the manner in which they responded to and complied with
the orders for exclusion."

Chapter 12

FARM PROPERTY

PERHAPS THE MOST COMMONLY MENTIONED HARDSHIP OF EVACUATION is the fact that so many evacuees lost both personal and real property. In some instances everything they had accumulated by virtue of hard work and great sacrifice. With evacuation came the threat of losing the labors of a lifetime. In addition to sale to junkmen and antiques dealers of household goods, of furniture and appliances, of treasured family heirlooms at ridiculously low prices, those evacuees who owned homes, businesses, and farms that were mortgaged were in danger of losing them because of their inability to keep up mortgage payments, not to mention tax assessments.

The loss of the property, personal and real, of the evacuees was perhaps the issue that roused most sympathy with the public. The widely reported stories of the loss of personal belongings in the Terminal Island evacuation, highlighted by the Tolan Committee hearings, brought strong criticism of the government actions.

We have already seen the problems faced by the Federal Reserve Bank in its mission of storing and/or protecting evacuee property. Those problems were relatively simple compared with those of the Farm Security Administration, which had been given responsibility for Japanese-owned or leased farmlands. General DeWitt's orders to the FSA were to "institute and administer a program which will insure continuation of the proper use of agricultural lands voluntarily vacated by enemy aliens and other persons designated by me, and which will insure fair and equitable arrangements between evacuees and the operators of their property." If the two charges were not contradictory, they hardly took account of the conflicts and tensions involved. Funds would be made available to carry out the general's directives and "to make, service and collect loans" in pursuance of the goal of keeping agricultural land in production. General DeWitt further wished to have a representative of the Agriculture Department on his Civilian Committee on Evacuation. What followed was an almost hopeless tangle of jurisdictions among the Treasury, War, and Agricultural Departments.

When Milton Eisenhower arrived on the West Coast to assume his responsibilities as director of the War Relocation Authority, he was dismayed at the general air of confusion that prevailed in regard to Japanese farm property. He wrote to the undersecretary of agriculture, Claude Wickard, that things were "in a turmoil." Few evacuations of farmers had taken place but those that had had demonstrated clearly that "the Japanese would suffer losses and production would decline unless the efforts already under way were backed up by some real authority. The perishable nature of truck crops," Eisenhower continued, "almost invites a stalling on the part of prospective purchasers who hope to get the property on the equity of the Japanese at a fraction of its true value. . . . The long and short of it is that the Japanese are selling for what they can get. Consequently everyone agreed that the power to freeze property and to operate the farms until fair value could be received should be vested in the Department of Agriculture." As things stood, the power to freeze prices was, as was noted earlier, vested in the Federal Reserve Bank, while the responsibility for recruiting people to "operate, buy, or lease farms" lay with agents of the Agriculture Department.

"Most of the Japanese farmers," Eisenhower continued, "have maintained their farms in excellent conditions. When they leave at the rate of two or three thousand a day . . . production is going to be a bit retarded. Evacuees must leave their household goods behind, with only a storage receipt which disclaims all responsibility; their cars, trucks, tractors, and other machinery are impounded. They move to assembly points and then on to the reception centers where, starting with sand and cactus, they hope to make a living."

Eisenhower's final observation was not atypical of the feelings of the officials charged with overseeing the evacuation or, more commonly, with protecting the property of the evacuees: "I feel most deeply that when this War is over and we consider calmly this unprecedented migration of 120,000 people, we are as Americans going to regret the avoidable injustices that may have occurred. . . . Here on the ground things are moving fast and are greatly confused. Consequently, our judgment may not always be sound."

By May 31, the Farm Security Administration had registered 6,664 farms comprising well over 200,000 acres. The FSA, assigned the virtually impossible job of attending to evacuee farm property and equipment, formed a subordinate body, entitled the California Evacuated Farms Association, which exercised the power of attorney for evacuee farmers. First, FSA agents were to try to find "tenants or operators" for farms surrendered by evacuees in order both to maintain production and to pass along monies generated by the operation of the farms in question once due loans had been met and taxes paid. The Division of Evacuee Property was charged with adjusting "differences arising out of inequitable, hastily made or indefinite agreements." It was also to supervise the actual operation of the farms in question by tenants and lessees to ensure that "no damage or waste was occurring."

The task of finding men to operate the farms of the evacuees proved a far harder one than anyone, including the Farm Security Administration, had anticipated. In the words of the report: "Doubts of venturing into this specialized sort of farming, a large-looming labor problem, and various other factors made potential operators hesitate." One solution was to combine a number of small Japanese farms into one large one with the formation of a corporation often connected with growers' and shippers' organizations. Such a "dummy" corporation would lease five or six farms and borrow money to put a crop in with the understanding that half or more of the profits were to go to the owner or to the evacuee who had leased the land originally. Sometimes, crops failed and the new lessees would default on their bank loans or fail to pay taxes. Each one of hundreds of variations on such a theme required intervention by someone, usually a lawyer, on behalf of the evacuee. If an evacuee could not afford the services of a lawyer, which, not surprisingly, was often the case, pools of lawyers willing to represent evacuees with minimum fees or, often, no fees at all, were formed in areas where Japanese agricultural land was concentrated.

A classic case in point was that of Northern Farms, a dummy corporation set up by the Nash-DeCamp Company to lease and operate twenty farms. A loan of $98,077 was obtained by Northern Farms to cover the cost of planting, maintaining, and harvesting the crops on these farms. Only five farms showed a profit. The total return on crops harvested on the twenty farms was $74,831. When the government loan had been repaid, a balance of $2,017 remained (50 percent of the profit on five farms) to be distributed to the owners of the farms that had turned a profit. But Northern Farms declared itself unwilling to make even this modest payment.

Farm Management, Inc. of Sumner, Washington, was another revealing case. Formed by five men who each put up $100, the corporation committed itself to farming thirty-six parcels of evacuee land comprising three hundred acres. The farms all had crops growing at the time they were taken over by Farm Management. The cash required to harvest and replant crops came in the form of a loan for $60,500. The mortgage was the crops and equipment on the farms. Upon securing the loan, Farm Management paid $19,794.65 to the evacuee owners for their equipment and $21,643.21 to the owners as one half of the estimated value of the as-yet-unharvested crops. The other half of the owners' share was to be 50 percent of the crop's value after harvest. The mortgage payment was due on December 15, 1942, and it was at once apparent that there "was not the slightest possibility," a report noted, that Farm Management could pay both its obligation to the evacuees and discharge its mortgage indebtedness. The consequence was that the Farm Security Administration, with its fetish about recovering its loans, asserted its claims over those of the evacuee owners.

These two examples will perhaps serve to give an indication of the problems faced in hundreds of such arrangements, which could hardly have been worked out under less propitious circumstances. By June 1, 1942, 722 loans totaling $3,120,243 had been made. One of the problems with the whole program was that the FSA became so preoccupied with getting repayments on the loans that that issue came to overshadow either the reasonably efficient operation of such farms or any kind of adequate return to the Japanese owners, although reserving a fair profit for the evacuees had been one of the primary objectives of the program.

At Cortez, California, most of the farmers belonged to a Japanese agricultural association at the time of the evacuation. The association hired a Caucasian manager to run the farms, "utilizing farm laborers who moved into California from the state of Oklahoma." Any profit was saved for the members of the association.

In addition to the land, leased or owned, there was often valuable farm equipment—trucks and tractors most commonly—that was needed to keep a farm in production. The equipment might not be of use in the type of farming more familiar to a prospective lessee. Or, not uncommonly, when leases were negotiated, the equipment was poorly maintained and lost much of its value during the period when its owners were relocated. Where machinery was "sold off of [a] farm it was to be retained in the community or locality."

One source of contention arising from the "firm collection policy" of the FSA was a stipulation that where evacuees leased their farms to substitute operators on a share basis, "the evacuees should receive their share of the crops produced *under any circumstances* [italics added]." This provision was essential, otherwise the substitute operators could incur various expenses and simply charge them against the lessors' share of the profits. Often, of course, there were no profits, simply deeper indebtedness.

It was soon evident that operators who found the management of evacuee farms beyond their capabilities and who had, in many instances, made substantial loans to lease the property, "believing that they have no opportunity of obtaining extensions of time or renewal of loans were simply abandoning the properties."

The bureaucratic tug-of-war between the Farm Security Administration under the Department of Agriculture and the Treasury Department made for a constant state of confusion and uncertainty that worked hardship on the evacuees. In the words of one report: "By the time the question of authority and jurisdiction was answered to the satisfaction of all agencies concerned, the exclusion orders were raining down upon a thoroughly bewildered people and trains and buses were carrying the evacuees who were permitted to take with them only what they could carry in their two hands—to half-constructed camps at Santa Anita and Manzanar."

A happier note was the experience of a Nisei with the pseudonym of Charles Nishimoto. Nishimoto and his sister, Sally, leased their 694-acre farm at the time of evacuation to a tenant for three years at $9,000 for the first year and $10,000 thereafter. The tenant got a loan of $22,050 from the FSA. Of this sum $16,000 was for the purchase of farm machinery and equipment and the remainder to cover the cost of growing and harvesting three hundred acres of tomatoes. At the end of the growing year the tenant announced that because of an acute labor shortage he had not been able to harvest his entire crop and consequently could not repay his loan but needed an extension. The FSA, with its "tough loan" policy, refused to extend the tenant's loan and expressed their determination to

seize all farm equipment in foreclosure proceedings. The unhappy tenant
then appealed to the War Relocation Authority office for help. The authority, anxious to protect the interests of the evacuee owner as well as to
keep such a large farm in production, appealed to the Farm Security
Administration, as one might say, for mercy. Meanwhile, the Nishimotos, doubtlessly disgusted with the whole procedure and now farming
successfully in Michigan, declared they had no intention of returning to
California. They authorized a real estate agent to try to sell their land for
$125,000, although it was considered substantially more valuable. The
evacuee property supervisor of the WRA's office in Sacramento advised
the Nishimotos to set a higher value on the property and undertook to try
to find a buyer. "We firmly believe," the WRA officer wrote the Nishimotos, "that your asking price is not in line compared to the way
properties have been selling." It was the opinion of the WRA office that
"someone in that area is 'knocking the place,' " i.e., trying to down-
grade its value, "by subdividing it into smaller tracts." The Nishimotos
were urged to come to California to take a direct hand in the sale of the
property. "Knowing that this ranch has meant a very large investment to
you," the WRA officer wrote, "I hate to see you dispose of it at . . . a
loss. If it were possible for you to gather up a crew of evacuees and had
enough finances to purchase the necessary equipment [the original equipment had been seized to satisfy the tenant's loan] I am positive that you
and your associates would make enough money in the next four or five
years to place your land bank loan in a current position."

The author of the War Relocation Authority report was obviously
pleased to be able to note that the Nishimotos returned to California, sold
the ranch for $100,000, a sum $30,000 above their indebtedness, with
which they purchased a three-story Stockton building "in which they are
operating a hotel and two shops."

That such accommodations were relatively rare is suggested by the fact
that some four pages of the War Relocation Authority's report on the
handling of evacuee property is devoted to the story of the Nishimotos.
But the author can hardly be blamed. It *is* an impressive story of time and
trouble (and personal concern) devoted to an attempt to do justice to an
individual evacuee (or, in this case, two evacuees), a story ending with
that triumphant sentence: "Mr. Nishimoto professes that he is 'satisfied
with the entire deal.' "

Until the centers themselves were closed, the War Relocation Authority was faithful in its mission. In January 1944 a conference attended by
various individuals concerned with evacuee property management was

held in San Francisco. Those attending were urged to be more aggressive in "investigating, reporting and documenting . . . cases of fraud, vandalism, pilferage, fire damage and serious mismanagement lapses." A new provision was adopted allowing the free transportation of five thousand pounds of fixtures, equipment, machinery, or tools "necessary to business enterprise whenever a family was unable to procure such equipment in the area of relocation."

Chapter 13

THE WAR RELOCATION
AUTHORITY

As HAS BEEN NOTED, SOON AFTER IT HAD BECOME EVIDENT THAT voluntary evacuation was not going to be successful, President Roosevelt issued Executive Order 9102, which created the War Relocation Authority. As described by its first director, Milton Eisenhower, the authority was responsible for "(1) aiding the Army in carrying out the evacuation of military areas, (2) developing and supervising a planned, orderly program of relocation for evacuees, (3) providing evacuees with work opportunities so that they may contribute to their own maintenance and to the national production program, and (4) protecting evacuees from harm in the areas where they are relocated. The first specific task of the Authority is to relocate some 100,000 alien and American-born Japanese evacuated from the military areas of the far Western states."

The director of the War Relocation Authority was a classic New Deal liberal. Milton Eisenhower had grown up, the youngest of five brothers, in the small Kansas town of Abiline. A shy, physically inept child, he had been teased by his older brothers for his lack of robustness. His brothers were all star athletes in high school while Milton's interests were primarily academic. To encourage his scholarly bent, his brother Dwight offered to give him a dollar for every A he got in high school. Milton recalled his brother's surprise when he presented him with a grade card with five A's. Milton also recalled that Dwight never paid up.

Milton Eisenhower's hero and model was Woodrow Wilson; as a young man Eisenhower had decided that his true calling was public service. After a stint in the foreign service, Eisenhower had gone on to a series of government jobs, from the Department of Agriculture's Office of Information in Calvin Coolidge's administration to Henry Wallace's right-hand man in the Department of Agriculture and a valued go-between with the President.

Early in March 1942 Eisenhower was summoned to the Oval Office. He was shocked at Roosevelt's appearance. The President looked gray and ill. There was none of the light bantering manner that had marked earlier visits by Eisenhower. Harold Smith, director of the budget, was present. Roosevelt's first words were, "Milton, your job, starting immediately, is to set up a War Relocation Authority to move the Japanese-Americans off the Pacific Coast. I have signed an executive order which will give you full authority to do what is essential. The Attorney General will give you the necessary legal assistance and the Secretary of War will help you with the physical arrangements. Harold," indicating Smith, "will fill you in on the details of the problem."

"And, Milton . . . the greatest possible speed is imperative."

Eisenhower, preoccupied with his regular duties at the Department of Agriculture, had only a sketchy notion of the Japanese American "problem." He remembered reading that General DeWitt believed that an invasion of the United States via the West Coast was a real possibility. He also recalled that the Tolan Committee had held hearings on the West Coast in connection with the plan to evacuate Japanese Americans from areas considered especially vulnerable.

Harold Smith briefed Eisenhower on his new assignment. After describing the general situation, Smith told Eisenhower that DeWitt was convinced that many of the West Coast Japanese were loyal to their homeland but believed that it was impossible to tell the difference between those who were loyal to the United States and those whose loyalty went to the Emperor. Attorney General Biddle and Assistant Secretary of War McCloy, Smith told Eisenhower, would be the individuals that he would be dealing with most directly.

In Eisenhower's memoirs, he noted that he was "deeply troubled" by his new job. "My instincts told me that the course we had embarked on was an extreme one. But I must confess," he added, "that I spent little time pondering the moral implications of the President's decision. We were at war. Our nation had been viciously attacked without warning. We had been badly mauled by the Japanese forces and the enemy had been rampaging almost without resistance in the Southeast Pacific." He had his orders and he was determined to carry them out as "effectively and humanely" as possible.

After his briefing by Harold Smith, who was only modestly informed himself, Eisenhower had a session with Biddle. In Eisenhower's words, Biddle assured him that he could "transfer the evacuees into private employment if that proved feasible and, in doing so, I could specify the conditions which would have to be met in such employment. If private employment proved impossible, I could establish evacuation centers, set up schools, develop work programs, create courts and all other facilities and procedures essential to making the relocation centers as nearly self-governing as possible."

Milton Eisenhower's first "West Coast" briefing was by Colonel Bendetsen—"straight, serious, grim, and completely confident in his own judgments."

It was Bendetsen who broke the news to Eisenhower that the voluntary evacuation program was a failure. In Eisenhower's words: "He insisted that the voluntary program be terminated and that compulsory evacuation of the entire Japanese population in Military Area No. 1 be undertaken at once. . . . I expressed dismay," Eisenhower wrote. "I strongly resisted the idea of complete evacuation, hoping some less dramatic solution could be found. . . . I insisted that the WRA, having been established only a few days earlier, was unprepared to cope with an immediate mass evacuation." Bendetsen's response was that the army had already formulated plans for the establishment of two centers, one in Arizona near the Colorado River, the other (Manzanar) in the Owens Valley of California, capable of containing thirty thousand evacuees. Within hours, Bendetsen told Eisenhower, "he could have a group of Nisei volunteers recruited from the Los Angeles area on their way to one of these camps to make preparations." The army was already setting up thirteen assembly areas to receive evacuees. Eisenhower asked Bendetsen for a few hours to consider the implications of what he had heard and "to consult with others."

For the next few weeks Eisenhower was frantically busy trying to put together a staff for his new agency. In the process he turned to the Department of Agriculture for most of his recruits, men and women he knew and trusted. It was soon apparent to Eisenhower that Bendetsen was correct about the volunteer program. Eisenhower and DeWitt met on March 25 at the Presidio in San Francisco and agreed that the volunteer program should be terminated immediately. Eisenhower found DeWitt "austere," confident that he was right in all his judgments, and a "machine gun" talker, barely stopping to catch his breath. He was still convinced that a Japanese invasion was not only a possibility but highly likely; he painted a lurid picture of the "chaos that, in his opinion, would result." In Eisenhower's words again: "He believed that a high percentage of both the Issei and the Nisei would support Japanese forces should they attack the West Coast, and he was adamant that one could not tell the difference between a loyal and a disloyal Japanese-American." Eisenhower added that he "sensed that General DeWitt had somehow blocked out the human implications of the evacuation. He wanted the area cleared at once so that he could make all feasible preparations for a possible invasion." Eisenhower got the impression "that [DeWitt] intended to evacuate German and Italian aliens as well." And indeed a few weeks later DeWitt renewed his call for a "limited collective evacuation of German and Italian aliens from Military Area No. 1."

Persuaded that the voluntary program was a failure, Eisenhower cast about for some alternative to mass evacuation. Would it not be possible to evacuate only men, leaving the women and children in their homes to carry on their husbands' businesses as best they could, "especially such businesses as florist shops, grocery stores, drugstores, and similar establishments where closing would involve serious economic losses?" The notion was more of a tribute to Eisenhower's heart than his head. Bendetsen was quick to point out the manifold difficulties of such a scheme.

Eisenhower's next move was to wire the governors of the intermountain states asking them to meet with him. His hope at this point was to initiate a program "to move the maximum number of evacuees directly into private employment. If mass evacuations were essential, at the very least it should be undertaken in a way that would permit families to stay together and the heads of those families to provide for their needs through gainful employment," Eisenhower wrote.

Meanwhile, the new director met with a delegation from the Japanese American Citizens League and asked them to constitute an advisory council to represent "those most affected by the President's executive order." Eisenhower considered this step "the wisest thing I did in that whole traumatic experience." The move marked the consolidation of the deep split between the "assimilators," represented by the league, and those Japanese Americans loyal to the Emperor.

The advisory council was headed by twenty-three-year-old Mike Masaoka, whom we have already encountered as secretary of the Japanese American Citizens League. A graduate of the University of Utah, Masaoka was a bright, self-confident young man. Eisenhower was charmed by him. "After the establishment of the advisory council," Eisenhower wrote, "I did not make a single major decision without first conferring with this young man." Eisenhower's dependence on Masaoka, while commendable in the sense of seeking advice and guidance from a Japanese American, revealed his lack of understanding of Japanese psychology; to have relied on a *very young man*, strongly identified with a particular and not very popular position among the Japanese generally, was a tactical error. However well intentioned, it was an affront to the Issei and a red flag to the enemies of the Japanese American Citizens League. It was certainly the case that Eisenhower (and his successor) were wise to seek the counsel of loyal Nisei but the choice of Masaoka, however brilliant an individual he may have been, was an affront to the Japanese respect for its elders. In a society that, however badly it may have been split on ideological lines, was at one in its veneration of age, to turn for advice to the son in disregard of the father was deeply offensive. At the same time it must be said that to have established a "more representative" advisory council would have been virtually impossible considering the bitter divisions that existed.

When Eisenhower met with the intermountain state governors at Salt Lake City on April 7 he did his best to sell them on the idea of welcoming the evacuees in their respective states as an important supply of notably hardworking individuals who would help harvest crops, especially sugar beets, in labor-starved areas. What Eisenhower had in mind was a kind of Civilian Conservation Corps made up primarily of young men who could provide a variety of useful services. "I was prepared to discuss policies about prevailing wages, health care, and other factors," Eisenhower wrote. But he never got that far. The governors literally shouted him down. One governor called out: "If these people are dangerous on the Pacific coast they will be dangerous here! We have important defense establishments, too, you know." Another governor shook his fist in Eisenhower's face and snarled: "If you bring Japanese into my state, I promise you they will be hanging from every tree."

Only Governor Ralph Carr of Colorado took a more moderate line. He would be glad to have loyal Japanese move into his state; he considered it the responsibility of citizens everywhere to cooperate with the War

Relocation Authority. Looking back on the abortive meeting, Eisenhower judged it "probably the most frustrating experience I ever had."

Resigned to the necessity of building centers for the evacuees, Eisenhower hurried back to Washington and called together representatives from the National Forest Service, Irrigation Service, Public Land Office, and National Park Service to enlist their support in locating sites for the relocation centers. Eisenhower also informed McCloy of his meeting with the governors and of the fact that he was resigned to the building of the centers "where people could live with modest comfort, do useful work, have schools for their small children, and thus retain as much self-respect as the horrible circumstances permitted." Eisenhower clung to his vision of "a kind of work corps, who could help in clearing and developing the land, who could plant crops and manufacture products for the war effort, such as tents, camouflage nets, and cartridge belts. These items could be sold to the government and the evacuees could share in the profits."

It was an appealing idea. The CCCs had been the New Deal's most successful and generally admired program. With the beginning of the war and the institution of Selective Service, those enrollees eligible for military duty (the vast majority) had been drafted into the armed services and the camps largely abandoned. To fill them with industrious young Nisei would be relatively simple (and inexpensive) as compared with providing places for them in the centers. Since they would be essentially the same facilities as those used a few months earlier by young Americans the concentration camp image would be largely avoided.

In addition to war-related "industries" in the centers, Eisenhower anticipated that each center would have a large agricultural component that would produce sufficient food for the centers and a substantial surplus to help meet the wartime need for food production.

Efforts to form a work corps modeled on the Civilian Conservation Corps, which so preoccupied Eisenhower, proved impractical. In fact, most of the efforts to involve evacuees in work projects that had some outside referent and that were intended to provide evacuees with additional income proved fruitless. Most evacuees resisted any notion of work that was not directly related to the life of the center. Many looked upon the centers as a time of vacation. Work for the sake of work had little appeal. Moreover, in the eyes of many evacuees it constituted a form of cooperation with the War Relocation Authority or the center administrations. One unanticipated problem was that any attempt to initiate a venture designed to produce something useful for the war effort was resisted by businesses and industries who feared competition from products turned out in the center. The only venture that enjoyed even a modest degree of success was the manufacture of camouflage nets at Manzanar. An effort to train evacuees to produce commercial ceramics attracted two experienced potters to Heart Mountain Relocation Center in Wyoming, but it, too, came to nothing. In the words of Dillon Myer, Eisenhower's successor, the work program was designed to "provide for the living requirements of the whole evacuee community to the fullest extent possible"; it was also to "develop land in the vicinity of the centers and improve its productive value" and to produce surplus food for sale on the open market, thus helping to defray the cost of maintaining the centers. Whatever profits might accrue would be shared by the members of the work corps. But the work corps did not work.

In early April, Eisenhower opened a War Relocation Authority office in the Whitcomb Hotel in San Francisco adjacent to the Wartime Civil Control Administration, and the two agencies agreed on procedures to phase out the WCCA and phase in the WRA. The preamble declared "the War Relocation Authority is an independent establishment created by Executive Order of the President, No. 9102, dated March 18, 1942, with a primary objective of relieving the military establishment of the burden of providing for the relocation of persons excluded from military areas." It was agreed that the actual construction of the assembly centers and the relocation centers should be the responsibility of the army; the equipment and original provisioning should be the responsibility of the WCCA. The agreement reaffirmed the role of the Federal Reserve Bank in acquiring "warehouse space . . . [and] civilian guards" to protect evacuee property and make an inventory of "goods stored by each evacuee."

The initial efforts of Eisenhower's staff were directed at planning for the governance as well as the practical day-to-day operation of the centers. Here the idealism so characteristic of the New Deal prevailed. The evacuees were to perform most of the necessary functions in the centers, including what we might call the "social services," the operations of the hospitals, schools, police, fire, and maintenance. One of the first memoranda that circulated to prospective center administrators (April 2, 1942) stated: "It is proposed to develop immediately a system of internal government which will place upon evacuees responsibility for the civic management of the colony and to organize health, education, recreation and other community services using Japanese personnel as far as possible." In a May 29 memo, much the same theme was stated: "The objective of the program is to provide, for the duration of the war and as nearly as wartime exigencies permit, an equitable substitute for the life, work, and homes given up, and to facilitate participation in the productive life of America both during and after the war.''

The next sentences struck an equally positive note: ''In the last analysis, each relocation community [not camp, not center, but ''community''] will be approximately what the evacuees choose to make it. The standards of living and the quality of community life will depend on their initiative, resourcefulness, and skill. Initially, the Government will provide the minimum essentials of living—shelter, medical care, and the mess and sanitary facilities—together with work opportunities for self-support.'' The rest would be up to the evacuees themselves.

A suggestion was made by a member of the planning staff that some mechanism be devised by means of which evacuees would be able to participate in the selection of personnel ''who would be employed to administer the policies set by the community councils.'' A Civil Service Commission of evacuees was proposed, made up of administrators and evacuees to classify positions and determine the qualifications of applicants. Evacuees, by one plan, would work with the project director on the preparation of the centers' operating budgets. A lawyer for the War Relocation Authority was consulted for an opinion as to how far the agency could go in allowing forms of self-government in the centers. He stated that it was ''possible to set up a procedure under which a 'mayor,' and a 'city council,' and 'courts' can be established within the relocation centers with much the same functions as they would have under the regular city form of government. In legal theory the project manager would merely delegate certain of his administrative functions to persons designated by election or otherwise by the Japanese. He would retain in that manner such degree of control or veto power as might be necessary for him to discharge his responsibility.'' At the end of May, the solicitor's office produced a document entitled ''Regulations Concerning Organization of Self-Government Within Assembly Centers and Relocation Centers.'' It called for election of a mayor, the establishment of a municipal court, the appointment of a chief of police by the mayor, and the organization of a police department by the chief of police.

A general policy statement described the basic purpose of the centers as ''the training of residents of the community in the democratic principles of civic participation and responsibility.'' The community government (what came to be called the community council) should (''shall'' the document read) ''assume the responsibility for the regulation of community life; it shall assume much of the responsibility for the formulation of policy and administrative direction of services and supply." This process was bound to be a gradual one as the centers settled into increasingly familiar routines and individuals suited to exercise leadership roles came forward.

Still another formulation set as a goal of the centers the establishment of organs of government and the delegation of power "commensurate with that exercised by an American municipality of approximately the same size." In other words, the aim was to turn the centers into hybrid American small towns. Among the early duties of a temporary council would be the framing of a "constitution," in much the same spirit as the original American Constitution. Such a constitution should lay out, within the center's guidelines, the powers and duties of the permanent council. The only limitations were that a council should be "democratic in form [elected] and should not place restrictions on civil liberties with the exception of the prohibition of the publication or distribution of materials in the Japanese language."

The temporary, constitution-making council would set up a number of commissions having to do with various aspects of the life of the community. Among those matters listed as coming under the jurisdiction of the council, or one of its commissions, was "the expending of monies, the regulation of the activities of religious groups, the appointment of a permanent staff for the council . . . public welfare, libraries and housing."

The principal agency of self-government in the centers would be the "community councils," elected again by the evacuees. The hand of external authority was exercised most conspicuously in the rule that the Issei could not hold elective office. Only the Nisei. The logic behind it was that everything should be done to make American citizenship attractive to the evacuees. The Nisei were thus to be "rewarded" for being citizens. In the words of the planning staff report: "A second consideration had a great deal to do with our decision. In general, the Nisei are much more Americanized than are the Issei. . . . We are of the opinion that if the Nisei alone are eligible for membership in the community council, the general character of the action taken by the community council will be more in keeping with American institutions and practices. . . .

"In addition to making elective offices open only to evacuees who are citizens of the United States, it is our intention to give them preference in considering application for leave from relocation centers, in assignment of work opportunities, and in other respects." Those supporting the policy of allowing only the Nisei to hold elective office pointed out that otherwise, "control might pass to those who were not in sympathy with the objectives of the Authority or with the war effort."

Since Eisenhower declared that he never made a "major decision" without consulting Mike Masaoka, it seems reasonable to assume that the ban on Issei being elected to the community councils was either proposed or supported by Masaoka and the other members of the Japanese American Citizens League advisory council. In any event, it became a source of bitter divisions in the assembly centers and, subsequently, in the relocation centers. At the same time the conflict may be taken to dramatize the generational struggle between the younger Nisei and the Issei and Kibei over the future of the Japanese in the United States.

The problem was that, as has been noted, the authority of the older men, the fathers and grandfathers—*oyakoko*—was one of the strongest elements in *Yamato Damashii*. It is probably not going too far to say that that rule alone condemned the community councils to failure and seriously compromised the hope of at least limited self-government in the centers. By giving such marked preference to the Nisei, the planners of the centers were, in effect, inviting them to be disloyal to their parents; in short to assume authority *over* their fathers and, in some instances, their grandfathers.

Some of the more practical members of the planning staff warned against giving too much authority to the evacuees; in their view it would be unwise to give the evacuees authority over the nonevacuee staff, that is to say, over the Caucasians on the staff and over such matters as the purchase of necessary materials, the type of streets laid out in the centers, and the methods of construction.

IN JUNE 1942, AFTER EISENHOWER HAD BEEN DIRECTOR OF THE WAR Relocation Authority for less than three months, Roosevelt asked him to become deputy director of the Office of War Information under Elmer Davis. Eisenhower, who calculated he had lost more sleep in those hectic days than in the rest of his life, was delighted to be relieved of the enormous burden of the War Relocation Authority. He recommended as his successor a friend, Dillon Myer, with whom he worked in the Department of Agriculture. Myer had a Bachelor of Science degree from Ohio State University and a Master of Education from Columbia. At the beginning of the New Deal, Myer ran the Agricultural Adjustment Administration program in Ohio and later served as the assistant chief of the Soil Conservation Service in Washington, D.C.

When he relinquished his office, Eisenhower wrote a memorandum to Roosevelt expressing his views on the future course of the WRA: "In leaving the War Relocation Authority after a few extremely crowded weeks, I cannot help expressing the hope," he wrote, "that the American people will grow toward a broader appreciation of the essential Americanism of a great majority of the evacuees and the difficult sacrifice they are making. Only when the prevailing attitudes of unreasoning bitterness have been replaced by tolerance and understanding will it be possible to carry forward a genuinely satisfactory relocation program and to plan intelligently for reassimilation of the evacuees into American life when the war is over. I wish to give you my considered judgment that fully 80 to 85 percent of the Nisei are loyal to the United States, perhaps 50 percent of the Issei are passively loyal; but a large portion of the Kibei (American citizens educated in Japan) have a strong cultural attachment to Japan."

Eisenhower proposed four steps to the President:

"(1) Recommend to Congress a program of repatriation for those who prefer the Japanese way of life.

(2) Issue a strong public statement in behalf of loyal American citizens who were now bewildered and wondered what was in store for them.

(3) Call for a more liberal wage policy for evacuees.

(4) Ask Congress to enact a special program of rehabilitation after the war to help the evacuees find their place in American life."

On the eve of Eisenhower's departure, he met for the last time with the JACL advisory committee, and Mike Masaoka presented him with a fifty-year-old dwarf pine.

Chapter 14

THE ASSEMBLY CENTERS

I T WAS LOGICAL TO SEND EVACUEES TO THE ASSEMBLY CENTER NEAR-est to their homes and so it was ordered in the main, although a good many Oregon and Washington evacuees ended up in California assembly centers (4,048 were sent to Pinedale and later went to Tule Lake).

Puyallup Assembly Center near Tacoma and Seattle was served, as were the others, by a network of roads and a convenient railroad line. Portland, as the name suggests, served the Portland area. Marysville, in Northern California, took in evacuees from a widespread farming area. Sacramento, Salinas, and Stockton Assembly Centers drew their evacuees from those towns and the rich farmlands adjacent to them. Fresno's evacuees came from that city. Tanforan, named for the racetrack, took in evacuees from San Francisco and the South Bay area while Santa Anita, another racetrack, was populated primarily by evacuees from the city and county of Los Angeles. Pomona, Turlock, Merced and Tulare in California, and Mayer, not far from Phoenix in central Arizona, completed the roster of assembly centers. Santa Anita was the first to open for business (March 27) and one of the last to fold up operations (October 27). It was not until the end of April that Puyallup, Tanforan, and Salinas began receiving evacuees. Puyallup stayed open until September 1942, as did Merced and Portland. Stockton, which opened May 10, remained open for six months (until October 17) while Marysville, Sacramento, and Salinas operated for little more than seven weeks (Sacramento from the sixth of May until June 26). Virtually all of the assembly centers experienced their peak populations in May and June. Santa Anita peaked August 23 with 18,719 evacuees. Generally the peak population at each center ran between 2,451, as at Marysville (June 2), and 7,390 as at Puyallup on May 25. Mayer brought up a distant rear on May 25. Not surprisingly it was closed a week later.

The physical arrangements of the assembly centers varied, of course, according to the previous use of the facility. Racetracks had stalls, for example, which initially were converted to rooms. Fairgrounds typically had exhibition halls, which became dining halls, gymnasiums, medical clinics, warehouses, schools, or repair shops for center transportation pools. At Portland Assembly Center virtually all of the evacuees were housed in the Livestock Exposition Pavilion.

Army-type barracks were the standard structures built to house evacuees. The barracks were divided into living spaces that could hardly be dignified by the name "rooms." They varied in size from sixteen feet by twenty feet to twenty feet by twenty-five feet depending on the size of the family to be accommodated. Such spaces were often divided by sheets to give a modest degree of privacy. Where the terrain and space permitted, barracks were arranged in "blocks," usually fourteen barracks to a block. The blocks became the basic social units of the assembly centers and, later, of the relocation centers. Typically, a block leader was elected by the residents of the block. He was usually an older Issei who had the respect of his fellow block members. Each block had its own showers, lavatories, and toilets. For the Japanese, with their passion for cleanliness, these spartan arrangements were one of the principal inconveniences (or perhaps more accurately, embarrassments) of the center life.

While the number of evacuees in a block varied to some degree from center to center, the standard number in each block was between six hundred and eight hundred. Thus an assembly center, or later, a relocation center, of eight thousand would usually have ten to twelve blocks. A kitchen and dining hall were also provided for each block.

Standard army steel cots, pillows, mattresses, and blankets (three to a person) were issued to evacuees when they arrived. Where evacuees did not bring their own linens or could not afford to buy them at the center store, they were provided. In the early days of the centers there were numerous logistical glitches that were the inevitable accompaniment of such a vast enterprise cobbled together in extreme haste; a shortage of numerous necessities; items that didn't work or worked poorly or broke down and languished for repair (hot water was a problem in several centers—no one had calculated how many baths the average Japanese took in a week). But after a few weeks of adjustment there was a measure of truth in the army's boast: "In short, the equipment and the supplies were those to be found in any well ordered community in sufficient quantity to maintain health, sanitation and reasonable comfort."

For families and individuals without their own financial resources, there was a clothing allowance that varied from $27.57 a year for children from ages one to five to $42.19 for "adult females." The total amount of clothing purchased by the WCCA for the assembly center evacuees came to $586,900. Charles Kikuchi's parents were incredulous when he told them they would each receive $2.50 a month for the purchase of necessities. "And the idea of getting free shoes and clothing is beyond them. Mom says that one Issei woman told her that we would never get anything free from the U.S., but that Japan is paying for our protection."

At the Stockton Assembly Center Mary Tsukamoto learned what it was to stand in long lines "for eating in the mess hall, standing in line in front of the latrine, standing in line for our bath. . . . For us women and children, this was something which we just couldn't . . . it was just a shock. I remember we got sick . . . we couldn't go . . . we didn't want to go. It was smelly, and it was dirty. In the shower, the water was poured over you, and there were no partitions, and it was so cramped that we almost touched each other. It was very humiliating. It sure helped when the kids had a variety show. Many were quite talented, and one night they made us all laugh, and we cried with laughter because it was so funny. There were five or six boys standing in a row, dramatizing the time when we go to the latrine."

Tsukamoto also recalled that sound carried so that you would hear everything that went on in nearby apartments. "We hear language from over the partitions," she recalled, "language I didn't want my daughter to grow up hearing. There was talking back to parents, young people shouting, fathers shouting and angry. All of that made me hate people, and I was ashamed of being part of a group of people who would be so hateful to each other . . . after a while we all got on each other's nerves. It was a terrible, terrible time of adjustment."

Tsukamoto's five-year-old daughter cried for a week—"she cried and cried and cried. She was so upset because she wanted to go home; she wanted to get away from camp. . . . I remember I always felt like I was dangling and crying deep inside, and I was hurt."

When the Reverend Allen Hunter, a Presbyterian minister, came to the center to preach, Mary Tsukamoto and some of her Christian friends asked him "to teach us how to pray. I said we feel like hating everybody; we just can't stand so many people around us."

One Nisei child was reported to have said on arriving at an assembly center: "Mother, I don't like Japan. I want to go back to America."

Helen Murao was a sophomore in high school when the evacuation started. An orphan, most of Murao's contacts had been with Caucasians. Thus at the age of fifteen she had her first sustained contacts with other Nisei. "I . . . remember taking walks with my sister's boyfriend and telling him how I felt, how angry I was at the Japanese people in general, and the country in general, the war, and everything. And that I wanted to have nothing to do with the Japanese people." To which her sister's friend replied, "You may feel different, but you aren't different. You're one of us. Like it or not, you are here. You chose to come here. Face it and live with it." For months Murao considered suicide as a way out of her misery and then she came to feel that "nobody's going to do this to me. *I'm going to prevail, my will is going to prevail, my own life will prevail.* I'm not going to kill myself, I'm going to prevail." And prevail she did. She got no "adult nurturing" because, in her view, the people in the center "were so wrapped up in their own misery. . . . In their own unhappiness . . . which is only to be expected, that nobody had anything to give to anybody else." What they had to give, and many did give, they gave to their families, who had the first call on them.

Rejected for induction in the army because he was "of Japanese ancestry," Minoru Yasui had done his best to get arrested for violation of the evacuation order but his efforts were frustrated at every turn and he finally found himself in the Portland Assembly Center. His most vivid memory of the center was the mess hall "festooned with yellowish, spiral flypaper hung from posts and rafters . . . black with flies caught in the sticky mess . . . horseflies, manure flies, big flies, little flies, flies of all kinds." There was even a fly-catching contest, the winner catching 2,462.

Yasui also recalled the constant buzz of conversation in the barnlike exhibition hall at night and then quiet except for the occasional coughing, snoring, giggles. Then someone would get up to go to the bathroom. It was like "a family of three thousand people camped out in a barn."

"When we got into camp," Tom Watanabe recollected, "it was a feeling of like, you're lost. You don't know what the hell to do. You don't know who to communicate with. I mean it's like some guy opened the door on a bus and put you out on a desert highway and said, 'Here it is, this is where you're going to live.' "

Miseo Hayashi and her husband were sent to the Santa Anita Assembly Center. Mrs. Hayashi recalled gratefully that Caucasian members of her YWCA chapter, visiting Santa Anita to inspect the conditions, discovered that the floors of the stalls were dirt and made such strong complaints that they were promptly covered with plywood, making the stalls somewhat more habitable.

Mabel Ota and her husband had volunteered to go in an advance party to help prepare Poston (formerly Parker) for the arrival of evacuees. A young gas station attendant whom they knew offered to buy their car and drive them and their possessions to Poston. When they stopped at Blythe for lunch, the restaurant owner refused to serve the Otas, and their Caucasian friend walked out with them in protest. At Poston, the Otas had a meal of nothing but "bread, potatoes, spaghetti, and macaroni" and "a breakfast of oatmeal that was full of . . . little black bugs."

Tom Watanabe recalled the dust at Manzanar: "You had the dust storm come through. You get a half an inch of dust. You either get in bed and cover yourself with a sheet or just stand out there and suffer. You couldn't even see three feet in front of you, and then when the dust storm was settled, you had at least half an inch of dust right on your sheet when you got under it." That and the cracks in the floors, cracks so wide you could see the earth underneath.

An initial shock for many evacuees was center food. The ration allowances for U.S. soldiers and military personnel was fifty cents per day. Since fish and rice, two relatively inexpensive foods, formed staples of the Japanese diet, the average cost of rations in the centers seldom exceeded thirty-nine cents per day. The Japanese fondness for rice was indicated by the fact that eventually 40 percent of U.S. rice production went to the relocation centers.

A serious problem was that Issei and Nisei had very different culinary tastes. One Issei recalled the food at the center where she was sent: "We ate bologna, weiners, cheese, cow's tongue, and all these weird things. Issei just looked at it and walked away . . . soon we could eat meat and better food." The standard army ration contained a large portion of navy or pinto beans, which most evacuees refused to eat.

In addition to rice and fish (and a substantial amount of beef) the center menus featured dry beans, beets, cabbage, potatoes, spinach, squash, and tomatoes. Where the number of persons to be fed exceeded the capacity of the dining hall, cafeteria-style eating was used. Where there was sufficient seating, the residents ate family-style. At the larger assembly centers each evacuee's meal period was indicated by a different colored ticket. The same rules and regulations for the preparation and handling of food prevailed as in regular army mess halls. Since most meats were centrally prepared, a school of butchers was set up with an eventual savings of an estimated eight cents a pound on meat. With hamburgers and sausage made in the center butcher shops, the savings were ten cents a pound. At Puyallup, Portland, and Tanforan, central bakeries were established, again with substantial savings. Special care was taken in the preparation of food for infants and small children. The formulas and menus were specified by the United States Public Health Service and the Division of Housing and Feeding of the Wartime Civil Control Administration.

That food was an indicator of "Japanese-ness" or Americanization is plain from an entry in Kikuchi's diary. He wrote: "There can no longer be conflict over the types of food served [as there has been in his family], everybody eats the same thing—with forks. We haven't had any Japanese food yet, thank God." Before long, due to the influence of the Issei, there was "Japanese food" in abundance; Kikuchi was soon complaining about having fish two nights a week. A red letter (or red meat) day for the Kikuchi family came when his father wangled a steak from the kitchen staff, brought it back to the family quarters, and cooked it. "This was the first time," his son noted, "we had dinner in a quiet family group," all nine of the Kikuchis.

Even with the best of intentions on the part of the assembly center (and, later, relocation centers) the quality and type of food was a persistent source of complaint. Feeding from six to eight hundred people out of a common kitchen does not make for the most refined cuisine. Beyond that, one of the most burdensome aspects of center life was the requirement that families eat in the center dining halls.

For most families the family meal is (or should be) the central family ritual, the reaffirmation of family unity and comity. To lose the family meal, especially in such a tradition-bound culture as that of the Japanese, was to lose the essence of family unity. When boys and girls began eating apart from their parents at Manzanar, parents objected to having the families separated at mealtime and the project director issued a rule (largely ignored) requiring that families eat together. As time went on many of the younger boys and girls shopped around at the dining halls in other blocks, trying to find the best food. Others went from dining hall to dining hall gobbling up a meal at each one.

When all is said and done the breakdown of the family meal may have been the most demoralizing aspect of center life. In the words of Jeanne Wakatsuki: "My own family, after three years of mess hall living, collapsed as an integrated unity. Whatever dignity or feeling of filial strength we may have known before Pearl Harbor was lost."

The young were far more resilient than their elders. Moreover, they had fewer responsibilities. Everyone in the Kikuchi family pitched in to try to make their stable quarters more livable. Charles and his siblings raided the racetrack clubhouse and tore the linoleum off the bar to put on the floor of their new quarters. Then his sisters wandered off "looking for boys." A few days after their arrival at Tanforan, Kikuchi noted in his diary: "The community spirit is picking up rapidly and everyone seems willing to pitch in. They had a meeting tonight to get volunteers for cooks and waiters at the new mess hall and this was done without difficulty. Rules were also made for each barracks such as radio off at 10:00 and not too many lights so that the fuses would not get overloaded." He added: "My first few days only make me feel like an American more, but that's something you can't go 'parading off.' I just feel that way, I guess. It may be an overdefensive reaction, but I think it goes deeper than that." On a more mundane level, Kikuchi was especially impressed by the quality of the toilet paper provided at Tanforan—"the kind that cost 3 for 25¢! I bet the Japanese never had this before. And I am sure that many Japanese are eating better than they ever did at home. And there is no eternal worrying over unpaid light and gas bills, etc. Yes, all this is fine, but—It always ends in the endless rows of buts. Can these things compensate for individual freedom of movement?"

One of the proudest accomplishments of the Wartime Civil Control Administration, an accomplishment passed on to the War Relocation Authority, was the medical care established initially at the assembly centers. Japanese doctors and nurses staffed the infirmaries and outpatient clinics prior to the arrival of evacuees. Since there were relatively few Japanese doctors and nurses they were parceled out among the various assembly centers. Under the supervision of Public Health Service "experts," a physician, in all cases a Japanese doctor, was in complete charge of the center hospital outpatient department, dental clinic, and other medical functions within the center. The buildings constructed as hospitals were provided with extra insulation, with screens and, for those hospitals in locations where the temperatures were high in the summer, an improvised system of sprinklers on the roof devised to mitigate the heat.

The Japanese American Medical Association of Los Angeles included some thirty-two doctors, most of them Issei. Dr. Fred Fujikawa volunteered to go to Santa Anita, where he found that a former saddling shed for the races had been converted into a crude hospital. There a staff of six was soon responsible for the health of some eighteen thousand evacuees. Men, women, and children were routinely vaccinated for smallpox and typhoid. Outside hospitalization was arranged for serious cases at the standard rate of $3.75 per patient day. The WCCA report notes "fees were neither charged nor accepted from evacuees for medical, surgical or dental treatment, or for drugs and supplies."

The dental clinics were the busiest sections of the health services as many evacuees, especially those from farm communities, took advantage of free dental care to repair the results of years of neglect.

Due perhaps to a dietary deficiency (an excess of rice in their diets it has been suggested) many Japanese suffered from near-sightedness so that the opportunity for optometric care was especially prized. At Tanforan, the optometry clinic issued over one thousand prescriptions in its six and half months of operation. A number of those visiting the optometry clinic each day came with broken glasses to be repaired or replaced. Some broken glasses were the result of the fights that were frequent between rival factions in the centers.

Pregnant wives and mothers with young children benefited especially from the center medical care. There were prenatal classes for mothers and those with infants received special attention. Formulas, scalding water for sterilization of bottles, nipples, and all other necessary items were made available in special diet kitchens and were delivered to mothers by evacuee attendants regularly throughout the day and night. A detail of trained evacuee girl attendants was assigned to each center to see that mothers requiring special baby formulas were supplied at the proper intervals.

Such attentions were bound to impress young mothers. By the same token the "evacuee girl attendants" prized their responsibilities and enjoyed their contacts with mothers and infants. Not only did they find pleasure in their nurturing role but they, like the mothers, received training in good nutritional practices.

Because of the shortage of Japanese nurses, some Caucasian nurses were enlisted to serve in the centers. At the same time a program was initiated to train young women in the centers "as aides in medical nursing, dental and dietetic duties." The lectures and classes included "instructions in nurse's-aide procedures, includ[ing] bed-making [those famous hospital corners], care of bedding, sponge baths . . . nursing ethics, personal health and hygiene, sickroom appliances . . . nutrition and diets, medication (place of drugs in therapy), counterirritants, enemas, hot and cold applications, communicable diseases, infant and maternity care . . . procedure for steam inhalation, procedure for preparing hypodermics . . . etc.'' A number of the young women so trained went on in the postwar years to become nurses and, in some instances, doctors. Almost 100 percent of the pregnant mothers in the centers registered for the prenatal classes and received regular medical checkups. Post-natal care was also routine, and well-baby examinations were conducted on a regular basis. Even premarital counseling was included in some centers.

With a large proportion of children, measles, mumps, and whooping cough were common. For adults, peptic ulcers were the most frequent ailments, doubtlessly due to the stress of center life. The centers suffered from time to time from epidemics (in one case from tainted shrimp) in others from flu viruses, but, considering the crowded conditions of center life and the high stress level as we would call it today, the health record was impressive, substantially better, in fact, than that of the general population outside the centers. In nine assembly centers that remained open three months or more, the count was 8.3 patient-days per 1,000 evacuees; they had a combined population of 58,299 evacuees served by 45 physicians, 43 dentists, 149 nurses, and 893 "other staff members," aides, dietitians, administrative assistants, and orderlies.

From March 21, when the first assembly center opened, until October 31, 1942, when the last center closed, there were, in all the centers combined, 504 live births, 6 stillborn, and 128 deaths.

ONE ASPECT OF LIFE IN THE CENTERS, THE IMPORTANCE OF WHICH CAN hardly be overestimated, was the predominately youthful character of their populations. Japanese American families, as noted before, tended to be large—five to eight or nine children was common. Over 8,000 children were under five (almost 8 percent); roughly 25,000 were under the age of fourteen (21 percent); 15,000 were fifteen to nineteen (14 percent), and an equal number were twenty to twenty-four. All told, 35 percent of the evacuees were under the age of twenty-five. The most volatile group were those aged fifteen to twenty-four. They numbered over 30,000 and included a number of Kibei. Among them were zoot-suiters who affected the style first developed by young Hispanics in Los Angeles—baggy trousers tapered at the ankle, conspicuous chains dangling from their pockets.

Because such a large proportion of the population of the centers were juveniles, the social life of the centers to a considerable degree revolved around children and teenagers. "The Thursday night talent show and the Saturday dances are jammed to capacity," Charles Kikuchi noted in his diary of May 16. The jitterbug was the dance of the moment for the young men who came to dances in "draped pants and bright shirts." They spoke "the special jitterbug language with the facial expressions which they copy from the Negroes," Kikuchi wrote. Parents were not immune to the Americanized behavior of their children. Kikuchi's "pop," urged on by his children, "tried to jitterbug . . . and was the hit of the evening."

A fad at Tanforan was for girls to wear boys' blue jeans. In the Kikuchi family it was decided that Alice's hips were too broad for jeans and that they made Emiko's stomach too big. One of the girls' social clubs, calling itself the Tanforettes, ordered red jackets and embroidered "Tanforettes" on the upper-right-hand side.

As time went on, the rooms that the school-age children shared took on the character of a typical American teenager's quarters, adorned with pictures of movie stars, college banners, and posters. Charles Kikuchi's room contained a shelf for his books and magazines and radio and a lower shelf "for the lamp, art objects, and diplomas." Although he was not a Buddhist, he had a small statue of the Buddha over his desk, his only concession to the Japanesy modes.

Sounding rather like the prospectus for a posh resort, the army report stated: "Under the guidance of the administration, a program was early set in motion to encourage all groups—child, adolescent and adult of both sexes, alien and American-born—to employ their stay in the Assembly Centers in useful and interesting activities." One of the problems, of course, was that the assembly centers were supposed to be just that— places where evacuees assembled for a few weeks on their way to the more permanent relocation centers. Planning lagged for such things as schooling, not due to start until the fall, when, it was assumed, the school-age boys and girls and their parents would be at Poston or Tule Lake or one of the eight other relocation centers that were on the drawing board or already under construction.

As soon as it became clear that transfer to the War Relocation Authority centers would be delayed, in some instances for five or six months, the Wartime Civil Control Administration went into high gear. The overall planning of a program of education and recreation was placed on the shoulders of the director of the Community Service Division, who was assisted in each center by a director of education and a director of recreation. All centers had unutilized buildings—booths for concessioners, exhibit halls, and the like—and these were quickly converted into class-rooms. In some cases where the climate was suitable, classes were held out-of-doors. Carpenters among the evacuees helped by building chairs and desks, tables and blackboards. State and county school boards supplied books. Paper, pencils, crayons, pens, and paintbrushes were contributed by sympathetic friends. The teachers were chosen largely from the evacuees. Many were college graduates and some held teaching certificates. Of twenty full-time teachers at Merced, more than half were university graduates and all had at least two years of university study. Tulare had thirty-seven teachers, four of whom had state certificates, and all others had done either state college or junior college work.

Girl Scouts were recruited to help in the nursery schools. There were a number of artists and craftsmen in the centers who taught courses that were especially popular with college-age men and women. The internationally known sculptor Isamu Noguchi was at Santa Anita for a time. Chuira Obata, a professor of art at Mills College, taught at Tanforan. From the music classes, orchestras were formed to play both symphonic and popular music for center dances. Tanforan opened a library three days after its evacuees arrived and had its education program up and running two weeks later. In Stockton it took ten days to start the first classes.

At Merced the subjects taught in first through sixth grades were arithmetic, reading, spelling, group singing, dancing, storytelling, drawing, and crafts. The junior high and high school curriculum included algebra, geometry, trigonometry, shorthand, bookkeeping, business training, elementary economics, commercial art, weaving, costume design, dance (folk and interpretative), music, handicrafts (paper, wood, and needle), child care, hygiene, etiquette, drama, gardening, and physical education. In the words of one report, "American history was stressed."

For the three and half months of Tanforan's existence, the enrollment in its classes increased exponentially. Out of a population of 7,800 evacuees, 3,650 were students and 100 were teachers.

Mary Tsukamoto, an experienced teacher, was engaged to teach English to the Issei. She was thrilled to find that there were "dear old ladies, and old men who could hardly hear, hardly see, hardly hold a pencil" who were anxious to learn English. One mother said: "I want to be able to write my son a letter. I'm always asking other people to write for me. When he's in the service and worried I want him to know I'm all right. I want him to understand from my own letter that I care for him and that I'm okay."

The handiwork of the students was exhibited at craft shows. Quiz shows were popular and parents crowded the commencement exercises that were held before families were sent on to relocation centers. At Fresno, three thousand parents and friends filled the amphitheater for a commencement exercise that was hardly to be distinguished from any such classic American event. Amateur theatricals were well attended and minstrel shows were especially popular. Several centers had swimming pools constructed by the evacuees. There were swings and slides for children, baseballs and bats of the older boys, volley balls, wrestling mats for judo and sumo and Greco-Roman wrestling, tennis and badminton courts, Ping-Pong tables, fencing foils (kendo was discouraged), horseshoes, fly-casting rods and reels, croquet sets—much of it contributed by church groups and civic organizations like the YWCA and YMCA.

Baseball was especially popular and leagues were formed with distinctive uniforms, names, umpires, official scorekeepers, the works. The Tule City Red Sox played the Modesto Browns and the Turlock Senators. In the basketball league there were Bulls, Bears, Pirates, and Panthers. While the younger leagues chose such names as Midgets, Kittens, Pups, and Papooses, girls team had such names as Bloomer Babes, Cabbages, Brussel Sprouts, and Zombies.

In Stockton a calisthenics class enrolled 350 older women.

One of the favorite events in the centers were beauty contests, and track and field days were also popular.

The Japanese delight in carnivals was evident. At Santa Anita on the Fourth of July the center gave itself over to three days of celebration called the Anita Funita Festival. The fact that something of a cloud hung over the very idea of Independence Day did not interfere with the festivities. The Boy Scouts paraded in trucks festooned with ribbons and banners and the drum and bugle corps made a fine noise. Three thousand evacuees entered the jitterbug contest and ninety-three babies were paraded in the "arms" and in the "toddlers" divisions; prizes were awarded on the basis of "health, disposition and individuality."

Fresno Assembly Center celebrated the Fourth of July by having an artist draw a large portrait of Abraham Lincoln, and a chorus recited the Gettysburg Address in the form of a classic Japanese verse poem. "Some people had tears in their eyes," Mary Tsukamoto reported; "some people shook their heads and said it was ridiculous to have that kind of thing recited in a camp. It didn't make sense, but it was our heart's cry. We wanted so much to believe that this was a government by the people and for the people and that there was freedom and justice. So we did things like that to entertain each other, to inspire each other, to hang on to things that made sense and were right."

Tanforan, finessing the Fourth, held a Mardi Gras over Labor Day. Tournaments in a wide range of sports were supplemented by folk dancing, garden and greenhouse displays, and exhibitions of arts and crafts. The Mardi Gras culminated in a beauty pageant.

Tanforan had two small lakes where sailboats made by ingenious Issei parents for their children or grandchildren sped back and forth. "They take a radio," Kikuchi wrote, "down to the lake and play it while sailing boats all day long. The wind makes them go fast as hell and it looks rather picturesque. The recreation department is planning to hold a regatta in the near future. . . . The Issei haven't anything else to do and I see them around all day long painstakingly carving out these boats." At Tanforan there were movies every Monday, Tuesday, Friday, and Saturday nights with some 1,500 people attending each showing. Sunday was the special day of games and center activities. Kikuchi described such a Sunday. "From where I was standing in the grandstands I could see about five baseball games in progress. Near the barber shop in the infield a lot of fellows were pitching horseshoes in the newly constructed pits. On the far side of the track a basketball game was in progress. Next to them and out of sight the *Sumo* wrestlers were occupied. About 100 persons were sailing boats on the lake. Great crowds stand around the edge of the lake looking on, especially at the man who gives rides to kids on the boat he has built."

A familiar figure was Henry Fujita, the National Fly Casting champion, with his son. At a newly built lake "couples go strolling over the bridge or sit on the benches under the transplanted row of trees around the edge of the lake. . . . Sunday is also a big day for tennis." Two courts had been laid out on the tracks up by the Post Office, and there were always golfers going around the small nine-hole golf course. For those who preferred milder activity, there were the weekly bridge tournaments. "The rest of the people go visiting each other or else have visitors in the grandstands. . . . Needless to say, the various churches draw capacity crowds on Sundays for those with nothing else to do."

Kikuchi, looking at the racetrack infield, saw "an interesting garden." "It is laid out beautifully," he noted, "and has some fragrant flowers already blooming. Around it is a sort of bamboo-like fence and right in the middle on a post is one of those Japanese lanterns. The whole thing looks like old Japan. Some people just can't divorce themselves from Japan and cling to the old traditions and ways. The garden is an outward indication of this sentiment for Japan. The odds are that the builder of the garden is pro-Japan, although he may have built it for cultural reasons.''

The most basic reality in the centers was, undoubtedly, the family. Everything involved and revolved around the family. We have already seen Charles Kikuchi's decision to stick with his mother and father, "Mom and Pop," to whom he had never been close, and with his younger sisters, whom he had only recently gotten to know. His younger brother, Jack, had made a similar decision. The four older Kikuchi children had moved out of the family home but they, like Charles, decided to be counted in the family unit in order to look after their parents and help with the younger children. "The more I think about it," Kikuchi wrote in his diary, "the more I become convinced that the family will not be a handicap but an asset. It is a stabilizing influence and will help prevent individual degeneration. . . . From an individual standpoint our family has not lost anything. We have been drawn close together as a group and everyone seems cheerful enough." He came back to the same theme again and again. "In reviewing the four months here," he wrote in his diary, "the chief value I got out of this forced evacuation was the strengthening of the family bonds. I never knew my family before this. . . . Pop and Mom have come through a very difficult adjustment period. Now I believe that they actually like it here since they don't have any economic worries.''

Robert Spencer, a Berkeley sociologist who had studied the evacuation, reflected at a conference on the relocation held at Berkeley in 1987 that he had failed to gauge the depth of family feeling and its importance in virtually everything that happened at Gila River Relocation Center (in Arizona) and, of course, at other centers as well. "In the all important question of marriage, for example, or in the heart-rending decision to leave the center and resettle somewhere in the permitted zones, the strength of the family made itself felt in prolonged deliberation and discussion and, quite generally in conformity to the wishes of the parental generation." Spencer also felt that he had underestimated the degree to which the Japanese disposition to form what he called in sociological jargon "extra-familial self-interest units," such as the dozens of *kai*, or associations, formed by the Japanese Americans in the pre–Pearl Harbor era, worked against the formation of centerwide communities.

One of the most striking aspects of assembly center social life was what we might call the emergence of the women. An important issue concerning the evacuation in general is the difference in the response of women and of men. That there were such differences is indisputable but they were muted by the subordinate position that traditional Japanese culture assigned women.

In the universal dislocation of family life women undoubtedly suffered more than men. On the other hand, their prescribed role was that of dutiful wife and devoted mother (and powerful grandmother). Since housekeeping was a special challenge in the cramped and awkward confines of the barracks, wives and mothers played a crucial role in making the centers livable and in looking after their husbands and children. At the same time, they experienced a welcome elevation in status. Although in American society women experienced discrimination, they had a far higher status and much greater freedom than their Japanese counterparts and this fact could hardly escape the notice of the female evacuees. Charles Kikuchi's mother told him: "Me glad come here, better than in Vallejo, no cook, just do laundry, I feel glad that all family together." Although Kikuchi's father talked from time to time about going back to Japan, his mother would hear none of it. The Japanese were far too conventional. When she yelled angrily at someone, "Hey you Jap," her older friends were shocked. At Tanforan, Kikuchi noted: "Mom is gradually taking things into her own hands. . . . For 28 years she had been restricted at home in Vallejo, raising children and doing the housework. Her social contacts have been extremely limited, and this has been hard for her because she is more the extrovert type of personality. Now she finds herself here with a lot of Japanese, and it has given her a great deal of pleasure to make all of these new social contacts. Pop on the other hand rarely leaves the house and he still retains his contempt for the majority of the Japanese residents. His attitude is intensified when he sees that Mom is gradually pulling away from him."

Kikuchi reiterated in his diary that his mother had made a much better adjustment to center life than his father: "Mom is taking things in stride," he wrote. "I have a suspicion that she rather enjoys the whole thing. It certainly is a change from her former humdrum life. She dyed her hair today, and Pop made some comment that she shouldn't try to act so young. One thing about these stables is that it does cut down on 'nagging' because people can overhear everything that is said."

Jack Nishida recalled that "until [his mother] went into the camp, she never had any time of her own. There, she learned flower arrangement."

"Old Mrs. Nagao" found a new career in teaching other Issei women to make crepe flowers. Quiet, mouselike Everett Sasaki took charge of the Victory Garden and produced more vegetables than the center could use.

In the words of an evacuee identified only as "A": "For the first time since their arrival in this country most [women] were experiencing an abundance of leisure, less isolation [than] in their own homes, and opportunities for daily association with other Issei women. For most their lives had steadily become richer and fuller than they had ever been." There were numerous women's clubs and classes in sewing, flower arranging, cooking, and, perhaps most important of all, learning to read and write in English. For mothers with sons in the army learning English suddenly took on a new importance since it meant being able to communicate with their sons. As one mother wrote in a tanka poem:

> *Fortunate me; Indifferent*
> *To the fierce fighting*
> *All over the world,*
> *Here I am, learning*
> *Flower arrangement, writing, and embroidery*

In "A's" words: When they left the center for "lives of work and relative loneliness" many had "a feeling of deep loss . . . many found themselves weeping."

Perhaps most important of all, women were treated by the War Relocation Authority as the equals of men. This was, for many couples, especially the Issei and the more Japanesey Nisei, a genuine revolution. In the centers, many of them experienced for the first time in their lives a relative equality with men. They went out to colleges and jobs as readily as men. They considered careers that would never have been available to them in most of the close-knit traditional Japanese communities of the West Coast. This was especially true of women belonging to one or another of the Protestant denominations represented in the centers.

BENEATH THE RATHER FRENETIC SOCIAL LIFE OF THE CENTERS LAY THE deep and bitter divisions that had characterized the Japanese prior to Pearl Harbor. Like most college-educated Nisei, Kikuchi was disconcerted by the depth of pro-Japan feeling he encountered in many Issei and Kibei. A few days after his arrival at the Tanforan Assembly Center, Kikuchi had met "the first Japanese nationalist who reacted violently. He said that Japan 'requested that we be put into a concentration camp so that we have to do it for the sake of Japan.' The man seemed pleasant and harmless enough at first but when he started to talk on this subject, I was amazed to see the bitter look of hatred in his eyes and face. He asked us point-blank whether we were for Japan or America and when we said 'America' on the basis of our beliefs and education, he got extremely angry and pounded on the table while shouting that we Nisei were fools and that we had better stick by Japan because we would never be Americans.''

Kikuchi confessed he was glad he didn't understand Japanese because it spared him the Isseis' anti-American tirades. "It makes me feel so uneasy and mad," he wrote in his diary, "it gripes me no end to think of being confined in the same place with these Japanists. If they could only realize that in spite of all their past mistreatments, they have not done so bad in America because of the democratic traditions—with its faults.'' Feeling as he did, he decided it was wise to keep his feelings about the war to himself. He wrote in his diary in early May, "I hardly know how the war is going now, and it is so significant [important] that the Allied forces win even though that will not mean that democracy will by any means be perfect or even justified. The whole postwar period is going to be something terrific." The same day "a funny feeling of loneliness" swept over him. He felt isolated and out of step with many of his fellow evacuees and for a time he gave way to an uncharacteristic feeling of self-pity. "I just can't help identifying myself with America; I feel so much a part of it and I won't be rejected.''

Kikuchi could reconcile himself to the evacuation of those Japanese Americans considered a danger but he felt that it had been "a big mistake to evacuate *all* the Japanese." Segregating the Japanese, pro-U.S. and pro-Japan, from the larger population was "the least desirable thing that could happen," he noted, "and it certainly is going to increase the problem of future social adjustments. . . . I am convinced that the Nisei could become good Americans and will be, if they are not treated with such suspicion. The presence here of all those pro-Japan Issei certainly will not help things out any. . . . These types of people should be evacuated, but why put all the innocent Nisei—99½ [percent]—in with them it burns me up no end." But it was soon evident to Kikuchi that a good many Nisei had a wait-and-see attitude toward the war. One Nisei friend told him that he wouldn't buy War Bonds because he didn't know who would win the war. "Such an attitude is inexcusable," Kikuchi wrote in his diary. "The Japanese [Issei] and Nisei are getting a raw deal but that does not mean that we should give up all of our ideals.''

He fretted that the Americanization process in the center was so slow. "We can't expect anything else, I suppose, under the circumstances," he wrote in his diary. "Ever since the Orientals have been in the U.S. they have had a difficult time. Denied citizenship and economic opportunities, it is not surprising that they have withdrawn and hung on to what they have brought with them. The cultural ties are stronger than the political ones.''

Kikuchi was especially indignant with the "little knots of Japanese men [who] cluster around the radios blaring the latest news and discussing the final Japanese victory. . . . A brave Nisei occasionally opens his mouth and he is shouted down,'' he added.

On May 6, General Jonathan Wainwright, hoping to spare his emaciated troops more suffering and casualties, had surrendered Corregidor; it was the most crushing defeat, Pearl Harbor excepted, in American history. It was made more bitter by reports of the so-called Death March in which, the story was told, brutal Japanese soldiers shot exhausted Americans and Filipinos who fell by the wayside on the evacuation from Corregidor to the Japanese prisoner-of-war camp. When the news of the fall of Corregidor reached the Tanforan center, Kikuchi heard an Issei say, "About time, no?"

As time went on, though, Kikuchi became more tolerant of the Issei. "They are Americans!" he wrote in his diary. "Sometimes they may say things that arise out of their bewildered feelings, but they can't throw off the environmental effects of the American way of life which is engrained in them. The injustices of evacuation will some day come to light. It is a blot upon our national life—like the Negro problem, the way labor gets kicked around, the unequal distribution of wealth, the sad plight of farmers, the slums of our large cities, and a multitude of things. It would make me dizzy just to think about them now.'' He wrote in his diary at the end of May: "I don't hate the Japanese here, but their conventional ways get me sometimes. Perhaps they would be better off if they were not so law-abiding. They should really let themselves go occasionally, but you can't tell what is going on behind the Oriental mask.''

For the most part, Kikuchi and his father avoided talking about the war. "Pop" irritated his son by stating that "Japan was fighting for the equality of the races. . . . He doubted the promises of the Allies to give more equality to all races. He based his conclusions on the results of the last war, plus the treatment of the Japanese and Negroes in the U.S.'' But Kikuchi insisted on probing his father's racial prejudices. First off the elder Kikuchi was an unregenerate capitalist. He distrusted the Germans. "Koreans are not the same as Japanese. A Jew is a cheating kike, a Filipino goes around raping women, and the Japanese in the U.S. are cutthroats. . . . Pop is a mixture of past fears and frustrations.'' "Mom borrowed a Japanese magazine this morning,'' Kikuchi wrote in his diary, ''and we ridiculed it as Jap propaganda, but she didn't mind. 'No can read American papers.' Although she does not realize it fully, she is closer to America than Japan. The family has completely democratized her.'' Emiko told her brother that she was glad that her parents were not '' 'Japanesy' like some of the Issei around here.''

On the morning of May 20, Charles Kikuchi lay in bed ''too lazy to arise'' and listened to the radio ''telling about the dangers of B.O.; how wonderful it was to eat Wheaties; please smoke Chesterfields; and Ladies, wouldn't you like to have a cheap skunk fur coat?'' When the thought struck him: ''Here we are living at the end of an epoch in a great transitional stage and a great war in progress which will mean much to humanity, and yet most of us don't feel much differently. . . . I can see and hear and read signs of the change all around me, but life seems to go along in its well-worn rut. Even the war is an event that one is deeply aware of yet so distant. The American public has not yet reacted fully to the significance of the whole catastrophe. . . . The world of tomorrow will be on a very different basis, but what?''

Kikuchi's Marxist friends were convinced that communism was the wave of the future and that Russia ''will be an example for the world.'' Kikuchi and his friends, Marxists and liberals (the Young Democrats) alike, agreed that ''here in our community we will have some sort of social revolution, not necessarily violent, after the war. That is certain; but there is no way of predicting its form.''

IN JAPANESE LIFE EVERYTHING DEPENDED ON CASTE AND CLASS. WHAT individuals did—their occupations primarily—were commonly advertised by the emblems on their clothes. In the necessary democracy of the centers, it came to be a matter of vast moment what job was given to whom. Kikuchi noted in his diary: ''There have been considerable 'personality difficulties.' The battle for prestige here is terrific—everyone wants to be someone, it seems—any kind of work will do as long as they get the official badges that distinguish them.''

One goal when setting up the assembly centers and, later, the relocation centers was that evacuees should be given the opportunity to perform all necessary tasks in the centers and be compensated for doing so, on a scale from ''unskilled''—laborers, dishwashers, assistant playground directors, cook's helpers, junior clerks among them—paid at the rate of $8 a month; to ''skilled''—accountants, senior clerks, motion picture machine operators, and cooks, among others—at $12 per month; and, "professional and technical"—physicians, dentists, engineers, chemists, teachers, and so forth—at $16 per month. No evacuee was required to work but once having accepted a job he or she was expected to carry it through; 27,000 persons, or 30 percent of the evacuee population of the assembly centers, were employed.

Charles Kikuchi and several of his Berkeley friends got jobs in the employment office. "It's very interesting to talk to the young Nisei that come in; they are so Americanized. . . . They are all fairly ambitious and think in terms of going on to school and then adjusting themselves here in the U.S. after the war," he noted. "A number of Nisei are complaining that the San Francisco gang is taking all the choice jobs and just working their friends in—a large part of which is true."

Being usually much more fluent in English, often being college-educated, and, not infrequently, Christians, the Nisei, not surprisingly, got the better and more remunerative jobs, while the Kibei were consigned to more menial tasks such as the kitchen help, grounds keepers, and farmhands. Some of the evacuees who came in for job counseling were annoyed to be spoken to in English. Kikuchi noted his irritation with them in his diary: "Most of them [the job seekers] can understand and speak English, surprisingly enough, and they should be made to use it more. . . . Now that we are cut off from the Caucasian contacts, there will be a greater tendency to speak more and more Japanese unless we carefully guard against it. Someday these Nisei will once again go out into the greater American society and it's so important that they be able to speak English well—that's why education is so important."

A source of unhappiness for the Issei lay in the fact that not only were they older and thus deserving of greater respect but many of them had been successful farmers and businessmen in the Japanese American community. In the camps they found themselves, in large part because of their inability to speak English, often limited, like the Kibei, to menial and physically demanding tasks. Inevitably, the Kibei and Issei made common cause against the Nisei.

After the initial trauma of arrival, life in the centers settled into a pattern. The older Issei found a kind of rhythm in long days of playing games, watching the kids playing baseball, playing golf or tennis themselves.

The Issei bachelor quarters were usually strongholds of pro-Japanese feeling in the various assembly centers. Kikuchi described a typical scene in the bachelor quarters at Tanforan. Some men were sprawled out on their beds "smoking or playing cards. A few asleep with their mouths open, snoring like mad, which adds to the general confusion. Over in a far corner, there is a lone but seedy looking minister with a dirty collar, who sits so straight in his bed reading a Buddhist prayer book. Flies buzz about him, but he pays no attention. This room is about the most colorful place in camp, but I am afraid that those Issei look to Tokyo rather than to Washington, D.C., for salvation.''

After visiting the Japanesy bachelor quarters at Tanforan, Kikuchi looked up and saw ''one of those new army bombers overhead.'' A little boy said to him, '' 'Gee, I bet they sure will give Tokyo hell!' I seconded the motion,'' Kikuchi wrote.

He described the ''toughs'' in the center as being made up, in the main, of former truck drivers and farmworkers. ''They don't seem to get along well with the girls,'' Kikuchi noted. ''Bunch was in the grandstands this morning. . . . They sit around telling dirty jokes and occasionally make wisecracks to the girls that go by. Sex is the one topic of interest and they go into all the details. The only mention of the war which I heard was: 'That bastard Hitler should be castrated because he brought us here'. . . . Not one of the group I saw this morning got beyond high school. They like to make remarks about female breasts. 'Look at that deflated set of cows. . . . If there is such a shortage of milk, why don't they milk that fat one?' Etc.''

If the older Issei, and more particularly the Issei bachelors, adjusted remarkably well, much the same was true for many of the Nisei. They, too, settled into routines that eased the discomforts and inconveniences of center life. In July, Kikuchi noted: ''Two months here and I'm not feeling so rebellious this week. Time certainly can go by fast. The days hardly seem long enough to do everything I want to. Got to thinking today that all of the things we have been striving for can hardly be blamed since we are living in a Democracy—and a Democracy is not supposed to have everything all planned out in a concentration camp. That's why they call it a *center*. If things were cut and dried, life would be unbearable. But the full day's activity makes things rather interesting.''

A month later he wrote: ''Three months in a concentration camp! Life goes smoothly on. I should be more dissatisfied and rebellious, but much against my will I'm forced to admit that I'm getting adjusted to this restricted life and falling into a smooth and regular rut.''

GAMBLING AND EVEN PROSTITUTION WERE PROBLEMS IN MOST CENTERS. In the Tanforan center, young bachelors often pressed their attentions too insistently on Nisei women. Indeed, the sexual issue in general was a major one in all the centers. "I know the sex problem is here to stay," Kikuchi wrote in his diary, "because one of the salesmen who comes in does a flourishing business in condoms, but nobody talks about this aspect of life here. It's swept under the racetrack. Because of a lack of privacy, it goes on mostly during the day and not at night."

The issue of contraceptives was a delicate one. Unmarried girls were under great pressure, needless to say, not to become pregnant and many married couples were anxious not to have children while they were in the center. At Tanforan the hospital was appealed to to sell contraceptives to the married couples who wanted them. The hospital refused; it claimed it had enough problems and insufficient staff. The ministers were then appealed to and, again not surprisingly, declined.

One of the evacuees proposed putting "a few of the professional women here on a Professional and Technical rating by the administration in order to protect the young girls [from overardent young men] as well as to keep the situation under control." The harassment of young women at Tanforan became such a serious issue that the community council took it up and pressed the administration to install more nighttime lighting.

Note has already been taken of the role of the various Protestant denominations both in missionary labors in Japan and the United States and in doing what they could to ease the traumas of the evacuation. Once the assembly centers were established, the churches played an important role in the lives of the faithful. Indeed, Riici Satow, a Baptist, had looked forward to life in the centers as a time of worship and spiritual renewal. "As I went there," he told Heihachiro Takarabe, "I was hoping to see Christianity dominate the whole camp. I was really thinking, if I may exaggerate a little bit, of filling the camp with the resounding echoes of hymns." He had hardly unpacked his bags before he was busy rounding up Christians. "We had morning service and evening service on Sunday," he recalled, "an officer's meeting on Monday, a prayer meeting on Wednesday and . . . there was another one, which I can't recall now. Anyhow, we had five meetings a week. Our new church was in full swing from then on."

The largest single Protestant denomination in the centers was the Methodists with roughly 12 percent. The Baptists were a distant second (7 percent), while the Presbyterians with slightly over 3,000 (6 percent) were third. Congregationalists, Episcopalians, Quakers, and Mormons were each under 1 percent. "Other denominations" totaled 1,053, and 2,199, or 2 percent, were Catholic. Traditional Shinto listed 442 members. *Seicho No Iye*, a modern cult that combined elements of Buddhism and Christian Science, had 37 members; 14,642, or 13 percent, failed to indicate a religious affiliation. Of the American-born evacuees over the age of fourteen (a total of 50,356), 25,000 described themselves as Buddhists and 18,000 as Protestants. Including Catholics, that meant 38 percent of all Nisei over the age of fourteen were Christians. That figure dropped to 22 percent among the Issei. The Episcopal magazine *Forth* estimated that "fully half of the Japanese Americans and a quarter of the non-citizens are Christian or pro-Christian." Although Buddhists outnumbered Protestant Christians two to one, many of the Buddhists were what the Reverend John Yamazaki has called "passive Buddhists," individuals who were Buddhists by way of not being Christians, who belonged to no Buddhist temple or congregation, and made no observances other than those called for in connection with the worship of the Emperor.

The fact was that sometimes the line between Buddhism and Christianity was rather loosely drawn. One morning when the third grade was holding its class in the Buddhist church, Charles Kikuchi heard them singing "God Bless America . . . at the top of their voices." Kikuchi heard an Issei say that his daughter was "in there because she was an American while he was a Japanese. He said it with a smile," Kikuchi noted, "and no trace of any bitter feelings. Most of the families here are that way," he added.

The official policy of the Wartime Civil Control Administration was that Japanese evacuees were "permitted to promote religious services within the various centers and to request such Caucasian assistance for coordinating religions, some Protestant denominations to have Caucasian ministers reside in the centers themselves." Caucasian ministers and missionaries who had constituencies within the centers were permitted to minister to their co-religionists at the invitation of evacuees. Japanese Protestant ministers and church workers conducted services wherever possible. "In those instances," the report tells us, "where there was not a Japanese qualified in this field, the group concerned might request assistance of Caucasian workers in conducting religious service."

Sunday services followed a familiar pattern with Sunday schools for children. Although the WCCA specified that all church services were to be conducted in English, in most centers an English service was conducted in the morning and a service in Japanese in the evening. In addition there were midweek prayer services and hours for meditation as well as panels discussing theological issues, and a wide variety of youth activities. Kikuchi noted in his diary: "Went to the College Fellowship tonight to hear the panel discussion on 'What Should the Nisei Attitude as Christians Be Toward the U.S. Government?' '' The mess hall was filled with college students from the Bay Area, but Kikuchi thought the discussion limited and constrained.

In addition to the life of the churches *in* the centers, a succession of renowned Caucasian divines visited virtually every center preaching to large crowds of evacuees, typically on themes of suffering and hope. The Reverend Sumio Koga, then a young student, recalls that E. Stanley Jones, head of the Federal Council of Churches, preached a stirring sermon at his center, declaring that the true spirit of Christianity was to be found, not in the world outside, but in the centers where love and faith and fellowship were abundantly evident.

Years later, June Toshiyuki recalled Jones's visit to the Santa Anita Assembly Center. "He talked about the eagle in Isaiah 40:31 and our experience. He said, 'Don't let this experience destroy you. Use it like an eagle to lift yourselves up. The eagle doesn't go against the storm clouds, it uses them to rise higher, giving it strength and this is what you people will have to do so you won't be destroyed.' '' That analogy always remained with Toshiyuki. John Yamazaki remembered that Jones pointed to nearby Mt. Wilson, telling his listeners that they must look on it like Mt. Zion or Mt. Horab. Others cherished other images from his talk.

One of Riici Satow's brightest memories was of the visit of a blind evangelist, the Reverend Niizato. The future of the Japanese in the United States, he told a large and attentive audience, "is promising and it is wide open for us. So don't ever be discouraged by anything. Once the war is over we are going to have our day."

Yoshiye Togasaki's warmest words were for the Quakers. Not long after she arrived at Manzanar, a Quaker doctor told her, " 'Togi, if there's anything we can do, let me know. We are going out to Terminal Island all the time, trying to find out what we can do to help them, but if you hear of any individual families that need help, let us know.' . . . the Quakers were always very steadfast. . . . Also the Catholic Mission fathers and sisters came in with the evacuees; they were committed too. And then some Episcopalians and Unitarians came to help very early too."

If there was at first an inclination for Christian ministers and Buddhist priests to cooperate, strains and tensions soon developed. An evacuee with the pseudonym of "Schoolboy" told Charles Kikuchi there was "a great rift between the Buddhists and the Christians. On the whole the

Christian group was more liberal and more aggressive. The Buddhists did not trust the Christians. I know that I was taught that the Christian Japanese were insincere and that they took on false airs and humbled themselves to Caucasians in order to gain their favor. The Christian Japanese mingled more with the *Hakujin*. The Buddhists kept entirely to themselves socially. . . . On the whole the Christian Nisei were not as backward as we were.''

The conviction on the part of the Buddhists that Christians enjoyed special privileges from the center administrators (Charles Kikuchi noted of Tanforan: ''All you have to do to get anything around here is to let Greene [one of the center administrators] know you are a church-goer'') aroused considerable hostility, especially among the more militant nationalists, who felt that the Christians were traitors to the Emperor. Many Christians were also active in the Japanese American Citizens League and thus doubly suspect. Like the JACL leaders, they were often characterized as *inu* (informer). In addition to being called *inu*, the Christians suffered other forms of harassment. Riici Satow recalled that human excrement was scattered in front of the quarters of some Christians, and one Christian, an evacuee named Kido, was badly beaten and only escaped more serious injury by shielding his head with his arms. Satow himself was threatened and slept with a club beside his bed. He remembered a defense tactic that he had been taught while working in the fields. If you are attacked by men with clubs and you have a club yourself, aim your blows at their legs, as they are the most painful and vulnerable parts of the body. Satow himself, although abused and reviled, was never physically attacked.

Harry Nishiura recalled that a zoot-suiter put a six-inch knife against his ribs in the block mess hall. ''I was shivering,'' he recalled. ''I know your father,'' Nishiura said. ''You know, huh,'' was the reply. ''And he kicked me on the shin . . . I never forget. I was scared. I had an overcoat on so he didn't see my knees shaking.''

A small but readily identifiable group in the centers were the college Nisei. We know a good deal about them from the diary of Charles Kikuchi. Like college students the world over, they engaged in constant bull sessions; they edited the center newspapers and conspired to win political power or at least to influence elections at the center. Many of the college Nisei at Tanforan were Berkeley graduates; some were from Stanford. They had their own poker games, often for high stakes, at least by center standards. University of California graduates posted a sign at

their barracks reading "U.C. Extension." It didn't seem to Kikuchi that
his friends did much studying. "They sit around and gab and listen to the
records," he wrote in his diary.

The situation was similar at Santa Anita outside of Los Angeles where
a number of UCLA and University of Southern California students hung
out together.

At Tanforan, Kikuchi and his college friends spoke frequently about
their concern that racist or "Fascist" attitudes might spread in the United
States. "Many of the American Chinese, Negroes, and Jews can see that
a dangerous precedent can be set, which could easily include them later
if this thing is not handled democratically." One of the problems could
well be that the Nisei might become increasingly Japanesy as a consequence of their treatment in the centers. The administration of the center
was "actually hampering Americanization" by its constant interference
in the life of the center and by its frequent censorship of the center
newspaper, the *Tanforan Totalizer*.

In one Tanforan bull session, Kikuchi noted, "The question came up
as to what we were fighting for. All of us agreed that Fascism was not the
answer, but there was a difference of opinions on whether an Allied
victory would be any solution to the whole mess." One of Kikuchi's
friends expressed the view "that it offered the most potentialities and
hope for the world. Would the solution include only the white races, or
will we be in a position to tackle the problem of India, China, and other
millions of 'exploited' peoples? . . . The problem is so immense that it
staggers the imagination." Kikuchi also wrote, "From talks with many
of the Nisei, I have found that most of the liberals show a fine degree of
understanding of Democracy as a fight for equality and freedom which is
yet to be attained. Their confidence in democracy has not been shaken
since they realize that there are millions of other North Americans in this
country who are with them in the struggle to achieve the potential ideals
of this country."

Not surprisingly, many of the discussions revolved around American
racial attitudes. There was general agreement that prejudice against the
Japanese was one reason a good many Nisei "were rejecting patriotism."
In one bull session, Kikuchi noted that there was a consensus that "a lot
of things would be cleared up if the Caucasian Americans showed their
good faith by letting the bars of immigration down and by giving the
Negro a democratic chance. Asia would never trust the U.S. unless we
showed good faith at home first. Ann [one of the most articulate Nisei]
thought that it was worth the fight to make democracy right and eliminate

the patronizing attitude of the white man. Whether America would shake off the stupid mistakes of prejudices was something that none of us could make a definite answer upon. We did not know whether economic greed would still be the dominant end of these nations at war. We hoped and believed that the world would be changed for the better, under a democratic system.''

A Nisei asked: ''What had I, or, as a matter of fact, what had the rest of us done, to be thrown in camp, away from familiar surroundings, and familiar faces? What had there been in my life that made such a thing happen? The only answer is, the accident of my birth—my ancestry. There is no other logical answer.''

Another of Kikuchi's diary entries described a bull session that centered on the degree of loyalty to the United States among the Nisei. When Kikuchi expressed his opinion that ''all of the pro-nationalist Japanese had already returned to Japan'' it ''drew a laugh'' from the others. Another member of the group expressed his concern that the evacuees would develop an inferiority complex in the centers that would inhibit their success after the war. ''Tomoto said we would either come out fighting and full of guts or else become a weak bunch of sissies. . . . It was agreed that the sudden release of 120,000 Issei and Nisei into the American community after the war would be tragic. We hoped that the government would carry the program right through to the final resettlement of the people, not forgetting the possibility that many may stay on in the relocation areas if they were made a success.''

The range of political opinion among the college Nisei was as varied as it was among young college-age Caucasians. Communists and socialists of various persuasions were represented but the largest group were the Young Democrats, New Dealers, most of them. Hatsune Helen Kitaji was a typical Nisei ''pink.'' An avid reader, an enemy of the Japanese military, and a member of a radical study group, she drew the attention of the FBI not because of her pro-Japanese sentiments, but rather because she was suspected of being a communist. The son of an Italian woman Kitaji was teaching English had reported her to the FBI, apparently because she spoke favorably of the Soviet Union.

Kikuchi thought that the communists, most of them graduates of Berkeley, were one of the more influential groups at Tanforan. ''They are intelligent,'' he wrote. ''They have direct contact with the Party, the CIO, and the Party Press. They are Ernie's Kitchen Cabinet [Ernie was the leader of the liberal wing in the Tanforan Assembly Center]. This group is important because they receive ideas from the outside.'' The "party line" was to do nothing to hurt the war effort, which sometimes made the communists rather difficult to distinguish from the stalwarts of the Japanese American Citizens League. Kikuchi's brother Jack said the communists were always distinguished by their "queer" appearance. It made Kikuchi take notice. "They do look different at that," he wrote. "There is something intense about them verging upon the fanatic." One of the dilemmas of the "liberals" was whether to "blacklist the 'Kremlin' bunch or not." Kikuchi noted that "the Comrades" were circulating petitions asking the War Relocation Authority to have only strong "anti-Fascists" for key administrative positions in the centers.

One of Charles Kikuchi's fellow evacuees was Hi Korematsu, whose brother was Fred Korematsu. He was at Tanforan on $1,000 bail for refusing to accept evacuation. The American Civil Liberties Union had chosen him to test the constitutionality of the evacuation. Korematsu was uncertain as to whether he should be a legal guinea pig. He sought the advice of his brother and his brother's friends in the center. The question discussed vigorously was would such a case help or hurt the cause of the evacuees by keeping the whole issue in the courts and perhaps further inflaming public opinion. Kikuchi urged Korematsu to stick with the case. It seemed to him that "we have everything to gain. We are not prisoners of war and our civil rights have been taken away without due process of law." The group who met to discuss the issue was, in Kikuchi's opinion, " 'a well-rounded' one, representing the 'radicals,' Progressives, JACL reactionary and church elements. . . .

"Afterwards the group started talking about the feeling of the Issei and I was disturbed to hear their opinion that the Issei still believed strongly— hoped—for a Japanese victory, and influenced the Nisei accordingly." One of the group told of being "grabbed the other day [by an Issei] and told to wise up as the only hope was a Japan victory and that the Nisei were only fooling themselves by calling themselves Americans. He said that the Nisei were a bunch of damn fools. Others cited similar experiences."

In the words of Toby, another participant in the Tanforan debate, "The Issei power is hard to buck. You know it is." Now the Issei, not realizing their limitations, wanted to reassert their leadership.

Kikuchi was not inclined to blame the Issei for their strong nationalist feelings but, he wrote in his diary, "we can't wait until they become Americanized. We have to work right now. The Army is wise in forbidding [the use of] Japanese in public meetings; that only encourages them to be more Japanesy." The Issei, Kikuchi (and many of his Nisei friends) felt were "too pro-Japan to be trusted with our future. The break with the past must be clean." The critical question was: "How to break down this attitude and yet not cast them aside? A lot of the feeling is defensive. They have been pushed aside here as far as self-government is concerned and they don't like it. I can't blame them for that but that should not be the basis for saying that they must get into control or everything will be a failure."

One Nisei expressed a more uncompromising view: "War is hell they say—it means breaking up homes and having heartaches. I feel it pretty strongly because I believe that the answer to the Japanese problem in America is to send all the Issei back to Japan and let those with citizenship start all over again."

Another contributor to the Tanforan bull sessions declared: "It's about time they [the Issei] realized that we can't always be bowing to their wishes. Some of us are getting to be 35 and 40 years old and why should we not try to develop the responsibility? The Issei as a group are too old and it will be the Nisei who are going to support them after the war. . . . A lot of the Issei have the idea that we are all going to Japan after the war and they want to lead us in the 'right direction.' They say that our citizenship is no good, etc., and that we should listen to them. I am not condemning the whole Issei group," Kikuchi's friend told him, "but the ones who want to get into control are often the more pro-nationalistic ones. We don't want that."

A Nisei who was not part of Kikuchi's circle expressed a different view of the struggle for political dominance between the Nisei and the Issei. His experience was that the Nisei themselves were "power crazy and they tried to rule with a dictatorial hand. I think that they were a little too harsh in thinking that they were superior to the first generation. The Issei were just as bad because they were out for themselves too. All this made me see that the Nisei and Issei were not a meek group. I lost the feeling that the Japanese were a sort of romantic people. I had pictured them previously as being a very special minority in this country and on a much higher moral and cultural level than other minorities. In camp I realized that the Japanese did not have a monopoly on human virtues, and that they could be just as greedy, just as selfish, and just as grasping as any other persons put into their position."

Ironically, Charles Kikuchi and his brother Jack differed sharply. Jack was inclined to taunt Charles about his Americanism. "He says," Kikuchi noted in his diary, "a Japanese victory is the only solution to the Asiatic problem since 'Keto' [white men] will continue to exploit these people regardless of what we say about democracy." "Pop," annoyed by their arguing, which he could not really follow, admonished them: "Brothers should not argue about the war."

The effort of the more numerous Nisei to present a more or less united front against the Issei failed. "If the people of this camp are an accurate cross-section," Kikuchi wrote, "there is not much danger of the Nisei voting as a solid group on anything. There are too many individual differences present."

One of the Caucasian staff members lectured to Kikuchi and Taro, one of his Nisei friends, that the Nisei were Americans "but you have not entirely worked into our melting pot, but preferred to stay in your isolated communities. Things are not so bad here and you can contribute to the war effort by not causing too much trouble. You can handle your educational and recreational system completely. And you Nisei have a large task ahead of you keeping the young ones Americanized and not falling under the first-generation influence. The Issei are hopeless."

BESIDES HIS DIARY AND HIS ACTIVE INVOLVEMENT IN THE POLITICAL AND social life of the Tanforan Center, Charles Kikuchi was happily involved as an editor of the center newspaper, the *Tanforan Totalizer*, a reference to its racetrack past. While he complained constantly of senseless center censoring and called the paper a "kept press," he clearly enjoyed working on it and boasted that copies were sent to the fifteen other assembly centers, the Library of Congress, the University of California Library, and the California State Library in Sacramento.

The fact is the centers were emotional pressure cookers of an unusually intense kind. Not only were factions in the centers constantly jockeying and competing for dominance, there were endless petty irritations and inconveniences that continually threatened to escalate into major issues between the directors and their staffs on the one hand and the residents on the other. And finally, there were the rumors. For a while, before he realized what a dangerous game it was, Kikuchi entertained himself by starting outlandish rumors and tracking how long it took them to circulate through camp with, of course, various embellishments. Of all the negative aspects of the centers (and there were certainly many) the endless circulation of rumors was perhaps the most demoralizing. This was in part at least because the rumors separated evacuees from the truth. If a rumor was denied by the administration it often served to give it greater currency. Enough of the rumors proved to be true, in part because a remarkably efficient system developed for picking up news of some impending edict from Washington, to encourage the rumor mills to keep grinding away. Since many evacuees worked in the administrative offices of the centers as secretarial and office personnel, they served as channels of information. A confidential letter left on a desk, a telephone conversation overheard and word could spread through a center like wildfire to the confusion and anger of administrators.

While many of the college Nisei were concentrated at Tanforan and Santa Anita because of the proximity of those two assembly centers to UC Berkeley and Stanford in the north and UCLA and USC in the south, there were, of course, college Nisei at the other centers as well and it is safe to assume that discussions similar to those so vividly described by Charles Kikuchi at Tanforan went on elsewhere. One of the most gifted of the college Nisei was at the Portland center. Minoru Yasui was about as assimilated as any Caucasian American. His father had an interest in some thousand acres of farm and orchard land in the Hood River Valley area of Washington State and by 1940 was a member of the local Rotary Club, a member of the Apple Growers Association, and a pillar of the local Caucasian Methodist Church as well as a founder of the Japanese Methodist Church. In his son's words, "He was a friend and neighbor of the local bank president, the most prominent lawyer in town, the editor of the local newspaper, and all 'important' people in Hood River, Oregon." Two of his sons were students at the University of Michigan. Minoru Yasui was a licensed attorney and a reserve officer in the U.S. Army. But both father and son had ties with the nationalistic Japanese Association, which automatically placed them on the FBI list of suspected subversives. Ordered, as a reserve officer, to report for duty at Camp Vancouver, Washington, Yasui stopped off at North Platte, Nebraska, to visit old friends. There he was intercepted by the town's police officer who asked if he was "a Jap." "No, I'm bog-Irish," Yasui answered. To which the officer replied, "Don't get smart with me! I'll throw your ass in jail if you fuck around with me."

Rejected by the army because he was "a person of Japanese ancestry," Yasui ended up at the Portland center, where he was soon an acknowledged leader.

Parker, Arizona, originally designated as a reception center for volunteer evacuees became, with the adoption of controlled evacuation, a relocation center. With its name changed to Poston, the center was divided into three separate camps known as Poston I, II, and III. Poston drew much of its staff from the Phoenix area and from the University of

Arizona. Like Tanforan and Santa Anita it had more than its quota of
college Nisei and budding intellectuals and, for a time at least, it enjoyed
the reputation of an intellectual center. One of Charles Kikuchi's friends
wrote him a glowing account of Poston: "The administrative staff as far
as the cultural and educational aspect of the center is concerned is beyond
reproach. The Ed. program has perspective and is going to be rich. It is
planned to have courses of Jr. College level. There are at present three
seminars on the great books. The teachers are all progressive and very
intelligent. Too good for the Japs; they're all Ph.D.'s from small universities like St. John's and the Meikeljohn school in S.F., where progressive education reigns. This guy Powell, for whom I work, is excellent—a
professor of philosophy at Wisconsin and the Meikeljohn school in S.F.—
talks the jargon of the longshoreman and thinks like the *New Republic*."

A sociologist named Alexander Leighton, with a commission as navy
captain, was also at Poston. Leighton's assignment was "not for history," Kikuchi's friend Mitch wrote, "but for improving life at Poston.
He is trying to get the kids on his staff university credit not only for an
A.B. but for Ph.D. Boy that is something—What a program!!!"

While the centers were in many respects remarkably permissive, they
(or more accurately the project directors) could, on occasion, act in
startlingly arbitrary fashion. One of the most sensitive points in all the
centers was the matter of contraband, objects evacuees were forbidden to
possess in the centers. Evacuees never knew what might fall under a ban
as contraband. At Tanforan it was records of Japanese military music
(pop music was acceptable). Books in Japanese were suspect, dynamite
and knives were of course forbidden. The issue of contraband came to a
head at Santa Anita where military police were ordered to make a search
for contraband. The consequence was what became known as the Santa
Anita riot, which began August 4, 1942. The center manager had added
hotplates to the list of contraband items and ordered them to be picked up.
Many were being used to prepare food for ill or ailing evacuees. There
were vociferous complaints and a spontaneous gathering of evacuees near
the administration building. One evacuee, suspected of being an *inu*, or
informer, was set upon and beaten, and the interior police were threatened. The military police were summoned, the crowd dispersed. The
center manager and interior security officer responsible for the handling
of the search were removed from the center.

Charles Kikuchi was distressed at the news of secret meetings of Issei
and Nisei at Santa Anita. One of the "conspirators" was the mayor of the

center. "We can't afford these things," he wrote in his diary, "and the safest way is to keep the Issei out of office."

WHILE THE WARTIME CIVIL CONTROL ADMINISTRATION HAD THE BASIC responsibility for setting up and equipping the assembly centers, the general management policies were set by the War Relocation Authority. The WRA planners, the reader will recall, were determined to encourage a maximum of self-government in the centers in line with their goal of making the centers schools of democracy. Democratic principles were to be practiced in the assembly centers as well as in the relocation centers. Democracy could never start too soon or be pursued too ardently. The centerpiece of the democratic governance of the centers was, of course, the community council (from which, quite undemocratically, the Issei were banned).

The first election of evacuees to the community council at Tanforan was a matter of great interest in the center. The Japanese American Citizens League indicated that it had every intention of filling the council seats with its own candidates while the more liberal Young Democrats hastened to put forth a ticket of their own. In Kikuchi's opinion, Henry Takahashi, one of the more prominent members of the JACL, "bootlicks like hell for personal advancement and should be given a kick in the rump and thrown out." Kikuchi accused Takahashi of trying to overawe the more suggestable evacuees by his degree in optometry and the fact that ten of his brothers and sisters got through the University of California. They were, after all, "the Berkeley Takahashis." Kikuchi and his Berkeley friends were not impressed. They threw their weight, and tried to recruit other Nisei to do the same, behind Ernie K., the leader of the Young Democrats. At the same time Kikuchi was well aware of the power of the JACLers. "We have to make every effort to work with them since their barking is fairly large," he wrote in his diary.

A few days later, Kikuchi accused the citizens league candidates of "red baiting" by spreading stories about the "radicals" (mostly the Young Democrats) who should be kept out of the council because they would cause trouble with the administrator of the center.

The strongest opposition to Henry Takahashi came from the Berkeley Methodist Episcopal group. They held a secret meeting and decided to put up their own candidate, "a prominent architect, liberal, and a member of the church group."

Kikuchi took note of the action of the Berkeley church: "The Christian group is another powerful faction, if they get well organized they can swing the election their way." That was a major concern of Ernie K., the Young Democrats' candidate. He thought that "the greatest trouble would come from the church groups. They would try to control the co-ops. If this happened there would be a lack of cooperation by the various church factions. . . . The Church attitude was not practical. . . . They believed too much in turning the other cheek, regardless of what happened." It was a theme to which Kikuchi returned several times. "These church people certainly must have a lot of faith in God, but I don't think they are practical enough in many instances. The church people around here get along so palsy-walsy with the administration—they get slapped down and then come back with the other cheek turned. As long as they don't try to solve this whole problem by religion they will get along in their own little sphere. The trouble is they try to include everyone. Nobu N. [a Young Democrat and a friend of Kikuchi] is going into a seminary because he thinks that religion is the only way the Nisei can carry their future heavy burdens."

As the campaign gathered momentum, all the features of a regular election were observed: flyers were printed and distributed and posters were stuck on walls and posts about the center. Speeches were made and potential voters canvassed. While Kikuchi was rather contemptuous of the whole procedure, he, rather patronizingly, considered it a good exercise for the Issei as "a subtle step toward Americanization." The victors in the election to the community council were a mixed group, dominated by the JACLers with some representation from the Young Democrats. But the election was clouded by the exclusion of the Issei from the council and the council was soon being accused by the more militant of toadying to the administration and by the administration of being uncooperative. After scarcely a month in existence, the council was dismissed. The whole episode had about it the air of inevitability.

Kikuchi felt that the members of the council had done their best under difficult circumstances. He listed their achievements: they had helped to settle a maintenance strike, gotten an improved laundry service, pushed for watch and shoe repairing services, spread information about the clothing and barber services, set up the movie committee, clarified the conditions of roll call and transfers, cooperated with the internal police and block managers in the control of gambling, oversaw adjustments in some of the social welfare cases, and tried to get the army to have books written in Japanese read for any indications of subversive material and cleared for return to their owners. They had the speed limit set at fifteen miles per hour, investigated the banking facilities, and had the banking hours extended. They had drafted a constitution for submission to the residents of the center. But all that had been brushed aside and the council dismissed.

Another tender shoot of community government saw the light in mid-May 1942 at Poston. There representatives of the first four blocks to be occupied met in a dining hall to discuss plans for a permanent center government. In the words of the WRA report *Community Government:* "The original meeting was conducted in an atmosphere of pioneers who were looking forward to creating a governing body for a peaceful and productive community." The meeting was presided over by the Reverend Mitani. A legal bureau, staffed by evacuee lawyers, was also organized and as each new block was formed representatives of the center staff met to explain the plan for block representatives. However, when a temporary community council was appointed, the block manager arrangement was abandoned. The primary reason seems to have been the arrival of the June 5 memorandum prohibiting Issei from running for the council.

The term "concentration camp" has been so persistently used in connection with the assembly centers and their successors, the relocation centers, that it might be well to consider briefly the nature of the security arrangements in the various centers. The phrase "concentration camp" is often combined with "barbed wire," summoning up the image of a fearsome Nazi-like death camp arrangement. While barbed wire was eventually strung around all of the centers it was more for definition and to control access and egress to and from the center than to prevent escape. At most of the centers, hundreds and sometimes thousands of evacuees came and went freely, along with visitors, purveyors of food, evacuees with outside jobs, teenagers on shopping expeditions (where there were nearby towns), athletic teams going to play Caucasian teams "outside," church groups visiting congregations in neighboring communities, and so on. Although soldiers were a constant presence, they were few in number (except at times of major disturbances in the centers) and, like the barbed wire, more symbolic than practical. The typical center had a complement of three officers and 124 enlisted men, hardly a force sufficient to guard between eight thousand and twelve thousand evacuees. The attitude of the soldiers toward the evacuees was anything but threatening. Kikuchi noted in his diary: "Sort of feel sorry for the soldiers. They are not supposed to talk to us, but they do. Most are nice kids. They can't get leaves and so have nothing to do. . . . One of the soldiers suggested that we get a volleyball team up and we can play each other over the fence, but the administration naturally would not think of such a thing." One of the soldiers was from Boston and "he thinks we are very American," Kikuchi noted. "He shoved a bologna sandwich into Alice's [Charles's sister] hands before she was even introduced. . . . What a funny world. They feel sorry for us in our present situation and we feel sorry for them because things are so monotonous for them right now."

At Tanforan the civilian head of the internal police charged with maintaining order in the centers was the soul of amiability. He was a large, jovial ex-Berkeley football star, "a pleasing personality," in Kikuchi's words. He told Kikuchi that he knew the Japanese well and that he always found them to be "honest, law-abiding, and peace-loving."

AN IMPORTANT FEATURE OF ASSEMBLY CENTER SOCIAL LIFE WAS THE stream of visitors who came on weekends, primarily at centers adjacent to large cities. At Tanforan near San Francisco and Santa Anita on the outskirts of Los Angeles the numbers of visitors strained the center facilities. There were so many visitors to Tanforan on Sunday afternoons that a man who owned property across from the racetrack opened a parking lot at fifteen cents a car.

Josephine Duveneck and her Quaker friends were among those visiting the Tanforan center every Thursday, bringing canned goods and home-cooked meals, toys for the children, approved books and newspapers. Among the visitors she wrote later were, "young housewives . . . professional people, businessmen, professors, Negroes, Mexican-Americans, ministers and priests—every conceivable sort of person caring enough about innocent victims of war hysteria to spend hours traveling and waiting in line for an hour's visit." Duveneck remembered standing in line with Mrs. David Jordan, wife of the founding president of Stanford University. Mrs. Jordan was waiting to see the houseboy who had served the Jordans for some twenty-five years. By July 1942 there had been over seven thousand visitors to Tanforan, including "many professors from U.C., Stanford, Mills, S.F. State and other Bay Area colleges. Many church and Y people came down," Kikuchi wrote.

The visitors brought so many books and sympathetic friends and organizations sent so many as well that by the time Tanforan closed shop, the original forty books that Charles Kikuchi had contributed to the center library had grown to some four or five thousand.

In late July, a month before Tanforan center was vacated, Kikuchi noted in his diary: "The attitudes of the people have settled down in many respects. From fearing and hating everything about the place, many of them have arrived at the point where they like it here and would not mind if they stayed indefinitely without moving on to a relocation center. Although the older people have a lot of spare time on their hands, they are taking up such things as gardens, sailboats, etc., to fill in. . . . The Issei as a whole believe that their status is a result of the war and have accepted it. Social barriers have also broken down and people are on a much more equal footing. Money and former position do not mean so much as they did on the outside.''

Tanforan, like the other centers, had taken on many of the aspects of a small town. "There were street lights," Kikuchi noted; "gardens had sprung up all over the place and vegetables were ready to eat.'' A hothouse provided flowers "for various flower projects. . . . All kinds of baseball, golf, and basketball fields dot the formerly vacant landscape. In front of many barracks are to be seen many fine pieces of architecture.''

Kikuchi looked forward to leaving the assembly center however. At the relocation center it would be up to the Nisei "to make or break . . . and leadership is bound to arise out of this experience. One of the dangers of the whole thing is the prospect of isolation and segregation of the Japanese. . . . One sure thing is that resettlement away from the . . . camps will break down a great deal of past volunteer and forced segregation of the Japanese community, since they will have to deal more and more with the great American public.'' The most significant words in Kikuchi's reflection are "past volunteer and forced segregation.'' "Volunteer'' refers to the disposition of many Japanese to *resist* assimilation and remain, *by intention*, outside the mainstreams of American life. "Forced segregation'' was, of course, the prejudice that Japanese Americans encountered when they did try to assimilate.

One of the unsettling issues in the assembly centers was which relocation center to ask to be sent to. There was a strong disposition, of course, to go to relocation centers as a family, as a congregation, or as part of an original community. College friends often wanted to go together and different political and/or social factions that had formed in the assembly centers generally wanted to stay together. The trouble was some members of a family preferred one relocation center, based often on its location and rumors about the climate, while others preferred another. Charles Kikuchi's father had diabetes and had little tolerance for hot weather. He feared going to Gila River in Arizona because it was reported to be as hot as Hades there. Charles, on the other hand, heard that there were several exciting studies of the relocation experience at Gila River, one under JERS, and a prospective gathering of intellectuals. And so it went. The longer an assembly center was in existence and the closer the ties that people had formed the more difficult it was to make decisions about where to request to be sent. One friend of Kikuchi told him that he wanted to go to Gila River to escape his mother and there were, doubtlessly, similar cases where Nisei children wished to escape the domination of Issei parents. But generally family solidarity and a sense of obligation on the part of children toward their parents kept families together.

Over all these often feverish discussions there hung the fact that, in the last analysis, the decision as to where people would go was in the hands of the War Relocation Authority. Although the authority was committed to keeping families together, it was not always possible to send families or even individuals to the centers of their choice.

"There is a mass dread of going to Arizona and the people are willing to believe the worst about it," Kikuchi wrote. With the Kikuchi family headed for the Gila River center, they began to pack their things. "I never knew we had so much junk," Charles noted in his diary. "Already we have about twenty boxes ready for inspection and shipment."

As we approach the end of the assembly center story we might note several things. Of the some 110,000 persons evacuated from the West Coast, 18,026 went directly to relocation centers, specifically Manzanar and Parker (Poston), and 91,401 to the assembly centers. Finally, there were a number of Japanese who had left the coast in the period of voluntary evacuation who applied for admission to assembly centers where they had family or friends. The Hiyakawas were one such couple. They had moved from California to Sante Fe, New Mexico, but they found life so difficult there that they applied for admission to Santa Anita.

In addition to those voluntary evacuees who found refuge in one assembly center or another there were a number of individuals who, like Jeanne Wakatsuki's father, had been placed in detention as suspected subversives but who had been cleared by review boards and released to join their families.

It is important to keep in mind that a good many evacuees spent more time in the assembly centers than in the relocation centers themselves. Some, as has been seen, went directly to relocation centers and some went from the assembly centers to indefinite leave from the particular relocation center to which they had been assigned without ever going to the relocation center itself. Some college-bound Nisei were never in a relocation center. As may be imagined, evacuees had widely, if not wildly, different experiences depending on what assembly center they were sent to, how long they stayed (sometimes as much as six months, sometimes as little as six days), and the relocation center to which they were assigned.

Obviously, under such circumstances, it is extremely difficult to generalize. What we can say with some confidence is that for many evacuees the assembly center experience was *the* experience. For those who spent five or six months in an assembly center and then went on for a few weeks or months to a relocation center, the assembly center experience loomed as large or larger than the relocation center experience.

By the middle of November the last assembly center was vacated. On November 22, 1942, General DeWitt "announced his conclusion that the evacuation program initiated by him the preceding March was completed, so far as his headquarters was concerned." In the words of the report: "The metamorphosis [from military to civilian] was complete."

As the assembly centers were vacated they were taken over by various army agencies, most commonly service schools for ordnance, signal corps, quartermaster, and so forth. In August, when Pinedale was closed as an assembly center, it was taken over by the Fourth Air Force. At the end of July the Sacramento Center was converted to a signal corps training school. The army report emphasized these conversions in order to point up the fact that the centers, far from being concentration camps in any conventional sense of that term, were entirely adequate for our own military personnel. Still, the best-appointed army facility is a far cry from home and the discomforts and inconveniences of the centers are well documented.

THERE WAS AN ABUNDANCE OF IRONY IN THE FACT THAT THE TWO MEN most responsible for the policies and the operation of the War Relocation Authority, Milton Eisenhower and Dillon Myer, were nonbelievers, so to speak. Eisenhower, the initial director, was a skeptic about the whole operation and spent much of his brief time as director pursuing alternatives to mass evacuation. He clearly passed on to his successor his doubts about the evacuation. Dillon Myer's determination to do all he could to alleviate the most onerous aspects of center life was apparent in the policies he and his planning staff developed.

The assembly centers had been in operation only a few weeks when the war in the Pacific Theater took a striking turn for the better. On May 7, 1942, the Battle of the Coral Sea took place. Japanese forces were threatening to invade Australia and New Zealand. An Allied fleet intercepted the Japanese and, in the course of the battle, sank over 100,000 tons of Japanese shipping, including troop and supply ships, between New Guinea and the Solomon Islands, effectively ending the threat to Australia and New Zealand. A month later (June 4–7) witnessed the Battle of Midway, one of the greatest naval battles in history. The Japanese suffered a crushing defeat, losing a number of battleships and aircraft carriers. The psychological effect of the Midway victory was somewhat offset, at least for West Coast residents, by the Japanese occupation of the Aleutian Islands of Attu and Kiska. But for anyone with even a modest knowledge of the logistics of naval warfare, the Allied victory at Midway dispelled the notion that the Japanese navy any longer had (if it ever had had) the capacity to mount an invasion or even a major raid on the West Coast of the United States. Yet the entire rationale of the evacuation had been based on the premise that the Japanese not only could but in all likelihood *would* make such an invasion or massive raid.

Once the implications of the Midway battle were clear (although never publicly acknowledged), the whole evacuation, an enormously complicated and expensive undertaking (without taking into account its human cost), became a huge embarrassment. But no one at this point could put Humpty-Dumpty back together again. It was left to Dillon Myer to deal with its consequences. The initial measure, designed by Myer and his staff to at least ameliorate things, was a plan for a generous leave policy for all evacuees in the centers whose loyalty seemed beyond reasonable question. If college students and college-age evacuees could be given leave from the centers to pursue their education why should not leave be granted on generous terms to all evacuees to encourage them to take up normal life outside the centers? In July Meyer announced just such a leave policy. There would be three categories of leave: short-term leave, work leave, and, finally, indefinite leave, the latter designed to enable evacuees to try the experiment of establishing themselves outside with the help of the War Relocation Authority.

Short-term leave, quite freely granted, might be for a few days or a week. Typically, an evacuee might wish to consult an outside medical specialist or a lawyer, to conduct business, or check on the condition of a farm that had been leased. Leave to visit friends or relatives in other centers was also granted.

At the Portland Assembly Center the Reverend Francis Hayashi joined forces with a Buddhist minister, the Reverend Terakawa, whom he had known at Stanford. With Terakawa and three JACL leaders they served as advisers to the manager of the center. Later, at the Minidoka Relocation Center in Idaho, Hayashi's committee was given charge of temporary leave, involving mainly those evacuees who wished to visit nearby Twin Falls.

Work leave was, as the term implies, leave granted to evacuees to work outside. Sugar beet growers were especially anxious to employ evacuee labor to harvest their crops. While the governors of the states in question were initially opposed to any evacuees entering their bailiwicks, the beet and sugar cane growers, desperate for workers, soon prevailed on the governors to sing a different tune. Agreement was reached with the War Relocation Authority to transport all temporary or seasonal workers to and from the assembly (and later, relocation) centers, to pay the prevailing wages, and to assure the War Relocation Authority that adequate housing, food, medical attention, and proper sanitation standards would be maintained. All recruiting was to be done by the United States Employment Service "on a strictly voluntary basis." Some 1,740 evacuees were released to the War Relocation Authority prior to the opening of the relocation centers for such farm labor. Of these, 332 returned to assembly centers to join their families after harvesting crops and the rest entered the relocation centers to which they had been assigned after their work ended.

Finally there was indefinite leave. Under the rubric of indefinite leave an evacuee approved for leave could go out to find a job and living accommodations and remain out, as the term implied, indefinitely.

Ichiro Yamaguchi was one of the first in his center to go out on a harvest contract. "We always left camp on a harvest contract," he recalled, "just so we could go out. We went on a sugar beet contract once and didn't get along with the boss so we left his place and went to a town in Idaho and worked in a packing house."

The seasonal agricultural work, after a rocky start, became so popular that during the 1943 harvest season, over nine thousand evacuees did agriculture work in eight Western states. Some evacuees were simply released from assembly areas on work furloughs and were never inducted into the relocation centers to which they had been assigned.

Indefinite leave was granted for a variety of reasons ranging from enrolling in a college or university or some other educational institution (1,105) to accepting employment, seasonal or otherwise (seasonal in the case of planting or harvesting). Some 7,600 evacuees were released on indefinite leave on what was described as "community invitation." Community invitation was further defined as "evacuees making arrangements to live in a hotel, hostels or in a private home approved by a Relocation Officer while arranging for employment or any evacuee going to an area pursuant to a notice from a Relocation Officer that the area was approved and that there were jobs available" (3,650). Other reasons for indefinite leave were "to join or accompany family" (7,697), to marry a Caucasian (113), to be interned by the Department of Justice as an intractable case (973), or for "voluntary internment" requesting to be placed in an internment camp.

The motives for seeking voluntary internment were clearly varied. For some it was the supreme gesture of defiance of the U.S. and of loyalty to the emperor. In addition, internees, as, in effect, prisoners of war, received, under international law governing the treatment of prisoners of war, a monthly stipend; they were with like-minded companions and free of the conflicting loyalties that characterized the Assembly Centers and, subsequently, the relocation centers. Some saw it was a preliminary step to repatriation to Japan.

Like college leave, the more general leave policy had the advantage of helping to mitigate the image of the centers as concentration camps, which were not notable for encouraging their inmates to leave. By the same token, the leave policy enraged those zealots whose principal criticism of the whole WRA operation was that it was far too lenient. Meeting at Kansas City early in September, the American Legion was highly critical of the efforts of the War Relocation Authority to get evacuees out of the centers on indefinite leave or on work furlough or on college leave. The Legion was inclined to focus on the latter group as the greatest threat to the security of the country. Various newspapers and politicians took up the cry. Bills were introduced into Congress to block the release of evacuees for any reason.

When representatives from Washington, D.C., and from the San Francisco office of the War Relocation Authority met in San Francisco in August 1942 there were substantial disagreements and considerable skepticism about the viability of the original plan, which had placed so much emphasis on self-government. The Washington staff clearly had growing misgivings about the viability of the centers themselves. One of Myer's most trusted colleagues, Tom Holland, had visited most of the assembly centers and had been, in the main, dismayed at the general atmosphere. He reported that "the general facilities were adequate but that the social/psychological situation was distressing." Morale was generally abysmal. "Normal social controls appeared to be breaking down. People of all ages were idle much of the time and there were serious conflicts between different factions in the centers.'' The notion of the centers as self-contained communities, harmoniously self-governing schools of democracy seemed to Holland hopelessly utopian. He felt that the only sensible policy was to get as many of the evacuees as possible out of the centers as soon as possible. One of his principal concerns was that rather than becoming schools of democracy the centers might very well have directly the opposite effect. The aggressiveness of the Issei, coupled with the respect that older Japanese enjoyed in the eyes of the young, might make the centers schools for the code of *bushido* and the worship of the Emperor. At the very least there was the prospect of a grim battle in the centers for the hearts and minds of the approximately fifty thousand evacuees under the age of twenty-one.

Another factor that had considerable weight was the conviction that the vulnerability of the Japanese in the United States was due, in large part, to their concentration on the West Coast and especially in California. If they could be prevailed upon to resettle in the cities of the Midwest and the East, they would be presumably be far more inclined to assimilate. In the words of Edward Spicer the original historian of the evacuation: ''The prevailing national prejudice against Japanese Americans as a collective abstraction would decline as Americans of different communities saw them in the flesh and came to know them as persons. . . . The relocation program really had three objectives: to get the evacuees out of the centers, to disperse them, and to integrate them into the communities where they settled.''

Taken together, the arguments for resettlement out of the centers seemed irrefutable. On September 26, 1942, Dillon Myer announced the resettlement program to take effect October 1. Again, in Spicer's words: ''The earlier objective of self-contained and self-supporting communities, schools of democracy so to speak, became subordinated to the point of view that the relocation centers were to be primarily temporary havens until it was possible for their residents to establish themselves in new communities or to return to their West Coast homes. There were to be created no incentives or symbols that would deter the outward movement.''

The War Relocation Authority's ground rules for relocation or resettlement provided: ''(1) the applicant for such leave must have a definite job offer *or some other means of support* [italics added]; (2) he must agree to keep the WRA informed of any changes of jobs or changes of address; (3) his record at the relocation center and with the FBI and the intelligence services must contain no evidence of disloyalty to the United

States; and (4) there must be reasonable evidence that his presence will be acceptable in the community where he proposes to make his new home."

In his history of the War Relocation Authority, Myer summarized the reasons for instituting the leave program:

"We recognized that loyalty could not flourish in an atmosphere of restriction and discriminatory segregation.

"It was recognized that such a wide and enforced deviation from normal cultural and living patterns might very well have long lasting and unfavorable effects upon individuals, particularly children and young people who made up a large part of the population.

"There was an obligation on the part of the War Relocation Authority both to the evacuees and to the people of the United States generally to restore all loyal citizens and law-abiding aliens to a normal, useful American life with all possible speed.

"Confinement in relocation centers fostered suspicion of evacuee loyalties and added to evacuee discouragements.

"We did not want to be responsible for fostering a new set of reservations in the United States akin to the Indian reservations."

To Myer's surprise and chagrin, the announcement of the resettlement program brought bitter denunciations from the evacuees themselves, who saw it as an attempt on the part of the government to evade the responsibility of caring for them by turning them out into a hostile Caucasian world.

As with the initial leave policy, those patriotic organizations like the American Legion who were unrelenting in their hostility toward the WRA for "coddling the Japs" renewed their clamor. To a beleaguered Dillon Myer it seemed as though he could please no one. It is not too much, I think, to say that Dillon Myer's experience as director of the War Relocation Authority gave a deeper meaning to the phrase "thankless job."

Chapter 15

THE NATIONAL JAPANESE AMERICAN STUDENT RELOCATION COUNCIL

As NOTED EARLIER, THERE WERE SOME 2,400 NISEI IN WEST COAST colleges and universities at the time of Pearl Harbor. A few weeks after the announcement that "people of Japanese ancestry" were to be evacuated from the West Coast, Robert Gordon Sproul, the president of the University of California, wrote to President Roosevelt about the plight of the Nisei students in West Coast institutions of higher learning, urging the President to take some steps to insure that they could continue their education. Roosevelt replied: "I am deeply concerned that the American-born Japanese college students shall be impressed with the ability of the American people to distinguish between enemy aliens and staunch supporters of the American system." Roosevelt was clearly dismayed to learn that the education of so many students was imperiled, and Milton Eisenhower believed that if the issue had arisen earlier it might well have resulted in Roosevelt forbidding mass evacuation.

Sproul also wrote to the president of the University of Minnesota, soliciting his support: "It is my belief that the efforts we expend now will be repaid a thousandfold in the attitude of citizens of Japanese ancestry in years to come. We look forward to a new and better world. . . . The world may look to us for leadership. Certainly our handling of this serious minority group problem will be looked upon as evidence of our intentions and a proof of the ideals we hold.''

Sharing Sproul's concern were Ray Lyman Wilbur of Stanford (which had a number of Nisei students enrolled in both undergraduate and graduate schools), Edwin Voorhees, dean at Berkeley, and Lee Paul Sieg, president of the University of Washington.

As is often the case in a democratic society when something needs urgently to be done, there are multiple responses and so it was with the challenge to protect the academic careers of the Nisei. Quite independently of Sproul's effort, leaders of the American Friends Service Committee began work to a similar end. On April 29, a few weeks after DeWitt's order for controlled evacuation, the Federal Council of the Churches of Christ in America (which, the reader will recall, had strongly opposed mass evacuation) joined forces with the Home Missions Council of North America to write President Roosevelt on their own account: "Many leaders of the Protestant churches are expressing their concern about our national policy with respect to American citizens of Japanese parentage which jeopardizes our democracy and has a bearing on a religious liberty."

The letter went on to deplore "such abrogation of the rights of citizens. . . . Here in the United States we have an uneasy conscience because this policy savors of totalitarianism and discrimination."

A month later the Northern Baptist Convention passed a series of resolutions challenging the constitutionality of the evacuation and declaring that removal of "citizens on the grounds that they belong to a race of a different color is not in accord with Christian principles." One resolution urged that "civilian hearing boards be immediately established to permit such citizens to establish their right to liberty." (In fact, such boards had already been established by Biddle and were working overtime to try to distinguish between persons of Japanese ancestry loyal to the United States and those loyal to the Emperor of Japan.)

Finally, the convention resolved: "That inland and Eastern schools and colleges study the possibility of receiving Japanese American young people who may wish to continue their courses of study."

Dozens of individual professors undertook on their own to arrange the transfer of Nisei students to institutions "in the interior" and in other ways to facilitate such transfers. University of Washington President Paul Sieg instructed the university registrar to provide free transcripts of Nisei student records for those seeking to transfer to midwestern and Eastern colleges. Since few Nisei students had any idea what colleges might be willing to accept them, the free transcript plan proved costly and relatively ineffective.

The result of these various efforts was considerable confusion and wasted energy. It was soon evident that a nationwide coordinated effort was essential if anything substantial was to be accomplished. As Joseph Conrad, a Quaker activist, wrote to C. Reed Cary, a member of the American Friends Service Committee in Seattle, "[excellent] work is being done in some areas, but the lack of information prevented other areas from doing likewise. Many jobs were being done in conflicting ways by groups not knowing what the others were doing. Many other needed jobs were not being done at all."

The Northwest College Personnel Association meanwhile met in San Francisco to discuss what could be done to assist Nisei in transferring to other institutions. The decision was made to constitute the association as a regional body for student relocation and a few weeks later the Pacific College Association, prodded by the regional office of the Student YMCA and YWCA, called a similar meeting. This time the entire West Coast was represented; the YMCA and YWCA officers joined with representatives of the American Friends Service Committee. Elizabeth Ann Dorn in her Yale thesis, "From Camp to College: The Story of the National Japanese-American Student Relocation Council," notes that "the majority of institutions considered for the Nisei . . . were ones well known to the participants of the meeting, mostly on the basis of personal contacts between colleagues, but also because of denominational affiliations."

The principal accomplishment of the San Francisco meeting was the establishment of the Student Relocation Committee. Joseph Conrad was chosen to serve as the executive secretary of the committee. The committee created by the Northwest College Personnel Association became an affiliated "northern" branch. One of the committee's first steps was to make up a questionnaire to be distributed to all students and prospective students (those Nisei graduating from high school, or recently graduated and not in attendance at a college). In the period of voluntary evacuation prior to mass evacuation, the committee assisted seventy-five students to relocate before travel was restricted; an unknown number of students had relocated at colleges outside the exclusionary zones prior to the May proclamation. At this point, no effort had been made to coordinate the efforts of the Student Relocation Committee with any federal agency. In a letter written on April 2, 1942, Robert Gordon Sproul raised the issue with California Congressman John Tolan, chairman of the Select Committee Investigating National Defense Migration. Sproul declared that it is "essential to the future unity of the country that these leaders [the Nisei] be given the privileges of continuing and completing their educations under democratic auspices, in order that their leadership shall not be influenced by bitterness or a sense of unnecessary persecution."

Sproul went on to propose that a central committee be established with the approval and support of the government to facilitate the placement of Nisei in Midwestern and Eastern institutions. He offered the University of California as the West Coast headquarters for such an operation.

The measures suggested by Sproul were already being undertaken by the Student Relocation Committee, but the letter, in effect, solicited the cooperation and support of the government. Milton Eisenhower, to whom Sproul's proposal was referred, was entirely in sympathy with its objective but instead of designating a West Coast organization as the proper body to carry out a student placement program, Eisenhower turned to Clarence Pickett, the executive secretary of the American Friends Service Committee. Outlining the plan (or rather the actuality) of the Sproul contingent, Eisenhower went on to give his own endorsement, adding, "It is not feasible for the War Relocation Authority to undertake such a university program for American-citizen Japanese, but this in no way detracts from the desirability of such an accomplishment. Consequently, I would like to ask that you establish a committee which would aid you in forming a set of policies and programs." When Eisenhower's request to Pickett became known to the West Coasters there was understandable irritation. They had taken the initiative and established an organization that had already given evidence of its ability to do the job. Now Eisenhower was asking Pickett *to form a committee* to draw up "a set of policies and programs."

There is no clear indication of Eisenhower's reasoning to, in effect, turn away from the Student Relocation Committee, but he may have felt that the American Friends Field Service, with its well-known track record in the field of social service, would be in a better position to rally widespread public and denominational support than a group sailing under what was, in the main, an academic banner. If that was Eisenhower's logic it proved sound. Thomas Bodine, a member of the Pasadena office of the American Friends Service Committee, told a friend that the Student Relocation Committee members were furious with Pickett for having "gone to Eisenhower and gotten Eisenhower to give [them] the responsibility. This! When a committee was already organized and functioning on the West Coast."

Clarence Pickett responded to Eisenhower's letter by accepting the responsibility on behalf of the Friends and calling a meeting in Chicago on May 29, 1942. Pickett invited presidents of many of the nation's colleges (Sproul and Lee Paul Sieg were among the college presidents attending), representatives of the YMCA and YWCA, the Japanese American Citizens League, and "a broad range of religious organizations and government agencies, including members of the Student Relocation Committee." Among the religious organizations were the Division of College Work of the Protestant Episcopal Church and Department of Cities of American Baptist Home Mission Society. Out of the May 29 meeting came the National Japanese American Student Relocation Council. Robbins Barstow, president of the Hartford Theological Seminary, was appointed director. The council was to have two main branches; the Eastern branch was located in Philadelphia, also the main headquarters; the West Coast section had four offices—Berkeley, Los Angeles, Seattle, and Portland. While the initial efforts of the council were concentrated on the task of arranging for the transfer of the 2,400-plus students attending the West Coast institutions at the time of the evacuation, it was soon broadened to include those high school seniors in the various centers who were qualified to go on to college, a considerable number as it turned out.

Since evacuees were under army control at this point (specifically the Wartime Civil Control Administration) it was necessary to get the army's approval for releasing Nisei from the assembly centers to attend college. Stimson and McCloy gave their approval and the army, anxious to draw attention to its enlightened decision, decided to dramatize the case of a University of California Olympic Gold Medalist named Harvey Itano. Itano had applied to the St. Louis University School of Medicine and had been accepted. The summer session was to start two days later. John McCloy thereupon flew to San Francisco to sign a release order. It was the Fourth of July and Itano was at the Tule Lake Relocation Center. Tom Bodine, a young Friend active with the relocation committee, drove to Tule Lake, picked up Itano, presented him with his release order, and then drove him to nearby Klamath Falls in Oregon to catch a train for St. Louis. The stunt got wide newspaper coverage and helped to publicize the relocation program. Harvey Itano, it should be noted, graduated from medical school with honors and became a surgeon in the U.S. Public Health Service and professor of pathology at the University of California in San Diego.

Meanwhile, the newly created (or re-created) council set up four departments: (1) records; (2) placement; (3) financial aid; and (4) leave. First, the students themselves had to be identified and persuaded to apply to a college. A student questionnaire covered the college last attended, high school record, foreign travel, religious affiliation, career goals, marital status, available funds, and three references.

Consent of the parents had to be obtained; because of the infatuation with education, such consent was usually forthcoming. The academic work of the prospective college student had to be certified to be of college caliber. All this had to be cleared, of course, with the War Relocation Authority administrators at the centers.

Once a student had expressed (or been prevailed upon to express) an interest in attending a particular college or university and been accepted, the next step was finding funds to cover tuition and fees, room and board, books, and the other essentials. Of the first 1,400 students qualified for relocation only 20 percent had sufficient funds to pay their own way. Raising such funds became the major concern of the council. Applications were made to all major granting foundations but with relatively little success, only the Columbia and the Carnegie Foundations giving substantial assistance and their gifts were primarily for the administration of the program. It soon became evident that the greater part of the required monies would have to come from the Protestant denominations, from Jewish groups, and from the Catholic Church. In the words of Elizabeth Ann Dorn, "the [council] relied mostly on the kindheartedness of various religious groups to provide scholarships for Nisei." As she also points out, the council relied on the same groups to provide the funds to operate the council. Although a great deal of the work was done on a volunteer or semi-volunteer basis, there were, of course, substantial costs in running such an extensive operation. Scholarship assistance was of primary importance. In the words of one council member, "initial scholarship aid had the effect of jarring a student 'loose,' encouraging him or her to go out and get a job to help cover the expense of an education."

Since the largest denomination in the centers was Methodist, it was not surprising that over 26 percent of the students who were relocated indicated that they were Methodist, approximately the same number whose religious preference was Buddhist. Roughly 75 percent of all student relocatees belonged to a Christian denomination, mainly (after the Methodists) Baptist, Presbyterian, and Episcopalian. Not surprisingly, there were problems. The Methodists wanted Nisei members of their congregations to receive priority in assistance. The Roman Catholics would not give scholarship support to Seventh Day Adventists, and the Evangelical and Reformed Churches were not inclined to help the Buddhists, while the Presbyterians, Baptists, and Congregationalists made no discrimination. Given those unexceptional constraints, funds were raised one way or another for all eligible students. Although there were few Buddhists among the first four hundred or so Nisei relocated, the World Student Service Fund, together with other church funds, gave financial support to Buddhists and nonchurch members alike. While the proportion of Buddhists increased, it never rose much above 15 percent. It should also be noted that many of the churches that contributed generously to the council had few, if any, communicants in the centers.

We can judge the extent of the churches' giving by the fact that students "successfully relocated by December, 1942, when the program had been in operation for less than eight months, had received $107,430 in financial aid." The Fellowship of Reconciliation was in the forefront of religious groups that rallied to help the evacuees. Among other things they published a bulletin entitled "Behind Barbed Wire: Convicted of No Crime."

The Protestant ministers in the centers played a crucial role in the operation of the student placement (or relocation) program. The Reverend John Yamazaki noted that his most time-consuming function had been "helping prepare for relocation outside, in employment and in school. For those going to work we must write letters to the employer and to the bishop and priest in their new diocese. . . . For our students who are leaving we have a large task in working with the Student Relocation Council, with our own Executive Council's college work division, and with the deans of universities." It sometimes took a year to place a student. Of the 150 students accepted in colleges from Gila River, twenty-four, Yamazaki reported, had been from the Episcopal congregation in the center. In addition, more than a hundred members of St. Mary's congregation from Los Angeles had been relocated in twenty-one states.

June Suzuki was one young Episcopalian who went out from Gila River with the encouragement of Yamazaki. Suzuki went to Pembroke College and after graduation returned to St. Mary's mission school on the Pima Indian Reservation at Gila River.

The Reverend Isamu Nakamura noted that "for the members of the [Presbyterian] church, I helped them by writing a few letters of recommendation to the church-affiliated colleges and universities, with assistance from the National Presbytery." Things, of course, did not always go smoothly. One young Nisei at Tanforan had been encouraged by the Mount Oliver Methodist Church to come to Dearborn, Michigan, to pursue his college studies. Getting wind of the arrangement, the Michigan Safety Commission and the mayor of Dearborn, led by the local chapter of the Veterans of Foreign Wars, announced that he could not come. The New York newspapers picked up the story and "Kenny M." was briefly a national celebrity and an embarrassed Dearborn ceased its resistance to resettling evacuees.

Ruth Asawa was encouraged to go out from Rohwer Relocation Center in Arkansas by a Quaker friend. Asawa went to college in Milwaukee, where she first worked for a German family and then found a job in a bakery. She got up at five o'clock every morning, worked at the bakery, and then went on to her college courses. During a summer vacation, Asawa and her sister, who had gone out to the University of Michigan, took a trip to Mexico City, where Ruth met the German Bauhaus painter Josef Albers. Albers was struck by Asawa's intellect, talent (and beauty) and encouraged her to go to Black Mountain College in North Carolina, the center of a brilliant coterie of artists and writers and composers who encouraged Asawa in her career as a sculptor.

Most of the Nisei who had attended West Coast institutions of higher education had gone to the great public universities, most typically the University of Washington and, in California, Berkeley and UCLA. Those institutions were less expensive than the relatively small number of private colleges in the West and they offered more of the preprofessional programs like business and engineering favored by Japanese students. In those large, impersonal institutions, Nisei formed their own subcultures, generally keeping to themselves in their student organizations. In the post–Pearl Harbor era, when the National Japanese American Student Relocation Council undertook to place the Nisei in colleges and universities outside of the exclusionary zone, the council was often frustrated by the fact that the army and navy would not allow students to enroll in institutions that had defense contracts. Since this excluded most of the larger and grander public and private universities in the Midwest and East, the council had, perforce, to turn to the smaller church-related, private colleges that were little known. On the other hand, these latter institutions were much more accessible through their denominational connections, which greatly facilitated the placement of Japanese students. The students usually found the private colleges friendly and welcoming, as classes were small and the professors actively involved with the students. Since there were not enough Japanese Americans in any one college to constitute a subculture they were, of necessity, much more integrated in the currents of student life. One evacuee student wrote: "I am not the *only* Japanese student on campus here. The atmosphere is definitely Christian. Already I have met some of the finest acquaintances I have known. Although there are only two of us here, we are not lonesome, as the Caucasians are more than friendly.''

A college Nisei wrote to a friend: "One hears so much about certain parts of the West being friendly. This is really one of them. This is really it! The people are fair, and for the most part unbiased in their opinions. . . . It has been an uplifting experience to have lived and studied in South Dakota.''

Similar testimony came from a Nisei woman at Smith College who was astonished at the friendly and helpful atmosphere so different from the large public university she had attended before the evacuation: "The professors actually get to know you; they say hello to you by your right name! . . . They announce their office hours and they keep them. . . . It took a considerable time to accustom myself to all this.''

An evacuee, accepted by Haverford College in Pennsylvania, wrote home: "To me Haverford is just perfect. I could not expect much more for I have been welcomed very cordially by the fellow students.''

Rhoda Iyoya remembered Eleanor Gerard as an excellent teacher who encouraged her to plan to go to college; a conscientious objector named Goodman taught biochemistry. "We all applied to go to colleges that would take us,'' Rhoda Iyoya recalled, speaking of her fellow high school graduates. Rhoda was accepted at Vassar. "All these arrangements were being made and my train fare and everything was taken care of. I went from camp after that summer without even a gap, to enroll in September at Vassar College. They took care of it all.'' During her college years Rhoda Iyoya was called on to go to churches in the area to talk of her experience in the centers. "In this way I knew who I was, what my background had been and how I fit into an American community and American history.''

Jack Takayanaki was a student at Chapman College, a Presbyterian church-related institution in California, when the war began. He and his fiancée, Mary, were sent to Manzanar, where with the help of the National Japanese American Student Relocation Council, he went out to attend Drake University in Des Moines. As soon as he was able he sent for Mary, and they were married. Takayanaki remembers that it was seven long months before the paperwork necessary for his leave was completed.

Toshiko Igarashi's husband was a Baptist minister. Their second son left Tule Lake for a scholarship at Colby College in Maine. Their third son also got a scholarship at the Presbyterian-related Kalamazoo College in Michigan. When the second son graduated from Colby College, Harvard offered him a scholarship to study at the Divinity School and from there he won one of the first Fulbright Scholarships to study in England.

Prior to Pearl Harbor only 16 percent of the Nisei were in private colleges. By 1943 62.7 percent were in non-state-supported-institutions. The number in Protestant colleges increased from 4.4 percent in 1941 to 34.5 percent in 1943. By 1943 61.4 percent were in colleges and universities in the Midwest, 5.7 percent in Southern institutions, and 9.5 percent in Mid-Atlantic states.

Needless to say, not all Nisei were attracted to the NJASRC program. A friend of Charles Kikuchi was scornful of their efforts. "He is very bitter," Kikuchi noted in his diary, "and thinks that the churches are capitalizing on gross injustices done the evacuees in order to win them over to the church. . . . He believes that the Japanese here do not need the spiritual leadership of some of the white reverends that come in and act so sympathetic. He would rather have them fighting mad in order to shake the whole group out of its lethargy and for them to make a very positive stand on the war and to hell with hurting the feelings of the Issei any more."

When several offers came to Kikuchi to "go out" to graduate schools he rejected them. To escape into "an Ivory Tower" was tempting but that would mean "to miss all this. Actually it is exciting and there are opportunities. Something fine will come out of all this, I am hoping."

In the summer of 1944 the NJASRC decided to send Nisei students who had made a successful adjustment to life on college campuses back to the centers to encourage more qualified young evacuees to relocate. After a five-day training course and visits to some of the major cities where students had relocated, those selected returned to the centers to meet with block managers, church groups, and various clubs to tell about their own experiences and answer questions from prospective students and their parents.

One evacuee, returning to his "home" relocation center, wrote that it was not the parents who were to blame for the reluctance of the Nisei to leave the centers but rather the Nisei themselves. "Unfortunately," she wrote, "it is a typical family custom not to speak openly to parents and exchange ideas and dissatisfactions back and forth." Many Nisei needed more self-confidence. Parents would listen to children "who show determination and initiative about their education." Indeed, with their passion for education, Issei parents were much more willing for their children to go out to college than to have them go out for jobs. One son wrote: "My father is old, 78 years old, and I know how he misses me. But as I left he strengthened me with these words: 'I am old, some day you will hear that I am dying, perhaps while you are still in school. Forget about me. Make my dying days happy in the knowledge that you are studying and preparing yourself for service. My life is in the past, yours is in the future. Go and be of good service to men.' "

A young Nisei woman wrote: "Little by little, college students left to resume their education. . . . After hearing of their fine reports, we felt the urge to seek the life of freedom again.

"I would sit at home and argue with Mom and Dad to let me out of camp, but they would stubbornly say 'no,' and tell me that we should stick together. 'The outside is not safe; but probably after a few months, conditions may improve,' Dad would say. 'A young girl should stay at home and be with the rest of the family.' " When her young brother began drawing airplanes featuring the emblem of the Rising Sun, she felt it was her "duty" to leave the camp and to try to get her brother out as well.

Evacuees in some of the centers, inspired by the example of the council, undertook to raise money from the residents themselves. Thus at Heart Mountain Relocation Center in Wyoming the Community Activities Section collected money for several scholarships for high school graduates, and at Topaz in Utah the Student Aid Fund raised $185,196 from various sources within and without the center, money that helped to send some thirty to various colleges.

A number of relocated Nisei contributed to the council's scholarship fund as well, and one Nisei soldier put aside part of each month's pay to help a woman student selected by the council with her college expenses. He called his contribution "the K.O. [his initials] Fund for an O.K. Girl."

It was not only conventional liberal arts colleges and universities that accepted students. Professional schools were also cooperative. A number of young Nisei women wished to have careers as nurses. Three hospitals in Rochester, New York, agreed to accept Nisei women as students. Frances Kirihara was among the evacuees accepted as nursing students at the Rochester General Hospital and she reflected years later that "many of us would not have been able to continue our education if it weren't for the different churches providing scholarships. I was able to go to Rochester because the Presbyterian church provided a scholarship for me to continue my training.''

The experiences of Frances Kirihara with *hakujin* in Rochester were ones she remembered with pleasure for years. A Quaker family, the Williamses, invited Frances and two of her Japanese friends to their home for Christmas, Thanksgiving, and Easter. Some of the Japanese students joined the conscientious objectors of the Fellowship of Reconciliation who were working at the hospital; they formed a congenial band, going out together to dine and dance. ''I think many people in Rochester made every effort to make the Nisei feel comfortable. Mostly they were church people and they were very sympathetic because we were treated unjustly. They were sorry that it happened.''

Osuma Doi worked as a nurse's aide and soon had an opportunity through the council and a Japanese family friend in Philadelphia to get a scholarship to attend the Lankenau Hospital School of Nursing in Philadelphia. Her sister enrolled at another nursing school. Doi's classmates welcomed her. An older student, she recalled, ''showed me the ropes and took me shopping for necessities. . . . There was no discrimination and I felt accepted.''

By 1944 there were over three hundred Nisei women in one hundred nursing schools in twenty-four states. Many were accepted in the United States Nurse Cadet Corps, which provided all expenses, including books, uniforms, and a monthly allowance.

The Nisei who experienced the good offices of the National Japanese American Student Relocation Council have emphasized that the attitude of the men and women they encountered in the often painfully long drawn out process of getting from camp to college was as important as the assistance itself. What we might call the organizational generosity of the council was matched by the personal kindness and generosity of those individuals responsible for carrying out its mandate. To Frank Inouye, a volunteer who worked for the council, it was ''no government agency looking down from its Olympian heights upon the masses below. It was a warm, human, friendly, sympathetic friend.''

Robert W. O'Brien, author of *The College Nisei,* summed up the Nisei college experience: ''They [the Nisei] held class offices of all kinds, were on the staffs of campus papers and yearbooks, took part in debate and athletic activities, joined fraternities, sororities, honorary societies and won [such] miscellaneous honors as 'Most Charming Girl,' 'Most Popular Boy.' ''

The council's true value, O'Brien wrote, ''can never be estimated statistically by the number of students helped or by the amount of financial aid rendered. Part of its technique for handling the students was to treat each as an individual, as a separate personality. . . . But the most significant aspect of the work was something even more intangible; the rekindling of the faith of a minority group. It meant hope, instead of despair, to six thousand relocated students.''

Part 3

LIFE IN THE RELOCATION CENTERS

Chapter 16

THE RELOCATION CENTERS

THE PROBLEM OF THE TRANSFER OF EVACUEES FROM THE ASSEMBLY centers to the relocation centers was another huge undertaking requiring elaborate planning and creating mountains of paperwork, a logistical nightmare that, on the whole, was accomplished with remarkable efficiency. Like the Kikuchi family, many residents of the assembly centers had accumulated personal belongings such as furniture, clothes, books, and phonograph records. These had to be packed and then inspected and trucked to the nearest railroad line. Evacuees were transported by rail in groups of approximately five hundred, with 171 special trains required (only 710 were transferred by bus). While a number of evacuees had been permitted to drive their own cars to assembly centers, only a few were allowed to drive from the assembly centers to the relocation centers.

Two baggage cars were provided for every five hundred evacuees, and those belongings that could not be carried by baggage car were sent by freight. Where two or more meals were required on the trip between assembly centers and relocation centers, dining cars were provided. One physician and one or more nurses accompanied each train carrying five hundred or more and sleeping cars were provided for infants and invalids who required special arrangements.

An effort was made to assign evacuees to centers as near as possible to their residences and to locations where the climate was similar to that of the area from which they had come. That these goals were often not met is not surprising.

The structures of the relocation centers were of a common plan. They were one-story wooden frame buildings covered with tarpaper and designed to accommodate 250 to 300 persons. Each section called a block contained fourteen barracks, with each barrack divided into four to six private units called apartments. The space allocated to smaller families— husband and wife and one child—was sixteen feet by twenty feet; larger families were given apartments measuring twenty feet by twenty-four feet. In addition to the apartments, each block had a dining hall, a recreation hall, men's and women's latrines, and a laundry room with eighteen tubs and twenty ironing boards. The number of blocks was determined by the population of the center. Manzanar, for example, with a population of over ten thousand, had thirty-six blocks.

In the face of wartime shortages, the War Relocation Authority was constantly stretched to locate and purchase needed equipment and supplies. In the words of an authority report: "Where to find enough lumber to buy to build boxes so that 12,000 persons could pack their personal belongings in them for relocation? Where to find tractors, farm equipment, feed, seed, and livestock? How to arrange for regular and sure deliveries of 50,000 tons of coal and have it unloaded and distributed . . .? How to handle ice deliveries from railroad cars at railheads 20 miles away when it was 120 degrees in the shade?" Where to get disposable diapers for mothers starting off on long train trips?"

Each center required some ten thousand items of equipment, material, and general supplies for the evacuees, all of which had to be ordered, kept in stock, and, eventually, when the centers closed, inventoried and disposed of one way or another.

While laid out on the same general plan, the relocation centers varied considerably in terrain and climate and, once occupied by evacuees, varied also in temperament or character, some being highly volatile, others relatively stable.

Heart Mountain in Wyoming was hot in the summer and chillingly cold in the winter. Granada (Amache), in southwestern Colorado, had a climate somewhat similar to that of Tule Lake in northeastern California— warm and dry in summer, cold in winter.

Gila River in Arizona was hot and desolate. Minidoka (also called Hunt), near Twin Falls, Idaho, was cold in the winter but comfortable in the summer. Topaz, Utah, was four thousand feet above sea level and had temperatures that varied between 106 degrees in the summer to the thirties in the winter.

Jerome and Rohwer were in far-off Arkansas in lightly wooded terrain and moderate climate.

Tule Lake, Minidoka, and Heart Mountain were on Federal Reclamation Project land. Gila River and Poston were on Indian reservations. We are already familiar with Poston and Manzanar; originally built as reception centers to facilitate voluntary relocation, they were afterward designated relocation centers. Located in the Arizona desert and uncomfortably hot in the summer, Poston's three units, officially I, II, III, were commonly referred to as Poston, Toastin', and Roastin'.

The populations of the relocation centers varied from some eight thousand at Topaz to eighteen thousand at Poston, and each center, with the exception of the two California ones, was one of the largest communities (or towns) in its particular state. Thus Topaz, with eight thousand, was the fifth largest city (or town) in Utah. Poston was the third largest city in Arizona, and Heart Mountain, with eleven thousand evacuees, was the third largest community in Wyoming.

The War Relocation Authority was not insensitive to the generally bleak settings of the centers and did its best to enhance the more desolate by planting trees and shrubs and by encouraging the residents of the centers themselves to grow plants and flowers. At Topaz the WRA planted 7,500 small trees and ten thousand shrubs.

The Gila River complex was divided into two separate centers or camps—Butte and Canal. The buildings at Butte were typical structures. In addition to the barrack blocks there were twenty buildings for administrative offices, staff living quarters, a hospital, a store, two churches, a library, schoolrooms, a Post Office, a building for the center newspaper, a firehouse, and high school buildings. Butte also had a recreation building with a room for judo. A large recreational area contained a sumo pit and an outdoor amphitheater. Canal Camp, four miles away, although much smaller, had essentially the same layout. The Post Office building at Canal was shared by a church congregation and a co-op store. At Gila River, between Butte and Canal, there were 1,400 buildings that served a remarkably wide range of purposes.

The buildings at both Gila River and Poston had double roofs as protection against the blazing summer sun.

In addition to the administrative complex and hospital, all centers had warehouse buildings, one of which was for refrigerated foods (a forty-foot-by-one-hundred-foot structure) plus twenty forty-foot-by-one-hundred-foot warehouses for dry storage.

Garages for the center's cars and trucks, various maintenance buildings, plus storage sheds for farm tools and equipment were also common to the centers.

Gila River had 350 vehicles of all kinds, 225 of them trucks. Some centers had so many vehicles that there were traffic problems. At Minidoka the number of evacuee cars driven around the center was so numerous that internal security decided they must be impounded. Their owners were indignant. Some simply parked their cars outside the limits of the center (in which case they were subject to vandalism), while others stored them in the center warehouse.

When evacuees had their furniture and personal belongings sent to them in the relocation camp, they often found that they had too much to fit into their cramped living quarters. In such instances, they had their surplus belongings stored in warehouses at the center. The centers thus served inadvertently as collecting points for large quantities of evacuee possessions. Heart Mountain, for example, had 450,000 pounds of such possessions in the center warehouse and 2,175,000 pounds in the barracks themselves. Poston had only 30,000 pounds in its warehouse but 4 million pounds in the barracks. Tule Lake had 950,000 pounds in the warehouse and 4,350,000 in the barracks, for a total of 5,300,000.

Food was issued to each block dining hall, based upon the weekly population figure. Evacuees who had owned or operated restaurants were usually responsible for preparing menus sixty days in advance. On this basis, requisitions for staples were prepared fifty days in advance, and, for perishable foods, fifteen days in advance. All this was based on wartime civilian rationing quotas.

Relocation centers had one or more food processing plants for foods favored by the residents. All the centers, for example, had tofu-making operations. There were also pickling plants for daikon, a large white radish popular with the evacuees. The Manzanar center made all the soy sauce that it used.

Farming took place at all the centers. Gila River farmed some 7,000 acres, 3,000 intensively in vegetable crops, and also had 2,000 head of beef cattle and between 2,000 and 3,000 hogs as well as 110 dairy cows and 25,000 chickens. There were herds of beef cattle at Topaz and Manzanar, which with Gila River produced over 3 million pounds of beef.

Together, the centers produced 110 million pounds of vegetables valued at an estimated $3,650,000.

A subject of much discussion in the War Relocation Authority planning staff had been what line to take in regard to internal businesses, such as stores selling groceries and sundries, clothing and gifts. The initial notion was to encourage individual entrepreneurs to set up business ventures and to rent them space but the notion of rent was unpopular and after some backing and filling, it was decided to have cooperatives as the common form of business enterprises in the centers. Patronage dividends or refunds were given at all the centers and by the closing of the centers the ten cooperative associations had opened a total of 270 "different enterprises or services . . . ranging from a single-employee watch-repair shop or shoe-repair shop to moderate-sized department stores stocking a wide variety of goods with many employees." Together the cooperatives did a gross business of $21,890,167 and paid out $2,298,830 while employing seven thousand residents.

As each contingent of evacuees arrived at the relocation center to which it had been assigned, it was greeted by those who had preceded it (sometimes with an improvised band) and welcomed by the head administrator of the center, the project director, who reviewed the rules and regulations governing the center and spoke of his hopes for cooperation and harmony. If the assembly centers had been a shock to many evacuees, the relocation centers with their remoteness, with their raw and seemingly endless rows of tar-paper-covered barracks and their unfamiliar landscapes, were even more disheartening.

In the words of Edward Spicer, "the occupation and adjustment period at every project was one of worry, inconvenience, shortages in essential supplies and services and general physical discomfort. Under these conditions, grievances were plentiful, crises common." An evacuee at Manzanar wrote bitterly of the conditions there: "The desert was bad enough. . . . The constant cyclonic storms loaded with sand and dust made it worse. After living in well furnished homes with every modern convenience and suddenly forced to live the life of a dog is something which one cannot so readily forget. Down in our hearts we cried and cursed this government every time when we were showered with dust. We slept in the dust; we breathed the dust; and we ate the dust."

Harry Nishiura had a special grievance. Nishiura and his extended family went from Los Angeles to the Pomona Assembly Center and from there to Heart Mountain. When he arrived at Heart Mountain he discovered that "they had misplaced my grandmother." "I got mad," he recalled. Rushing into the center office he announced, "If you don't find my grandmother, I'm going to knock every one of you." With this challenge, the Japanese police in the center made a search and found Nishiura's grandmother, cold, frightened, and alone.

The basic social units of the relocation centers were the blocks. Most were occupied by evacuees from the same town or church congregation or city neighborhood. They were, in effect, small neighborhoods. In one block the residents were all from Salinas, California. Ichiro Yamaguchi was strongly pro-U.S. but he experienced little hostility because his block was made up primarily of friends from Salinas. "They were all nice people," he added. "After all, we all knew each other."

One Issei woman recalled that "our block at the Amache [Granada] camp of 7,500 people was very peaceful, because everyone came from Cortez. There were very little problems. . . . Of course we heard of lots of problems in other blocks, though. I heard about adult fist fights. We never had such problems, because our block was just like family members."

Another block was made up largely of evacuees from the rural, strawberry-growing town of Florin, California, and inclined to the pro-Japanese side.

Those centers whose residents, by chance or choice, were predominately from rural towns such as Norwalk, Florin, and Cortez (those whom Charles Kikuchi referred to patronizingly as "backwoods country people") were apt to be the most strongly pro-Japan.

Over 21,000 evacuees were relocated out of communities with prewar populations of 2,500 or less; 11,335 from communities of under 5,000; and 25,672 from communities of between 25,000 and one million. Over 23,000 were relocated out of cities of over a million (i.e., Los Angeles), 31,141 coming from Los Angeles County, of whom 396 ended up in Tule Lake. In Placer County, by contrast (as in Sacramento County), out of 1,827 relocated, 1,807 ended up in Tule Lake. Most of those relocated out of Santa Cruz County (1,419) went to Poston (1,222) and 88 ended up in Tule Lake. In Orange County, of 1,887 evacuees, 1,636 ended up in Poston, 58 went to Gila River, 77 to Manzanar, and only 30 in Tule Lake. Of the 5,014 from San Joaquin County, 815 went to Gila River, 3,516 to Rohwer. The 12,848 relocatees from the state of Washington were divided between Minidoka (7,240) and Tule Lake (4,366). King County, the location of Seattle, had 8,879 evacuees, 6,801 from Seattle; most went to Minidoka. Of the 3,531 evacuees from Oregon, 2,305 went to Minidoka.

One frequent source of tension in the centers was the conflict between those evacuees who came from California and those from Washington and Oregon. An evacuee from Seattle wrote: "What's the matter with these Californians? They're so crude, and they don't have any manners. No wonder the Caucasian Californians wanted to get rid of them."

A college Nisei from the Northwest wrote of Manzanar: "The people here are different from others. They are more Japanesy. Coming from such areas as Terminal Island, San Pedro, and San Bernardino, they are known as the 'tough' bunch. And how true when you hear some of the Issei talk! Even the children have acquired vulgarity in their ways of speaking and acting."

There were, of course, numerous other elements that affected the tension level of any given camp—the percentage of Christians versus Buddhists being a major one. Tule Lake and Manzanar were at the pro-Japan end of the spectrum, Minidoka at the pro-U.S. end.

An indispensable element in the drama of the relocation centers was the Caucasian staff. Numbering from 150 to 275 at one time, they came in the aggregate, over the history of the centers, to perhaps three or four thousand men and women. They were recruited constantly, since many could not tolerate the psychological pressures of the centers and, as we would say today, burned out. Wherever possible the authority employed husbands and wives. The staff quarters at the centers were rented at "reasonable rates" and were, in the words of the WRA report, "somewhat better than the accommodations provided for the evacuees but not outstandingly so. The main difference was that cooking and sanitary facilities were available in each apartment." Almost half of the appointed employees were teachers. The authority paid teachers $1,620 for a twelve-month year which some critics of the centers declared was too high.

A number of the teachers were, like Ralph and Mary Smeltzer, members of one of the peace churches and so were conscientious objectors who came to the centers to do their alternative service. They were idealistic young men and women who felt great sympathy for the evacuees and dreamed of helping them create "peaceful and harmonious" communities. Some were students and admirers of Japanese culture. A number had backgrounds in social work. Some were Quakers.

Aside from the teachers there were a number of Caucasians, especially in the early days of the centers, who were engaged in clerical work. Caucasians also filled most of the supervisory jobs. At Gila River there were 210 appointive employees and 4,000 evacuee employees. Dining hall operations, preparation, and serving of food, kept 1,500 to 1,800 evacuees busy.

By the time the centers closed, in the words of WRA's final report, virtually all of the "clerical, stenographic, semi-supervisory and laboring work was done by the evacuees. A system of hours of employment, sick and annual leave . . . was devised for the evacuees that very closely paralleled the rules, regulations, rights and privileges of the appointive employees under Federal civil-service rules. . . . From this work at the centers, there were developed a rather large number of employees among the evacuees who were later employed by the Authority in its offices outside the centers."

The relationship between the Caucasian supervisors and the evacuee workers was an extremely delicate one, especially in the area of manual labor, in construction and agriculture most notably. In the words of one evacuee: "After 2 years many [staff members] had developed their rules of thumb for getting a maximum amount of cooperation in the jobs the agency set them to do." A Caucasian foreman in one center expressed this acquired wisdom: "You've got to treat them all as if they were volunteers. If you do that everything is all right. If the work crews were allowed to set their own pace and determine their own rest periods they would not only complete their tasks reasonably efficiently but pitch in in an emergency."

The head administrator of each center was called "project director," a harmless enough designation. He had three assistants in "operations," "administrative management," and "community management," a "reports officer" of rather vague responsibility, and an attorney. The community management division included education, health, recreation, internal security, family welfare, community analysis, and community government.

The operations division was responsible for construction and maintenance, the building of roads, utilities, agricultural work, "industry," and transportation (industrial activities remained, as we have noted, nugatory). Administrative management presided over procurement, accounting and budgeting, employment, dining, and personnel.

The operations division was also responsible for evacuee records. They grew by a kind of compounding—employment records, medical treatment records, property records, records regarding registration, clearance review, leave, transportation, communications about jobs and college placement. When the centers closed over a thousand boxes arrived in Washington, all to be sorted and classified and filed once more. The task took three months and when it was finished the mountain of paper occupied 450 filing cabinets.

Caucasian staff members were frequently distressed to discover that most evacuees wished to keep them at arm's length. Desiring to be friends, they were often rebuffed. "There is a very clear cut line between the Caucasians and the other colonists," an evacuee wrote. "At the evening meeting, everyone brought sandwiches and we served tea. Some Caucasians came in before we were through and were distinctly 'frozen out' and made to feel most uncomfortable. There is very little social life between the two groups."

In the words of one evacuee, "the staff in general constituted a segregated minority living at the margins of the relocation center communities." They had their own social life, their own relocation facilities, their own internal strains and stresses, their own differences of opinion on the problems that were common to all the centers. Again in the words of the evacuee: "The consciousness of the evacuee world, massive and solid around them . . . loomed large for staff who rose every morning to see it stretching out before them and whose daily work dinned some aspect of it into them constantly." At those times when fear and anxiety gripped the evacuees over some new War Relocation Authority policy, or the rumor of a new edict, the staff echoed the evacuees' response. Staff at such times felt rather as though they were sitting on a powder keg.

There were, of course, bad staff members as well as good ones, as well as some individuals who by their very attentiveness and desire to please struck some evacuees as patronizing or insensitive. Generally speaking, however, the staff were an unusually able and dedicated group. A Nisei college student at Topaz recalled the kindness of one of the Caucasian staff members. "The most amazing part," she wrote, "was that he never showed his disappointment in spite of the setbacks and hardships we had. He did not like to have me say that I was working for him, for he said we were working together for the good of 10,000 people. We worked night and day, but I did not mind, for I was working with a man who could not have been finer." Such testimony, it may be said, was not infrequent.

One of the most significant staff positions was that of the community analyst. He (and in one instance, she) was typically an academic, a sociologist or anthropologist, charged with observing and analyzing the situation in each center and making weekly reports to the Community Analysis Section of the WRA in Washington. The intention was to make such modifications in the operation of the centers as would be to the benefit of the evacuees.

The problems that community analysts encountered in the centers are well illustrated by the experience of one of them, Asael Hansen. In Hansen's words: "The reason for setting up the Community Analysis Section within the War Relocation Authority . . . was the belief, or hope, that trained social scientists with no other duties would learn enough about the internees to improve their situation." At Heart Mountain, Hansen hoped to establish such rapport with the evacuees that he could inquire into the thinking, feeling, and behavior of the camp residents. "Then, assuming sufficient skill in organizing basic data, my reports would represent some of the realities of evacuee life."

Hansen took on his assignment under awkward circumstances. The director of Heart Mountain made it clear that he would prefer not to have a community analyst in his center. Moreover, some of the Nisei who worked in the administration building had already read Hansen's records and were familiar with both his background (he was on leave from the University of Miami in Ohio) and the nature of his task. One of Hansen's most helpful contacts was with a Christian Issei who had a bachelor's degree in economics from Columbia and was married to the daughter of a Japanese Methodist minister. After five months of wooing by Hansen, his new friend told him, "I liked you from the very first. I felt certain that you were a professor on leave and not a spy of some kind that many people in the camp think you are. And I thought you were a good man. But it was not clear to me what you really intended to do here. Were you here only to collect information on the Japanese to report to your WRA bosses in Washington? You explained that if Washington had good information on us, they could understand us better and administer us better. But I couldn't be sure. And then I wondered if you intended, as a professor of anthropology, to study the Japanese as if we were guinea pigs and to write some articles and maybe to get some raise in salary. . . . What I had to settle in my own mind was that you really *cared* about the Japanese and that you were sincerely and deeply concerned with their future. I had to feel that the welfare of the Japanese was more important to you than your professional career. . . . A few weeks ago I . . . made up my mind that you really did care. So tonight I assure you that, from now on, you can ask me questions; I will tell you what I know. If I believe that there are better informed persons in this camp, I will seek their counsel."

Incidentally, Hansen's Issei friend's suggestion as a way for him to win the confidence and friendship of other Issei was to sponsor a Kabuki play.

The only unequivocal benefit of the weekly reports of the community analysts is that they afford a marvelously detailed daily account of the centers.

Other eyes were also watching. At the beginning of the evacuation, Dorothy Thomas, a professor of sociology at the University of California at Berkeley, decided that the evacuation presented a golden opportunity for social scientists to observe the forced migration of a people. Thomas thus devised what came to be called the Japanese Evacuation and Relocation Study, known more commonly as JERS. She was notably successful in raising large sums of money to hire researchers (observers), most of them Nisei graduate students at Berkeley, Stanford, and UCLA, who were, of course, also evacuees. These observers wrote regular accounts of center life, and Thomas or one of her Caucasian associates visited the centers on a regular basis to discuss their observations and exchange information.

One of Dorothy Thomas's informants was James Sakoda. Sakoda's background was, as he put it, "that of a 'Japanesy' Nisei with strict moral values, Japanese language school after regular school, attendance at a Buddhist church and judo lessons." Sakoda's father was a hog farmer. When hogs in the area were killed by government agents to prevent the spread of hoof-and-mouth disease, Sakoda's father took the lump-sum government payment and returned to Japan, where the young Sakoda became more Americanized than he had been in the United States, in part as a consequence of being in the Hiroshima Nikkei Club with other Nisei "under the auspices of a Christian Church." Sakoda and his three brothers returned to the United States and Sakoda enrolled at Pasadena Junior College and, subsequently, at the University of California in Berkeley.

Charles Kikuchi was another JERS observer. A number of JERS evacuee observers went on after the war to become college professors.

In time the centers became small cosmoses. They had all the agencies and instrumentalities, as we say, of any community. And some more uniquely their own. They had religious services, social organizations, hospitals with doctors, nurses, operating rooms (the residents of one center, dissatisfied with their chief of medicine, petitioned the administration to have him fired), cooperative stores, small business ventures such as barber shops, tobacco stores, internal economies, and, as we have seen, largely unsuccessful attempts as modest war-related industries. They had schools, recreational facilities, social programs, transportation and communication systems, construction crews, paid workers, labor boards.

Villages, towns, small cities? One hardly knows what to call them. Cosmoses.

Chapter 17

TROUBLE IN THE CENTERS

O NCE THE EVACUEES WERE ESTABLISHED IN THE RELOCATION CEN-
ters, the social and political atmosphere changed dramatically. The assembly centers had been understood as a kind of limbo, an interval of
tentativeness and uncertainty. The very air of impermanence militated
against outbreaks of violence among the evacuees or against the administrators of the centers. The time in the assembly centers was a "wait-
and-see time," a time of rumors about where and, above all, when,
evacuees would be dispatched to the relocation centers, their semi-
permanent homes. Once in the relocation centers, though, every issue
that had become evident in the assembly centers—food, the quality of
medical care, the availability of water, rules governing leave, wages, and
working conditions—now became a political issue. The first assignment
for the directors from WRA headquarters in Washington had been to
involve the evacuees in organizing evacuee-run center governments
based, it was assumed, on the community councils. But there was trouble
at once over the rule banning Issei from election to the councils. By
denying Issei, "the respected elders," the right to be elected to the
community councils, the War Relocation Authority virtually guaranteed
that the councils would be a bone of bitter contention.

At Poston I, acting on the WRA's assurance that "it will be up to each community to plan its design of community life,'' the director and the evacuees had agreed on a civic planning board made up of Issei and Nisei to draw up a constitution for the center. At that point they learned of the June 5 memorandum from the WRA that stipulated that Issei were barred for election to the community councils. The planning board thereupon disbanded and was replaced by an "elected" community council made up of thirty-six Nisei, all but one of whom were under forty. Amid denunciations as "administration stooges" the council undertook to function as an intermediary between the evacuees and the administration. At Minidoka no council was elected at all because of the staff's unwillingness to fly in the face of general resentment at the exclusion of the Issei. An Organization Commission, which had been set up to draft a charter of self-government and which contained a majority of Issei, functioned in lieu of a community council. Seven members were chosen from a list of candidates nominated by delegates elected from each block. The council had an executive committee of seven members and a consulting and advisory body of thirty-five, most of them Issei. The fact was, the notion of an advisory board of Issei indeed enjoyed a degree of popularity as one way of getting around the ban. At several centers it soon became clear that the Issei advisory board rather than the Nisei community council exercised the real power.

Manzanar went its own way. Rejecting the form of a representative community council, it relied on a kind of town hall of block delegates who served as an advisory group for the project director.

At Heart Mountain and Granada the evacuees undertook to form a kind of two-house legislature. The upper house, composed of Issei, would advise the lower house, composed of Nisei. When this plan was forwarded to Washington, it was vetoed as an evasion of the community council. At most centers the Issei ban resulted in a series of proposals intended to give proper weight to the Issei. When one was rejected by Washington, another designed to accomplish the same end was proposed. It became, in some centers, a kind of game. If it was not exactly what the planners had in mind, it was certainly democratic.

Gila River evacuees drew up a resolution protesting the ban on the election of Issei. After arguing that the rule tended to divide the centers along generational lines, the drafters observed a little disingenuously that the noncitizens had "assimilated many of the finer American ideals''; that they had "worked continuously in America ever since coming to this country; they brought up their children to be loyal American citizens, many of whom now serve in the Armed Forces of the Nation; they also bought property and invested heavily in War Bonds with the intention of permanently making this country their home.''

The resolution was forwarded to Dillon Myer, who replied with an explanation of the reasoning behind the rule. It had been decided that citizenship should be given special recognition so that it would be more valued by the alien Japanese. "We understand," Myer wrote, ". . . that a few among the alien evacuees have been taunting the young Nisei with [the] fact [that their citizenship] . . . was valueless. It is our intention, therefore, to help make up for this fact, as much as possible, by giving special recognition to the citizenship status of the Nisei.'' Myer's reply only added fuel to the fire.

It was at Heart Mountain that the whole notion of the self-governing community was most directly challenged. The "charter commission" at Heart Mountain raised a basic question: "Is this real self-government, or is it only so-called self-government?" The commission then stated "if it is going to be real self-government, then it is O.K. If it is going to be a self-government in name only, we do not want it.'' The latter was clearly the case. In all final decisions, in all matters directly affecting the center's future, the administration had the final world. That being the case, the commission asked itself, and by extension the other residents of the center, "Why is it that members agreed to support a document which they know is not really self-government?" The answer offered was: "First, within a relocation center where freedom of the residents is restricted, is it possible to ask for self-government? Secondly, perchance that such complete self-government is granted, is it advisable for the evacuees to fully exercise such right?" "After thorough discussion" the commission decided that it was impossible to ask for complete self-government and if, by some odd chance, the residents were given complete self-government, they would be unable, through inexperience and a wide variety of constraints, to exercise it effectively.

With the blocks as the basic social units of the centers, it was perhaps inevitable that "block managers," originally appointed by the directors to perform a kind of liaison function between evacuees and the administration, should become increasingly political. Those chosen were almost invariably evacuees who could speak English. Their responsibility was "to distribute supplies and materials, to maintain records, to conduct censuses, and to perform a myriad of other tasks which had direct relation to the welfare and comfort of the residents of his block." It was a logical step for the residents of the blocks to demand that the block managers, if they were to represent the blocks, be elected by the block residents rather than appointed by the directors. Once elected, the block managers soon became a consultive or advisory body. When they had assumed that function they were clearly competitors with the community councils.

The block managers were initially resisted by many of the program directors and their staffs because they constituted a form of internal "government" opposed to community councils. An additional complication was that the block managers were usually, in line with Japanese respect for the elders, Issei, who were not allowed to be elected to the councils. In Heart Mountain, Masuo Akizuki, who had organized a San Jose baseball league before Pearl Harbor, was chosen block manager. He taught the use of sewing machines and became chief of the "electrical department." That office enabled him to hook up an illicit shortwave radio that kept the residents informed of the claims of the Imperial Army of countless victories.

Finally, there was the fact the block managers represented their blocks "monolithically." That is to say, if a majority of the members of a particular block, or the more powerful and influential members of a block, held a certain point of view or represented a certain position, it was generally represented as the opinion of the entire block. In other words, there was little or no room for individual expressions of opinion (Kiuni Sugiyama recalled that some block managers were referred to by evacuees who disagreed with them as "blockheads").

The Gila River center developed a block council composed of one representative of each barrack elected by the residents plus the head chef. The block council was to work for "the improvement of the grounds of the block, recreation for the residents of the block, health and sanitation for the block, the need of preventing fire hazards, the adjustment of problems that arise among the residents of the block."

The intriguing aspect of this development was that while it ran counter to the planners' intention to develop the evacuees' experience in democracy—the notion of the centers as "schools of democracy"—the block management system, devised primarily by the evacuees, or at least developed by them, demonstrated precisely that democratic spirit that the planners had hoped to engender and was thus a far better lesson in democracy than a system, however democratically structured, that was imposed from above.

True to the history of such ventures, it took some time for the administrators to accept this spontaneous expression of democracy in preference to the preconceived ideas of how the centers could best stimulate democracy. Some never did and continued to try to make the community coun-

cils function in accordance with the plan. It must also be said that the
block councils had their obvious limitations. There were, from the point
of view of the administration, many issues that required to be addressed
by the center's evacuee population as a whole and this plainly could best
be done by some form of community council.

Under pressure from Washington, the project directors did their best to
promote community councils. One of the principal tasks of the councils,
once they were in operation, was to appoint an "organization commission," whose duty it was to organize the centers, a formidable undertaking. At Gila River, ten commissions were established: a judicial
commission, a juvenile board, juvenile guidance commission, recreation
association, health board, public relations committee, manpower commission, resettlement advisory committee, food committee, and community fund committee. At Rohwer, there were committees for agriculture,
education, food, fuel, investigations, and welfare, a judicial commission,
and a labor relations board.

In the effort to protect the principle of self-government, one notion
after another was advanced. For virtually every problem or every function
of the center administration an evacuee committee was proposed. Besides
the board of police commissioners, evacuee boards were proposed to be
concerned with the purchase and preparation of food (there being constant complaints about the type of food, commonly not enough fish) and
its preparation, along with a committee on "future planning" (as though
the centers were to have any future) and library use and resources.

The judicial committee in the different centers varied widely in effectiveness. For the most part, the committees were concerned with minor
infractions of rules or with discouraging behavior viewed unfavorably by
the residents. Cases involving traffic violations, gambling, petty theft,
and assault were heard and punishments meted out. At one center, juveniles who were considered troublemakers were forced to give up their
modish zoot suits and required to have their hair cut.

At another center, the community council recommended the use of
community funds to construct a building to show movies but the residents
of the center voted against the proposal, perhaps because they suspected
the movies would, directly or indirectly, be propaganda for the U.S.
cause.

At two centers, community councils adopted resolutions limiting the
amount of money that could be given as gifts at weddings, funerals, and
on other occasions. The intention was to discourage lavish gift giving,
which, it was felt by the council, was inappropriate in the relatively

spartan conditions of the centers. Since gift giving was one of the most basic Japanese social customs, the resolutions had little effect.

In the matter of evacuees taking responsibility for their own affairs, this was expressed initially, and thereafter more or less continuously, in the form of requests for goods and services that the evacuees found missing or deficient. Thus at the Gila River center in August 1942 a resolution, generated by the evacuees on their own initiative, requested street lighting; completion of a water system so that the grounds could be watered and their appearance thereby improved; that tables and chairs be provided for the apartments; and the screening of windows and laundry rooms. The group also requested the establishment of a canteen that would be owned and financed by the evacuees and operated on a nonprofit basis. That was certainly an exercise in democracy. The request for the purchase and distribution of wearing apparel and even such a simple item as scarcity of laundry soap got their attention. They requested recreation programs and the prompt establishment of schools for the children. There should also be provision for religious services for the various faiths represented in the center. A reference to "religious gatherings" (as contrasted with services) suggested that at least some of the evacuees were already caught in the social life of the typical American congregation. One of the most significant requests was for the speedy completion of hospital facilities.

Finally, in a complaint that was common to all the evacuees in all the centers, the Gila River group protested strongly the exclusion of noncitizens, the Issei, the parents and elders, from elective office.

One of the most arresting comments in Spicer's report *Community Government* is the observation that no substantial number of the "residents" were "either entirely in favor of or vitally interested in" the establishment of self-government in the centers. "The vast majority . . . remained disinterested spectators."

The evacuee identified only as "A" echoed Spicer's observation. "A" estimated that out of the roughly nine thousand evacuees in each center, no more than seventy or eighty were actively involved with center government. These were, in the main, block managers and the more experienced and confident individuals who spoke English and who had had businesses or professions that brought them in contact with Caucasians in the years prior to the war. They constituted the liaison between the Issei in the blocks and the administrative staff. But in the volatile emotional state that prevailed, they walked a narrow path filled with potential hazards. Those who preserved their leadership roles developed complicated strategies for keeping their balance between the various evacuee factions and the administration. If they appeared to be too cooperative, too active in representing an administration point of view or in trying to persuade the residents of their block or ward to accept any new War Relocation Authority policy, they risked being accused of acting as tools of the administration, of being administration "stooges," or "dogs." Conversely, if they pressed the wishes of the evacuees too aggressively with the administrators, they were apt to be written off as troublemakers. In the best of circumstances, these liaison men, whether elected by their blocks or appointed by the project director, developed a bond of trust and understanding with both the project directors and evacuees.

In the words of one evacuee: "Most blocks at first had at least a few outspoken men or women who were vigorously anti-administration in attitude. In block meetings they urged resistance to . . . most things that the administration wanted done. . . . They urged flat resistance and always found some support from among block people." The liaison men, in contrast, did their best to try to convince the residents of their blocks that such tactics were self-defeating and, if followed, would destroy any hope of creating "peaceful centers." At the same time, the liaison men "had constantly to be aware of the need for obtaining some concession from the administration, however small, in any moves that threatened the stability evacuees had so far attained in the centers." In other words, close bargaining was a requirement for a liaison figure to retain credibility with the residents of his block.

The would-be leaders who most rapidly lost credibility with their fellow evacuees were those who urged cooperation with the center administration. In Spicer's words: "It was evident that certain types of men could not for long function in positions of community leadership. Men who vigorously pushed unconditional participation in the American war effort, who followed without question all the features of the program as laid out by the Government agencies, who attempted to take seriously the regulation excluding the Issei from elective office, or who were insensitive to the Issei problems of status in Japan and the United States—men with such beliefs or qualities could not function effectively as leaders."

The successful liaison figures were not usually men who had been prominent in the Japanese social and patriotic associations. Those leaders were, typically, Issei, who seldom spoke or understood English. Many of them were known to the FBI and other intelligence agencies because of their leadership roles in patriotic organizations; they had, in many cases, been picked up by the FBI, incarcerated for a time, and released to an assembly or, later, relocation center. For the most part such individuals lay low in the centers and while they had considerable influence, particularly on the side of noncooperation, they did not become visible until the last phase of center life.

AS NOTED EARLIER, THE WRA'S RESETTLEMENT PROGRAM, DESIGNED TO get evacuees out of the centers and into jobs and homes, caused an uproar in the centers. Dismayed by the resistance to resettlement, Dillon Myer went to Poston early in November to explain and defend the program. The volatile state of evacuee emotions was demonstrated soon after his arrival. His speech was received tumultuously; it turned out that John Collier, commissioner of the Bureau of Indian Affairs, whose agency was operating Poston under contract with the WRA, had spoken at Poston a week earlier and had emphasized the importance of building a strong community committed to a program of irrigation and land development, a project, he stated, that would benefit the Indians on the reservation for generations to come. Collier's talk was reassuring to the residents since it implied that they would have a safe haven on the reservation for the duration of the war. Myer's speech, which defended the resettlement program, in effect contradicted Collier. The more militant evacuees made much of the contradiction as an example of government perfidy and arbitrary action. The Myer visit thus added fuel to the fire of general dissatisfaction. Edward Spicer blamed the "combination of heat, dust, primitive facilities, broken promises and factional conflict" for the eruption that followed.

Factional conflict was clearly the spark that ignited the conflagration. One of the members of the community council, a prominent JACLer, had been the target of angry militants. On November 18, he was so severely beaten that he had to be hospitalized. The FBI was called in to arrest the attackers. Not surprisingly, no one would talk. After some poking about, two young men were arrested and put in the center jail. One was a popular judo expert; the other was described as "a civic-minded young man . . . active in community affairs." In any event, evidence against them was scanty and the arrests caused general outrage in the center. The feeling was that both men were innocent but had little hope of justice if they were tried in a regular civil court. There were demands that the two be released at once. The community council after several feverish sessions requested that they be released "until such time as an evacuee court could hear the charges against them." The project director was absent and his understudy felt that he did not have the authority to act in his place. Request refused. The members of the community council thereupon resigned along with the Issei advisory board. The residents formed their own body, a committee of seventy-two, with one Nisei and one Issei from each block. This body decided on a general strike although it was not clear at first what form such a strike would take.

After heated discussions it was decided to block access to the center jail, thereby preventing the removal of the two men. The speed and efficiency with which the residents' organization moved to assert itself was impressive. A central executive committee composed of four Issei and four Nisei took over the day-to-day direction of the strike. The staff was at a loss as to what course to take. Some urged that the military police be called in to disperse the crowd with tear gas and restore order but cooler heads prevailed and the project director, Wade Head, turned his attention to finding some way to initiate negotiations with the strike leaders. Meanwhile, the center was organized into round-the-clock watches at the jail. Blocks assigned members to maintain the blockade and flags were made bearing the insignia of each block. Pictures of individuals who were believed to have been too compliant with the administration were posted around the center. The situation was ideally suited for the noncooperators. They gave frequent inflammatory speeches, denouncing the evacuation, the policies of the government, the conditions in the centers, and the personal character of the director. Japanese music blared over the public address system; those individuals who tried to speak in English were shouted down. There was a kind of wild outpouring of Japanese spirit, an invoking of old gods and sacred symbols. For the moment, divisions were forgotten or suppressed. Staff members who tried to visit friends among the evacuees were coldly received or asked to leave lest their presence cast suspicion on the evacuees as collaborators. They might be beaten if they were friendly with Caucasians. A line had been drawn and in the words of Edward Spicer, the author of *Impounded People:* "No one crossed the line even for a moment without intense consciousness of it."

After a feverish week of negotiations, the strike leaders and the project director reached agreement on a number of issues. The strike leaders insisted that what they wanted was genuine representation of the residents whatever such a body might be called. They agreed that law and order must prevail and that violent acts could not be condoned. One of the suspects was released for lack of evidence and it was agreed that the other should be tried by the center's judicial committee.

The director gave a conciliatory talk to the crowd, still guarding the jail, and the strike was declared over.

The Committee of 72 proposed a series of committees or commissions. An honor court was to be established as well as a labor relations board. A city planning board was given broad powers (vetoed by the administration). For a time the focus shifted from specific demands to political issues when a faction of the nationalists tried to overthrow the central executive committee and failed. For the rest of the life of the center, the "pattern of organization" developed during the strike persisted. The community council, for all practical purposes, was dead at Poston. Isuma Nakamura noted that as a result of the strike, which he, incidentally, did not sympathize with, the food improved noticeably: "We got a boiled egg, toast and coffee for breakfast. For lunch we had rice with a side dish of cooked vegetables with a sprinkle of meat."

News of the Poston I upheaval spread to all the other centers and exacerbated already tense feelings. Manzanar was a pot waiting to boil over. There the block managers had constituted a semi-official governing body called the Block Leaders Council made up of Issei and Nisei that maintained liaison with the director. The center simply ignored the June 5 instruction barring Issei from election to the community council; the Block Leaders Council changed its name to the Block Managers Assembly and functioned as before.

Manzanar had more than its share of militants. Their leaders included three evacuees we have already met: Joe Kurihari, the World War I veteran, embittered by the evacuation; Henry Ueno, a Kibei; and Tom Watanabe. Watanabe's wife died in childbirth in the Manzanar hospital, as did the twin daughters she gave birth to. Her death increased his bitterness. A member of the center staff named Campbell had done his best to persuade Ueno to go out, promising him a good job with a millionaire friend, but both Ueno and his wife had no intention of leaving. Ueno taunted Campbell; he was happy in the center; he had a following; he had influence. He would soon demonstrate his influence.

Frank Masuda and Mike Masaoka, both prominent in the JACL, had formed the Manzanar Citizens Federation with the avowed purpose of trying to work harmoniously with the administration of Manzanar. All they got for their pains were accusations of currying favor with the director and betraying their fellow evacuees. On December 5, 1942, Masuda, a former restaurant owner, was seriously beaten. The next day several evacuees identified by Masuda as among those who had beaten him were arrested. They included Dick Miwa, a Kibei who was a cook and who had been active in organizing a union of kitchen workers. Miwa had accused the Caucasian chief steward of being in cahoots with the assistant project director in stealing sugar from the center to sell on the black market. Miwa was arrested and put in jail in nearby Independence. Joe Kirihara at once called a meeting of all evacuees, set up a public address system, and announced a series of "demands" to be presented to the director. The principal demand called for the unconditional release of Miwa and action against Masuda and other *inu*. During the meeting death lists of other suspected *inu,* most of them identified with the JACL, were read out to the crowd. Among them were Togo Tanaka and Joe Grant Masaoka, the older brother of Mike Masaoka. One speaker announced that he and his allies would "do a lot of killing tonight unless Miwa was released," declaring defiantly that as "true Japanese . . . we should not be afraid to die in this cause as our brothers are dying for justice and permanent peace and the new order in Asia." The charge was made that Miwa had been framed by Masuda and the director because of his demand for an investigation of the alleged sugar thefts. The crowd then voted to go on strike the next day unless Miwa was released. The director, Ralph Merritt, met with the leaders of the protest and agreed to bring Miwa back to the center but insisted that he must be kept in the center jail until the charges against him had been investigated. Dissatisfied, the protesters called for another meeting at six in the evening.

By one account, the evening meeting was turned into a celebration of the Japanese victory at Pearl Harbor. The JACLers were once more denounced as "dogs" and the cry was raised, "Let's go and kill those guys."

A night of terror followed. Ralph and Mary Smeltzer were conscientious objectors and teachers at Manzanar when the riot started. In Mary Smeltzer's words: "A friend two doors down from us came over frantically asking Ralph to find her husband who was hiding from the mob at his brother's apartment and to take him to the guard house for safety." Ralph found the frightened man, had him crouch down on the floor of his car, drove without lights through the center, and then "made a beeline across a field to the outside-guard house. . . . About sixty were rescued from the camp during the night and housed in the military compound," Mary Smeltzer recalled.

"That night," Watanbe declared later, "they had a meeting in Block 2 mess hall, and the Issei, you know them diehards, they say what we should do is go against the MPs and take away the rifle and this and that."

At a meeting the next morning, the mood of the crowd was still decidedly rebellious. The call was made for the assassination of some eleven or twelve *inu.* The first name read off was that of Masuda. He should be taken from the hospital and killed, one speaker declared to loud applause. At that point the crowd split, with one group headed for the hospital to kill Masuda, the other for the project jail, where Miwa was now imprisoned as a concession to the militants. Masuda was hidden under a hospital bed, doubtlessly saving his life. Frustrated there, the crowd searched randomly for other *inu,* and failing to find any on the death list, turned back to the jail, where a squad of frightened MPs was drawn up around the jail. At this point Merritt authorized the commanding officer of the military police to declare martial law, and soldiers were called in to protect the MPs and force the crowd back from the jail. Someone remembered the sergeant in charge yelling to his jittery, young MPs, "Hold your line. Remember Pearl Harbor."

Pushed back from the jail by the soldiers, the crowd jeered and taunted them. The soldiers thereupon put on their gas masks and threw tear gas grenades at the crowd to disperse it. People fled in every direction, then regrouped and returned to the fray. At that point a soldier fired without orders. Again evacuees fled. One evacuee started a parked car, placed a weight on the accelerator, put the car in gear, headed it for a machine gun, and leaped out. The car veered away and crashed into the police station while the machine gunner fired several bursts at it as it careened across the yard. Ten evacuees were hit by bullets fired by the soldiers and one evacuee died shortly after he was hit. When the dead and wounded were brought to the hospital, the crowd tried to force its way in, but Frank Chuman, an evacuee employed in the hospital, stood them down, insisting that only hospital staff could enter.

The Nisei who was killed had a brother serving in the United States Army. A second evacuee died five days later. Military police and National Guardsmen patrolled the center while the evacuees rang bells in the blocks all night long.

The next morning black armbands were distributed to evacuees by the rebel leaders and strong pressure was brought to bear to force all residents of the center to wear some article of mourning until the funeral of the Nisei who had died. Mothers were told that their children would be treated as *inu* unless they wore the bands.

A few days later Masuda, Masaoka, Tanaka, and some twenty others on the death list were taken with their families to an abandoned Civilian Conservation Corps camp in Death Valley and subsequently resettled. Miwa, Joe Kurihara, and other ringleaders were arrested. The Issei among them were sent to Department of Justice internment camps as enemy aliens and the Nisei were sent to a War Relocation Authority isolation camp at Moab, Utah.

The fact that so many of those supporting the administration had to be sent out of the center was in itself a serious setback to Merritt and his staff. It seemed to many people in and out of the center that he had in effect capitulated to the pro-Japanese faction and tacitly acknowledged that he was unable to protect those evacuees who had been outspoken in their support of him. The conclusion seemed to be that as long as there was no further outbreak of violence, the center would be firmly in the hands of the anti-administration if not anti-U.S. faction. And it was essentially on those terms that a degree of order was restored.

Like most such episodes there are a dozen versions of what took place, among them that the crowd had been ordered to disperse and was doing so when the MPs opened fire. Even the number of dead and wounded is in dispute. Three dead and twenty-three wounded, some accounts say. Two dead and nine wounded, say others.

In the investigation that followed a crucial question was whether the crowd was advancing on the MPs with the intention of mobbing them: Had the killed and wounded been shot in the front of their bodies (in which case the assumption would be that they were advancing on the soldiers) or in the rear (which would support the contention that they were withdrawing in response to the order to disperse)? The doctor doing the autopsy reported that all of the victims, the dead and the wounded, had been struck in the side and back. According to Frank Chuman, an effort was made to persuade the doctor who had performed the autopsy to change his report from side and back to front, and because he refused he was relieved of his duties as chief of the medical staff.

As may well be imagined, the events at Poston and Manzanar caused much soul-searching on the part of the War Relocation Authority. In late December 1942 the director's office issued a memorandum that showed a clearer understanding of the real situation of the centers than earlier such documents. After reviewing the difficulty of preserving the remnants of self-government in the face of the "disturbances," the memorandum went on to state: "Significant government, after all, should not consist of an enumerated list of specific powers, but be the opportunity for people to concern themselves with the problems which are of major importance in their lives. Let us examine some of these problems and see which of them might possibly become a function of government." The paragraph was a kind of tacit admission that the original plan for self-government had proved impractical for reasons, in the main, beyond anticipation by the planners and, subsequently, beyond the control of the administrators.

The project directors were asked, among other things, "who among the evacuees was either opposing or favoring community government?" All of the project directors were in accord that the barring of Issei from holding elective office was the greatest barrier to any sensible notion of self-government. In the words of one director: "The Issei refuse to accept the administration's opinion that citizens alone can hold office. They feel that citizenship status is irrelevant in a relocation center and since all Japanese were relocated and treated in a similar manner, all should be entitled to hold office. Had Issei been permitted to hold office, much of the present unrest would have been obviated, the Issei stated. Issei participation would have enabled them to direct [evacuee] energies into productive, loyal channels." Whether or not the influence of the Issei would have directed the energies of the Nisei into loyal channels, the Issei may very well have persuaded the Nisei to be more discreet.

The same director noted that "the Nisei felt that the present organization tends to intensify the growing cleavage between the two groups. This cleavage is so significant that at times all issues are decided within the community solely on that basis without reference to substance."

Ralph Merritt, the project director at Manzanar, wrote that the agitation of a majority of the evacuees for further self-government "deserves serious open-minded consideration by the Authority." The evacuees questioned "the sincerity of any plan of self-government prepared and limited by the authorities above, whose authority includes the maintenance of a barbed wire fence as visual evidence of the actual complete lack of the fundamentals of self-government. Their view boils down to the conclusion that it is silly for mature men to spend time playing with dolls."

Wade Head, director at Poston, took the opposite view. He reported that a number of staff members shared the opinion that self-government was a sham and believed that it complicated the running of the centers. It would have been, they declared, "easier to have run the center dictatorially with all rules and policies established by the administration and without consultation with the residents, and that the [existence] of community government, democratic practices and evacuee participation increased the difficulties of administering the center."

A memorandum to John Provinse, a member of the WRA staff, from Solon Kimball, head of the Community Management Division, on January 8, 1943, expressed an increasingly common point of view: "My observation,'' Kimball wrote, ''has been that our administration has been too 'good,' too perfect. We have over-planned and over-directed. We have not allowed sufficient outlet for aggressiveness through actual participation in running a project, so that the aggressiveness when expressed is against the 'loyal' group, and I suspect in the future may be directed against us. I think we need to loosen up our administrative organization to permit more of the planning (and mistakes) to come from the bottom.'' Kimball recommended ''the creation of evacuee committees to study special problems and make recommendations.'' Kimball conceded that the ''Issei may be and probably are the real power in the community.'' Functioning in an advisory capacity ''they could provide advice to the younger and more American Nisei group.''

In Poston, the Nisei who emerged as chairman of the community council wrote a memorandum entitled ''One of Poston's Problems.'' In it he attacked the performance of the Caucasian staff, arguing that there were evacuees who could carry out these responsibilities much more efficiently than the administrators. The Poston council was so pleased with the memorandum that it had it mimeographed, distributed to the Poston staff, and dispatched to the councils at the other centers. The project director responded sympathetically to the memorandum, stating that he supported the idea of giving the evacuees as much responsibility as possible and reclassifying all positions that evacuees could fill satisfactorily.

The action of the Poston council chairman encouraged like-minded evacuees in other centers to take a similar position. They in effect rejected the original model developed by the War Relocation Authority of close cooperation between center staff and evacuee leaders in favor of a more adversarial approach. ''Demands'' gradually replaced ''requests'' and the tone of the centers became more argumentative with leaders on the alert for issues that offered political leverage. Evacuee ad hoc committees were formed to evaluate staff performance in various areas of center life.

In Edward Spicer's words, the events at Poston and Manzanar ''affected the other eight centers profoundly.'' Their principal effect was to deepen existing divisions and heighten tensions between evacuees and center administrations. Now every issue in the centers—food, the quality of medical care, the water supply, the disposal of garbage—became a political issue. In Poston the Union of Kitchen Workers anchored the radical wing of the evacuees. One would be tempted to say that the riots marked the ''end of innocence'' in the WRA staff were it not for the fact that, as subsequent events were to indicate, the WRA's innocence was invincible. There were, of course, further consequences of the Poston and Manzanar events. Widely reported in the media, the riots provided welcome ammunition to those hostile to Japanese Americans in general. There were renewed calls for "internment" as opposed to "relocation," and for the army to take over the centers on the grounds that the War Relocation Authority was too soft on the evacuees. A far more serious consequence was that the attitude of the War Department itself hardened; Gullion, Bendetsen, and DeWitt pressed the WRA for greater restrictions. The resettlement effort was slowed down and, most serious of all, any hope for lifting the exclusionary ban on Military Areas No. 1 and No. 2, a move essential, in the view of Myer and his staff, to the success of the resettlement campaign, was indefinitely postponed.

THE CHAIRMAN OF THE TOPAZ COMMUNITY COUNCIL IN MARCH 1943, IN cooperation with his counterpart at Poston, drafted a letter to Dillon Myer making four principal requests. The first was that the evacuees have a representative in Washington to advise on policy at the source. In addition there was a request for transportation expenses to "job destinations" for evacuees relocating and for "machinery to secure temporary loans after arriving" because most evacuees were without sufficient funds to set themselves up in new locations. The most poignant request was that the government not penalize " 'teenage' youths without giving them the opportunity to correct themselves." This request pointed to one of the most agonizing aspects of Nisei rebellion—the fear among the Issei parents that whatever their own loyalties, their sons were hopelessly compromising their futures in America in the event of an Allied victory. Finally, the chairman was concerned that the policy of relocating evacuees out of the centers would cause a severe manpower shortage in the centers themselves.

On April 19, Dillon Myer lifted the ban on Issei serving on community councils, and it was announced in the centers a few days later. Thereupon new community council charters were drawn up in six centers and approved by vote of the residents. It was soon evident that the change, which was understandably taken by the evacuees as a triumph over the authority, did little to improve the effectiveness of the councils. Their members were keenly aware that they were sailing in rough waters. They were, for the most part, determined to avoid any effort by the center administrators to use them to effect political ends.

In Spicer's view, the residents of the centers expected the community

councils "to maintain toward administrative action [which is to say toward the administration] an attitude compounded of latent hostility and
eternal vigilance, and to make occasional strong protests." The project
administrator, on the other hand, saw it as a group "created to explain
policy and procedure in favorable terms to the residents and to assist the
administration in achieving its objectives." In short, there was a hopelessly irreconcilable difference in the way the two parties, administrators
and evacuees, viewed the role of the community councils. In the words
of one unhappy project director: "From all appearances the council seems
to be undergoing that process of disintegration which besets every attempt
to set up a liaison group between the administrator and the administered.
Because of necessity the administration must rule by fiat, the residents, at
first optimistic, soon recognize the fact that the liaison has not the power
to enforce the residents' interests when these interests are counter to the
administration's. The net result is that the liaison group, afraid of arousing the residents' overt animosity, becomes progressively more cautious
and, as its reliance upon buck-passing increases, progressively less effective in furthering administrative policies."

Another serious problem that developed in the centers and that contributed directly to an overheated political atmosphere was the fact that
evacuees were employed in various tasks having to do both with the
internal operation of the centers and, as we have seen, with industrial and
agricultural production on a large scale. Many of the evacuees, especially
those with attachment to the Emperor, did not wish to work or cooperate
in any way with the center administration. The initial plan of the WRA
had assumed that everyone in the centers would be engaged in some
productive work. As has been noted, the War Relocation Authority planners had the naive notion that the evacuees could be employed in cottage
industries that would contribute to the overall war effort. This hope was
soon abandoned but there was still, in most centers, a kind of compulsion
to have evacuees working, in part on the not unreasonable assumption
that the devil makes work for idle hands. Most of the evacuees, however,
had no interest in or intention of doing any work other than that necessary
to keep the centers going and contribute directly to their own comfort and
welfare. In the words of one block leader, "the people [of his block]
regarded work as something for the welfare of the community and nothing more. . . . Work that went beyond the routine needs of the center
residents was the administration's interest, and evacuees had no particular
obligation in connection with it."

The attitude of the project directors, on the other hand, was that if the evacuees were unwilling, for example, to collect the garbage, the garbage would lie uncollected until they undertook to collect it. When orders came down from Washington that gasoline must be conserved in the centers and driving curtailed, the drivers of various vehicles protested vigorously, even threatening to strike. In this instance, the problem was resolved by patiently explaining to the drivers that they had an obligation to the other residents to conserve gas so that essential operations such as the delivery of food to the dining halls, the transportation of workers to their job sites, and the use of vehicles for funerals and weddings could be carried on. In the words of the report, "With only minor protests from some of the evacuee drivers, a marked reduction in the consumption of gasoline was achieved." In a similar vein, "threats on the part of . . . drivers of coal or food trucks to strike unless their demands were met were frequently ignored [by the program directors] who took the position that this was an operation of direct concern to the community, and if coal was not delivered or food provided to the mess halls, then the people would freeze or starve."

A classic case of project director–community council deadlock occurred at Minidoka, normally one of the least contentious centers. It involved the construction of a gymnasium and when the controversy was over there was more than enough discredit to go around.

A gymnasium had been requested by the residents, plans drawn up, and construction started. Building lagged because of a higher priority given to hog pens and hen houses. When complaints began to filter in from impatient residents, the project director responded by suggesting a "Build the Gym Week" in which everyone would pitch in to complete the structure. The response was negative. Only a few staff people appeared and no residents, the latter presumably believing that it was the responsibility of "the government" to provide the labor to build the gymnasium. At this point, the project director announced that if the community, through the council, was unwilling or unable to muster the labor to complete the gym, it would simply be boarded up and left uncompleted. This diktat offended the members of the community council, who felt that they were being coerced. Their honor impunged, they threatened to resign because of the "dictatorial" attitude of the project director. The chairman of the council pointed out that the losers in this case would be the residents themselves and especially the children and young people, who would be the principal users of the gymnasium. At the same time the council addressed an indignant letter to the director, stating: "The council has gone on record, unanimously as regretting and resenting the fact that you have chosen to approach the council with an 'or else' ultimatum. . . . We fail to understand the psychology which prompted you to adopt such tactics in dealing with the council; surely you are not so naive as to believe that either the council, or the evacuee residents as a whole can best be moved to action under the brunt of dictatorial ultimatums.''

Another paragraph followed laying the blame squarely on the shoulders of Harry Stafford, the project director, but ending by agreeing to recruit additional workers and doing all in the council's power to speed the project.

Stafford, in his report to higher headquarters, noted that his ultimatum "put the council members on the spot insofar as they were, for a change, unable to pass the buck either back to the administration or on to any other group of residents. This is not to say they did not try. . . . The gym . . . will be completed December 30.'' The prediction proved premature and the reason is also worth noting. The evacuee foreman resented the unwillingness of Caucasian supervisors to accept his directions. He quit and the evacuee crew quit with him. At this point the council addressed the national director as follows: ''The council was required to accept responsibility for the construction of the gymnasium, but it was never consulted thereafter before changes were made, and its advice calculated to avoid trouble was not accepted. The prolonged attempt to reconcile the stands of the administration and the workers has resulted in general demoralization of those who took part in the arbitration, and a further reduction of confidence in the council on the part of both the administration and the residents. If this final attempt at settlement of a relatively minor issue fails, it is clear that the usefulness of the council in aiding a smoother relationship between the administration and the residents has approached its end. With a number of difficult problems already in sight, there seems to be little use for the present members to stay in office if this matter cannot be solved.''

The Washington office, understandably, refused to intervene, the council stood on a point of honor, the gymnasium was not completed, and the indignant residents held a mock funeral for the chairman of the council and wrote on his "tombstone" "an administrative stooge and dog,'' whereas the chairman was convinced that he and the council had been acting to uphold the dignity of the residents against an authoritarian director.

Under such circumstances it was hardly surprising that the beleaguered project directors often wondered who was in charge, the directors or the evacuees.

Undoubtedly, one of the factors that contributed greatly to the "unmanageability" of the centers (aside from the fact that the WRA officials in Washington and the center staffs hadn't, in the main, a clue to the Japanese psychology) was the extraordinary social and economic diversity of the evacuees (the JERS staff identified eighty-eight subgroups). They ranged in class from the despised *eta* (the lowest social class in Japan) to families of ancient samurai lineage like the Wakatsukis; from largely illiterate Issei bachelors to wealthy farmers, businessmen, lawyers, doctors, professors, artists; the rich and the poor and those in between; the Christians and the Buddhists (and a few Shintoists). Moreover, the leaders of the nationalist factions were often former Japanese army and navy officers who enjoyed great prestige among the humbler ranks and were thus able to exercise influence far beyond their numbers.

Chapter 18

RESETTLEMENT

A FRUSTRATED DILLON MYER SOON DISCOVERED THAT HIS HOPES FOR prompt resettlement and a rapid phasing out of the centers were doomed to disappointment. Like everything else, resettlement became a political issue. The militant nationalists denounced it unsparingly and did all they could to dissuade other evacuees from resettling. There were, of course, formidable practical difficulties, the foremost of which was a widespread hostility to the Japanese, who were perceived as allied, in one degree or another, with the enemy. How were evacuees to find jobs and places to live in cities and towns where anti-Japanese feeling was often strong?

The WRA was well aware of the problems involved. H. Rex Lee, a member of the War Relocation Authority staff in charge of the seasonal (or work) leave program, was assigned the job of establishing the first area resettlement (or relocation) office in Salt Lake City. The first Midwestern field office was opened in Chicago on January 4, 1943, followed by offices in Cleveland, Minneapolis, Des Moines, Milwaukee, New York City, and, subsequently, a number of other cities. By June 30, 1943, field offices had been opened from Spokane to Boston. The first job of the offices was to create "favorable community acceptance." In Myer's words, "The officers gave talks to business, professional, social, civic, church and fraternal groups. They met with employers individually and in groups, enlisted the aid of unions, and spoke to employees in plants where the employment of Japanese was contemplated.'' Most important of all, perhaps, they formed committees of local residents to assist (and sometimes to virtually take over) the relocation of evacuees. ''We would spend the most of our energy on locating interested people, advising on the organization of committees, providing educational material on evacuation and relocation, and supplying local sponsors with information about the occupational background of evacuees who wanted to relocate.''

Baffled by the resistance of the evacuees to resettlement, Myer was determined to persevere. In Edward Spicer's words: ''It was felt by many [of the planners and administrators] that a combination of pressure, salesmanship, and incentives would do the job.'' But only a trickle of evacuees responded. Perhaps more counselors were needed. More were trained and dispatched to centers. Perhaps more translators. More were provided. More monetary incentives. More were offered. A family counseling service was hastily instituted but as one of the series of memoranda made clear, the purpose of the family counselor was not to apply pressure ''to force people to relocate. Its major objective was the transmittal of reliable information . . . and through the interviewing technique, to relieve [the evacuees] of many psychological blocks.'' Evacuees were assured that if they resettled, they would have all the possessions that they had accumulated in the centers shipped to their new homes, as well as whatever household furnishings and personal belongings they may have been fortunate enough to have found secure storage for prior to their evacuation. Job training, legal advice, assistance in negotiating loans to start up business ventures would also be available. Each evacuee relocated out got $50 for expenses to his or her new location (one could hardly say ''home''), $75 if there was one dependent, $100 if there were two or more, $3 per diem while en route, plus coach fare.

However benign and well-intentioned the counseling program was, it involved an interview process and the collection of data about the evacuee and his or her family. It thus appeared in the minds of many evacuees as an unwelcome intrusion in their private lives. It did not occur to the planners of the WRA, habituated, like most Americans, to mountains of forms and endless questionnaires, that their Japanese clients might react with resentment and suspicion. Each new effort to explain to the evacuees the advantages of resettling, advantages that seemed so evident to the authority and its representatives, appeared to the residents, as they might now well be called, as attempts to bring more pressure on them to leave the centers. Their resistance called to mind a popular Broadway play of the era called *The Man Who Came to Dinner*. The man who came to dinner because of various, on the whole fanciful, ailments, refused to leave and became a most unwelcome guest in the household of his hosts, lingering on long after he had outworn his welcome. The matter was reminiscent of the guests of Uncle Sam who, however reluctant to accept his invitation, turned out to be equally reluctant to vacate.

To Japanese who had lived securely in their own cultural enclaves for decades, who had been sustained in a strange land by a network of extended families, of *ken* and patriotic *kai*, by a culture of great antiquity, order, and beauty, to be told they were free to go to Denver or Little Rock or Salt Lake City was a bit like telling them they were free to go to hell.

In the face of evacuee indifference or open hostility to the resettlement program, the Washington WRA staff issued a series of directives, urging more democratic participation by the evacuees—"a progressive relocation program," one such directive read, "can be achieved only through the full and complete participation and cooperation of the evacuee population." It was "essential" that they be "involved in relocation planning." The phrases "thorough understanding" and "complete acceptance" run like a litany through the directives, memoranda, letters of amplification, and other agency documents. Month after month the welfare counselors and the relocation counselors, the project directors, their staffs, visiting bureaucrats, consulting psychologists, all did their best to speed resettlement.

Still, most evacuees resisted, "in spite," as one staff member wrote, of "desirable economic opportunities, good public acceptance, and the continued relaxation of security measures by the Army." Indeed, resistance to resettlement soon passed from passive to active. The classic statement of the position of the nonmovers, as we might call them, came from a self-appointed group at Minidoka. Entitled "Spiritual and Mental Welfare of Evacuee Residents," it was sent to the Spanish consul, who handled all matters between the United States and the Japanese government, for forwarding to both parties. Under "Relationship Between WRA and Residents," it read: "The evacuee residents of this project with a sincere desire to abide by the laws of the United States, to preserve peace and harmony within the project, and pursuing a policy of patient forbearance, have at no time resorted to improper conduct. It is fully realized that in view of war conditions, our feelings of dissatisfaction and uncertainty are to a certain extent unavoidable. But it is indeed regrettable that certain segments of the American people, press, politicians and government officials have deliberately and maliciously fanned the flame of anti-Japanese prejudice. We in these relocation centers have been used by them as a 'political football,' and to spread false and inflammatory reports designed to harm us. Within the center itself, the overbearing attitude of racial, social, and intellectual superiority assumed by most of administrative officers, high and low, in violation of the announced formula of mutual cooperation, has undermined the morale of the residents. All of these factors have severely tested our confidence in American justice and our sincere desire and willingness to abide by its laws. With a view to removing these and other causes of our feeling of uncertainty from our daily existence, we earnestly desire a clarification of our wartime status and in particular our relationship with the WRA administration.''

The second section of the ''Spiritual and Mental Welfare of Evacuee Residents'' tract declared: ''Early in the evacuation stage, the Government announced that for the protection of the evacuees themselves, it will retain them in relocation centers for the duration, and guarantee them food, clothing, shelter, and also recreational facilities. Despite this promise, the Government abandoned this original policy, and began to enforce a policy of persuading evacuees to leave the center and resettle in American communities. The existence of intense anti-Japanese feelings and its threat to the personal safety and livelihood of the evacuees are well-known to the authorities in charge of the evacuees' welfare. Despite these and other unfavorable circumstances, the Government, acting through the WRA, has undertaken to impose upon the evacuees a policy of sprinkling them unnoticeably across the length and breadth of the country.''

The statement was signed by sixteen Issei leaders. It seemed to Harry Stafford, the Minidoka director, a bit disingenuous, since several of the signers had been functioning as advisers to the director on community issues.

Feelings of the staff caught between the War Relocation Authority's policy of relocation or resettlement and the residents' determination not to be persuaded or forced to leave are reflected in the views of a staff member of Minidoka. ''Careful observers in camp,'' he wrote, ''have long been aware of a strange paradox in resident thinking, namely, that almost one hundred per-cent of the evacuees express themselves as opposed to relocation in theory, though in practice a sizable minority obviously approve the policy since hundreds actually join the immigrant train. Thus, even the very mention of the word 'relocation' makes residents resentful and makes some bristle with indignation.''

A Kibei who clearly spoke for a number of his fellow evacuees, advised a friend: "I think it's best not to go out. There's been broadcasts from Japan saying that the Japanese people should stay inside the center. If you go out, then Japan will assume that you are loyal to the U.S. and they won't do anything for you. That's why I think it's better not to go out. . . . The war can't last very long now. America is going to be invaded soon. And when Japan wins they won't be able to keep us in jail. The trouble with the administration is that they think America is going to win."

When a family of Nisei children who had relocated to Chicago wrote their father at Minidoka, urging him to join them, he declined, giving as his reasons: "As things are, I feel it is better for us to remain here for the present. We would be a burden on the children if we went out, but right now we don't need any money and we don't have to depend on anyone else." When and if the West Coast was opened up, he and his wife could go directly back to their home in Seattle. He would be more inclined to go out "if I thought Japan were going to be defeated in this war, but it's evident that Japan is winning the war." (This was a constant refrain by the Issei.) Since Japan was winning, there seemed little point in leaving the centers. There were rumors that when peace was negotiated, the Japanese government would require that every head of family be given $10,000 by the United States, a sum that would be matched by the Japanese government. An additional matching $7,000 would be paid for each child.

In many families, children wished to go out but their Issei parents were reluctant or unwilling. A Nisei block manager at Heart Mountain stated the problem succinctly: "My kids want to go east. I finally put a stop to the talk. I want to go back where I came from. I know the situation there and I have a lot of friends. All these incidents don't scare me. I'm sure my old friends are still my friends. Besides, my parents won't hear of going anywhere except California."

Two centers, Rohwer and Gila River, had "relocation commissions," made up of evacuees and staff members, to answer questions and encourage evacuees to apply for leave. Pictures of smiling "relocatees" were posted on bulletin boards along with copies of letters attesting to their satisfaction with their relocation experience and their new lives. Often these were defaced or removed. Some centers invited back relocatees who had been especially successful in getting reestablished. Often these were individuals with special skills or people who had found well-paying defense jobs and when they returned they were commonly regarded with suspicion or ill-concealed contempt for cooperating with the

War Relocation Authority or, equally reprehensible in the minds of some, accepting assistance from the enemy.

The Heart Mountain council revealed one of the main bases of resistance to relocation by proposing "the establishment of small family-type hostels in key cities to house from 50 to 100 families." In other words, to reproduce as far as possible the general atmosphere of the centers themselves. It is to be doubted if the entire relocation period produced a more instructive document. As there has been occasion to note any number of times, most Americans thought in terms of "the individual"; the Japanese thought in terms of family and community, or, more precisely, of a community of families. The notion was for groups of families and friends who had come from the same town or rural community to establish themselves as a group, ideally in some farming region where the climate and soil was similar to what they had known on the coast.

AS IN THE FORMATION OF THE STUDENT RELOCATION COUNCIL, THE American Friends Service Committee had anticipated the problems to occur. There was no doubt in the mind of Homer Morris, one of the officers of the committee, that the War Relocation Authority could not handle resettlement on its own. The task was simply too vast. "Every effort should be made," he wrote in September 1942, "to have the [relocation] centers depopulated of able-bodied people by the end of the war. If this can be achieved, it will do more to soften the blow that has befallen our Japanese friends than anything else could do. This liberal policy of the W.R.A. deserves the support of all friends of the Japanese. It offers a place where *we can begin at once* in order to demonstrate our continued friendship." An American Friends Service Committee *Bulletin* reminded Friends everywhere that "we have before us those age-old obligations—those privileges of Christians which the historic Church calls the 'spiritual and corporal works of mercy—to counsel the doubtful . . . to comfort the sorrowful . . . to visit the sick . . . to clothe the naked . . . to harbor the harborless.''

In October 1942 a group of church representatives met in New York and agreed to establish the Committee on Japanese American Resettlement. This committee would work closely with local committees on resettlement. George Lundquist, a publisher and a Quaker who had given up his business interests to serve as a volunteer with the New York Church Committee for Japanese Work was made executive secretary of the newly formed committee.

Lundquist put out the *Resettlement Bulletin,* which was issued every few months to all participating churches and individuals. In the case of student relocation, the churches had organized and funded the program on their own. In the far larger WRA resettlement program, they stepped in to help the WRA, which appeared to be at its wit's end in trying to dislodge evacuees from the centers. The principal asset the Committee on Japanese American Resettlement brought to the resettlement effort was its contacts with ministers and laity in the various centers. Evacuees who viewed the WRA with distrust as an agency of a government that had uprooted them from their homes and communities, had far more confidence in the good faith of the churches where denominational affinities were frequently reinforced by personal friendships. Evacuee ministers were in an ideal position to reassure anxious members of their congregations that the committee stood ready to do all in its power to assure a successful transition to life outside.

Ralph Smeltzer wrote a friend after the resettlement program was announced: "It is good to know that you are definitely interested in aiding job relocation. From your position you can help most by finding job openings and organizing local committees to assist the Japanese when they arrive. From our position [at Manzanar] we can help most by selecting the best candidates and preparing them for relocation and assimilation."

To the Smeltzers, Ralph and his wife, Mary, must go credit for proposing (and helping to put into effect) one of the most important elements of the resettlement effort, the establishment of hostels to provide temporary quarters for evacuees seeking jobs and permanent housing.

The proposal for establishment of the hostels was presented to Dillon Myer in December 1942 by the Smeltzers. Myer readily agreed to the plan and a few weeks later, Thomas Temple, a member of the United Brethren Church, left for Chicago with thirteen young Nisei. They were to be quartered at the seminary of the church while they tried, with the help of the Brethren, to find jobs and more permanent quarters. The Brethren hostel was an immediate success. The young Nisei soon found jobs and homes or apartments. An encouraged Ralph Smeltzer wrote to Leland Brubaker of the Brethren Service Committee (February 20, 1943): "The task ahead of us is tremendous . . . hostelers must be properly selected . . . they must be gotten to the hostel . . . they must be properly accommodated . . . we must help provide them with jobs . . . [and] adequate and satisfactory living quarters must be found for them . . . they must be followed up in their jobs to assure community acceptance and happy living arrangements.'' With the United Brethren and the Friends leading the way, other denominations followed suit.

A hostel in Cleveland had been a fraternity house; rented with money from the Baptist World Emergency Fund, it accommodated thirty Nisei who stayed an average of two weeks before moving to more permanent quarters. The hostel, a Baptist minister noted, eventually served as a headquarters for five hundred or so evacuees, many of them students who lived in the Cleveland area.

In most communities the fact that the hostels were established under the wings of local churches won them reluctant acceptance but there was often at least initial opposition. When the United Brethren and the Friends established a hostel in New York City in a residential neighborhood, a loud cry of protest went up. Even Mayor La Guardia, usually on the liberal side of every cause, joined in the clamor. Secretary of the Interior Harold Ickes, rich in the rhetoric of denunciation, declared: ''In the past two weeks, the American people have heard three high public officials giving voice to opinions that seem ominously out of tune in a nation that is fighting for the principles of democracy and freedom.'' There was nary a peep out of the chastened officials but protests continued as various groups tuned in with predictions of doom if the hostel remained open. At the same time some thirty groups came to the support of the hostel and its occupants. Given police protection, the hostel persevered and was soon functioning without opposition.

While a general ecumenical spirit prevailed between the different denominations, a natural division of labor fell along denominational lines. The Caucasian Baptists in, say, Minneapolis, took responsibility for Japanese Baptists in Poston or Minidoka. The Presbyterians did likewise, as did the Methodists. Since evacuees who belonged to a particular Protestant church (and congregation) in prewar days often went to an assembly center and subsequently to a relocation center as virtually intact congregations, the process of resettlement in such instances was greatly facilitated. Often those who were given ''indefinite leave'' with the assumption (or hope) that they would put down permanent roots were soon able to assist their friends and fellow congregants to resettle. In addition to those evacuees who received assistance from the major denominations represented in substantial numbers in centers, denominations with very few, if any, members in the centers undertook to come to the aid of fellow Christians as well as Buddhists and those evacuees with no declared religious affiliation. Most prominent in this area were the American Friends Service Committee and the United Brethren wing or branch of the Moravian church.

As soon as a kind of "critical mass" of Nisei settled in a city, forming their own organizations, it was easier for other less assimilated Nisei to resettle there, confident of help. Certain cities became resettlement centers for evacuees from Minidoka or Granada or Topaz. If a young Nisei found a job in Detroit or Dearborn, he or she would do his or her best to find jobs for friends and to send, as soon as possible, for their parents. I think it is safe to assume that most, if not all, of the Issei in say, Detroit (294) were the parents or grandparents of the 1,355 Nisei in that city.

Chicago, with more than ten thousand resettlers, was known as the "Mecca of Relocation." In that city, twenty-five Caucasian and evacuee ministers joined forces in a committee called United Ministry to Evacuees.

By July 1943 the War Relocation Authority had received requests for ten thousand evacuees in the Chicago area alone. In many instances seasonal leave, which seemed far less final to evacuees, turned into indefinite leave or, for all practical purposes, resettlement. By December 1943 3,900 persons had relocated in the Salt Lake City area and three thousand in the Denver area, some 40 percent of the total relocatees. Soon employers who needed a number of workers began sending recruiters to the centers to talk with evacuees. One of the most successful recruiters was a large farm corporation, Seabrook Farms in New Jersey.

Jeanne Wakatsuki's older brother, Bill, and his wife, Tomi, decided to go out with their child and lined up a job with Seabrook. They were followed by Jeanne's sister and her husband; four more Wakatsuki children soon departed. Ray, the youngest son, joined the coast guard, Woody was drafted, Eleanor was in Reno, and her husband was in the army in Germany. When the war ended, Bill Wakatsuki continued his career with the company. The International Harvester Company and the Stevens Hotel chain were also successful recruiters. Government agencies got into the act, especially ordnance depots and railroads.

One of George Lundquist's *Resettlement Bulletins* noted in the fall of 1943 that over fifteen thousand evacuees had been "restored to normal American communities" since the resettlement program had begun, many, if not most, with the assistance of the Committee on Japanese American Resettlement. They were living in practically every state outside of the evacuated area and working in a wide variety of jobs, "in munitions' factories and airplane plants, as well as in many government offices including the War Department.'' A number were employed by the committee itself just as the student relocation program had employed a number of Nisei in their various offices.

Lundquist noted that the ''exodus'' of evacuees over the past year had been largely a youth movement. The challenge that lay ahead, he warned his readers, was to relocate in the coming year as many as possible of the 75,000 remaining in the centers. These would be mainly ''family units or groups'' and they must, like their predecessors, be given to understand ''that democracy and Christianity work'' as ''practical principles of our daily lives.''

The issues of the *Resettlement Bulletin* carried reports from members of the committee in various cities, human interest accounts of, typically, social gatherings of young Nisei. Dorothy Brauninger reported for the Kansas City Council of Churches that when the opinion was expressed that Kansas City had no Japanese evacuees, the city's churches put on a lawn party. Invitations were sent to the Nisei and ''thirty-five Japanese, twelve Negroes and more than a hundred young people from thirty-four churches showed up to socialize and play badminton, tether ball, Ping-Pong, shuffle board and soft ball.'' Two gypsy fortune-tellers told fortunes and a strolling accordian player led community singing. The *Dayton Daily News* was quoted on a get-together party of thirty-four young Nisei men and women at the home of the Lynton Appleberrys.

For Christians, who made up the greater proportion of those evacuees resettling, there was a kind of push-pull effect in operation. The push was the frequent harassment by the militants in the centers, the pull was encouragement they received from their co-religionists who had gone out before them.

In addition to the Committee on Japanese American Resettlement, some eighty-seven organizations throughout the country undertook to assist the evacuees in resettling, and 222 community agencies assisted the evacuees in some aspect or another of resettlement. Those Nisei who had the strongest ties through their denominational affiliations to the larger society often passed out of the centers expeditiously.

One consequence of the indefinite leave program was that the proportion of Issei and of the more intractable Nisei and Kibei in the centers increased as the actual or potential cooperators and compromisers, responding in part to the continuing tensions of life in the centers, departed.

In June 1943 the Washington office of the War Relocation Authority announced a plan to cut back on the number of paid jobs held by evacuees in the centers. Put forward as a necessary economy measure, the an-

nouncement was interpreted by already understandably paranoid evacuees as a ploy to put more pressure on them to accept leave. Such a
reaction was one of the things that made the directors of the centers gray
before their time. Even the simplest suggestion or directive was endlessly
discussed and debated in the search for some hidden intent, prejudicial to
the interests and well-being of the evacuees.

Many different motives impelled evacuees to go out. Kazuko Hayashi
recalled in conversations with Heihachiro Takarabe that in order to avoid
the endless gossip and recrimination that took place at the laundry house
in her block at Poston, she would get up very early in the morning to do
her laundry before the other wives had congregated. She did her best to
get her three daughters out of Poston as quickly as possible. The oldest
girl got a job in Chicago not long after the family arrived at Poston and
helped find positions for her sisters. The youngest daughter was accepted
at a nursing college in Philadelphia and her mother left the center with
her. Her oldest son had meanwhile volunteered for the army. "When my
youngest daughter and I left the Camp," Hayashi recalled, "people
laughed at us. They said, 'What are you going to do outside? If you stay
in the camp, they will feed you. It is so comfortable here. Are you
looking for trouble outside?' " Kazuko Hayashi and her children had
arrived in Poston in August 1942 and the last of the family (the mother
and youngest daughter) left at the end of 1944. Her three daughters and
two sons all eventually were admitted to universities. In Chicago, the
Hayashis' landlord was a Mrs. Tyrell, who, in Kazuko Hayashi's words,
"thought that my sons and daughters were her family members." She
presided over the wedding of the younger Hayashi son.

Riici Satow was among those at Poston who decided that it was time
to get out. He was concerned about the education of his nine children.
"Another thing that made me think that the time was ripe for us to get
out," he told Heihachiro Takarabe, "was that a lot of people there started
making too much fuss and commotion over nothing." That worried Satow. If they were making so much trouble in the center when Japan
appeared to be winning the war, Satow was apprehensive over how they
might behave if Japan started losing. "I didn't want to be around when
the news of Japan's defeat would reach our camp because anything could
happen at such times. Of course, the rumor that someone was out to get
me in the camp [for his Christian activities] had been worrying me."
Friends in Colorado found work for Satow, and in April 1943 he left
Poston. He had been in the center for ten months and he left with a sense
of relief. The Satows settled in Keenesburg, a small predominantly Ger-

man beet-growing community some twenty-five miles from Denver, and the Satow children were enrolled in the Keenesburg schools. The family stayed there until a year after the end of the war.

David Yutaka Nakagawa was the son of a fisherman on Terminal Island and was thus swept up in the first forced evacuation on the West Coast. Nakagawa's father was one of the first Issei picked up by the FBI. From Santa Anita, Nakagawa went to Granada, or Amache, as the evacuees preferred to call it. There as a volunteer assisting Nisei ministers or organized church groups, Nakagawa felt the pressure of evacuees who accused him of "kowtowing" to the center's director. Nakagawa, in consequence, was glad to have an opportunity to go out to Dayton, Ohio, to work at the YMCA in that city and attend the "Central Y College" there. Drafted from Dayton, Nakagawa was sent to the 82nd Airborne Division (paratroops) at Fort Bragg as a physical instructor.

When Pearl Harbor was bombed, Frances Kirihara was in the University of California at Berkeley's School of Nursing. There were twenty-one other young Japanese Americans in the school, and they were told that they would have to leave. Because of her training at Berkeley, Kirihara was drafted as a nurse at Granada, a position she found rewarding. But life in the center was difficult and she left as soon as she could find a job outside. In Denver, she found lodging with a Presbyterian minister and worked at the Colorado General Hospital.

The Niwa family stayed at Manzanar until her son Nobu graduated from high school. Then, with the aid and encouragement of their church, Nobu and his father went out to Milwaukee and after son Aki graduated the next year, Haruko and Aki joined them. The train that Haruko and Aki took to Wisconsin was full of soldiers but, Haruko recalled, "they are very sweet and gracious and nice to us. Next to my seat was a soldier and he offered coffee, and whenever the train stop and he hop out for lunch or something, he say, 'May I get you a sandwich or something?' "

In Milwaukee, Aki got a job in a tire recapping plant and went to college while Haruko worked as director of the local resettlement association.

Donald Nakahawa's sister went out soon after the family was relocated at Topaz. With the help of her church she attended the University of Rochester in New York. When Donald and his mother left Topaz, they were encouraged by "the church people" to settle in Rochester with Donald's sister.

After helping to start the elementary school at Poston, Helen Kitaji went out to teach Indian children at a Navajo reservation at Window

Rock, Arizona. There she was dismayed at the demoralized state of the Indians. It made her think of her experience at Poston. She wrote a friend, "just having the government give is bad for any group. Respect for property, for themselves, and others goes way down. It is true, I see, and saw it happening to those at Poston."

Determined to get out of Minidoka, Helen Murao wrote to a woman she knew in the Baptist Home Missionary Society. She must get out of camp at once. "There's something that's marvelous about being young and ignorant," she reflected years later, "you just ask and somehow things materialize." The friend "had access to homes throughout the country willing to take students. She sent me a list of several." Murao chose the family of a Presbyterian minister in Madison, Wisconsin. "They wanted an evacuee. I didn't stop to think whether that was going to be all right or not; it just meant getting out. So I went. They were a terrific family. When I came out of camp, they gave me the support that I really sorely needed, and they have been friends ever since." One of Murao's brothers became a doctor, another earned his Ph.D., and she got her master's degree.

Henry Kazato noted that "the camp authorities began to say they'd like to see us get out of camp as soon as possible, so we began to look around for places to go." Kazato found a hospital in Detroit. It turned out to have been an excellent decision on his part. He was paid $225 a month rather than the $19 he had earned at Poston.

Jobo Nakamura was at Tule Lake. He had been a student at the University of California Berkeley at the time of evacuation and at Tule Lake was an editor of the *Tulean Dispatch*. He decided reluctantly to resettle. "Now that I have made plans to leave the project," he wrote, "I feel like staying here a little longer. Life here has made me soft and indolent. I'm clothed, sheltered, and I don't have to worry about where my next meal is coming from. I feel as though I've become part of the dust. . . .

"There is no economic pressure living in a socialized world such as here, and I am living day to day in purposeless drifting, planning frivolous things to do tomorrow. It's funny . . . I want to prolong this sort of life but [if] I procrastinated I'll be here for the duration and I don't want to be here when the war ends. My better conscience tells me that the sooner I re-establish myself in a normal American community, the better I would be prepared to meet the postwar future.

"I must go out and make my living the hard way again. Yet doubt and fear disturb my mind. Would I be jumping out of a frying pan into the fire? Will I be happy outside in a strange community? To go out means to depart from my life-long friends. It means to tear myself away from a life of comparative ease and security to start life all over again. It makes me feel weary. I hope this will be the last time I have to move again.''

If a young, college-educated Nisei with a superior command of English felt such doubts and misgivings about going out, it is hardly surprising that evacuees far less able to cope with life in general felt even more reluctant to give up the relative comfort and security of the centers for the uncertainties and hazards of life outside.

Miyo Senzaki's experience illustrated another problem. Senzaki's parents were the prosperous owners of five produce markets. Her three older brothers and five sisters were employed in the markets when the war came. The markets were hastily disposed of at considerable loss and the family found itself first at Santa Anita and later at Rohwer. Miyo Senzaki felt for the Issei especially. ''I had a husband, I was in love; and as long as I was going to be with him I could take it.'' But when she got pregnant for a second time, she was filled with despair. ''I'm not going to have this child in camp,'' she thought. ''I don't know what but we're getting out of here.'' Perhaps she could get an abortion. Finally resigned, she told her husband: ''Well, I'm having this one in camp, but no more kids, unless you get me out of here.'' Her husband applied for indefinite leave and got a job at a tool and die plant in Minneapolis that had a contract with the army. He sent for Miyo and she had her second child in a Minneapolis hospital.

When Miyo tried to return to Rohwer to be with her parents, she encountered resistance from the center director, who announced that she (and other servicemen's wives who wished to return to Rohwer) would have to pay sixty cents a day as a visitor's fee for room and board. The director insisted that she should stay outside and have her parents join her, rather than coming back to the center. The episode pointed up what threatened to become a serious problem—the inclination of some evacuees to use the centers for rest and recreation between jobs outside their home center. That was the case with Harry Nishiura. When Nishiura's wife became pregnant and was in poor health, he decided to leave Heart Mountain and go to Billings, Montana. Nishiura, who had learned the art of ''chick-sexing'' from a fellow evacuee in the Heart Mountain hatchery, easily found a job at the Yellowstone Packing House at $600 a month, substantially more than the $19 per month he made at Heart Mountain. After the baby was born, the Nishiuras tried to return to Heart Mountain but the policy there, as at all the other centers, was that once a person or a family had gone out and demonstrated ability to get work and function outside, they could not return unless they agreed to pay room and board. An indignant Nishiura refused. He smuggled his wife and child back into the center and slipped in himself. After two clandestine months in Heart Mountain, Nishiura learned that his chicken-sexing talents were in demand in a hatchery in Omaha, Nebraska. When he tried to go out once more, the center director discovered that he had sneaked back in and was irate. Nishiura bought an "old, junky 1927 Plymouth" and headed for Omaha, where the family lived in a converted service station. It was there, he recalled, that "we heard on the radio that Japan surrendered, and I cried. It was hard to take."

Late in 1943 a Poston staff member wrote: "In a recent conference which I called to consider child welfare and youth guidance procedures the familiar dilemma became evident: whether the project services should stand back to be called upon by the residents, or the professionals in the project administration should reach down into the blocks to direct the living of the residents along the lines which we approve. In the discussion several interesting observations were offered by a young Japanese-born, American-educated block manager who has had social work experience in connection with a California Juvenile Court.

"He agreed that the life of the project is now sharply separated in its orientation around two opposite poles: the California Japanese culture, which, as he reminded us, is at least 20 years behind the social progress of the Mother Country which these people left at least 20 years ago, and the professional Americanism of the schools with their curricular, their recreation and activity programs, and their appointed teachers from all over the country. The first pole represents the orientation of what he called 'the core of the community.' To belong to this core, one must have been for years a member of one of the Japanese cultural clusters from which the residents came. The process of relocation [out of the centers] he said, has simply drawn off the individuals who were farthest from the core-like molecules escaping by evaporation from the surface of a liquid . . . the young people who are left . . . are increasingly reabsorbed into the culture of the core. They are learning more about Japanese—with or without Adult Education's sanctions; are conforming more closely to family expectations; are marrying rather unexpectedly with non-English speaking Kibei; and for the most part, are 'postponing' their plans for relocation to some indefinite date."

The analysis was a shrewd and informed one and it pointed up the ironic fact that the longer the evacuees remained in the centers the more Japanese most of them became. The process was exactly the reverse of what the War Relocation Authority had planned and anticipated. At the same time, it did vindicate in a way their altered policy of encouraging evacuees to relocate in the interior. Those individuals "farthest from the core" were indeed "drawn off." Each crisis in the centers, while spinning off more of the Americanized, at the same time strengthened the core community by making its members more dependent on one another and more inclined to support the core leaders, the more militant and aggressive or, if one prefers, these evacuees with the deepest sense of their Japaneseness.

Some evacuees were concerned about the consequences of affirming loyalty to the United States in the event that the Japanese won the war. Someone produced a Japanese criminal code that provided two years' imprisonment for any Japanese citizen who voluntarily aided an enemy alien in time of war. The acceptance of resettlement was interpreted by some as voluntarily aiding the enemy, the United States; the question was raised in various meetings, if Japanese were deported to Japan after the war would their cooperation with evacuation be interpreted in Japan as "voluntary aid," and thus be subject to punishment? If word of "cooperation" reached the Japanese authorities would the relatives of evacuees living in Japan be prosecuted?

One Issei expressed his uncertainty in a Senryu, a traditional three-line poem:

> *Balancing the war news*
> *With his own future—*
> *Dilemma of Dilemmas*

On January 1, 1943, there were 110,240 Japanese Americans in the various relocation centers. Six months later (July 1, 1943) the number had dropped to 103,282 and from then on until the centers were closed the evacuee population declined by roughly 10,000 every six months. Almost 35,000 evacuees were given indefinite leave from various centers. Minidora, with some 12,000 residents, of whom 4,368 were given indefinite leave, led the way. Tule Lake, with 29,467 evacuees, had only 2,291 on indefinite leave. After December 20, 1944, the category of short-term, seasonal indefinite leaves was abolished and all leaves were considered terminal.

One of the consequences of the leave and resettlement programs was that the evacuees who remained in the centers experienced what we might call "spatial expansion." As individuals and families moved out, the vacated space was quickly appropriated. In Block 28 at Manzanar, the twelve Wakatsukis had four rooms due to Ko Wakatsuki's enterprise in moving to occupy space vacated by evacuees who had gone out.

Indefinite leave (and resettlement) were the centerpiece of the War Relocation Authority's program. That they were a failure, at least as far as rapidly emptying the centers of their residents, was Dillon Myer's bitterest disappointment (among many it must be said). At the same time the resettlement of some 35,000 men, women, and children outside the exclusionary zone throughout the Rocky Mountain West, Midwest, and the East was a remarkable accomplishment. It changed, often for the better, the lives of those who were resettled; equally important, it involved tens of thousands of Caucasian Americans who by assisting in that process bore witness to the most basic values of a democratic society.

Chapter 19

REGISTRATION

As the reader may recall, the selective service act was passed September 16, 1940. Under its terms a million young men were drafted into the army of the United States. Among them, in the ordinary course of events, were a number of Nisei. Others, like Minoru Yasui, were reservists who had gotten their commissions through the ROTC and were called up with their units. On June 17, 1942, the War Department discontinued the induction of Japanese Americans and all Nisei were classified as IV-C, not acceptable because of ancestry. However, the need for bilingual Japanese to act as translators with army and marine units in the Pacific was so great that exceptions were made and some 160 Japanese were recruited and rendered notable service in the Pacific Theater.

As early as July 1942, less than a month after the announcement of the ban on enlisting Japanese, Dillon Myer began pressing McCloy to change the army's policy so that Nisei could volunteer to serve in an all-Nisei unit. There was already a Nisei Hawaiian National Guard unit known as the 100th Battalion that was sent to Camp McCoy in Wisconsin in the fall of 1942 for special training. Myer and others, including a Colonel Fielder, an intelligence officer who had served in Hawaii, pressed for a policy that would utilize the 100th Battalion in combat.

Myer found an ally in McCloy, who took up the idea of an all-Nisei unit with Stimson. At a JACL meeting in Salt Lake City in November, attended by representatives of the War Department and the War Relocation Authority, Mike Masaoka, his brother Joe Grant Masaoka, Ted Slocum, and other JACLers urged that Nisei be allowed to volunteer for an all-Nisei unit like the 100th Battalion. They were convinced that such a demonstration of loyalty would have a salutary influence on public opinion by dramatizing the fact that thousands of evacuees in the relocation centers were ready to sacrifice their lives for their country.

The proposal was given a certain urgency by virtue of the fact that the American Legion, in the aforementioned Kansas City meeting, besides opposing the college leave program, had passed a resolution urging that "All Japanese both alien and native born be ordered confined to concentration camps for the duration of the war." Another resolution took the line that all Japanese east of the Rockies had "escaped." Therefore: "Resolved that those Japanese escaped to states east of the Rockies be taken into custody and placed in these different camps or that they be placed under military control in their present location."

The negative publicity generated by the Poston and Manzanar riots was also on the minds of Myer and the WRA staff.

The principal outcome of the Salt Lake City meeting was a decision to call for volunteers for an all-Nisei unit that would be combined with the 100th Battalion. The decision was also made to accompany the call for volunteers with a four-page registration form, Form DSS 304A, to be used "as a basis for determining eligibility of volunteers for service in the combat team, for certifying individuals as eligible for work in defense industries," and "to facilitate the War Relocation Authority leave program."

All male evacuees seventeen years of age or over were required to answer questions 27 and 28. Question 27 was "Are you willing to serve in the armed forces of the United States on combat duty, wherever ordered?" Question 28 was: "Will you swear unqualified allegiance to the United States of America and faithfully defend the United States from any or all attack by foreign or domestic forces, and forswear any form of allegiance or obedience to the Japanese emperor, or any other foreign government, power, or organization?"

The question for women read somewhat differently: "Will you swear unqualified allegiance to the United States of America and forswear any form of allegiance or obedience to the Japanese emperor, or any other foreign government, power, or organization?"

The War Department and the War Relocation Authority were so

pleased with questions 27 and 28 that they decided to propose them in somewhat altered form to Issei men and women. The questionnaires for the Issei were labeled "Application for Leave Clearance." The notion was that the registration forms for the Nisei women and Issei men and women would be used to determine their suitability for resettlement. An earlier questionnaire had been issued for those evacuees who might wish to apply for leave "in order to re-establish themselves in normal life outside the centers." But this form was voluntary and needed to be filled out only by those wishing such leave; as we have seen, only a small percentage of the evacuees made application. The military registration, by contrast, was obligatory. The army was responsible for registering males over seventeen, the center administration for registering all others. Conscious of the furor caused by Myer's announcement of the resettlement program, the army and the WRA were determined to proceed in a manner that would convince the evacuees of the good intentions of the government and allay any apprehensions. Officers assigned to go to the centers to explain the purpose of the registration were given special training. An attempt was made to anticipate questions about the implications and consequences of the appeal for volunteers and the registration itself. Each officer was given a speech to read that said in part:

"We are here on a mission. . . . The effort is not a campaign or a drive. . . . Its fundamental purpose is to put your situation on a plane which is consistent with the dignity of American citizenship.

"You may object that this—your life here—is not free. . . . The circumstances were not of your own choosing. . . . The only answer which needs to be made to such an objection is that if there were not millions of Americans who agree with your point of view we would not be here and this statement would not be made.

"The present undertaking is of itself an acknowledgement that the best solution has not been found for you during the present war emergency in your relation to the United States, which is the country of your birth and of your residence.

"Your government would not take these steps unless it intended to go further in restoring you to a normal place in the life of the country, with the privileges and obligations of other American citizens."

Some of the anticipated questions went: "Will my family be permitted to return to the West Coast [if I volunteer]?

"Answer: Not for the time being.

"Question: What happens to my father who is not a citizen of the United States?

"Answer: Like all other persons now in relocation centers, he may file an application for leave which will be acted upon by the War Relocation Authority. It is fair to say that his chances for favorable action will be better by reason of your going into the service."

On January 28, 1943, Secretary of War Stimson announced that the War Department was prepared to create a volunteer Nisei combat team to be made up of Nisei from Hawaii, from the mainland United States in areas where Japanese Americans were subject to no restraints, and, finally and most importantly, of Nisei in the relocation centers. The army teams were scheduled to arrive between February 6 and February 10. The Authority and the Army, considering themselves by this time experts on the Japanese psyche, were confident that many Nisei would "welcome the opportunity to strengthen their claims to the rights of citizenship."

If the War Relocation Authority had had the most malevolent of intentions it could not have found a better way to sow dissension and worse among the inhabitants of the centers. The centers were immediately in an uproar. Not only was the hated form an invasion of the innermost privacy of a very private people, it brought to the surface the divisions between Japanese and Japanese; these already touchy and dangerous matters were brought out into the bright light, as it were, and exacerbated in the process.

It was soon evident that there were three possible responses: (1) whether to answer "yes-yes" or "no-no" to questions 27 and 28; (2) whether to refuse to register at all; or (3) to reply to 27 and 28 conditionally as, for instance, "I will be loyal to the United States *if*. . ." The if, typically, was "if my full rights as a U.S. citizen are restored to me and I am allowed to return to my West Coast home."

The Issei, not being citizens, had a different problem with registration. They could not claim that their rights as citizens were being infringed but they were certainly conscious of the fact that citizenship had been denied them. They felt a special irritation at being confronted with question 28, which, in effect, asked them to renounce all ties and loyalties to their homeland. Even for those few Issei who had become more or less assimilated the question was offensive. They were, in fact, citizens of Japan. To answer yes to 28 would mean to reject their Japanese citizenship without becoming American citizens. Several of the center directors saw the contradiction as soon as they went over the registration forms and the director at Manzanar wired the Washington office of the War Relocation Authority, pointing out the awkwardness of the question for Issei.

The response was immediate. The question might be changed to a more appropriate one. At Manzanar the question read:

"Are you sympathetic to the United States and do you agree faithfully to defend the United States from any and all attack by foreign or domestic forces?" With this change most of the Issei at Manzanar, many doubtless with some private reservations, answered affirmatively.

The same problem arose at the other centers and Washington offered an alternative: "Will you swear to abide by the laws of the United States and to take no action which would in any way interfere with the war effort of the United States?" Since the Issei were hardly in a position to take any action at all for or against the United States the question was relatively easy to answer in the affirmative.

Another problem for the Issei was the fact that the form given to them was headed "Application for Leave Clearance." This title alarmed the Issei, who, having, for the most part no intention of leaving the centers, not unnaturally believed that the form was simply a ruse to get them out. When this problem was explained to Washington the heading of the form was changed to read "Information for Leave Clearance" and it was explained to the Issei that the information was solicited for use in the event that they *decided* that they wished to go out on leave. With that modification most of the Issei agreed to fill out the registration forms. Moreover, since "allegiance" in Japanese is *Chusei* while "loyalty" is *Chugi*, some Issei took the position that they could have "allegiance" to Japan and "loyalty" to the United States. Beyond all that, asking a Japanese nationalist to forswear allegiance to the Emperor was rather like asking a devout Christian to forswear faith in God the Father *plus* devotion to his own specific father. One young Kibei declared that "the Emperor was like his father; he could never go against the Emperor."

In addition to the question of whether or not to register and how to answer questions 27 and 28 (those who answered no to both were known as the "no-nos" and, correspondingly, those who answered affirmatively were the "yes-yesers"), there was the far more serious question of whether to volunteer for the all-Nisei combat team. The pro-volunteer position was ably argued by the editor of the *Minidoka Irrigator:* "Our utterances have always been loaded to the limit with professions of faith and unequivocal loyalty. . . . The simple question now is: Are we to eat our words, or are we going to make them good? . . . If we are to be embodied in the American grain so conclusively that we can never again be smeared and reviled by the bigots and home fascists, there is no course for the eligible among us but to try like hell to get into the uniform of Uncle Sam's fighting forces.

"What we face is the acid test. . . . The simple fact is that a major concession has been made to nisei demands and rights. Criticism and sniping at this date . . . come in poor grace. . . .

"Consider further that the tremendous publicity value and potential of a homogeneous nisei group would be reduced, if not completely lost, in the event nisei soldiers were scattered . . . in the broad and deep ranks of the regular units of the Army. And let's remember that favorable publicity is our greatest need."

Despite the editorial, there was strong opposition to volunteering at Minidoka and the life of the editor of the *Irrigator* was threatened.

One of the evacuees at Minidoka was a young Kibei named Matsuda who had spent eight years in Japan and returned to do graduate work at Berkeley. Prior to the registration crisis he had been looked up to in his block as a leader. When he urged people in his block to register and registered himself with ten of his friends, he became a pariah, "a marked man, a leader of the opposition. At present," James Sakoda noted, ". . . hardly anyone in his block speaks to him . . . he goes to the mess hall, eats silently, without talking to anyone. Formerly he had many friends in the block—now he has practically none. One good family friend even told him not to come to see them."

Riici Satow drew "hatred" on himself by arguing that "since we were living in this country, we had to abide by the law of the land by all means. You can't live while resisting the country that you live in. I maintained that we should follow whatever course this country might set and that the question of who was going to win the war should be dealt with separately."

Yoshisada Kawai's feelings were typical of those Issei who felt some attachment to America. "I felt deep in my mind," he told Heihachiro Takarabe, "a turmoil, because I did not want my sons to take arms against my mother country and shed blood. I just could not bear the thought of it. On the other hand, I have received so much from this country and I owe it a lot. . . . I was crushed between *giri* and *ninjo-Jooai* [duty and affection/love], and I had to take an absolutely neutral position. It was the only way out for me."

In the feverish excitement generated by registration, the most serious episode took place at Jerome, Arkansas. There the Reverend John Yamazaki, who was bilingual, had agreed to act as translator for the army officer who came to explain to the evacuees the nature and purpose of registration. That night militants sought Yamazaki out and beat him badly, whether because he was a leader of the Christians in the center (half of his congregation from St. Mary's Episcopal Church in Los Angeles were at Jerome) or because of his role as translator is not clear. He also offended by having two sons, James and Peter, in the U.S. Army. Yamazaki's son John, an Episcopal priest at Gila River (with the other half of St. Mary's congregation), came to Jerome. His sons got leave from the army and the three met to give what aid and comfort they could to their badly beaten father. The center was placed under martial law by Paul Taylor, the director, and, at Taylor's insistence, Yamazaki, his wife, and small daughter left Jerome for Chicago, where he assisted evacuees in resettling. His son John, faced with similar hostility at Gila River, went out to Cincinnati with his wife.

Yamazaki's beating was a foretaste of a controversy that kept the centers in an uproar for weeks. June Toskiyuki felt it acutely because her husband was an Issei. Like many others, his wife noted, "he thought Japan was winning the war. His dream was that Japan would send a ship and take all of us back to Japan." His response to the registration crisis was to withdraw completely from center life and even from attention to his family. He stayed in his quarters and played melancholy tunes on a flute while June was left to care for the children. The tension between them was heightened by the fact that June's brother Joe volunteered for the 442nd. Every night June, her mother, and the other members of the family would gather to light candles and pray for Joe's safe return. June's mother was convinced that her prayers had resulted in her son missing the troop ship that was to take him to France and that was sunk by a German submarine.

At the Granada center, the project director prevailed on the evacuees to fill out the form but he was alarmed when a nose count showed that one hundred Nisei had answered no to the question of their loyalty to the United States and only thirty had volunteered for the 442nd. At this point the chairman of the community council was prevailed upon by the director, James Lindley, to talk on the phone to officials of the WRA in Washington in an effort to explain the reaction of the evacuees at Granada. A series of stormy meetings followed in which the volunteering program was fully discussed. These tactics resulted in 152 Nisei answering yes to the loyalty question while the negative answers dropped to twenty-seven.

At Heart Mountain, when the center newspaper, the *Heart Mountain Sentinel*, supported registration, the *Rocky Shimpo*, a bilingual Japanese newspaper published in Denver, denounced the editors for having "purchased a seat in the great gallery of bigots, racists, demagogues, autocrats, and fascist-minded. . . . It has deserted justice, fair play."

A Nisei group that called itself the Citizen's Congress conducted a kind of open forum to debate the issue. A rough consensus was reached at least by those involved in the debate (by no means all of the residents) that registering should be conditional on guarantees of "release from the centers and the right of all evacuees to return to their homes." As "the speaker" put it: "The minds of many of us are still shrouded in doubt and confusion as to the true motives of our government when they invite our voluntary enlistment at the present time. It has not been explained why some American citizens who patriotically volunteered at the beginning of the war, were rejected by the Army. Furthermore, our government has permitted damaging propaganda to continue against us. She has also failed to reinstate us in the eyes of the American public. We are placed on the spot, and our course of action is in the balance scale of justice; for our government's honest interpretation of our stand will mean absolute vindication and admission of the wrong committed. On the other hand, if interpreted otherwise by misrepresentations and misunderstandings, it will amount to renewed condemnation of this group.

"Although we have yellow skins, we too are Americans. We have an American upbringing. Therefore we believe in fair play. Our firm conviction is that we would be useless Americans if we did not assert our constitutional rights now; for unless our status as citizens is cleared and we are really fighting for the high ideals upon which our nation is based, how can we say to the white American buddies in the armed forces that we are fighting for the perpetuation of democracy, especially when our fathers, mothers and families are in concentration camps, even though they are not charged with any crime?

"We believe that our Nation's good faith is to be found in whether it moves to restore full privileges at the earliest opportunity."

There was certainly an element of the disingenuous in the speech, which was obviously carefully crafted not so much for the Heart Mountain Citizen's Congress but for distribution to the media, to the government, which is to say, to the War Department, to the War Relocation Authority, to all social service organizations thought to be sympathetic to the Japanese American cause, and to the other centers in the hope of prevailing on them to join forces with the Heart Mountain protesters in a universal refusal to register. The charge that the government had "permitted damaging propaganda" implied that the government should have prohibited any negative comments about Japanese Americans. Such a charge was hardly reassuring as an indication of the drafters' understanding of democracy. Nor was the charge that it was the government's responsibility to "reinstate us in the eyes of the American public." That was, of course, exactly what the government, in the form of the War Relocation Authority, had hoped to accomplish by registration. It certainly was true that the registration plan put the Nisei on the spot but that had not been its intention. It wished, if anything, to get them off the spot by giving them the opportunity to affirm their loyalty to the United States.

For a time, anarchy seemed to threaten the Heart Mountain center. When the director, Guy Robertson, issued orders, they were simply ignored. Ironically, it was an Issei block manager, excluded from elected office, who persuaded the members of his block to fill out the forms. Other blocks fell into line.

At Topaz a Committee of Nine sent a telegram to Secretary of War Stimson requesting assurance of a complete restoration of rights before continuing the registration. The Topaz telegram received a prompt response that read: "The present program is not complete rehabilitation but it is the first step in that direction." The conciliatory response to the Topaz telegram heartened the Topaz "cooperators." After an internal debate, the character of which we can only guess at, the Topaz Committee of Nine was superseded by the Committee of 33, which wired the War Department on February 16: "We accept this registration as an indication of the Government's good faith."

That was not, of course, the end of the matter. The Committee of 33 had no more authority than the Committee of Nine but in most centers (Tule Lake and Manzanar being the most notable exceptions) majority opinion gradually shifted toward compliance, that is to say, toward registering. Still the bitter struggle went on. The frequency with which many Nisei changed their minds told more eloquently than words of the internal conflict in the centers and in the hearts of individual Nisei. Fierce emotion-charged exchanges took place far into the night and there were certainly many sleepless nights for evacuees of all persuasions. The moderates constantly reverted to the theme that the future of all Japanese Americans in the United States was at stake and reminded their fellows that refusal to register would play into the hands of their detractors in the larger society. Refusal to register would also compromise thousands of Japanese Americans who had left the centers on indefinite leave and were trying to establish themselves in towns and cities where they were dependent upon the assistance and good will of their new neighbors. The

Christians remaining in the centers were especially conscious of problems poised by intransigence since a high proportion of those who had left the centers on indefinite leave were Christians, extremely vulnerable to the shifting tides of public opinion.

In some centers Issei took the lead in trying to quiet fears and encourage registration. At Minidoka an Issei leader declared: "Americans are not exceptions to the adage that 'it is human to err and divine to forgive.' But when they find they are mistaken, they have the courage to try to correct it. If they have made mistakes in the past, your children, as American citizens, should share the consequences of those mistakes. My advice is to forget the past and look to the future. Let the Nisei do their duty toward the country in which they were born and to which they have allegiance. . . .

"The principle involved here is that since our children were born here, they belong here. Morally speaking, they do not belong to us, but to their country. I believe our attitude towards this principle will be extremely important for the future welfare and happiness of our own race in the United States. We should look to our own moral code in this matter."

Still the soul-searching went on. A twenty-three-year-old Kibei, asked why he had answered no to question 27, replied in honest bewilderment: that he did not see how he could forswear his allegiance to the Emperor of Japan no matter what his feelings were toward the United States. "How can a Kibei be comfortable in a U.S. uniform when his convictions lie elsewhere?" he asked the official questioning him. A Tule Lake Kibei expressed a similar feeling: "If I change to Yes, I won't be able to walk down the streets of Tokyo with a clear conscience after the war."

Jack Nishida was "one of those 'No-No' boys. My folks felt that they were going to leave this country and go back to Japan. If that was the case, I was the only boy in the family so I had to go with them." Nishida's father repeated like a litany: " 'If Japan should lose the war, I'll take poison and die. Japan will never lose the war.' We used to argue about it through the night. We used to be really angry at each other." On several occasions, father and son were close to physical violence and Mrs. Nishida had to step between them. Finally, Jack Nishida's attitude became one of indifference. He left it to his sister to fill out the registration papers.

Woody Wakatsuki's father was entirely opposed to Woody volunteering for the 442nd. He repeated the argument that for the Japanese becoming a soldier or a sailor was tantamount to death. That was why the Japanese were such famous warriors; they fought with complete abandon.

After warm debate, father and son reached a compromise. If and when a draft came Woody would accept the draft. By then the war might even be over.

The campaign against the loyalty questions was especially vigorous in Tule Lake. Speeches were filled with angry denunciations of *keto* (hairy ones), a derogatory expression for Caucasians, and, in Frank Miyamoto's words, "flaming expressions of pro-Japanese nationalism." When a motion was made that everyone should refuse to answer the questions, Miyamoto rose to protest that the decision about the questions should be a personal one. As he sat down he heard a Kibei say: "Let's bag this guy, beat him, and roll him in a ditch!" That night Miyamoto and his wife locked their door and put a chair against it. Miyamoto placed a hammer, his only weapon, beside his bed. An Issei minister was severely beaten as well as a Kibei editor and translator for the center paper, the *Tulean Dispatch*. Another Christian minister escaped a beating by barring his door. The attack on the Christian minister and the thwarted attack on his colleague sent shockwaves through the Christian evacuees in Tule Lake and strengthened the determination of many of them to get out of the center as soon as they could.

Although the project directors were instructed to remind the evacuees that interference with registration was punishable under the Espionage Act by fines of up to $10,000 and/or twenty years' imprisonment, at Tule Lake those opposed to registration went from block to block arguing, exhorting, and threatening. A concerted effort was made to get blocks as units to refuse registration, pressing again and again the refrain "We are all Japanese together." Anyone who broke ranks imperiled the solidarity of the group and brought discredit on "the Japanese people." Petitions stating the evacuees' refusal to register were distributed at mealtime when maximum pressure could be brought to bear on reluctant individuals to sign. Those individuals who spoke up in favor of registering were hooted down and denounced as *inu*. Again and again that fateful, hateful word was used to harass and intimidate. On February 24, a large meeting of Kibei drew up a petition demanding that they be taken from the center "at bayonet point" as the men from Block 42 (the heart of resistance) and that they be treated as "Japanese nationals." Those who stated their intention to register in spite of the bullying were segregated in the mess halls at special tables, received written threats, and were often followed by children barking at them like dogs.

When a group of Nisei persisted in their campaign to prevent other evacuees from registering, Harvey Coverly, the director, ordered them arrested on the grounds that, as American citizens, they were required by Selective Service to register. The arrests were responded to by a delegation from three blocks who appeared at the director's office to announce that they wished to reject their American citizenship and be sent back to their homeland. In the words of Edward Spicer, "day by day opposition to the registration became more highly organized and more bold."

An Issei who refused to register declared: "The main thing is that the war's got to end soon. Japan will probably attack the mainland, but still I suppose it might take some time for Japan to win the war. America was sure dumb in thinking that she could beat Japan in a couple of months. . . . Japan used China as a sort of practice ground for her Army. But America was not smart enough to see that. She's [America] losing all over the place. You can't believe the news you read in American papers because all they do is tell lies. One reason Americans are so weak is that they don't have any guts. . . . Japan won't weaken now, because look at all the resources she has at her command. . . . I'm staying for the duration. When the war's over I can go back to Japan. Of course it depends on the kind of peace that is made, but America is losing the war."

A Nisei woman who was questioned as to whether she was disloyal replied, "Yes." "Why?" "Well—no reason. If I say 'loyal' will they take me or leave me here?" "We don't split families," she was answered. "If one member is on the segregation list the others in the family are given the choice of leaving or remaining." "Then it doesn't have anything to do with staying?" "No . . ." "Then I'm loyal."

Morgan Yamanaka explained his no-no vote as a protest against being in the Tule Lake center. His brother and sister were in Japan—"do we fight them?" The notion of loyalty was a slippery one for Yamanaka. "Up to the issue of loyalty, my plans, my ideas, were you must be a good citizen. But you see being a good citizen for me didn't involve fighting against Japan. You do whatever you can to be a good American citizen, but it never occurred to them that you might have to fight your brother or uncles. . . . So when I answered no-no on the questionnaire, the basic reason was that . . . I would not want to fight [my] brother."

One of the arguments for refusing to register at all (as opposed to registering as a no-no) was that if an evacuee answered no-no, Congress and the army "could define all of us as disloyal, they could cancel our citizenships, making us enemy aliens . . . [and thus] confiscate legally our properties."

A Nisei girl declared: "I am going to say 'no' to anything as long as they treat me like an alien. When they treat me like a citizen, they can ask me questions that a citizen should answer." A young Nisei said, "You people are just not loyal to us; so that's the way we feel."

One of the most difficult problems for the WRA officials to deal with was the conviction on the part of many evacuees that the Japanese government was informed of virtually everything they said or did. At Tule Lake when the new director, Ray Best, assured the evacuees that their answers to the questionnaire would be kept secret, the statement was greeted with scorn and disbelief.

Further complicating matters was the rumor that the Selective Service draft would soon be instituted among the Nisei in any event. If that were to be the case, what was the point of voluntarily enlisting? When the point was sufficiently emphasized that a decision about instituting the draft had not been made and would depend, in large part, upon the success of the program of voluntary enlistment, a number of evacuees who had resisted enlisting decided to do so.

Dillon Myer hurried to Tule Lake soon after the rebellion against the registration broke out there. The director arranged for Myer to address the evacuees. It was a tense time. Myer's talk was translated by an Episcopal minister, the Reverend Dai Kitagawa, and after Myer's talk questions went on until eleven at night. Finally, an old Issei farmer rose to complain about not being able to buy whiskey or beer at the center. The crowd burst out in laughter and the tension was broken, at least for the moment. Myer felt that he had addressed the most serious concerns of the residents and won over the greater part of his audience. "When the meeting broke up," he wrote, "many of them came up to shake my hand. This was for me a memorable moment." But Myer's visit did little to reconcile the more militant Tule Lake evacuees. Of the male population of Tule Lake, seventeen years of age or older, 49 percent of the Nisei and 42 percent of the Issei responded negatively to the famous questions or simply refused to answer them at all.

In all the centers taken together, there was a total of 77,842 Japanese over the age of seventeen eligible to register. Of these, 20,982 were "male citizens," or Nisei, and 19,212 were "female citizens." "Male aliens," or Issei, numbered 22,275, not quite 1,500 more than the Nisei, while "female aliens" were recorded as 15,373. Of the total, 3,254 refused to register primarily on the grounds that to register was an act of submission to government authority. Of those refusing to register, 1,260 were male Issei and 588 female Issei. Some 65,000 answered question 28 in the affirmative, 2,083 qualified their answers by writing "yes, if . . ."

Most of those refusing to register at all were at Tule Lake (3,218 out of a total of 3,254). Gila River, Tule Lake, and Manzanar had the largest numbers answering question 28 negatively (1,238 at Tule Lake and 1,204 and 1,582 at Manzanar and Gila River respectively). A few months later over 2,000 switched from no or a qualified yes to yes, bringing the number of yeses to 68,000. Typical of the switchers was Frank Chuman at Manzanar. At the time of Pearl Harbor, Chuman was going to the University of Southern California Law School and working for the Los Angeles probation department. Shipped to Manzanar, he was bitter over the interruption of his education and when the registration crisis came, he signed no-no. Almost immediately he regretted his impulsiveness. As a friend of the director, Ralph Merritt, Chuman asked if he could withdraw his nos. Merritt, who traveled often to Washington, promised to do his best. It took several forays and an appeal to Dillon Myer to have the nos replaced by yeses. Merritt's effort had the indirect effect of reopening the whole issue for those evacuees who might, like Chuman, have second thoughts. With his record clear, Chuman was determined to try to resume his law school career. With the encouragement of Merritt and the help of the National Japanese American Student Relocation Council in the persons of Tom and Betty Emlen, who had recently graduated from Haverford College in Pennsylvania, Chuman was accepted at the University of Toledo Law School. Ralph Merritt urged him to accept. "After that," he told Chuman, "there is nobody, not even the military, that can prevent a United States citizen from going to the Eastern Defense Command without the clearance. You are free to travel throughout the United States. . . . There's nothing to prevent you from going out of camp because I am the one that will allow you to go out and go to the Midwest."

The turmoil produced by the registration crisis had a profound effect on the Caucasian men and women who constituted the administrative staff. One of them wrote of his own experience: "My part in the show was organizing and running the machinery of registration. I saw the whole show, back-stage and front. Registration itself went off smoothly and quickly. The team captains and block managers did a good, business-like job of lining up the residents and running them through on time. The interviewers were, for the most part, patient and fair and accurate. It was conducted on the whole with dignity and good feeling and an appreciation of the gravity of the issues. . . .

"Now we're standing around looking at what we've dredged up. All of us I think have been startled by the sweeping repudiation of loyalty to this country, or of hope of any future here. You expected it among the Kibei, but not among the citizens [the Kibei were, of course, citizens by virtue of having have been born in the United States even though they had been educated in Japan]. And to find, by the hundreds, products of our high schools and colleges who've never been in Japan answering No to the loyalty questions they gave, was shocking. Our first reaction, mine anyway, was anger. I wanted to wash my hands of the whole traitorous bunch and consign them to any concentration camp the public wanted to set up.

"Now that I've had time to reflect a little, and have talked with well over a hundred about their attitude toward this country, and seen the real anguish that accompanied many of their decisions, and the fears that prompted others—well . . . I want to see if anything can be salvaged from the wreck."

One Manzanar staff member spoke of "the jungle depths" and "the dark, tangled conflicts" that registration had brought to the surface. In the words of a community report: "Many of the administrative staff . . . were extremely apprehensive of the danger of future mass uprisings. Some staff members were skeptical, disillusioned, or simply disinterested in their attitude toward community government." Some of the center staffs, under constant strain from trying to enforce some degree of law and order while at least paying lip service to the principle of self-government, became increasingly contemptuous of the evacuees' own agencies for maintaining order. As the story went, some were ready to take the line: "It's our job to tell the Japs what to do and shoot the bastards if they won't."

The disenchantment of the center staffs was reflected in the attitude of the evacuees toward the administration of the centers: in many instances they became highly critical of the administrations. An Issei at Jerome declared: "I heard [the project director] say that since registration he has lost faith in the Japanese. . . . I think it would be a good idea to get rid of most of the Caucasians here and let the evacuees run the center themselves. They have the experience of the Co-op [the center store] and I am sure they could run the camp democratically. When this feeling of compulsion goes away then the people will cooperate more." In Edward Spicer's words, the evacuees "made critical appraisals, not only in terms of competence and relative ability as compared with evacuees working under them, but also of attitudes toward evacuees in general. They were looking about, spotting the ones who seemed to them to be tainted with racial prejudices and therefore unfair in their dealings with evacuees."

At Heart Mountain, the evacuees tried to bring pressure on the director to fire staff members that they found unsympathetic. The director rebuffed them but the effort indicated the degree to which the evacuees had come to assert themselves. In the rather patronizing words of one evacuee at Granada (in May 1943): "Most of the appointed staff are all right. They try to do the right thing. Many times they don't understand the psychology of the Japanese Americans and consequently make mistakes, but they are honestly trying to help the evacuees. . . . They have only two or three Hitlers among the staff here [and, presumably, no Hirohitos], and while they make it hard work for us sometimes, we know we can trust and work with most of the appointed staff."

Many discussions of the relocation program have slighted the very important class and economic differences among the evacuees, often speaking of them as if the evacuees were a socially and economically homogeneous group, which clearly was not the case. Seldom mentioned is the fact that those Japanese with substantial real property had a much stronger incentive to affirm their loyalty to the United States than those with little or no property. Those with property holdings had been assured by the War Relocation Authority that everything possible would be done to protect their property; moreover they had, in many cases, witnessed the efforts of the Division of Evacuee Property of the War Relocation Authority and the Wartime Civil Control Administration before it, to make good on that promise. An evacuee with a formerly successful business in mothballs or leased to a Caucasian operator, or a farmer with property to the value of thousands of dollars similarly on lease, had every reason to suppress feelings of grievance, outright hostility, or nationalist leanings and join the yes-yesers. On the other hand, an elderly Issei couple who had worked much of their lives as farmhands, often for prosperous Japanese farmers, and laid little by, had every reason to wish to return to the scenes and friends and relatives and memories of child or young adulthood. This assumption is confirmed by Spicer. Among the no-nos, according to Spicer, was a large proportion of rural folk who had not prospered in the United States, who were ready to return to Japan for their later years, and pleased at the prospect of having their fare paid by the U.S. government. The Tule Lake staff felt that the center had a number of evacuees who were "less well off economically, less courageous, less confident in their ability to make a living for themselves than the average of the evacuees."

Plainly, the registration crisis led to the resettlement of many of the more moderate evacuees. In the words of the authors of the JERS volume *The Spoilage*, they left behind "a disproportion of Californiana, ruralities, Kibei Buddhists, immigrant bachelors, the dispossessed in general, as well as a very large number of families, usually with many children."

Among its many other side-effects, registration made the situation of those evacuees employed by JERS awkward in the extreme. James Sakoda, an observer at Tule Lake, wrote to Dorothy Thomas that the registration issue had destroyed his credibility there. "The registration has hit a great many people rather badly. I and a great many other young leaders in the community no longer feel that we belong to the people anymore." Transferred to Minidoka, Sakoda found the atmosphere much less threatening. There were, to be sure, a series of strikes there—the pickling plant strike and the warehouse strike—but everyone was anxious to avoid the kind of conflict that had occurred at Tule Lake and Manzanar. Even at Minidoka there had been a "gradual change," Sakoda reported to Dorothy Thomas, "from the most 'loyal' center to one close to pre-segregation Tule Lake. . . . In a way this change can be considered the triumph of the Tule Lake ways over the Minidoka ways." One thing that contributed to the radicalization of once peaceful Minidoka was that a disproportionate number of moderates, and especially Christians, went out, leaving the centers increasingly in the hands of militants. Sakoda, who had felt obliged to be a yes-yeser, confided his anxieties to his diary. "When this war is over," he wrote, "this whole incident is going to make very sad reading—it is going to read like a real tragedy—and the writing of such a chapter should not be left up to the WRA or any Caucasians who do not understand what the Japanese people are really feeling. The whole incident is going to make the Japanese people look very foolish if all of the factors going into disturbing the minds of the people are not brought out."

Rosalie Hankey Wax was another member of the JERS staff. Wax's contact, Jack Nishimoto, told her much the same thing. The Nisei simply did not wish to be drafted. In Nishimoto's mind all of the JERS people, Dorothy Thomas included, as well as the WRA staff, "labored under the same limited view. They refused," Nishimoto wrote, "to see what the evacuees were really like." That, of course, was the heart of the problem—the inability of the Caucasians, however good their intentions, "to see what the evacuees were really like."

It seems to me that Edward Spicer, the community analyst at Poston, a staunch friend of the evacuees and the relocation's most sympathetic historian, gives us an important clue to the thinking of many of the evacuees who refused to register or who were no-nos. Spicer, in his introduction to the reprint of *Impounded People*, published some twenty-five years after the centers had closed (and after his initial report had been printed), spoke of the fact that many evacuees looked on the centers as "neutral havens," places where they could "wait out" the war. Since most initially believed that Japan must win or, later, when the evidence that the Allies were prevailing was incontrovertible, that there must be at the very least a negotiated peace that would protect their interests, they had no incentive to cast their lot, so to speak, with the United States. By doing so they would seriously compromise their hopes of a handsome postwar settlement.

Beyond that, the Japanese are inveterate gamblers. In the centers it seemed to many of them that they were in an ideal position to cover their bets. The reaction to registration was so extreme because, in their view, the rules of the game had been changed. Suddenly they were asked to put their cards on the table. In the poker player's jargon, "their bets were called." It seems to me that only such a hypothesis can explain the furor that the registration issue created. As both Sakoda and Nishimoto insisted, it was not for most Japanese an issue of loyalty or disloyalty, it was a matter of changing the rules. Even those Japanese who favored the United States, who hoped that the United States would, if not exactly win, at least stave off defeat, wished to cover their bets. The game had hardly begun. It was arbitrary and unreasonable to change the rules. The outside Americans, on the other hand, could not imagine such a state of mind. For them it could only translate into the simpleminded dichotomy, loyal or disloyal, and since they insisted on seeing it in the largely irrelevant black-and-white terms, they succeeded in pushing the Nisei especially, who felt most vulnerable, further and further in the direction of covert opposition or open hostility. It was not so much that the Nisei cast their lot with Japan because they so profoundly resented being herded into the centers (which to be sure they clearly did) but that they were indignant at being forced into a corner that they had not anticipated. In one sense, the evacuation program had been a kind of odd reprieve. "Persons of Japanese ancestry" were, by the relocation, relieved of the necessity of making thousands of difficult individual choices, the principal one being: "Am I willing to be drafted to fight in the armed forces of the United States against the Emperor and my homeland?" Assuming that the majority would have answered that question in the affirmative, it must, nonetheless, have been something of a relief not to have had to make it; the centers were more bearable as neutral havens. And then the neutral haven was snatched away and the draft-age Nisei found themselves confronted with decisions they had hoped never to have to make. That, in their view, was the final betrayal.

For those evacuees whose natural bent was subtlety and indirection, intense reserve, and family and "clan" loyalty, the experience was especially painful and in many instances inflicted wounds that would never heal. The carefully maintained facade that, in the main, had concealed the depth and degree of conflict among the Japanese themselves was permanently shattered. There had certainly been abundant clues and hints of conflict before the fateful registration but the staff and evacuees of various persuasions had a vested interest in minimizing such tensions. Had that not been the case, the War Relocation Authority never would have mandated the registration. Its purpose was to provide grounds for getting evacuees out of the centers, not for further complicating everything having to do with the relocation program.

Perhaps the greatest mistake was combining registration with a call for volunteers for an all-Nisei combat unit. It seems evident in retrospect that a much clearer procedure would have been to simply appeal for volunteers for what was to be called the 442nd Combat Team, leaving "registration" for another time and divorcing registration completely from anything to do with leave or resettlement.

So inept and so uncomprehending of the Japanese psyche were the architects of the whole process that one might be tempted to believe that it was all intended to place the evacuees on the defensive and present them to the public in the worst possible light were it not for the fact that the War Department and the WRA had everything to lose and nothing to gain by such an unfavorable outcome. Both parties clearly went into the venture with a sublime confidence that it would work to the advantage of the evacuees *and* thereby to the advantage of the WRA and the army.

One of the most ironic (and tragic) aspects of the registration crisis was that the whole issue of volunteering for the 442nd Combat Team, the ostensible reason for having registration in the first place, was obscured. The relative handful of those volunteering were harassed and denounced. Mike Masaoka, adviser to Milton Eisenhower and, subsequently, to Dillon Myer, and an officer of the Japanese American Citizens League, was the first to volunteer. Ichiro Yamaguchi noted that "JACL was very unpopular. They were the ones who answered volunteer service for the Army. A lot of people didn't like that either."

When Shig Doi, a veteran of the 442nd, was interviewed by Jack Tateishi in the early 1980s, his bitterness over the treatment of the volunteers by the militant nationalists was still evident. One of his friends had been ridiculed for having been a member of his college ROTC and when it was known that he had volunteered for the 442nd, the irreconcilables at Tule Lake put a bone on his plate in the dining hall with the supreme Japanese insult appended to it—*"Inu ga koko do taberu"*—"Dogs eat here."

Shig Doi and his brother had both suffered abuse for volunteering. "I'm glad I served. I did what I had to do. And I have no regrets." His detractors had said no-no. "Well, how many who went back to Japan came back here? All of them. The 442nd wrote the history for the Japanese. It was a good stepping-stone for the Buddha-heads, and we paid dearly for it. It's something that we left that the future generations can be proud of." What Doi could not forgive was the persecution that his parents suffered as a consequence of the fact that Doi and his brother volunteered. "That's what hurt me most," he told Tateishi. "I don't know, I guess it's because they were back there enjoying the benefits of my protection, and my dad, my dad must have died with a broken heart. He died young. My mom died young, too. I did what I had to do, and I have no regrets. But people made it tough for my family. And that's what hurts me most."

The mother of a Nisei who volunteered told of the abuse that she and her husband suffered from their son's decision. "We were really scorned by many people," she told Heihachiro Takarabe. "It was the most difficult thing which happened to us in our entire life. But we said to our son, 'We understand you. We want you to do whatever you feel right. If you want to be a loyal citizen of the U.S.A. and be patriotic, we think it is a very good thing.' So we gave our blessing and sent him out. . . . My son went to Italy and fought fierce battles, but he came home alive."

Tom Kawaguchi was sent to Tanforan initially and then on to Topaz. Topaz seemed to Kawaguchi like the end of the world. "I thought, oh my God, I gotta get out of this place. I was going to try to get out one way or another." The way Kawaguchi and his brother chose was volunteering for the 442nd. When people asked Kawaguchi why he wanted to volunteer, he replied: "I don't understand what the argument is. Our country is being attacked and I want to defend it. It's that simple." His friends looked at him and said: "You must have holes in your head." Kawaguchi speculated that the reason he felt as he did may have been because since childhood he had mixed primarily with Caucasians. "When issues come up," he told Jack Tateishi, "I don't look at myself as a Japanese; I just look at myself as a person that wants to say what he wants to say."

John Kanda was a junior in high school at the time of the evacuation.

"The day we left [were evacuated]," he recalled, ". . . I was sad. I thought it couldn't be happening, and believing what was in the textbooks and all on government and the Constitution, I just said, hey, this can't be happening to us; but it was." John Kanda and his brother volunteered for the 442nd.

Wilson Makabe was another Nisei who volunteered for the 442nd. Makabe went from an assembly center to seasonal leave, and after being assigned to Tule Lake continued to work outside as a farmworker for a county commissioner named Kenyon Green who provided Makabe with a house on his ranch and then drove to Tule Lake to pick up Matabe's brother, two sisters, and father with whatever luggage they could carry in the car. Hearing about the formation of the 442nd, Makabe took a bus to Salt Lake City and enlisted. Seriously wounded in northern Italy in the campaign to break through the so-called Gothic Line into the Po Valley, Makabe lost one leg and the other was badly injured.

We will hear more of the 442nd. The War Department had hoped to find some 3,600 volunteers; they got 1,200. It was a thin harvest, reaped at incalculable cost. But, quite miraculously, it would prove enough.

Chapter 20

SEGREGATION

THE REGISTRATION CONTROVERSY, REPORTED IN DETAIL IN THE PRESS, often with lurid embellishments, had the predictable effect of renewing the calls for putting the "Japs" in concentration camps rather than "pampering" them in the relocation centers, which were often made to sound by the press as vacation resorts. The *Denver Post* was one of the worst offenders in this regard. It carried a series on the Heart Mountain center, the first of which was headlined: "Food Is Hoarded for Japs in the U.S. While Americans in Nippon Are Tortured." Much was made in the papers about the cruelties and hardships suffered by Americans interned in Japanese prison camps. One story in the *Post* announced that a reporter had unearthed $12,000 worth of baby food at Heart Mountain with only five babies in the center hospital. The reporter failed to point out that there were many other babies in the center not in the hospital. When the Granada center served turkeys on Christmas day (most of the turkeys had been raised at Poston), word got out to the media and considerable outrage was expressed over the fact that many Americans had to go without turkeys due to wartime shortages in poultry.

There were calls in Congress for investigations of the centers and a series of House and Senate hearings were held. There were suggestions that all Japanese who had left the centers on any form of leave or in the resettlement program be required to return to the center to which they had originally been assigned.

All of this was, in turn, faithfully reported in the Japanese language press and, not infrequently, in the newspapers published in the centers. Such reports certainly did nothing to moderate the paranoia that most evacuees felt.

One of the proposals that received a good deal of support in Congress was to turn the centers back to the War Department. Mon Wallgren, a Washington senator, introduced a bill to that effect (SB444). Another proposal was to segregate into one center the evacuees considered loyal to the Emperor, primarily the no-nos, the "renunciants" (those who specifically renounced their American citizenship) and those who had requested repatriation to Japan. The loyal evacuees would thereby be freed from the pressure of the militants.

Dillon Myer was opposed to both proposals. His reaction was to publicly state what he considered the case for the evacuees and to press Secretary of War Stimson to lift the Exclusionary Ban on the West Coast. Myer clung doggedly to his conviction that the ban was the root of all the problems experienced by the War Relocation Authority. The evacuees could never be prevailed upon to leave the centers until the ban was lifted.

In January a subcommittee of the Senate Committee on Military Affairs, under the chairmanship of Senator A. B. (Happy) Chandler of Kentucky, began hearings on SB444, the bill calling for the transfer of the relocation centers to the War Department. Chandler, who visited several of the centers, had issued a succession of critical comments; Myer was apprehensive about the committee's final report.

At this point, the President himself was recruited to bolster support for Myer and the WRA. Washington is a city that is acutely aware of the weight of symbolic acts. When Eleanor Roosevelt spent a day at the Gila River center south of Phoenix, the event was well covered by the press and the message to Washington political circles was not missed. To underline this support, the President invited Myer to have lunch at the White House. At lunch on the White House lawn, Myer told the President of the various trials and tribulations that the authority was subjected to, mentioning, in particular, Senator Chandler's hearings. Roosevelt listened attentively (which was not always his wont) and regarding Chandler told Myer: "I think I can help you with that." That the report of Chandler's committee was surprisingly mild, given Chandler's longstanding hostility, Myer credited to Roosevelt's influence with the committee's Senator Joe O'Mahoney of Wyoming.

The Chandler Committee had hardly concluded its hearings when the Dies Committee, headed by Martin Dies, Jr., of Texas, cranked up its own investigation, appointing a subcommittee of John Costello of Los Angeles, Karl Mundt of South Dakota, and Herman P. Eberharter of Pennsylvania to look into conditions in the centers. The composition of the House subcommittee was not encouraging: Costello was chairman; he had been an early advocate of mass evacuation; Mundt had made his reputation as the scourge of the reds; only Eberharter was of liberal persuasion.

J. Parnell Thomas, a member of the full-committee from New Jersey, got into the act in May 1943, traveling to Los Angeles to hold a press conference at which he announced that the evacuees were being too well fed and that he had evidence (which he did not reveal) that scattered among the southern California Japanese American community at the time of Pearl Harbor was "an organized division of the Japanese army." Thomas called for an end to the "WRA policy of releasing disloyal Japs."

Someone by the name of Townshend appeared as a witness before the subcommittee. Townshend had been in charge of the motor pool at Poston, had decamped at the time of the Poston strike, and subsequently been fired. He told the subcommittee that there had been "over 1,000 Japanese officers and soldiers at Poston" at the time of the strike and described the center staff as "poor simpletons, cowering Caucasian employees standing around like whipped children." He failed to mention that he had panicked and fled for his life.

At the full committee hearings in Washington, Dillon Myer asked for permission to testify in defense of his agency. He reminded the committee that the WRA program "is being watched in Japan, where thousands of American soldiers and civilians are held as prisoners or internees; in China, India, Thailand, Burma, and many other countries whose collaboration we need if we are to defeat our enemies with a minimum loss of life." The manner in which the problem of the Japanese American was handled had vast international repercussions. "The program of the War Relocation Authority has been under investigation for the past eight weeks in such a manner as to achieve maximum publicity of sensational statements based on half-truths, exaggerations and falsehoods; statements of witnesses have been released to the public without verification of their accuracy." The result had been to stimulate public distrust and to provide the enemy "with material which can be used to convince the peoples of the Orient that the United States is undemocratic and is fighting a racial war;

"Undermining the unity of the American people;

"Betraying the democratic objectives which this nation and its allies are fighting to preserve;

"It may lead to further maltreatment of our citizens who are prisoners or who are interned."

Myer's testimony was given considerable publicity and he followed it in March with what he called an "Anniversary Statement" in which he reviewed the situation in the centers and acknowledged the tensions that existed between those evacuees who were pro-U.S. and those who were "actively pro-Japanese." He argued that it was of great importance to assist those evacuees who were pro-U.S. to get resettled. He reminded his readers that many of those who had resisted the WRA's authority were "loyal Americans [who] have chosen various means of expressing their protests over un-American treatment which they have received." Such protests were "easily misinterpreted." But of one thing the director was sure: "After many months of operating relocation centers, the War Relocation Authority is convinced that they are undesirable institutions and should be removed from the American scene as soon as possible. Life in a relocation center is an unnatural and un-American sort of life. Keep in mind that the evacuees were charged with nothing except having Japanese ancestors; yet the very fact of their confinement in relocation centers fosters suspicion of their loyalties and adds to their discouragement. It has added weight to the contention of the enemy that we are fighting a race war; that this nation preaches democracy and practices racial discrimination. Many of the evacuees are now living in Japanese communities for the first time, and the small group of pro-Japanese which entered the relocation centers has gained converts." It was this last point that clearly preyed on Myer's mind and on the minds of many others closely connected with the relocation. To what extent was the relocation experience turning loyal American citizens into pro-Japanese dissidents?

Ten days later (March 11, 1943) Myer and his staff decided to address Henry Stimson himself and plead for the lifting of the ban of the Exclusionary Zone. In his communiqué to Stimson, Myer reviewed in considerable detail the history of the evacuation. The policies of the War Relocation Authority, Myer wrote, had been based on three major assumptions. "The first of these is that all evacuees of Japanese ancestry, except for those who request repatriation and those who may be deported for illegal activities, will continue to live in the United States after the close of the war. The second is that the United States has no intention of conducting the war on a racial basis and that the education program should be carried out at all times in harmony with this principle. The third assumption is that all American citizens and the law-abiding alien residents of the United States should be treated by the government, insofar as possible under wartime conditions, without racial discrimination.''

Myer went on to describe the negative aspects of the relocation centers in some detail. One of the most serious problems, he noted, ''arises from the fact that we have thrown together in closely-packed somewhat rudimentary communities thousands of people who have a common racial ancestry but who are highly heterogeneous in almost every other respect. Citizens are mixed in with aliens; the well-to-do with the poor; farmers with city dwellers; the highly educated with the near illiterates; those whose cultural background is primarily Japanese with those who have never visited Japan and have no desire to go there. This mingling of people with widely varying economic status and cultural backgrounds under the conditions of relocation center life has created many conflicts and has intensified others which existed prior to evacuation. It has produced a widespread feeling of individual and collective insecurity and has led to frustration, fears, and bitterness. . . . In the atmosphere of tension that prevails almost constantly at most of the centers, a few active agitators have been able to produce results out of all proportion to their numbers.''

Another serious problem was ''the gradual breakdown in the pre-war structure of Japanese-American family life. Older women who have spent virtually all their lives in hard physical labor are now reduced to idleness and find time hanging heavy on their hands.'' Myer then went on to describe quite vividly the problems of the children and young people in the centers. One of the most serious problems was that the artificial life of the centers, which required relatively little work and much of that done grudgingly, was inimical to the famous work ethic of the Japanese. Minor tasks, indifferently performed, had become the norm in some centers. In brief, the whole atmosphere of the centers was deeply demoralizing. For Myer, it followed from this analysis that the sooner the evacuees were returned to normal life outside, the better. Every month spent in a center compounded the problems of the War Relocation Authority and further demoralized the evacuees.

The solution that Myer pressed on Stimson was to lift the Exclusionary Ban on the West Coast so that a major effort could be mounted to get evacuees out of the centers and back at least to those general localities from which they had been so rudely snatched. The first and best reason to lift the ban was that the "danger of invasion has undoubtedly receded [if it ever existed]. Another is the increasing seriousness of the manpower problem. A third is the need for pushing food production and other production activities to the utmost. And a fourth consideration is the high desirability of eliminating, insofar as possible, all discriminatory actions against American citizens and law-abiding alien residents of the United States at a time when we are fighting abroad for the principles of freedom and democracy."

With these things in mind, Myer had "three possible plans of action." Plan A was to simply proceed as on the present course getting as many evacuees out into the interior as possible while also providing seasonal leave for agricultural work in areas not too remote from the centers.

If this plan were followed, Myer estimated that over the next four to six months between 10 to 25 percent of the evacuees could be resettled.

Plan B would "involve the removal of all those regulations and restrictions which now apply only to Japanese Americans and not to the American population at large. It would mean elimination of the evacuated areas as such, immediate reinstitution of selective service for all male citizens of Japanese descent, and release from the relocation centers of all evacuees" except those for whom there was some substantial basis for believing that they were security risks.

Plan C was presented as "a middle-ground approach." Under C the evacuated area would not actually be eliminated but "all American-citizen evacuees" judged not to be security risks would be screened and allowed "to return to the evacuated area and would be recommended for work in war plants. . . . Evacuees cleared by the joint board [representing the War Department, Department of Justice, and Naval Intelligence] for work in war plants and for return to the evacuated area would no longer be subject to discriminatory restrictions and regulations."

Any talk of raising the Exclusionary Ban alarmed General DeWitt. To do so would call into question the validity of the whole evacuation. He was equally opposed to the notion of "loyalty reviews" as the basis for enlisting Nisei into the U.S. Army. He wrote to McCloy: "We wouldn't have evacuated these people at all if we thought we could determine their loyalty." But Colonel Bendetsen had serious doubts. He said to one of McCloy's aides: "Of course [the fact that loyalty is hard to determine] is probably true of white people, isn't it? You know that old proverb about 'not being able to look into the heart of another'? And not even daring to look into your own.' '' And to another aide he remarked: ''Maybe our ideas on the Oriental have all been cock-eyed. . . . Maybe he isn't inscrutable.'' Still it seemed to Bendetsen as to DeWitt that to lift the Exclusionary Ban would be to ''confess to an original mistake of terrifically horrible proportions. . . . I would find it very hard to justify the expenditure of eighty million dollars to build Relocation Centers, merely for the purpose of releasing them again.''

Stimson's response was a rebuke to Myer. The secretary noted ''A serious deterioration in evacuee morale . . . in recent months. This unsatisfactory development,'' Stimson continued, ''appears to be the result in large measure of the activities of a vicious, well-organized, pro-Japanese minority group to be found at each relocation project. Through agitation and by violence, these groups gained control of many aspects of internal project administration, so much so that it became disadvantageous, and sometimes dangerous, to express loyalty to the United States. The fact that these groups were permitted to remain in power not only shook the confidence of the loyal in their Government, but also effectively stifled the expression of pro-American sentiment. It had been, and remains the opinion of the War Department, already frequently expressed to you, that much trouble could have been avoided if these troublemakers had been removed from the relocation centers and placed in rigorous confinement. . . . It is significant that the evacuees themselves propose segregation as a necessary step too long delayed, and volunteer the opinion that the situation will grow worse at an accelerated rate if action is not taken immediately.''

A bitterly disappointed Myer drafted a prickly and argumentative reply to Stimson. After a rather perfunctory thank-you—''I wish to thank you for the support which the War Department has given the program of the War Relocation Authority generally,'' Myer went on to imply that the War Department had caved in to the reactionary views of the Western Defense Command. ''If mass segregation on a fair and individual basis is so simple'' that the War Relocation Authority is to be criticized for not accomplishing it, ''it is difficult to see why a wholesale evacuation of all persons of Japanese descent was ever necessary. If the dangerous and potentially dangerous individuals may be so readily determined as your letter implies, it should have been possible to evacuate only the dangerous from the Pacific Coast area.'' The War Relocation Authority had been from its inception opposed to the notion of judging ''categories of people,'' as loyal and disloyal. ''The evacuation,'' he reminded Stimson, "was justified by military urgency, but military necessity would not justify segregation on categorical basis as proposed to the Authority." The real cause of bad morale in the centers was not the failure of the War Relocation Authority to act decisively against "troublemakers" but evacuation itself "and all the losses, insecurity, and frustration it entailed, plus the continual 'drum drum' of certain harbingers of hate and fear whose expressions appear in the public press and are broadcast over the radio.

"However," Myer concluded, "if it will help to secure the acceptance of the relocation program [that is to say, apparently the resettlement program], we are willing to accept the consequences of segregation in the centers."

It was a bold letter. In effect Myer bargained away his resistance to segregation (which, had he stubbornly retained it, would doubtlessly have led to his being sacked) for an assurance that the resettlement program could continue.

The project directors, thoroughly unnerved by the registration controversy, were unanimous in favor of segregation when they met with WRA staff in Washington on May 31. The fact was that Stimson had directed Myer to undertake segregation so that much of the May 31 meeting was devoted to discussions about how that process could best be carried through. With the registration crisis very much in mind, the WRA staff was determined to make every effort to anticipate evacuee objections and allay anxieties. After weeks of rumors, the decision to segregate was announced in early July 1943.

Once the decision had been made to segregate, Tule Lake became the obvious candidate to be the center for those to be segregated, primarily on the grounds that it already contained the largest number of "refusers" and dissenters. The plan was to relocate all the no-nos from the nine other centers *to* Tule Lake and move *from* Tule Lake all those "cooperators" who wished to be moved.

In all discussions of segregation, the contrast between loyal and disloyal was played down and segregation was referred euphemistically as "regrouping of people according to their national sympathies." It was emphasized that transferring the segregants to Tule Lake was not conceived as punishment "for past acts or expressions" but a move to try to restore (or in some instances, create for the first time) peace and harmony in the centers. All evacuees' belongings, including those in storage, would be sent with them to their new centers. Semi-revived community councils were appealed to for assistance in reconciling residents to relocation, and it was pointed out to them that those who did not wish to be relocated to another center might want to seriously consider being relocated out. Block managers were also utilized to inform residents of their blocks. In Topaz, the community council was given a major share of responsibility for planning the move. A Transferee Committee was formed to facilitate the transfer. Even the so-called segregants, many of whom welcomed the prospect of being with those of their own disposition, pitched in.

Segregation was a vast undertaking; the logistics were formidable. Out of the Tule Lake population of some eighteen thousand, approximately eight thousand yes-yesers had to be moved, bag and baggage (all belongings, furniture, and other property), to another center, and some eight thousand no-nos from all the other centers had to be moved to Tule Lake. First of all, the no-no goats had to be separated from the yes-yes sheep, a very considerable task in itself that involved interviews with the evacuees and mountains of paperwork. Segregation meant, among many other things, further soul-searching by many evacuees—in effect another identity crisis since evacuees were permitted in many instances to change their no-nos to yes-yeses.

A major obstacle to the success of the whole enterprise developed at Tule Lake where some four thousand yes-yesers dug in their heels and refused to budge. This meant that four thousand no-nos in other centers could not be accommodated at Tule Lake. The WRA wracked its collective brain. All its powers of persuasion were employed to prevail upon the Tule Lake yes-yesers, many of whom it may be said were older Issei with large families, to transfer or go out. The whole considerable network of WRA regional and local offices along with the considerable resources of the Committee on Japanese American Resettlement would be available to them. Only a few hundred could be pried loose. The fact was the yes-yesers who declined to move had made their peace with the no-nos. Tule Lake, perhaps because of its more turbulent history (Manzanar was its only serious rival in that respect), had developed a kind of esprit. It thought of itself as superior to the less notorious centers. For such residents leaving Tule Lake meant a step down in the center world. Also, just as going to Tule Lake from Rohwer and Jerome meant a step in the right direction, i.e., toward the West Coast, going from Tule Lake to Topaz, Poston, or Heart Mountain was a step (or two or three) in the *wrong* direction, away from the West Coast.

Some Issei pleaded for exception from moving on the grounds that their health was too bad to permit them to move. Others balked because of the rumor that movement out of Tule Lake was preparatory to moving them out of the centers altogether. Another was that those remaining at Tule Lake would be reclassified as prisoners of war and receive $50 a month. Oddly enough, this was an incentive to stay. There were threats of a sit-down strike of residents, who would have to be forcibly moved with all the attendant bad publicity for the War Relocation Authority. Speakers went to all the wards (groups of four blocks) to answer rumors and reassure the prospective transferees; all, finally, to little or no avail.

As the weeks went by, those residents of Tule Lake who were to be transferred became obsessed with rumors about where they were to be sent. Rumor had it that bands of Indians would attack the center at Jerome (near an Indian reservation), that mosquitoes there were the size of sparrows, that the center was situated in a swamp, and that in rainy weather the entire center was flooded.

Nonetheless, the transfers to Tule Lake from the other nine centers went far more smoothly than registration had. Evacuees were involved in planning for the move and given responsibilities in connection with the actual entrainment and the trip. At Topaz the project director placed the major responsibility for the management of the campaign to relocate out on the community council, which worked closely with a staff group called the Administrative Transfer Committee. Thirty-four blocks sent representatives to the Transferee Committee. These elected a chairman who, in turn, appointed a Community Cooperative Committee of five members. It was the job of the Transferee Committee to facilitate the movement of the segregants out of Topaz to Tule Lake. The General Transferee Committee, on the other hand, had overall responsibility both for those being transferred out of the center and those being transferred in. The segregants chose a "train monitor," "car captains," and others having responsibilities during the trip to Tule Lake.

The Special Events Committee of the community council was given the responsibility of arranging a welcome for the newcomers from Tule Lake, who were met at the center gate by the Boy Scout drum and bugle corps "and escorted to the induction center where light refreshments were served." This classic American ritual observed, they were then directed to their quarters and oriented to their new home. Much the same procedures were followed at the other centers.

From the middle of September to the middle of October 1943, 6,289 nonsegregees were transported out of Tule Lake to one of six other centers, and 8,559 persons classified (usually by their own testimony) as segregants and their family members were brought to Tule Lake from the other centers. In all, 18,711 evacuees were moved between centers in the segregation program. Fifty-three railroad carloads of personal belongings of Tule Lake evacuees were moved with their owners to six centers.

With segregation completed, the residents of Tule Lake included a number of so-called segregation parolees (men, in the main) who were paroled to Tule Lake from the Department of Justice internment camps and who were not free to leave until released by the Department of Justice. These were individuals considered especially disposed to acts inimical to the United States. Also included were those men and women who had requested expatriation or repatriation. Finally, and most poignantly, there were those "family members" of the segregants who, though not themselves segregants, were loyal to those members of their family who were. In this category might be included, for example, the wives of husbands who had answered question 28 in the negative, but who themselves had answered the female version in the affirmative, and minor children and parents.

Topaz sent 1,459, of whom 1,069 were Nisei and 390 Issei; the Nisei were between seventeen and thirty-nine years of age, the Issei from forty to sixty-four. Poston sent 1,427, of whom 1,043 were Nisei and 384 Issei. Gila River sent 2,005 and the ratio of Nisei to Issei was about the same as that of Granada, one of the smaller centers, which, with a population of 7,656, sent 215 men and women, but even after adjusting for the much larger size of Poston (18,039) and Gila River (13,420), there were far more segregants proportionally at Poston and Gila River than at Granada. Jerome with 7,932 (only a few hundred more than Granada) sent 2,147. Jerome had a high percentage from Hawaii; the Hawaiians were notably bellicose. Minidoka sent only 335, divided evenly between Nisei and Issei (167 to 168).

Virtually all of the Christians at Tule Lake chose to transfer to another center. Some were permitted to travel to their new homes by car. The Igarashi family, given permission to travel on their own to Jerome, Arkansas, rented a car and held prayer meetings along the way.

Tule Lake, now populated by evacuees who had cast their lot with Japan (except, of course, for those troublesome four thousand yes-yesers who had refused to be moved), became a "concentration camp" of a kind (if only in the sense that the Japanese nationalists were concentrated there). There were, of course, numerous other distinctive features—more interior police, more soldiers, tanks, far more limited movement in and out (this was especially true of residents on parole from internment camps). One Jewish staff member, tormented by the analogy with Nazi concentration camps, resigned but the fact was that the WRA rationale for Tule Lake was that the Japanese nationalists were now free to pursue what was generally referred to as "a Japanese way of life"; this proved to be an ambiguous phrase.

Chapter 21

TULE LAKE

THE TULE LAKE CENTER AT WHICH THE SEGREGANTS ARRIVED IN October 1943 was hardly what most of them had expected. It was a grim and desolate setting, barren of the touches of greenery and flowers found at most others. It was badly crowded and a recreational building had been converted into a barracks for single men.

Some three thousand of the twelve thousand in other centers who were slated to transfer to Tule Lake had to remain in their home centers because there was no room for them at Tule Lake due to the refusal of the large number of yes-yesers to relocate. Two thousand of the three thousand scheduled to go to Tule Lake remained at Manzanar, next to Tule Lake, the center with the largest number of no-nos.

When the segregants were collected at Tule Lake a survey of their backgrounds was made with specific reference to the number of years individuals had spent in Japan, apparently in an effort to establish a relationship between time spent there and the degree of loyalty to the Emperor, the presumption being that there would turn out to be a close correlation between the two. The results seem to indicate otherwise. Of a total of 10,765 men and women segregants, 4,502 had never visited Japan while somewhat over 4,000 had spent seven or more years there. Among 6,940 American-born Japanese males at Tule Lake 4,330 had spent no time in Japan.

A Nisei no-no who transferred to Tule Lake wrote to a friend at Topaz: "This center compared to Topaz is a center from all parts of the West Coast—not just from the East Bay region of California. You always had some former friends around at Topaz. But here it's very hard to get to know people. In my particular block, there are people from almost every center and every part of California.

"You just can't make friends with just anyone without knowing a little about their background. Thus it's hard to get the least bit congenial with your block people, ward people, center people. One noticeable thing about the Japanese here, though, and that is if the Issei came from the same 'ken' in Japan they are more apt to become friends."

The proponents of segregation had anticipated it would have two principal consequences. First, life in the other centers would be more harmonious once the no-nos and other dissidents had been segregated. Second, the Tule Lake segregants, having been, in a sense, authorized to pursue "a Japanese way of life," would themselves be more tractable. But the latter expectation was not to be. Four days after the last segregant had arrived at Tule Lake a truck carrying farmworkers and driven by a sixteen-year-old Nisei turned over trying to pass another truck. All of the farmworkers riding in the truck were injured and one man named Kashima died shortly after the accident.

The episode provided the occasion for airing a host of grievances by the farmworkers. Kashima's funeral was made a political event. The director, Ray Best, was instructed to attend the funeral and his refusal to do so was added to the list of grievances. Eight hundred farmworkers declared themselves on strike, imperiling thousands of dollars' worth of ripening crops—alfalfa, potatoes, cabbage, cauliflower, lettuce, turnips, beets, spinach among them. The farmers refused to harvest the center's crops on the grounds that some of the harvest was scheduled to go to other centers. "They wanted . . . Tule Lake labor and produce to be used only for Tuleans who had determined to be Japanese and not for the other evacuees who had determined to be Americans."

Sixty-five block representatives were elected to negotiate with Best (the so-called Negotiating Committee). The Negotiating Committee showed considerable political astuteness by focusing its attention on specific grievances such as dust control, better facilities, better preparation and service of food—practical day-to-day issues. Initially at least, they played down the ideological themes.

While various specific grievances were being negotiated between Ray Best and the Negotiating Committee, Dillon Myer arrived at the center on

November 1. While Myer was meeting with Best and the members of the
Negotiating Committee in the administration building, the Negotiating
Committee put out a call for all residents to go to the building to hear of
"important developments." The consequence was that a curious crowd
estimated at ten thousand gathered. When nothing seemed to be happening some of the crowd started to drift away but they were herded back by
supporters of the Negotiating Committee. Some of the organizers of the
crowd had spread the word that the meeting was to concern "bad food."
Others described it as a rally. In the words of one witness: "It was the
biggest and best organized demonstration of evacuees that had taken
place in any center. It was also the most premeditated and least spontaneous demonstration."

Meanwhile the negotiations went on. Among the Negotiating Committee's demands was an insistence that the status of the Tule Lake
evacuees be more clearly defined. Were they prisoners of war? If so,
there was always that potential $50 a month called for by international
law. If they were being treated as aliens, that was illegal since they could
not be divested of their citizenship unless, as some had indeed done, they
formally requested the withdrawal of their U.S. citizenship. Under those
circumstances, the Kibei who had joint Japanese and American citizenship would become Japanese citizens and thus prisoners of war. In addition to such tendentious legal points the Negotiating Committee
demanded the ouster of the project director and his five top assistants.

In an atmosphere of growing tension, Myer, showing considerable
courage, emerged from the meeting to address the crowd, assuring them
that all legitimate grievances would be given consideration. He was followed by the Reverend Abe, a Buddhist priest, who declared: "We have
been here a long time. A great many things have been discussed [with
Myer and center officials] and no conclusions have been reached. We will
have to enter into further negotiations. . . . You people must remember
that you are Japanese and must act as Japanese to hold together for the
sake of the Empire and the Emperor."

Frank Miyamoto, the JERS contact at Tule Lake, later recalled how
angry cries erupted from the crowd during Myer's visit: "We are people
of Imperial Japan! We're not a people to be forever pushed around by the
damned Whites!" When a Nisei foreman called out in English for more
light someone called out: "This is Japan. Who dares to speak English
here?" A roar of approval rose from the crowd. One evacuee who witnessed the event from his hospital window wrote a friend: "There exists
within the center a common idea of unity that no other center can achieve.

The leaders are all men of ability, high caliber and possess diplomatic talents similar to the crowd that occurred during the Santa Anita riot. During the three hours 20,000 of us waited eagerly, as from time to time one of the representatives would state, 'Now's the time for united spirits, we must not fail or else the whites will take advantage.' We should be proud of our race. We sure brought up the morale.''

During the negotiations, a band of militants went to the center hospital and severely beat the chief medical officer, a Nisei known to be unsympathetic to the Negotiating Committee faction. Some staff members, blocked from leaving their offices, became alarmed at what they felt was the generally menacing spirit of the crowd; rumors swept through the center that an attempt had been made to set several buildings on fire. While Myer did his best to cool the situation, outside tradesmen who had been in the center left and reported that a riot was in progress and that the agitators had taken over the center. A few nights later "a group of young men" hearing the rumor (false as it turned out) that trucks were to leave Tule Lake with fruit and vegetables for other centers, determined to stop the convoy. Searching for the trucks, they encountered internal security officers and a fight took place. The leader of the internal security force called on the officer in charge of the military police for support and soldiers and a tank were soon on the scene. One of the internal security men had been badly beaten and when several of the militants were captured they received severe beatings at the hands of the outraged security men. The next day a reinforced contingent of soldiers arrived. Tanks were stationed at strategic locations and some 350 of the more militant segregants were arrested and confined in a stockade in the center of the center.

The Tule Lake newspaper, the *Tulean Dispatch*, encouraged its readers to believe that help was on the way. Under the headline "Tule Lake Japanese Intimidated by Tanks," the paper announced that the fact that a tank had entered the Tule Lake center had been promptly reported to Japan and that Radio Tokyo had announced the fact, adding that "the Japanese in the center are holding out by displaying their *Yamato Damashii*."

After the demonstration at Tule Lake and the arrest of the ringleaders, the military police took over the running of the center. The tactic that the police had to deal with was "withdrawal and passive non-cooperation." When the military police assumed control of the center, the commander, accompanied by an official of the War Relocation Authority, summoned the residents to assemble at the open-air theater to hear the proclamation of military control and the regulations that were to accompany it, but no evacuee appeared and the address was delivered over the public address system to sullen residents who remained in their blocks. It was an augury of things to come: passive noncooperation with the army and the WRA. This was called *genjo-iji*, or "status quo."

Out of the Tule Lake episode came renewed calls for the military to take over all the centers. Twenty-two of thirty-three West Coast congressmen petitioned the President to fire Myer and replace him with a tougher director. The *San Francisco Chronicle* joined the chorus of critics, calling the War Relocation Authority administrators "phonies" and "bad public servants, examples of two-bit men pitchforked by bureaucracy into four-dollar jobs," a reference to the fact that most of the top WRA staff had been recruited from the Department of Agriculture.

At a Los Angeles Town Hall session, Dillon Myer faced an inquisitorial audience. In the question-and-answer period, a man in the audience asked: "Mr. Myer, if the thing that happened at Tule Lake had happened in Japan, what do you think the Japs would have done with the troublemakers?" Myer replied that they undoubtedly would have shot them but, he later wrote of the incident, "I thanked God we were living in a country that does not believe we should shoot people for what we think they are thinking."

Among the segregants themselves, there were rancorous divisions. Some residents supported the militants in their demand that the strike be continued until the stockade was closed and the men inside released. Others believed that the strike served no purpose other than to make daily life difficult and inconvenient. A vote showed the center almost evenly divided, with a slight majority in favor of ending the strike. A Coordinating Committee was thereupon formed to try to work out some sort of compromise, and the military police returned control of the center to the project director. But as with so many similar bodies at other centers in other crises, the Coordinating Committee found itself in an increasingly awkward position between the administration and the evacuees. Every effort at compromise was interpreted as a sign of weakness or betrayal. The members of the Coordinating Committee were denounced as *inu*. Since a number of the members of the committee were active in running the center store, they were accused of profiteering. After three of four months the committee dissolved amid further recriminations.

It was succeeded by the *Sokuku*, or Young Men's Association for the Study of the Mother Country, founded by the Buddhist priest the Reverend Aramaki. The *Sokuku* described itself as dedicated "to increase the appreciation of our racial heritage by a study of the incomparable culture of our mother country.'' The *Sokuku* also pledged ''to refrain from any involvement in center politics.'' Far from refraining, the *Sokuku* did all in its power to prevail on center residents to comply with its program of Japanization. Bugles and uniforms were supplied and young evacuees engaged in constant drilling, drumming, bugle-blowing, shouting ''Wash-ho! Wash-ho!'' as they marched about. A Nisei woman gave cautious approval to the *Sokuku*, saying that they had ''worked out some good things to educate young men. . . . The *Sokuku* says, 'We must train these boys.' And I think that's right. You must do something with these zoot suiters.'' A *Sokuku* pamphlet declared that the future of all ''true Japanese'' was in Japan. They were ready ''to sacrifice everything . . . to the country we dearly love.'' To do this they must ''uphold highly our Japanese spirits and increasingly endeavor to cultivate ourselves both mentally and physically in order to fulfill the principle of being nothing but a real Japanese.''

The pamphlet was followed by a petition demanding repatriation. In the words of one unsympathetic evacuee: ''When they circulated this petition they said, 'If you sign this paper you won't be drafted into the Army and you'll be free to get on the exchange boat.' So everybody signed it.''

The campaign against anything Western was tireless and ingenious. The Kibei were busily breaking up dances where the style of dancing was ''not Japanese.'' Some went so far as to enter women's showers, announcing that the Japanese custom was for men and women to bathe together. Nisei girls, serving as clerks in the center housing office, were rebuked for aiding the enemy and slapped and pushed about. One night all the windows in the housing office were smashed. Such treatment of young Nisei women, recalling as it did traditional Japanese attitudes toward women, was offensive not only to the women themselves, to their parents and brothers, but to many other Japanese in the center. A young Nisei woman wrote soon after her arrival at Tule Lake: ''Anything can happen in this dump. It's almost as bad as being in Germany. You wonder why you were born. No fooling, these guys have no respect for women, and boy, do they believe in Gestapo methods. You can't use your own mind. You gotta be alert of what you say, and on top of that you gotta respect the Kibeis.'' The moderate Nisei called the nationalists the ''rah rah boys of Tojo with ears pinned to the short wave.''

Meantime, Congress passed a bill, the result, in large part, of the Tule Lake turmoil, to permit U.S. citizens to renounce their citizenship under procedures approved by the attorney general (Public Law 405 of the 78th Congress, signed by the President July 1, 1944). The intention of the bill was to relieve pressure in the centers by recognizing the reality that a number of Japanese Americans were ardent Japanese nationalists. As reported in the JACL paper, the *Pacific Citizen*, the act was "designed to provide legal means to denationalize between 300 to 1,000 persons of Japanese ancestry at the Tule Lake segregation center who had expressed a desire to renounce their United States citizenship and have asked for repatriation."

Sokuku hailed the legislation. "Fortunately," its newsletter declared, "the government whose national policies are based on democracy, humanity and liberty has now proclaimed by legislation that it officially approves our inclination. We are indeed delighted with this recognition." The Society to Serve the Emperor for Speedy Repatriation, *Sokuji Kikoku Hoshidan*, was formed to press all Nisei to renounce their U.S. citizenship and apply for repatriation to Japan. One project of the *Hoshidan* was to buy an island in the South Pacific as a refuge in the event that the United States won the war.

The emphasis at Tule Lake now shifted from trying to compel all adult residents to request expatriation or repatriation to Japan, to pressure for renunciation of citizenship. A Nisei declared, "I never wished to renounce my citizenship but to stop my parents pleading and sobbing I went to an interview for renunciation." Another Nisei, appealing to revoke his renunciation, declared, "Everybody around me renounced. Or at least they said they did. They wouldn't speak to me. They treated me like an outcast. I felt alone and powerless in a huge dark place." Another Nisei wrote to his lawyer, "Everybody told me that I must renounce my citizenship of the United States, otherwise I will be forced to go outside the camp to be murdered." The established formula for Nisei renouncing their citizenship in "renunciation hearings" was: "I renounce because I want to be Japanese." The Kibei version was: "I renounce because I am Japanese with Japanese face and hair."

A Nisei girl remarked that quite a few of her friends were renouncing because they wanted to accompany their family to Japan. "You know why the boys are renouncing?" she added. "They are dodging the Army draft." Before the renunciation proceedings were over at Tule Lake seven out of every ten Nisei had requested "denationalization." In 80 percent of the families where anyone renounced, every member who could renounce did so.

Looking back on the renunciation, one Nisei, not himself a renouncer, wrote: "It was funny the mentality of the people in here then. I mean both Issei and Nisei. . . . The Justice Department gave the hot-heads their reason for defiance when they began sending hundreds of renouncees to internment. To defy that, internment became an honor. Anyway, it meant no relocation and no draft." The wife of the Reverend Aramaki told a friend that she was happy that her husband had been sent to the internment camp at Santa Fe "because it made him a real Japanese."

Japanese traditions and Japanese culture were one thing, the establishment of the Greater East Asia Co-Prosperity Sphere School was another. Other Japanese schools were organized, none quite so inflammatory as the Greater East Asia, but all having that bent, and strong pressure was brought on parents to enroll their children in the schools. Ben Takishita, fourteen years old, was required to attend the Japanese school against his will. He recalled being forced by one of his older brothers, a teacher in the school, to sit on the floor for an hour, "and if you move you got hit on the head. This kind of thing . . . their purpose was to teach us Japanese and forget English. . . . All day we were in Japanese school. We were learning the language and being hit. The school forbade speaking any English; you had to speak only Japanese even at home. The boys had to cut their hair, 'bozu' style and the girls wear pigtails. Every morning they would do 'wasshoi-wasshoi'—very political thing—pro-Japan."

Hissho Kigan Shiki, "Ceremony to Pray for Victory," was observed by the *Sokuku* on the eighth of every month as "the day our motherland declared war against the allied nations. On this day the people of Japan offer a fervent prayer for total victory at any cost." The ceremony was preceded by a cold shower as an expression of physical fortitude and cleansing. *Meiji Setsu*, the celebration in honor of the birthday of the Emperor Meiji, the grandfather of Hirohito, was carried off with much ceremony at Tule Lake; some ten thousand residents participated. A Kibei at Tule Lake wrote to a former teacher that the militants "shout loudly 'Banzai to the Emperor!' and even the police, it seems, are afraid to cross them. If you are caught at anything like [American] dancing you are likely to be practically killed." One group of militants refused to enter a gate to a section of the center until an American flag, placed there by the Boy Scout troop, had been removed.

The segregants were increasingly at odds with the less militant, primarily with those yes-yesers who had refused to move and had little sympathy with the militant nationalists. In the words of one of the female Kibei at Tule Lake: "I was disappointed when I found a great number of Yes-Yes people. . . . We had expected just one group and had expected to run this camp as we wanted to. We had high hopes for that.'' An editorial in the *Tulean Dispatch* pressed the same idea: ''We are here because we wish to be JAPANESE, because we desire to do things as Japanese. Our future does NOT lie in the American way of life; our future is in the Japanese way of life!''

When the militants found that they could not prevail on a number of Nisei at Tule Lake to renounce their citizenship and seek repatriation, they began to agitate for what soon came to be called ''resegregation.'' They wished to be sent somewhere where they could pursue the ''Japanese way of life,'' or have ''a Japanese face'' as some put it, uncontaminated by the less ardent or doctrinaire. Soon rumors began to circulate that the ''true Japanese'' were going to be segregated once more, at their own insistence. Word even came over the camp radio that the ''disloyals'' (now a word of positive connotation) would be sent either to Alaska or to Jerome. An elderly Issei woman said, ''People heard it over the radio and the blocks are very upset. Children are crying. I have moved four times already and I don't want to move again.''

The resegregationists ''emerged from the underground'' and assumed the name of *Saikakuri Seigan* and circulated the so-called Ishikawa Petition, which urged separation from ''a large number of heterogeneous elements with whose thoughts our ideas would never harmonize.'' The resegregationists collected 6,500 signatures, many through the exertion of considerable pressure, including physical violence. A Nisei from Topaz reported, ''I was pressured into signing up with the Resegregationist Group along with many others. We signed in order to prevent physical harm to ourselves and to the members of our family.'' In the words of one skeptical Nisei: ''Though they believe themselves to be the only 'true Japanese' in the center, this claim is received with skepticism on the part of the majority of the residents who believe their actions to be contrary to their words. Indeed their actions are often contrasted with the ways of the old Japanese samurai 'who kept their word once it was spoken, and never drew a sword unless for a purpose.' Parading and flag-waving in a center still under lenient care is looked upon as cheap exhibitionism and a disgrace to the Japanese people. The majority believe in working things out in a gentlemanly fashion 'as a proud people of a first-class nation.' ''

In the early summer of 1944, the manager of the center store, a man named Hitomi who had been active on the Coordinating Committee, was stabbed to death. The most notable consequences were the silencing of any opposition not only to resegregation and the complete dominance of the ''back-to-Japaners.'' It came to be more and more the case that any appearance of reluctance to embrace the return-to-Japan movement brought ostracism and threats of violence. The issue of the stockade tended to be eclipsed by the fervor of the resegregationists. The men in the stockade undertook a hunger strike that failed to budge the administration, but when it was over the decision was made by the War Relocation Authority to close the stockade and send the more intractable individuals to an internment camp.

By November 1944 the War and Justice Departments had resolved to step up the pace of renunciation and repatriation and take the resegregationists head-on. There would be no more drills, no more public exercises designed to intimidate other residents. The only resegregation would be the shipping off of the most intractable *Hoshidan* to military jails, where they would find life far more difficult than in the centers. Even as groups of renunciants were being shipped to incarceration centers, the drills for boys and girls were held on Sunday mornings at nine o'clock in defiance of the Department of Justice edict.

The Greater East Asia Co-Prosperity Sphere Language School simply changed its name to the Japanese Language School and special Japanese studies and observances were merged with the normal activities of the center. Hollywood movies replaced the mandatory Japanese films and the project director was invited to throw out the first baseball of the season. Some renunciants attempted to join the U.S. Army as a way of expressing their reconciliation to America. American-style boxing and wrestling replaced sumo, kendo, and judo for school-age boys, and the beginning of the baseball league was a welcome distraction.

On December 20, 1944, an army contingent of twenty officers arrived to hold renunciation hearings. As in so many previous occasions, wholly misleading rumors circulated. The most persistent one was that those evacuees renouncing their citizenship would not be forced to resettle out of the center while those who failed to renounce would be forced to relocate. In the words of one Nisei, "My brother said at this hearing that he wanted to renounce his citizenship, because he figured he could then stay at Tule Lake." The *Hoshidan*, of course, did all that it could to spread the story hoping thereby to greatly increase the number of renunciants. Residents of the center were told to seek internment as the surest way of demonstrating loyalty to Japan. For the resegregationists, internment was the ultimate triumph over "the system." Thwarted in their original intention of resegregation by a purging of the less militant and the yes-yesers, they were now able to use "denationalization" to achieve a de facto resegregation in internment camps. There resettlement and induction into the military were no longer threats. There they could enjoy perfect rectitude.

At the end of 1944, a Nisei at Tule Lake summed up the feeling in his block, a feeling he believed was typical of the center in general: "This block, like all the others," he wrote, "has a few people who might be called relocation prospects. Because people are loyal to the United States, have property or other holdings 'outside' or believe that democracy is the proper form of government, they will eventually desire to relocate and start life anew. Now they are waiting for the present war hysteria and racial prejudice to subside or be controlled. They are a minority group in the block, but so far as their loyalty is concerned, there can be no doubt. Many of these families have already given their sons to the war effort of this country. They are willing to fight and stand by their principles. . . . Some are bachelors and have relatives elsewhere. These people are cool towards all actions aggressively aimed at the WRA, and they consistently follow the group that is conservative, if 'political' pressure makes it seem necessary to follow a given course. Sometimes these people are referred to as the fence-sitters, who are waiting for the clouds to clear."

Another conservative group was made up of people who had requested repatriation or expatriation to Japan at the earliest date. Our Nisei analyst estimated this number at about three-fifths. "Although," he wrote, "there is no question of their loyalty to Japan, they feel that the countries involved are at war and that people are sacrificing their lives to protect their respective nations. While many were evacuated from their homes in a sudden action which often resulted in their losing everything they had, they figure that this is now so much water under the bridge and that it's too late to do much about the past. Now that they have chosen to become Japanese subjects, they believe it is up to them to comport themselves in peaceful and law-abiding fashion. Being thankful for the shelter and food provided by the Government, and realizing that the tax-paying citizens of this country are being deprived of many luxuries, this group is anything but wilfully antagonistic. . . . They ask no favor but to be left alone to pursue their ambition of returning to Japan.

"These two groups do not under any circumstance desire to relocate. Because they fear forced relocation and compulsory draft, they are taking whatever action they believe helpful to prevent such situations. They frequently state that such action on their part is necessary because of the inconsistencies in the policies of the U.S. Government. Though both groups have similar ideals in mind, their means of obtaining their goals are altogether opposite. These two elements constitute the majority who command the respect of the people of the center. Of the two, one is radical in its views and actions, while the other is conservative and law-abiding.''

On the other hand, if the War Relocation Authority should act in a way deemed by the conservatives to be arbitrary or unjust, these conservatives would "no doubt respond in a manner of utmost hostility." Such individuals kept our Nisei's block on an "even keel." They wished to be able to say when they finally embarked for Japan that "they left friends in the United States who regarded them as decent, self-respecting individuals. They think hopefully of a better future abroad, but do not turn away from this nation in hate and passion."

Finally, there was the group that our Nisei analyst termed the radical group. "These people show their complete hate and distrust of the U.S. Government by drastic actions that are . . . detrimental to other law-abiding Japanese within the center. . . . Although it is a minority group when compared with the 'conservative' disloyal group, the individuals are high-strung and uncontrollable. Their stock remark is that they are the only 'true Japanese,' although the great majority of the residents hardly agree. The radicals even go to the extent of using force and violence within their own group to hold it intact. . . . They further exhibit hostile and disagreeable attitudes which make social functions impossible in many blocks." In the opinion of our Nisei, the majority of the membership in the most radical group came from "country folk who respond to the pressure of a few extreme leaders."

In this atmosphere "some of these who considered themselves loyal Americans were inclined, by the pressures as they perceived them, to relocate, to move rather in the direction of going to Japan as an alternative to being dumped out on their own to sink or swim in an uncertain and generally hostile environment." Thus, there was one more irony added to an already abundant supply: the effort of the War Relocation Authority to empty the centers had the effect of pushing some evacuees in the direction of repatriation.

It seems to me that we can only understand the events at Tule Lake (and, by extension, at the other centers) in the light of the historic culture of Japan. We might recall the experience of Yukichi Fukuzawa, the Japanese scholar who lived in constant fear of assassination simply because he was a student of Western history and culture. There was, obviously, a bright side and a dark side to *Yamato Damashii*. On the bright, the devotion to art and learning, to duty and service and loyalty; on the dark side, the grim determination to force conformity—one's own conformity—on everyone else, the essence of totalitarianism. Marius Jansen, the reader may recall, described the code of *bushido*: "The romantic overtones of the cult of the swordsman—the wise and courageous samurai, eye ever fixed on the ultimate objective with a heart as pure as his shining blade, trained to set aside all personal considerations, cultivating self-perfection in order to be a more perfect instrument of justice. . . . There was cruelty as well as courage in the conduct of the *ronin* swordsman. . . . Since they took for themselves the highest of morality and duty, their enemies could be dismissed with hatred and contempt." This is the spirit in which the assailants of John Yamazaki, of Mike Masoda, of Togo Tanaka and countless others acted. Those who were "wrong," those who were disloyal to the Emperor, must expect to pay with their lives. Confident that they embodied the noblest spirit of Japan, the nationalists dismissed "their enemies . . . with hatred and contempt." Setting out to demonstrate the superiority of traditional Japanese culture over the strange hybrid called American democracy, a hybrid they were profoundly contemptuous of, the "true Japanese" succeeded in doing exactly the opposite—they demonstrated the darker side of autocracy. The endless plots and mindless cabals of Tule Lake bring to mind Kurosawa's films of feudal Japan. What one disenchanted Nisei called the "priesthood from Heart Mountain [referring to Buddhist priests from that center] and the fallen stars from Manzanar and Poston" conspired against the Tuleites and, finally, against one another.

Chapter 22

THE DRAFT

W ITH THE INTRACTABLES OR MILITANTS OR JAPANESE NATIONALISTS (whatever we may wish to call them) segregated at Tule Lake, there was every reason to hope for relative tranquillity at last. For one thing, Christmas, a time of peace and joy for Christians, was in the offing. It seemed a favorable augury. December 25, 1943, was the first "real Christmas" in the centers. Christmas 1942 had slipped by in the process of getting settled and in the unrest produced by the riots at Poston and Manzanar. Now different Protestant denominations and church groups took it upon themselves to send toys to the centers to brighten the children's holiday. The *Heart Mountain Sentinel* of December 18, 1943, carried the story of such gifts: "Busy, tired hands are preparing gifts for distribution at the Block 18 Community Christmas Committee headquarters where hundreds of gifts are arriving daily as church groups and individuals throughout the nation manifest their desire to share Christmas with children of this center . . . the gifts are from girl reserves, missionary societies, Sunday School classes, ladies aid guilds, most of which are affiliated with the Presbyterian churches. The Presbyterian Church of America selected Heart Mountain and Tule Lake Centers for its gift-giving project."

Yoshiko Igarashi recalled that at Heart Mountain "used clothes were sent to us from churches all over America. . . . When a load came at Christmas time, we sorted it out according to the ages, and the men distributed them around.''

The *Minidoka Irrigator* noted ''Outsiders are showering the project with Christmas gifts for children. . . . Groups of carolers of all ages . . . serenade every block, the shut-in, the sick, the others.'' Although Minidoka was one of the least contentious centers, it had its quota of irreconcilables. In the midst of excited preparation for Christmas, an anonymous warning appeared in the form of flyers scattered around the center. One flyer addressed to two ''cooperators'' read: ''To Jim Sagamoto, Iwao Hara: Give order . . . Cancel all Christmas collections. If you do not take this order, we shall sabotage.''

A similar note read: ''Blindman Sagamoto, you and all your group: We are ready to take action. Our group is determined to risk any jail sentence. We will sacrifice anything. It is the terrible time of war.''

Still another flyer declared: ''Pro-American people leave this camp immediately. If not, danger fall upon you. 6,000 pro-Japanese.''

The year 1944 started off promisingly enough. It was almost a year since the registration crisis had shaken the centers to their core and now evacuees seemed anxious to settle into the normal routines of center life. Confident that the resisters of military service were segregated in Tule Lake, Secretary of War Stimson announced on January 20, 1944, that all draft-age Nisei in the centers would be subject to the draft like other young American males through the agency of the Selective Service. The rationale of War Department and the War Relocation Authority was to build on the favorable sentiment that had been created nationwide by the 100th Battalion's sterling performance in Italy. Without some replacement system, the 100th and the 442nd must eventually be lost by attrition; there was bound to be unfavorable comment if new recruits could not be found from among the thousands of draft-age Nisei still in the centers.

To the dismay of the War Relocation Authority, the announcement of the institution of the draft in all the centers except Tule Lake caused another upheaval in the centers. Although long anticipated by many Nisei (Woody Wakatsuki had been dissuaded by his father from joining the 442nd with the understanding that he would wait to be drafted), there was once more the feeling, especially among the Kibei, that the rules had been changed in the middle of the game.

The whole draft issue was complicated by that streak of fatalism in the Japanese that there has often been occasion to refer to. The typical Japanese attitude was that if a son was called to serve in the army or navy it was simply assumed that he would be killed, whereas the average American draftee or enlistee had every hope of returning. To most Japanese having a son drafted into the army was like a death sentence.

In the words of one Nisei: "We are taught that if you go out to war you should go with the idea that you are never coming back. That's the Japanese way of looking at it. . . . I listen to white boys talk. They look at it differently. They all take the stand that they are coming back, no matter who [else] dies. It's a different mental attitude. . . . My mind is made up. I know my father is planning to return to Japan. I know he expects me to say 'no' so that there will be no possibility that the family will be separated. There isn't much I can do for my father any more; I can't work for him the way I used to. But I can at least quiet his mind on this." The same attitude was expressed by another Nisei resisting the draft. "If I and my brother," he told an interrogating officer, "get killed what happens to my family? My brother and I are the only ones old enough to help support the family."

Issei who held property in the name of their "citizen children" were afraid that if their sons went to war and were killed they would lose their property. An Issei at Tule Lake declared, "I'd be willing to go out now if it weren't for the draft. I have one son in the Army now, and I don't want my other sons to be drafted one by one. . . . I'd be glad to see them go, but it makes you mad when you've been discriminated against so much. Ever since I came to America there wasn't a day when I wasn't made to feel small because I was a Japanese. I've lost all hope of a future in America. . . . I've lost everything. . . . Unless you are a parent you can't tell how we Issei feel."

The more extreme Nisei urged that the proper course was to simply refuse to serve; the moderates, prompted by lawyers who were experts in the area of civil liberties, took the line that petitions should be drawn up and submitted to the War Relocation Authority and to the army stating the legal grounds for opposing the draft. These objections or "demands" were, in essence, that until *all* the constitutional rights of the citizen Nisei were restored to them and they were compensated for any losses suffered in the original relocation, they were under no legal or moral obligation to respond to the Selective Service calls. The petitions (it had been decided to call them "petitions" rather than "demands"), which were so similar as to make clear that there had been close cooperation between the Nisei in the various centers, started off with expressions of loyalty and then went on to list the conditions that the Nisei felt should be met before the government could, in good conscience, call on them for military service.

"We believe, however," a typical petition read, "that the rights and privileges of citizenship, in all justice, be combined with the duties and obligations of citizenship." Nisei should not be assigned to special segregated units (as the men of the 100th Battalion had been) but serve in mixed units. Moreover, all citizens should be free to travel wherever they wished including in the West Coast states from which they were still excluded. There should be a guarantee of the physical safety of the Nisei and their families and "adequate economic means for those who resettled." Voting rights should likewise be guaranteed and it was suggested in several of the petitions that arrangements should be made to grant citizenship to the Issei. The petitions were also utilized to record the resistance of the residents of the centers to resettlement. Those who were employed in the centers should receive wages based on U.S. Army standards. Included was a request that any restrictions on admission to graduate programs at colleges and universities be removed. And then a calculated knife thrust: the government should take steps to "protect any and all minorities against the possibility of future mass exclusion and evacuation." The evacuees thus presented themselves as the champions of the constitutional rights of all minorities.

A petition from the Issei at Heart Mountain was sent to Dillon Myer, to Stimson, and to President Roosevelt. It inquired about the status of returned veterans, asked for prompt return to the West Coast, requested government allotments for dependents and the elimination of special clearance procedures for Nisei who wished to work in war plants.

A petition from Minidoka included "a request for special military training in colleges and universities, equal opportunity for advancement, and equality of employment in industry." Like the Topaz petition, it asked that the Issei be reclassified as "friendly aliens," and that they receive financial restitution for any losses that they had suffered as a consequence of relocation. In addition, they urged a government-initiated program against anti-Japanese discrimination in every area of American life. There was certainly a degree of disingenuousness in the petitions. Their primary purpose was clearly to derail the program of drafting Nisei.

One consequence of what we might call the petition episode was that the number of sympathizers among those groups and organizations concerned with humanitarian and civil rights issues grew substantially. Moreover, as a result, at least in part, of the agitation of the militants, over two hundred Nisei in the various centers refused to report for induction or for physical exams. Jack Tono at Topaz was among those refusing to report. U.S. marshals arrested Tono and some sixty-three Topaz Nisei and distributed them among county jails in Casper, Laramie, and Cheyenne. The charge: "failure to report for a physical." Tono and the others were tried, convicted, and sentenced to three years in a federal penitentiary—"which didn't faze me a bit at that time," Tono declared. Tono went to a prison on McNeil Island near Tacoma; the older and married men and their relatives went to Leavenworth, Kansas. Sent to do farm work, Tono encountered some hundred or so Jehovah's Witnesses who had refused to serve in the army on religious grounds.

On the other side of the fence, so to speak, where the JACLers who had supported the plan for the 442nd at the Salt Lake City conference in November 1942 and had urged the War Department to institute the draft in the centers. They were as dismayed at the Nisei resistance as were Dillon Myer and the War Relocation Authority. Some of them now did their best to persuade their fellow Nisei to accept the draft. We have earlier encountered Minoru Yasui, who had such a notable exchange with the sheriff of North Platte, Nebraska. Yasui had gone from the Portland Assembly Center to Minidoka. There, after some sixty days of wrangling, he was allowed to go out. He headed for Salt Lake City, the headquarters of the JACL, and then for Denver, where he joined up with Joe Grant Masaoka, the older brother of Mike Masaoka, and an officer of the JACL. Joe Grant was, in Yasui's words, "very concerned about Nisei refusing to register for the military draft reinstituted for Nisei—to give us an opportunity to prove our loyalty and patriotism to the United States of America. Because the JACL had, in effect, caused these young men to be caught in a situation where they felt they must defy the military draft orders, JACL felt a deep sense of responsibility to these young men."

Masaoka persuaded Yasui to join him in trying to persuade the Nisei to accept the draft. A number of young Nisei were in prison at the federal correctional institution at Englewood, Colorado, awaiting trial for refusing to register. Yasui and Masaoka tried to prevail on one of them to change his mind, pointing out to him: "Son, you're ruining your life. You're still a young man, and you'll have a criminal record that will hold you back for the rest of your life. Please reconsider and cooperate with your draft board."

The Nisei replied: "Why should I when the government has taken away our rights and locked us up like a bunch of criminals anyway?"

"But you've got to fulfill your obligations to the government."

"Look, the government took my father away, and interned him someplace. My mother is alone at the Granada camp with my younger sister who is only fourteen. If the government would take care of them here in

America, I'd feel like going out to fight for my country, but the country is treating me worse than shit!''

And so the conversations and exhortations went, much the same from camp to camp, with Joe Grant Masaoka and others doing their best to persuade the Nisei to register and the Department of Justice to be lenient.

When Yasui and Masaoka turned their attention from the internment camps to the relocation centers in the hopes of dissuading Nisei not to defy the draft, the atmosphere crackled with hostility. At Granada, military police had to protect the two men from violence at the hands of the audiences they addressed. From Granada to Gila River to Poston, the result was the same—indifference or hostility. At Poston they were not allowed to address an assembled group on the grounds that such a gathering might turn violent.

Once the inevitability of the draft had been accepted by the majority of those in the centers, the actual process of induction often served as a unifying event. Some of the centers organized farewell parties for the inductees with the USO providing entertainment. While the numbers were small from each center (in June 1944, 166 Nisei responded to Selective Service calls), by December 1944, 1,543 had been drafted out of the various centers. Many of those who were taking basic training returned to the centers on furlough to visit their families, a move encouraged by the War Department. Seeing their sons in American uniforms aroused pride. The warrior image was so powerful in the Japanese psyche that even an American uniform stirred strong emotions and it was certainly the case that many of the parents of Nisei soldiers had cast their lot with the United States. USO offices had been opened in some of the centers and they helped to crystallize sentiment favorable to the United States. Each soldier who returned for a visit became something of a celebrity. Women wove one-thousand-stitch belts as good-luck charms for the protection of young men in battle according to an old Buddhist tradition. The senryu poets began to compose poems to the soldiers. In addition to the soldiers visiting home on leave, word was received in the centers of the prowess of the 442nd fighting in Italy and when news came back to centers of those killed and wounded in battle, Buddhist and Christian ministers joined in ceremonies for the dead. In Spicer's words: "The relocation centers were now like normal communities outside with their honor rolls, and memorial services for war dead.''

In July an Issei mother wrote to a friend who had ''gone out'': ''You know things are a lot different than they were a while ago. People really rebelled at the time of registration. They said awful things about the government and they spoke of the boys who volunteered almost as if they were traitors to the Japanese for serving a country that had treated the Japanese so badly. When Selective Service was reinstituted all one heard was that the Government had no right to draft men out of a camp like this. At first when the boys left, their mothers wept with bitterness and resentment. They didn't think their sons should go. This week five have gone from our block. I tell you I'm surprised at the difference. Wives and mothers are sorry and they weep a lot. But now they really feel it is a man's duty to serve his country. They wouldn't want him not to go when he is called. When they talk among themselves, they tell each other these things. They feel more as they did before the evacuation.''

Much the same thing was happening in the blocks. In the words of a block leader: "At first our block was a little slow in giving some recognition to the boys who went for induction. Then we started giving $10 to each inductee, provided they left from the block. But many of them took indefinite leave after they passed their physicals in order to get the cash grant and trip somewhere at WRA expense. These youngsters are smart boys. Last week we held a block meeting to decide if our policy was right. There was a lot of women present. They were interested in this question. We voted that all boys would receive a block present whether they went on indefinite [leave] or not. After all, they were going to the Army. So now, before a boy leaves for induction or goes out of the center on indefinite leave after passing his physical, five or six leading men of the block dress up in their good clothes and call on him to present the gift and the best wishes of the block.''

"The feelings of the mothers were more and more a factor to be reckoned with in block opinion," Spicer added.

The same procedures were followed in drafting evacuees in the relocation centers as were followed for all draftees. A draft board reviewed requests for deferment or exemption.

The process of drafting out of the centers was greatly complicated by the fact that a large number of the draft-age evacuees were on indefinite leave and the process of tracking them down proved a complicated and time-consuming one. Of those who received induction notices, 2,795 were inducted from one of the centers, 852 were placed in 1-A but not drafted prior to the close of the centers, 1,446 were rejected for one reason or another, and 315 were arrested for refusing to report for a physical examination or induction.

From the beginning of the draft in November 1940, to December 1945, 25,778 Japanese Americans were inducted into the armed forces, 438 officers and 25,340 enlisted men. An estimated 13,500 were from the continental United States and 12,250 from the Hawaiian Islands.

The record read:	Killed in Action	569
	Died of Wounds	81
	Wounded	3,713
	Missing in Action	81
	Total	4,444

With the draft no longer an issue, an effort was made to revive the community council, but the genie, it turned out, could not be returned to the bottle. The militants, the nationalists, the dissenters in general used the councils to their own ends. The sophistication attained by those residents who accepted leadership roles in the centers is perhaps best indicated by the address of the chairman of the community council in Topaz. At the ceremony inducting a new council, he outlined his view of the council's function:

"The community council realizes that the problems of today and problems to come are and will be much graver and more serious than those of the past two years. With this fact in mind, the present council has begun their serious thinking in terms of the welfare of the residents.

"The council is not and will not work for the self-interest of any individual or group of individuals but for the mutual and general welfare of all. We will welcome any suggestions and criticism that are constructive and helpful at any time, through your councilmen or direct to the office of the council in Block #1.

"We will use every means available to inform the residents on every subject that is brought to us, the action that is being taken, and the progress and the final decision. We will make every effort to follow through on every problem and issue so that we may be able to write its finale to the satisfaction of the residents.

"The present council has decided that in order to perform its duties for the general welfare of the residents, it is necessary that we have: (1) solidarity of councilmen; (2) support and confidence of every resident; (3) support and confidence of every organized group in the center.

"To the members of the administration—

"There may be times when the residents' request be considered unreasonable. We want the administration to appreciate the fact that these requests will be made only after thorough and careful investigation, study, and analysis. Only those which we believe are reasonable shall be presented.

"Any request the council determines is out of reason will not be brought to the administration. We believe this is the council's responsibility.

"Once we determine it is a reasonable request we wish the administration to appreciate this fact and grant us favorable consideration, otherwise, the council shall be placed in a most difficult position. Mainly, because of lack of confidence which will be greater on part of the residents. In case our request cannot be granted, we expect the administration to give us justifiable facts in black and white.

"I believe there must be a mutual understanding for better relationship.

"With mutual understanding between the residents and the council, between the administration and the council, I, as chairman, can assure the administration of the council's sincere desire to put forth every effort toward the harmonious and peaceful operation of the center.

"On this basis then, this council hopes to be able to leave a record to be proud of."

The rhetoric was impeccably democratic but the action, it turned out, ran in the old confrontation channels. It could not, in fact, be otherwise.

Chapter 23

SOCIAL AND CULTURAL LIFE

IN THE SPRING OF 1944, WHEN THE FUROR OVER THE DRAFT HAD DIED
down, an uneasy truce settled on the centers (Tule Lake excepted, of
course). So many evacuees had gone out (over 25,000) that some centers
had the air of declining towns. Jerome, the scene of the Reverend John
Yamazaki's brutal beating, had sent 2,417 no-nos to Tule Lake, among
them the troublesome Hawaiians, leaving fewer than five thousand behind. Jerome had subsequently been closed and the evacuees distributed
to other centers (Dillon Myer considered the closing of Jerome a kind of
dry run for the persistently hoped-for closing of the other centers).

A former staff worker at Topaz wrote in February 1944 on returning to
the center: "The most striking impression on revisiting Topaz, a year
after registration, is the remarkable sameness in the black tar barracks,
the lack of trees, the biting frosts, and the isolated circular thinking of the
residents."

Edward Spicer believed that 1944 had been an important year for the
centers. Through most of that year there were no dramatic announce-
ments of new policies to stir up the residents of the centers; they had for
the most part settled into routines of center life that, as we have seen,
were not without their agreeable side. The War Relocation Authority had
fixed its baffled attention on trying to prevail on the evacuees to vacate,

using all the blandishments, cajolings, and cautious pressures that it could to try to budge the residents. When it became evident that this policy was not only not succeeding in relocating or resettling substantial numbers of evacuees, but rather providing an issue around which resistance to virtually all administrative initiatives formed, the project directors and their staffs quietly desisted.

As Spicer put it, an adjustment had been worked out to the relocation center way of life. In Washington, the War Relocation Authority officials had come to the conclusion that relatively little could be done to get evacuees out of the centers until the War Department revoked the Exclusionary Ban on the West Coast. The more confident and self-reliant evacuees had already taken advantage of the resettlement program; many of those remaining would not budge until they had the assurance of returning to more or less familiar scenes, the "West Coast state," as Edward Spicer called it.

In the anonymous "A's" words: "Life in the center had been accepted by the majority of older people as an interlude. It had become more than bearable. For many it had become pleasant as it took on meaning through association with other Issei, but it was still felt to be an interlude between acts in their real lives. This sense of its unimportance, of its lack of meaning in relation to real life, colored most of the activities in the centers. . . . The leaders and the liaison men . . . moved from the ideal of 'model cities' to the conception of 'play-toy councils,' as the realization of the artificiality of the communities grew more clear. Life in the centers led nowhere in particular; it was a waiting. Nevertheless the time could be passed pleasantly."

Nineteen forty-four saw an effort to revive the community councils. The ban on Issei had been lifted in the spring of the previous year and Issei leadership generally accepted as the JACL leaders enlisted in the 442nd or went out to college or to jobs.

As noted earlier, there were three levels of center life that manifested themselves in the assembly centers: the practical, day-to-day material aspects of life—food, shelter, heat, medical care, and so forth; the social and cultural life, including education, recreation, the arts; and the political or ideological aspects. Here particular attention shall be paid to the social and cultural aspects of center life that did so much to mitigate the more intolerable aspects of the centers.

One of the most striking aspects of *Yamato Damashii* is its aesthetic element. Art, in its widest manifestation, is integral to the Japanese character. It is not something to be "appreciated," a kind of "embellishment," the preoccupation primarily of the more prosperous and better educated members of society as is so often the case in the modern industrial world. Art, like loyalty and honor, obedience to parents, like the work ethic and "individualism" to the *hakujin*, was, and to some extent remains, an essential part of the character of the Japanese people of whatever class or degree. In the centers one of the most appealing aspects of *Yamato Damashii* was this same impulse to turn everything into art, to enhance the natural beauty of the world, and to create an endless array of aesthetically satisfying *things*. That impulse is perhaps stronger in the Japanese people than in any other race or nation.

Allen Eaton's book *Art Behind Barbed Wire* covers many of the traditional Japanese arts that were practiced in the centers. Embroidery was one of the most popular forms. Poetry, music (the *biwa* notably), dance, ceramics, and *kobu*, the discovery of hardwood roots and limbs, especially of cypress trees, that suggested human or animal forms. Wood carving was another very popular art form as was the making of traditional Japanese furniture. Since the Japanese love competitions and exhibitions, these were frequent in the centers and between centers. Shows of calligraphy and flower arrangements were often combined—the flowers arranged with an appropriate poem in calligraphy behind them and perhaps an ink brush painting of a scene related to the flower arrangement. Many of the objects fashioned in the centers were made to enhance the bleak barracks or the cramped living quarters of the evacuees. Artistic mail boxes were something of a fad and most striking were the classic Japanese gardens that sprang up wherever the soil and climate allowed. Where flowers were reluctant to grow, classic arrangements of rock and dried wood had to suffice.

The musical associations typically tried to plan productions that appealed to all segments of the center. They made or ordered from outside elaborate costumes and rehearsed classic Kabuki plays as well as popular modern Japanese musicals. A *fujiyose*, or variety show, was given at Minidoka in March 1944. The program, with notes by a Nisei, offered:

1. Vocal solos entitled "Cucaracha" and "El Rancho Grande" (. . . sung by a Kibei in Spanish.)
2. A Japanese modern comedy entitled "Borrowed Wives." (This is the story of two men who made a wager that the woman he married would be better [looking] than the other. In order to win the wager, both men substituted good looking women to pose as his wife. The climax of the play was reached when it became known that both men had borrowed wives.)

3. A modern dance by a Kibei. (A Kibei dressed as a Chinese girl danced to the tune of a recording entitled "A Flower-Vendor of Nanking.")

The climax of the evening was the Star Band, which was composed of Kibei boys. The band included saxophone, harmonica, and guitar and featured "vocal solos which were extremely popular with the audience." The program was in Japanese and the audience was largely Issei. For the more sophisticated, there were musical societies that practiced "utai singing," the intoning of classic Japanese poetry. Katsusabura Kawahara took advantage of his enforced leisure to study the *chikuzen biwa*, a traditional Japanese stringed instrument, and he carefully preserved a picture of his *biwa* class.

The making of dolls with their intricate Japanese robes was another popular art and the Girls' Day Doll Festival was a special event in the centers.

Topaz was located in an area where there was an abundance of semi-precious stones. These were collected on the long walks that helped to relieve the monotony of center life—walking was the main form of recreation for the older Issei in most of the centers (and the fashioning of carved walking sticks, a popular craft)—and then cut out and polished in the lapidary center. The most common stones were agate, obsidian, fluorite, jasper, calcite, and, of course, topaz.

In Heart Mountain there were several groups of Kabuki performers and "four mandolin bands," modern variations on the classic *shamisen*.

At Manzanar and some of the other centers, there were classes in ballet and in the classic Japanese dance of *odori*. Jeanne Wakatsuki visited an old geisha woman, tiny and elegant-looking, who had adorned her room like a Buddhist shrine and taught the discipline of the geisha to young girls who came to her.

Poetry is (or was) a part of the language of Japan. Every literate Japanese man or woman was a poet. After his contingent arrived at Minidoka, Yoshisada Kawai remembers that he "stood outside of the house by myself, hearing the cry of coyotes in the vast, vast plain, looking at the flowing clouds and shining moon. I thought about my sweet native town and the very fragile human life. I thought it must be man's destiny to go through such a difficult time. I remembered a poem . . .

> *"I am here, and where is God?*
> *The stars are shining very*

brightly but it is a very lonely
night.''

Most centers had poetry clubs where members wrote and read to others
the classic Japanese and senryu poems. The senryu were three-line poems, each line having a fixed number of syllables, five in the first, seven
in the second, and five in the third. The members of the poetry society
would decide, with the assistance of a teacher or leader, on a particular
topic and the group would gather to write poems on that theme. The
theme of acclimatization inspired a senryu that read:

Inured to penury,
The sixteen dollars
Is more than sufficient.

The topic "servings" evoked:

At the hospital—
An angel of mercy
At $16.00 a month.

Others touched on various aspects of center life:

Now, after two whole years,
Everyone can distinguish
The sound of his own messhall gong.

Tomorrow in some other form,
A piece of scrap lumber
Is laid away today.

The cooperating block
Rings harmoniously
With laughter.

When soldiers of the 442nd began to suffer battle casualties, one senryu
entitled "Worry" read:

Trembling hands
As the mother opens
The V-Mail.

And another, similar in tone:

> *The cream of the crop—*
> *Nisei soldiers—raised*
> *By wrinkles on the parents' brow.*

The relocation "out" controversy prompted:

> *Relocation—*
> *To the east, to the west?*
> *Folded arms.*

The senryu poets, men and women, contacted poetry groups in other centers. Poems were exchanged and on January 15, 1944, the *Rowher Outpost*, the center newsletter, printed poems by the winners of a Continental United Senryu Mutual Selection contest. There were a number of entries from both the centers and evacuees who had resettled outside.

Poston published its residents' poems in the *Poston Bungei*. Also published were *Popil* (Poppies) *Popii Kushu*, a haiku collection, at Topaz in 1945; and *Sauki Irei kushu* (*A Book of Memorial Verses*), haiku in honor of the 442nd Combat Team, at Salt Lake City in 1945.

Equally important, in those centers adjacent to towns, musicians and artists from the centers gave concerts and displayed their artwork in churches and community halls. The core of the Minidoka Massed Choir of eighty-three voices was the Seattle Methodist Church Choir of fifty-six voices. Augmented by other evacuees, the choir gave a concert at the nearby Jerome High School sponsored by the Jerome Ministerial Association. Some eight hundred people jammed the school auditorium to listen to a program that included Beethoven, Liszt and a selection of spirituals—"Deep River" and "Everytime I Feel the Spirit" among them.

An exhibit of brush paintings was put on in the basement of the Twin Falls Public Library. Sponsored by the Union Church Association of Twin Falls, the exhibit drew over three thousand residents of Twin Falls. Indeed, the center's resources for entertainment seemed endless; the male quartet sang at four Twin Falls churches and at churches at Jerome and Buhl.

At Topaz, the Caucasian wife of the head of agriculture, a Mrs. Roscova, helped organize a choir to sing Handel's *Messiah*. Koji Murata remembered it with delight some forty-five years later.

*   *   *

NEXT TO THE ARTS, SPORTS DOMINATED THE SOCIAL SIDE OF CENTER LIFE
and baseball reigned supreme. Of all the elements of American life that
worked to "Americanize" the Japanese, baseball was in a class by itself.
Every center had a number of baseball teams. In some cases, each block
might have several—a Little League team, a girls' team, one for teenage
boys, and even "old men's leagues."

There was fierce rivalry between the baseball teams at Poston I, II, and
III and at Gila River between Canal and Butte. Ichiro Yamaguchi recalled
that baseball players in Poston I who had a game with players from
Poston III would try to hitch rides on funeral cars going from one camp
to another.

The pride of Minidoka (which preferred to call itself Hunt after the
local Post Office), was its high school baseball team. When the center
team played the Twin Falls High School team at Minidoka, the Minidoka
team won by a score of 16 to 4 while some four thousand enthusiastic
evacuees (almost half the population of the center) cheered their team on.
The next night the Minidoka team played before a large crowd in Twin
Falls and the result was the same, a 16 to 4 Minidoka victory. The beat
went on. The Filer High School team was Hunt's next victim. Having
defeated seven high school teams from nearby towns, the Hunt team
traveled 175 miles to Idaho Falls to play in the state championship. There
they were beaten by a team whose pitcher, it was said, had recently
pitched for the New York Yankees, a ringer. The Hunt team claimed that
a third of the spectators cheered them on. Perhaps the sweetest victory
was at home against the military police team from the center. With the
score 14 to 1, the game was called as no contest.

Sumo and judo were poor seconds to baseball but both sports had a
considerable following as traditional Japanese martial arts. Most centers
had tennis courts and pitch and putt gold courses, which were in constant
use when the weather permitted.

The older men, the Issei, spent their time, like old men in any American (or Japanese) small town, playing cards and talking and drinking
home-brew sake. To the scandal of the more straitlaced, gambling, always popular with the Japanese, flourished. The bachelor barracks and
the laundry rooms were social centers where games of goh went on
interminably. Leagues were formed and formal competitions held. As
"A" put it, "the goh clubs became the focus of the social life of the older
men." The men played hana (flowers), a traditional card game, as well

as poker. Indeed, as noted before, most of the older Issei made no bones of the fact that they viewed their time in the centers as a compulsory vacation. Many of them had worked too hard all their lives to have ever had a proper vacation. Confident that Japan would soon achieve victory in the war, they resigned themselves to center life as an unfortunate interlude that should be viewed philosophically. With Japanese victory, they would be restored to their former ways of life and substantially rewarded for their loyalty to the Emperor.

Many evacuees deplored the influence of the Issei bachelors, who spoiled the children and set a bad example for them with their foul language and crude manners. A college Nisei wrote of one center: "The language here is vile. The children won't learn good English and they won't learn good Japanese."

James Sakoda described the Issei bachelors in a more sociological way. For them "camp life was . . . ideal. Living in a bachelor's quarters was not much different from living in a pre-war laborer's bunkhouse. Meals were served three times a day. The men could get together in the boiler room and talk about how Japan was faring in the war [winning] or play games, such as *shogi*."

In addition to the organized recreational and cultural activities, there were innumerable individual initiatives that contributed in one degree or another to the common life. At Topaz, H. Niva, a violinist, trained wild birds and a pair of orioles shared his cubicle to the delight of children at the center. Every block at Minidoka built a classic deep tub Japanese bath (*ofuro*) but it turned out that they spread infections and were eventually banned.

Most conspicuous perhaps were the innumerable gardens lovingly nurtured in unhospitable soil. At parched and barren Gila River, Don Sukushima, a graduate of the University of California at Berkeley, demonstrated the virtue of initiative. Drawing on a pick and shovel from the center warehouse, he began scratching out a rough ditch. Soon he was joined by other evacuees. When the director of the center inquired as to the meaning of this activity, he was told that its intention was to hook up to the canal in order to bring water into their block so that residents could have gardens. Thereupon the director ordered earth-moving equipment in and the ditch was dug in short order. The consequence was an explosion of gardens. John Yamazaki, the son of the John Yamazaki so badly beaten at Jerome, himself an Episcopal priest, reported in the Episcopal Church's magazine *Forth* on the beautification of the Canal camp at Gila River: "No longer merely a barren desert with a row of monotonous barracks,'' he wrote, ''this Gila River Relocation Center has been converted into a beautiful community camp, with lawns, trees, and vegetable gardens.'' Jeanne Wakatsuki remembered the ''small park'' at Manzanar ''with mossy nooks, ponds, waterfalls and curved wooden bridges.''

Much the same process took place in other centers. Indeed, it was said that the state of morale in various centers could be judged by the state of the gardens and little parks that the evacuees created. Manzanar, at the threshold of the Sierras, had perhaps the most naturally beautiful setting. The Japanese love mountains and believe they have a profoundly spiritual quality. Mt. Whitney loomed in the distance, serene and lovely. It reminded George Wakatsuki of the sacred Fuji in his homeland. His daughter Jeanne, walking the graveled path in the fading light of evening and looking out to the ''darkening mountains,'' felt as though ''suspended in some odd almost lonely land you could not escape from yet almost didn't want to leave.''

At Poston, Hatsune Helen Kitaji met Bob, the young Nisei she would marry, at a New Year's party in January 1943. From then on they met almost every Sunday until she left the center. ''We hiked to the river, we swam, slept, ate, wrote and played—such carefree days,'' she wrote in her diary.

The contacts with the Caucasian world outside were not limited to cultural activities, sports, or the churches. For perhaps a majority of the evacuees work leave or work furloughs were the principal form of contact with the outside. Some evacuees lived in Twin Falls on indefinite leave and worked at Mesa Orchards and over a hundred were transported to Walla Walla, Washington, to work in a canning company there. Some five hundred evacuees commuted to work each day from the center while another 1,800 lived and worked outside, in contrast to three thousand employed in the center itself.

Two of the most common contacts with the outside were through the Boy Scouts and the YWCA. At Twin Falls on National Boy Scout Day, the Boy Scout Drum and Bugle Corps of Minidoka outnumbered other troops by four to one and some spectators conceded the Hunt band was decidedly the best.

In Idaho the Magic Valley Girl Reserves, a branch of the YWCA, held a state conference at Filer that was attended by a delegation from Minidoka. One of the Minidoka delegates, Toshie Wakamatsu, was elected vice president of the state Girl Reserve.

There were, to be sure, frequent tensions between the centers and nearby communities. An episode at Twin Falls is revealing. It involved the use of the Japanese language by young evacuees visiting Twin Falls to make purchases in the city's stores and stroll the streets. Storekeepers (and others) complained about the evacuees speaking Japanese. They considered it rude for Japanese to speak English to them and Japanese to each other. The Kiwanis Club protested to the project director, Harry Stafford, who took the complaint with the utmost seriousness. The center newspaper, the *Irrigator*, was enlisted to explain to evacuees the feelings of the townspeople and the delicacy of the whole issue. The ministers, block managers, and Buddhist priests were also recruited to help; educational forums on the subject were scheduled, posters placed around the center, and notices put on bulletin boards. Stafford urged "that this entire program be carried out with good judgment and respect for the customs and habits of the center residents. . . . If properly conducted," he added, "this campaign should result in a great degree of Americanization of the center residents." That, he pointed out, was the way democracy was supposed to work—talk, discussion, explanation, respect for the opinions of others.

It was generally agreed, after much discussion, that the problem lay primarily with young "smart alecs," who had an "overbearing attitude . . . walking along the streets in large groups, talking in loud voices." The offenders were almost exclusively boys, behaving, it may be said, in the way young males of mating age are inclined to do. After much discussion, the "boys" from Minidoka were prevailed upon to be more considerate of their hosts.

Minidoka's relations with neighboring towns were facilitated by the friendly attitude of the editor of the *Boise Statesman*. An evacuee at Minidoka wrote of his gratitude to the editor for "sticking up" for the evacuees. Some Caucasian editors, he noted, "go out of their way to stick their necks out. I hope none of it ever brings them any harm."

THE CENTERS WERE YOUTH- AND CHILD-ORIENTED, AS HAS BEEN AL-ready noted. For one thing, Japan itself is one of the most child-oriented cultures in the world. I once asked a Japanese friend how such pampered children could turn into such disciplined adults and he replied with one word—"grandfathers," by which, he explained, he meant that grandfathers were the strict disciplinarians who injected some iron into the grandchildren to counter the indulgence of the parents. The anecdote also made the point that most traditional Japanese families were three-generation families. At the same time that physical affection was seldom demonstrated, it was the parents' code that "everything was for the children," *kodomo no tameni.*

At the Gila River center, June Toshiyuki loved to walk to the cattle-yards with her three children. She recalled that she felt rather like the Pied Piper because the other children in her block would tag along and when they came to the cattleyard the children would climb the haystacks and dive off into the new-mown hay. "If they saw a canal, the boys would jump in and swim. We had so much fun together."

At Manzanar, the recreation leaders organized events for the children in the center. On weekends Jeanne Wakatsuki and her friends took hikes with the recreation leaders to camps where brush had been cleared and tables and toilets built. The first camp was a mile or so from the center, the most remote some three miles into the Sierras. One of the leaders of the expeditions was a *hakujin*, a Quaker named Lois who wore her hair in braids and was in love with a handsome Nisei named Isao. Lois and Isao took the opportunity provided by overnight hikes to pursue their courtship.

The younger children played the games that Japanese children had played for centuries plus a number of American ones. Many Nisei children were delighted to be spared the Japanese language schools that their parents had insisted that they go to. "This means," Charles Kikuchi wrote, "that Japanese will be used less and less as the younger children grow up. . . . And if these schools were a source of propaganda for Japan, they have now been eliminated."

At the same time, it must be said that center life introduced many tensions into the relations between grandparents, parents, and children. One cause of rifts between parents and children was the disposition of some children to blame their parents for the fact that they were in the centers and not outside living the lives of normal American teenagers (although the life of teenage boys and girls in the centers was almost a replica of that of American teenagers outside). Among the girls' clubs were the Starlites, the Bombadettes, and the Exclusive Blues as well as chapters of the Girl Reserves, Brownies, Girl Scouts, and the Young Women's Christian Association. Hikes, parties, dances, and movies were all part of their lives. Like all twentieth-century children they irritated their elders by playing popular music too loudly and by reading foolish and frivolous magazines and books. "Their world," "A" wrote, "was still the world of American schools, movies, comics, radio, sports, and socials—not the world of the Issei." Jeanne Wakatsuki's sister Lillian was in high school singing with a hillbilly band called the Sierra Stars.

Her oldest brother, Bill, led a dance band called the Jive Bombers. At Minidoka, Louis Sato and his twelve-piece band called the Harmonaires played for Twin Falls High School dances and, most notably, for a Halloween dance at the Odd Fellows Hall.

When all is said and done, dances were the most popular entertainment for the young unmarried Nisei. Since the blocks used their dining halls as dance halls, the evacuees often gave them such mocking names as Starlight Terrace and Crescent Ballroom.

Food remained a central preoccupation of the evacuees, young and old. The residents of Jerome and Rohwer were much envied because the proximity of the Gulf of Mexico made it possible for them to enjoy shrimp tempura. Manzanar means "apple orchard"—a few neglected apple and pear trees were still growing in the now dry soil when the center opened. Jeanne Wakatsuki's father pruned and cared for the nearest trees and stored the fruit in a root cellar underneath the barracks where the family lived, and where he kept the improvised still he used to make the potent rice wine, sake.

WORK WAS A FESTERING SORE IN MOST CENTERS. THE READER WILL recall that the original plan had been for all center residents to be actively, if not exactly gainfully, employed and to some extent that was indeed the case. The men in Jeanne Wakatsuki's family had various jobs. Her brother Woodrow, or Woody as he was called, worked as a carpenter. Her brother-in-law was a roofing foreman, a critical job in the jerry-built barracks, which often leaked. Another was on a reservoir crew, charged with keeping the center's reservoir clear and water flowing to the center. Jeanne's mother worked as a dietician. But there were many makework jobs for little money where little was actually accomplished. The effort to cut down on boondoggling by eliminating unnecessary jobs was resented in the centers. One evacuee "racket" was to quit a paid job in the center and then draw unemployment compensation. Unemployment compensation was thereupon eliminated except for those assigned to a job who were unable to work because of injury or illness.

Most centers had an evacuee employees fair practices committee to arbitrate disputes or other problems among the evacuees, or between evacuees and the appointed staff, but they soon became as politicized as most other aspects of center life (the arts and education being perhaps the most notable exceptions). The fair practices committee was under heavy evacuee pressure to decide disputed issues in favor of the evacuees. The

WRA report "Administrative Highlights" notes dryly: "One receives in most instances just about what one pays for; and although 7 or 8 hours may have been spent on the job by each evacuee, and reported as such, it is fair to say that in the majority of instances, only a good 2 or 3 hours of work per day were actually derived from the average evacuee."

As noted earlier, the ambitious plans for war industries in the centers came to nothing. Some cottage-industry-type enterprises enjoyed a modest degree of success: garment "factories" at Manzanar, Heart Mountain, and Minidoka, cabinet shops at Manzanar and Tule Lake, a mattress factory at Manzanar, and food-processing plants at all centers.

The center cooperative stores were a valued and essential element. In the words of one evacuee: "Former business men took increasing responsibilities for the community stores, keeping abreast of the market, and learning new fields." Who ran the stores and who was employed in them were often political issues. As we have noted, the manager of the Tule Lake store was assassinated by his enemies.

A LINE IN A POPULAR SONG OF THE 1930s WENT: "LOVE AND MARRIAGE . . . go together like a horse and carriage." Certainly that was true in the centers. During the life of the centers, there were numerous marriages and almost six thousand births. Charles Kikuchi had noted in the months prior to evacuation: "Lots of kids getting married off on the theory that they have to protect their vested interests when and if morals get loose in camp."

Center marriages turned out to have an unexpected complication. Among the more traditional young Japanese women in the centers it was impossible under center conditions to go back and make the customary exhaustive search of the genealogical records for several hundred years of the prospective groom. "Certain clans are taboo," Charles Kikuchi noted, "and social ostracism will result in Japan if married into." The stigma attached to the *eta*, the lowest in the Japanese social scale, survived immigration. One *eta* (*burakumun*) family in Berkeley offered $5,000 and a home to any Nisei who would marry their daughter—"but no takers."

In the Minidoka center the Federated Church Youth Fellowship sponsored a well-attended forum on the topic "Should Evacuees Marry?" Unfortunately, we do not have a record of the discussion but whatever the obstacles, over 2,800 evacuees were married in the centers and seventy-eight divorced. Most of those who married had known each other before the evacuation; their families had often been friends; they not uncommonly had met in high school or college and frequently belonged to the same church congregation or, at least, were both Christians or both Buddhists.

Weddings, births, and deaths took place in the centers with all the attendant observances. There were, for example, 5,981 live births at the various centers during the life of the camps and 2,862 deaths in the same time period.

THE MOST FAITHFULLY OBSERVED HOLIDAYS IN THE CENTERS WERE THE traditional Japanese holidays of the Emperor's birthday, the day celebrating the Forty-seven *ronin*, and Girls' Doll Day. The project directors did their best to promote Americanization by encouraging the celebration of days associated with American history, such as Washington's birthday and the Fourth of July. At Minidoka the director set April 30, 1943, as the day for the dedication of the center's American flag. A visiting politician spoke, followed by the center director and then Mike Hagiwara, "speaking for the residents." Hagiwara declared: "Our flag represents to me ideals and principles which are truly American; for us, Americans, to cherish and protect and for the world to enjoy.

"Our Federal government, our administration, staff, our neighbors in the nearby communities of Twin Falls and Jerome . . . our friends throughout the United States, have in their actions and considerations, exemplified beyond question, those ideals and principles.

"We have discovered in a way that no other Americans have, how real, and how precious these ideals and principles are. It is in losing and then regaining that true values are discovered."

AFTER SEGREGATION, CHRISTIANS, FREE FROM THE PRESSURE OF THE more militant Buddhists, asserted themselves more confidently. At the same time, as more and more Christians went out, the numbers diminished proportionately in the centers. At Minidoka approximately 55 percent of the Nisei evacuees were Christians (or "preferred Christianity over Buddhism"), while some 20 percent of the Kibei were Christians (or preferred Christianity), and 26 percent of the Issei males (34 percent of the Issei females).

Not surprisingly, at Tule Lake the residents were overwhelmingly Buddhist. There only 20 percent of the Nisei were Christian, 5 percent of the Kibei and roughly 10 percent of the Issei. In all the centers the proportion of women Christians was 5 to 10 percent higher than that of men.

Perhaps the greatest Caucasian hero of the evacuation was Herbert Nicholson. Nicholson, a lay missionary in Japan who spoke Japanese fluently, was tireless in his visits to the centers. He knew hundreds of the evacuees from prewar days and he visited many of them regularly, bringing news of friends and family in other centers and supplying needed items not available in the center co-op stores. An Issei at Manzanar gave Nicholson the title paper to his truck and Nicholson used it on his trips to Manzanar, Poston, and Gila River, "bringing whatever the internees wanted: organs for the churches, books, furniture, personal belongings." On one occasion, Nicholson brought in a large bottle of what was purported to be vinegar. When it was discovered by a center staff member to be sake, Nicholson was banned from Manzanar for six months.

Before visitors' quarters were built at the centers, Nicholson often had to spend the night curled up in his truck. Always eating with the evacuees in their mess halls, he was a familiar figure, playing with the children, telling stories, visiting with the older Issei. At Manzanar he was something of a thorn in the side of the director, Ralph Merritt, who resented his direct involvement with evacuees but did not dare forbid it.

At Topaz, Rhoda Iyoya recalled, "We had a very nice church youth group. Mr. Nugent came in from the outside and stayed with us throughout the duration of the camp. He would take us into the community. We were able to get permission to go out to Wasatah Academy, a Presbyterian School in Utah. . . . We would visit and participate in their student life. . . . We had a school choir that one of our musicians led. . . . We took the glee club choir to the nearby Utah community and sang in their schools so there was a lot of relationship with the Utah community. In general the Utah people felt pretty good about us."

In Poston, Jitsuo Morikawa, a Baptist minister, organized a vacation bible school that enrolled eight hundred children for a two-month session with five-day-a-week meetings, and another five hundred children for a month's session. A hundred teachers were enlisted from the evacuees. At Easter time eight days of conference, prayer, and worship were planned. Posters were put up around the center, trucks carried signs throughout the three camps advertising the conference, a common meeting place was prepared surrounded by mesquite trees, and paths were cut for easy access. In Jitsuo Morikawa's words, "Instead of calling in some great preacher to lead the meetings the evacuee ministers did the preaching. Every night eight hundred to a thousand people attended and on the final night among the fourteen hundred people who were present two hundred young men and women . . . accepted Christ as their Savior.''

At Gila River, before he was forced out by the militants, the younger John Yamazaki reported that Issei and Nisei communicants worshipped together and a Caucasian volunteer, Camilla Butterfield, from the Diocese of Texas, ran the Sunday School. Eleven evacuees were baptized during the year and Yamazaki presided over five marriages and three burials. The Episcopal bishops of Arizona, Arkansas, and Los Angeles had visited the center with their wives, and Bishop Gooden of Los Angeles had preached an inspiring sermon, "One Father, One World, One Blood," using the biblical text "Of one blood God made all the nations of the earth."

Yamazaki reported that, as director of religious education, he had thirty-five volunteers and 350 pupils enrolled in classes.

At Manzanar, two Maryknoll nuns, Sister Mary Suzanne and Sister Mary Bernadette, ministered to the Catholics in the center, conducted classes for those wishing confirmation, and did their gentle best to convert the younger evacuees. Before the war they had run an orphanage for parentless Japanese children. In the center they set up what was called the "Children's Village," and assisted Father Steinback, a Catholic priest, who had come to the center to live and minister to Catholics there. Jeanne Wakatsuki, drawn to the rituals of the church, longed to be confirmed but her father forbade it.

In the centers, Baptist minister Morikawa wrote, "We . . . discovered that life and its true meaning were not totally dependent on what we ate or wore or the kind of houses we lived in. . . . We found the preciousness of human friendship, the presence and the reality of God. . . . We give thanks to God when we remember how the evacuation and internment of Japanese Americans brought to the surface the true conscience and courage of the church." As in the days of the abolition movement, of the Confessing Church in Nazi Germany, of the civil rights movement of the postwar period, the "church courageously responded to the time of our evacuation. . . . Acts of heroism were performed all over the country, some known, mostly unknown."

Morikawa added: "The Christian evacuees found this discovery that God went with them into the relocation center. They were evacuated out of the Pacific coast but they could not be expelled from the Great Commonwealth of God's friendship and grace. . . . Somehow God seemed nearer in those bare barracks than in the well furnished apartment in the city."

For Christians in the centers their churches remained their mainstay and an essential link with the world outside. A conference of Japanese ministers was held in Denver in December 1943. Mark Dauber, the executive secretary of the Home Missions Council of North America, gave the keynote address. In it he challenged the delegates, Japanese and Caucasian alike, to use the conference sessions to "determine not only the future of the American Japanese church but of the whole Christian Church." Dauber's words subsequently reverberated in many sermons in the centers and gave dignity and a sense of purpose to the lives of the faithful. To suffer and endure, to be humble and forgiving, to sustain hope and help those in need, these classic Christian tenets were doubtlessly more often observed in the centers than in the Protestant congregations outside.

AS IN THE WORLD OUTSIDE, THE ELEMENTARY AND HIGH SCHOOLS WERE the principal agents of Americanization. More than thirty thousand students were enrolled in the center schools and seven thousand graduated from the high schools. The fact that, initially, most of the center schools had to scrimp and scrape (students arrived at most centers in the late summer or early fall just at the time that the 1942–43 school year was starting) gave them a kind of esprit that is often the consequence of having to improvise. At Poston, the largest center, where no facilities had been provided, schools were opened in October 1942 without tables, chairs, books, paper, or blackboards. The teachers and students helped to build their own chairs and tables and painted plywood black to serve as blackboards. Teachers were recruited from the Indian reservation, from retired missionaries who had been in Japan, and, as Dillon Myer's account puts it, "any other source available."

One of Poston's special prides was the fact that the school buildings of Units 1 and 2 were built of adobe by the evacuees. While equipment was initially lacking for science classes, enterprising biology teachers utilized the surrounding terrain for their classes, surveying drainage ditches and small creeks adjacent to the centers. In time, sympathetic outsiders brought considerable equipment to schools in all the centers.

Mary Lind, a Caucasian, supervised the kindergarten teachers, and teacher-training classes were started as soon as the center opened. Much the same pattern was followed in other centers. At Poston there were some 5,200 students. Many first-year students had to-be-expected language difficulties but by the third year at Poston, the pupils rated above their grade level in virtually all subjects.

"Our teachers and people in responsible positions," Rhoda Iyoya recalled, "were very caring people and did the best they could to provide us with the things we needed. For a student, life was pretty normal. We kept busy. We didn't realize the hardships the older people had to face. As young people you can really ride with that."

In Minidoka teachers came from diverse backgrounds—the Civilian Conservation Corps, the National Youth Administration, the Indian Service, the Work Projects Administration, and other New Deal agencies. Jessie Sistermans, a native of Berkeley, was teaching high school in Los Angeles; she and a friend, Edith Waterman, "followed their students into exile." Minidoka's high school principal was Jerome Light, a graduate of Stanford and an advocate of progressive education. Indeed, if there was a favored class in the centers, it was the teachers. In Jerome, June Toshiyuki, as a teacher and president of the center YWCA, had many privileges. She came and went much as she pleased, visiting Little Rock and participating in the USO shows put on for soldiers of the 442nd Combat Team at Camp Shelby, Mississippi. Ed Izumi, a set director from MGM, helped Toshiyuki design sets for a pageant she put on with her pupils. The fact that the children of the center's director were in Toshiyuki's kindergarten class helped facilitate matters. "We had a large rhythm band of children," she recalled. "All these were nursery and kindergarten children, yet they put on shows for the whole center. . . . One Halloween, all the teachers went on a hay ride." The Caucasian director of the mess halls also had children in Toshiyuki's nursery and kindergarten and would, in consequence, "let us have practically anything we needed. That was the highlight of my camp days."

Kimi Sugiyama recalled, "Living in Jerome wasn't bad at all. We got along well. I taught school. Other people had other talents like crocheting, knitting, painting, etc." When Jerome was closed in June 1944, Sugiyama went to Gila River and taught school there.

In Minidoka, the graduating seniors requested the publication of a traditional high school yearbook and the administration assisted in getting it out. High school graduations were major events in the centers with all the panoply of such occasions outside. There were invocations by the clergy, guest speakers, often distinguished outsiders who were known to be friends to the evacuees, musical interludes by the center band, and addresses by the valedictorians. At Amache, the valedictorian at graduation spoke of the nation's history: "Sometimes America failed and suffered. . . . Sometimes she made mistakes, great mistakes. . . . America hounded and harassed the Indians, then remembering that they were first Americans, she gave them back their citizenship. She enslaved the Negroes, then remembering Americanism, she wrote out the Emancipation Proclamation. She persecuted the German Americans during the First World War, then recalling that America was born of those who come from every nation seeking liberty, she repented. Her history is full of errors, but with each mistake she has learned. . . . Can we the graduating class of Amache Senior High School believe that America still means freedom, equality, security, and justice? Do I believe this? Do my classmates believe this? Yes, with all our hearts, because in that faith, in that hope, is my future, our future, and the world's future."

In the words of Thomas James's *Exile Within: The Schooling of Japanese Americans, 1942–1945*: "Realism, tolerance, and hope ran through nearly all the commencement speeches and essays that have survived from graduation exercises in 1943."

For the Nisei or Sansei (third generation Japanese), graduating from high school usually meant resettlement out. For many, as has been noted, it meant going on to college or professional school; for others, leaving for some secretarial or clerical position. Some who wished to remain with their parents took jobs in the offices of the center administration.

Auxiliary to the high schools were the center libraries. At Topaz, Toyo Suyemoto Kawakami took the library as her special province. It opened on December 1, 1942, and "the next day presented a concert of classical recordings. The audience was so enthusiastic that concerts were given every Wednesday with mimeographed information about the composer, the selections, and the next week's program. One room served as a bindery. A selection of titles was borrowed from the Salt Lake City Library and arrangements were made with the University of California Library for interlibrary loans. When attendance at the library exceeded 450 a day, it was kept open in the evenings. The library had fifty-two magazine subscriptions as well as the *Oakland Tribune* and *San Francisco Chronicle*."

As in the assembly centers, adult education classes were an important feature of center life, not only in the arts but in a broader range. Courses in business administration were popular and, most of all, English language courses for the older Issei. When Charles Kikuchi's mother wanted to enroll in an English class her husband forbade her. In Kikuchi's words:

"He doesn't want her to get ahead of him and he thinks she is just doing it for social purposes, which is undoubtedly true." After a few weeks' holdout Kikuchi's father decided not only to acquiesce in his wife's taking an English class but to join her: "Humph, what the hell. Me 67 years old. Too old to start school, but me smart and learn fast like Miyako [his oldest daughter] in the head."

Tom, Charles Kikuchi's youngest brother, a high school sophomore, undertook to teach his father to pronounce English words and the father picked up writing with surprising speed. "He practices about 6 hours a day," Charles wrote. "His tenacity is amazing. He says he is doing it for my benefit so that he can explain his thoughts better to me."

English-speaking Issei made excellent English teachers. Katsusaburo Kawahara improved his uncertain English and noted that "quite a few women never had a chance to learn English . . . and they figured when they got out they could communicate with their younger ones."

Part 4

THE RETURN

Chapter 24

CLOSING THE
RELOCATION CENTERS

DILLON MYER, CONVINCED THAT THE RESETTLEMENT PROGRAM could never accomplish its goal of clearing the centers until the ban on the West Coast had been lifted, revived the issue in a letter to John McCloy on October 16, 1943. Myer reminded McCloy that the question of the constitutionality of the "continued exclusion" of evacuees from the "evacuated areas" was before the courts and there was reason to believe that they might soon declare the ban unconstitutional. In light of that fact, Myer argued, it would be an appropriate time to have it lifted. A copy of Myer's letter was forwarded to the new commanding general of the Western Defense Command, General Delos Emmons, who had taken over from DeWitt. Emmons took issue with Myer. The Tule Lake episode had created so much hostility on the West Coast, Emmons stated, that he thought the time unpropitious to return evacuees to the area. "I think it would be very good policy . . . to let this feeling subside before any considerable number of Japanese are returned to the Coast. I would like to suggest to Mr. Myer that it would be good policy for him to endeavor to obtain the support of [newly elected] Governor Warren . . . on a sound plan for relocating Japanese. . . . I am quite sure that if we ram down their throats any plan to return Japanese to the Western States such political opposition would be aroused as to completely nullify even a perfectly sound plan.'' Emmons, whose record as commanding general of the Hawaiian Command had been a commendable one, free certainly of any implication of racism, doubtlessly had a point. The Tule Lake outbreak had been taken as confirmation of the most extreme anti-Japanese positions.

Near the end of 1943, Attorney General Francis Biddle came to the support of Myer. ''The important thing,'' he wrote to Roosevelt, ''is to secure the reabsorption of about 95,000 Japanese, of whom two-thirds are citizens and who give every indication of being loyal to the United States, into normal American life. The present practice of keeping loyal American citizens in concentration camps is dangerous and repugnant to the principles of our Government. It is necessary to act now so that the agitation against these citizens does not continue after the war.''

Biddle did Myer another important favor, although it did not appear so to Myer initially. Biddle recommended to the President that the War Relocation Authority be placed under Secretary of the Interior Harold Ickes. Myer, busy warding off calls for the military to take over, was uneasy. He protested to Biddle, who did his best to reassure him. Still not satisfied, Myer called James Byrnes, director of war mobilization, to protest. Byrnes heard him out and then said quietly, ''I think you should go to Interior.'' On February 16, 1944, Roosevelt signed Executive Order 9423. It may well have been the single most significant move in the troubled history of the War Relocation Authority. Harold Ickes was an old Progressive Party warhorse reincarnated as a bulwark of the New Deal. Gruff and high-tempered (the press liked to refer to him as a ''curmudgeon''), Ickes, with Frances Perkins, the secretary of labor, was keeper of the President's conscience and a member of the New Deal's inner circle, which included Ickes's rival, Harry Hopkins, Benjamin Cohen, and Tommy (the Cork) Corcoran. Biddle realized how vulnerable the War Relocation Authority was, especially in light of the troubles at Tule Lake. With the authority under the wing of the Interior Department, its enemies would have to go through the formidable Ickes, unfalteringly liberal on civil rights issues, to get to Dillon Myers and his agency. Few people in Washington had the stomach for taking Harold Ickes on. Equally important, Ickes, who played cards regularly with the President, had his ear as few other people in the capital and was thus in an ideal position to both present the authority's side of any particular case and recruit the President, as well as the tireless Eleanor Roosevelt, as allies in the cause. On a personal level, as it turned out, Dillon Myer and Harold Ickes would get along, in Myer's words, ''exceptionally well.''

On March 6, 1944, three weeks after the War Relocation Authority had been transferred to the Department of the Interior, Myer, still determined to press for the lifting of the Exclusion Ban, wrote Ickes stating that "if the exclusion orders were revoked, except for Tule Lake, by July 1, 1944, the War Relocation Authority could be liquidated by July 1 of the following year." A month later (April) another memorandum was sent to Ickes headed "A Plan for Bringing the Relocation Program to a Conclusion." Again, the critical point was lifting the exclusion. A month *later* in May (Myer could not be accused of lacking in persistence) another memorandum made essentially the same points (it was a tactic that might be compared to the Chinese water torture, a memorandum at a time).

A few weeks later, Stimson recommended to the President that the exclusion be ended. In Biddle's words: "The Secretary of War raised the question of whether it was appropriate for the War Department, at this time, to cancel the Japanese Exclusion orders and let the Japs go home. War, Interior, and Justice all agreed that this could be done without danger to defense considerations, but doubted the wisdom of doing it at this time before the election."

Ickes wrote the President on June 1, 1944: "The continued exclusion of American citizens of Japanese ancestry from the affected areas is clearly unconstitutional in the present circumstances. . . . I understand that the Department of Justice agrees that there is little doubt as to the decision which the Supreme Court will reach in a case squarely presenting the issue."

Ickes's most telling point concerned the children in the centers, who were exposed solely to the influence of persons of Japanese ancestry. "They are becoming a hopelessly maladjusted generation, apprehensive of the outside world and divorced from the possibility of associating—or even seeing to any considerable extent—Americans of other races." And, as a parting shot: "I do say that the continued retention of these innocent people in the relocation centers would be a blot upon the history of this country."

A new commanding general of the Western Defense Command, General C. H. Bonesteel, also checked in, writing to McCloy on July 3, 1944: "My study of the existing situation leads me to a belief that the great improvement in the military situation on the West Coast indicates that there is no longer a military necessity for the mass exclusion of the Japanese from the West Coast as a whole." Bonesteel's optimism about "the great improvement in the military situation" was based on the continued success of Allied and especially U.S. forces in the Pacific. On

June 16, U.S. B-29 Superfortresses, flying from Saipan, bombed the Japanese home island of Kyushu; it was the beginning of massive bombing attacks on the principal Japanese industrial centers. Bonesteel was bold enough to question Roosevelt's policy of distribution. He believed that the great majority of evacuees would want to return to their former haunts where they could resume "the religious, social and cultural contacts to which they are accustomed and which the Japanese particularly treasure."

The issue boiled down to the question of whether lifting the exclusion might lose California for the Democrats (and thus, perhaps, the election) in the upcoming presidential campaign. Edward Stettinius, Jr., the new secretary of state, who had succeeded Cordell Hull, summarized it for the President: "The question appears to be largely a political one, the reaction in California, on which I am sure you will probably wish to reach your own conclusion." Roosevelt's response was to propose putting more money and effort into relocation, "dissemination and distribution," in his words. "Why not," he asked Ickes and Stettinius, "proceed seriously along the above line—for a while at least." If the Exclusionary Ban were to be lifted prior to the elections, the reasoning ran, it would almost inevitably become a campaign issue with unpredictable consequences for other Democratic politicians besides the President and especially for liberal congresswoman Helen Gahagan Douglas, who was running against a Republican newcomer named Richard Nixon who had already implied that Douglas was a tool of the Communist Party. Douglas had been an outspoken champion of the Japanese Americans and inserting the resettlement issue into her campaign might be damaging to her as well as to the whole question of resettlement. Disappointing as the decision was to Myer it was probably the correct one.

Anticipating the announcement of the lifting of the Exclusionary Ban after the November election, Myer sent out a five-page letter to all project directors to be distributed to the evacuees at the time of the official announcement (meantime to be kept confidential). Headed "Summary of WRA Policies and Procedures for the Final Phase of Relocation Program," it read in part:

"The lifting of the blanket exclusion orders by the Western Defense Command is undoubtedly the most significant event since the evacuation both in the lives of the evacuated people and the program of the War Relocation Authority. To the great majority of the evacuees, it means full restoration of the freedom of movement which is enjoyed by all other loyal citizens and law-abiding aliens in the United States. . . . Largely as a result of the splendid record which your sons, brothers and husbands have achieved in the armed services, the American public has come increasingly to a recognition of the essential good faith and loyalty that characterize the great majority of people of Japanese descent. Today the evacuees as a group have more friends and supporters throughout the Nation than at any previous time. They are being accepted as fellow-workers, friends, and neighbors.''

Myer went on to assure the evacuees that ''in view of the funds that are available and the arrangements that are being made, the War Relocation Authority feels wholly confident that no evacuee will be deprived of adequate means of subsistence by reason of the closing of the centers.'' Myer urged those evacuees settled in the interior to stay where they were rather than to hurry back to the West Coast thereby immeasurably complicating the resettlement of those who were still in the centers.

Then came a statement that would create another uproar among the center residents. All centers would be closed ''within a period of six months to one year after the revocation of the exclusion orders.'' But no center would be closed without at least three months' notice to the residents. There were more reassuring words about the assistance the authority would afford all those leaving the centers.

The rumor that such a move was pending prompted an alarmed editorial in the December 13 edition of the *San Francisco Chronicle,* which reported that the state Senate Committee on Japanese Resettlement ''strongly urged'' President Roosevelt, the Western Defense Command, and the War Department ''not to permit the return of Japanese to the Pacific Coast, and particularly to California, for the duration of the war. . . . We believe that because California is required to make an all-out war effort, that to allow the Japanese to return during the war is inadvisable because it would cause riots, turmoil, bloodshed and endanger the war effort.'' The editorial writer pointed to Tule Lake as proof of the paper's long-standing contention that many Japanese Americans were loyal to the Emperor and therefore a threat to the United States.

On December 17, 1944, the official announcement was made that the Exclusionary Ban had been lifted and the next day Myer announced the schedule for closing the centers. The ban had been lifted three years and ten days after the attack on Pearl Harbor and approximately two and a half years after the last Japanese had been evacuated from Military Area No. 1.

Former state Attorney General Earl Warren, now governor, in part at least because he had not strongly opposed evacuation, called on ''all Americans'' to comply ''loyally, cheerfully and carefully'' with the War

Department order revoking the mass Japanese evacuation. Warren further notified "chiefs of police, sheriffs and all public officials to join in developing uniform plans to prevent intemperate actions and civil disorder." Harold Ickes added his voice, warning that "any interference with the [evacuees'] 'right' to resettle on the west coast would be met with the full force of the Government."

Among the evacuees the announcement that the centers were to be closed brought another wild emotional upheaval. Once more mess hall bells rang, summoning residents in the various centers to feverish discussions. The outraged reaction was perhaps best expressed by a Nisei girl at Minidoka who exclaimed: "This is a town. You can't close a town!" It might be said that the evacuation and relocation of Japanese Americans included five great traumas. The first, of course, was the evacuation itself with its attendant confusion, uncertainty, and loss of property; the second, and in some ways the most severe, was registration; the third was segregation; the fourth was the draft; and the fifth was the announcement that the centers were to be closed in 1945 independently of the course of the war that many of the evacuees were still confident that the Japanese Imperial forces would ultimately win. An Issei declared: "I was afraid this was going to happen. They said that we can go any place we like, but that's not so good. This is even worse than being evacuated."

The storm of protest that greeted Myer's announcement was the final irony of the whole strange drama. The hated had become familiar; the remaining centers had indeed taken on much of the character that the young Nisei woman at Minidoka described, as towns. Once more Dillon Myer and the WRA had misjudged evacuee reaction to an Authority initiative designed to expedite resettlement. Myer had so convinced himself that the Exclusionary Ban was the principal obstacle to resettlement that the angry outcries of the evacuees once more caught him by surprise (how little the liberal imagination understands of the vastness and mystery of the world and yet how endearing it is in its innocence and goodheartedness!).

Soon there were the now familiar protests and petitions. The centers couldn't be closed. Many of the people remaining in them were Issei men and women too old to start over, people with no particular place to go, parents whose sons were in the army or in college, whose daughters were secretaries in Chicago or Minneapolis, who spoke little or no English. People began to talk of these men and women as "residues," individuals who would be left and for whom the centers, or at least one center, must be kept open indefinitely.

One evacuee who had been planning to resettle angrily canceled his plans. He would hang on until he was "shoved through the gate." Talk went around of a sitdown strike. The cry was raised, for the final time, about being "pushed around." The evacuees had been pushed around innumerable times, or so it seemed to them, and now they were to be pushed one final time—out. In the minds of a surprisingly (at least to the WRA) large proportion, it was one push too many. They wouldn't go. An Issei wrote: "I don't want to be the first one to go back and get killed. I'm not a fool. I wonder what's going to happen to those who refuse to go out. I suppose they're going to become like Indians." Permanent wards of the government.

As in the other center crises, there was a determined effort on the part of the more militant to force everyone into conformity to the nationalist line—which was to simply refuse to leave. Those who seemed inclined to accept the inevitable and leave, however reluctantly, were derided as pliant and acquiescent, as traitors to the Emperor. They would suffer for their submissive attitude when Japan was victorious. In a Heart Mountain evacuee meeting, an Issei declared: "The trouble with a lot of evacuees is that they are two-faced and weak-kneed. When they talk to us they say one thing, and when they talk to WRA officials they say another. . . . A bunch of *inu*. . . . If the evacuees would just stick together, if nobody would budge out of here, we would get somewhere. We could force the government to keep the centers open or give us some real assistance. . . . Worse, a lot of softies leave here for railway fare and $25. And now that the WRA has said it is going to close the centers, probably more will crawl out of the place like beaten animals."

A councilman from one center noted: "Many . . . of my block people have asked me if I thought the WRA would really close the centers. I always tell them the same thing—the future of the centers and of the evacuees is no longer under the control of the WRA. WRA itself is being abolished by the Government. It can't help what it is doing. It is actually [a] peewee organization—set up by the President and Congress to take care of the evacuees, now to be wiped out. It may be that the WRA had more to do with closing the centers than this indicates. I try to protect the WRA a little. I do not do this because I like the WRA or because I think it has done all it could or should do for evacuees. But I don't want people to blame the WRA too much. WRA can do some things to help, and it will work out better if people do not hate the administration too much. I don't know what other councilmen tell their block people."

In addition to the natural reluctance to leave what had become familiar, there was the satisfying if not exhilarating feeling that refusing to budge was also a political statement that brought sympathy and support from friends outside. At Heart Mountain, one of Asael Hansen's Issei friends who had resisted resettlement assured him that he intended to remain in the United States after the war. He even had a cemetery plot in Los Angeles. "I do not know what to think about the United States," he told Hansen. "This country excludes me from citizenship. But I feel that I am a Californian. Even more strongly I feel that Los Angeles is my home city." It was a position common to many evacuees who did not wish to resettle prior to the end of the war but who had no intention of returning to Japan.

Apparently spontaneously, four centers requested that a conference be called to discuss the problems that might result from the closure of the centers. The response from Washington was that such a conference had to be planned and financed by those in the centers and must be held outside of any particular center. Masaru Narahara, chairman of the Topaz community council, thereupon took the initiative of contacting all other community councils to invite them to attend a meeting in Salt Lake City in February. Only Manzanar held aloof. After some debate and misgivings, the other centers joined in plans for the conference. Some groups expressed a determination not to cooperate in any way with the WRA and urged other centers to follow a policy of noncooperation.

Elections were held at each participating center for delegates to the conference and resolutions were drawn up directing the delegates to support one position or another. Some project directors viewed all this activity with apprehension. They were alarmed at the evident intention of a good many highly vocal residents to try to organize opposition to the closing of the centers, in some instances by making clearly unacceptable demands as the price for relocation. One director expressed his concerns as follows: "Most of us here on the staff including me are of the opinion that the conference idea is very ill-advised and will produce far more harm than good to the program. Unfortunately there are those most interested and those who are likely to be sent as delegates are the anti-administration, disaffected, demanding and petitioning Issei type who will gain no other end but to destroy much of the good attitude which has been created here." Myer, who had been invited to attend, put his weight behind the conference and agreed to go.

When the All Center Conference opened on February 16, 1945, there were thirty representatives from seven centers. Invitations to attend had been issued to Friends of the American Way, the Japanese American Citizens League, the Citizens Committee for Constitutional Rights, the

American Civil Liberties Union, Christian and Buddhist churches, the American Friends Service Committee, the Pacific Coast Committee on American Principles and Fair Play, the Protestant Commission, the Maryknoll Mission, the American Red Cross, the YWCA, and "numerous individuals interested in the welfare of the evacuees."

There turned out to be considerable differences among the delegates. Edward Spicer divided them into three identifiable groups. First, "the hopefuls," a group made up primarily of Nisei and some of the younger Issei who had reconciled themselves to prompt relocation and were anxious to secure the most favorable possible terms for themselves and their families. "They were convinced," in Spicer's words, "that there was a future for them in this country and that they had the ability and the courage to make a living for themselves and their families."

"The desperates" were largely the middle-aged and older Issei. "They were the middle-class respectable small businessmen and farmers," Spicer wrote. "They had insurance and real estate agencies that catered to a Japanese urban and rural population. Their success had depended upon a Japanese community. They had no confidence in their ability to establish themselves in situations where they would depend on a Caucasian clientele. They felt they were too old to start in and work their way up. Life outside was full of hazards they felt incapable of coping with. This group was, in the main, cooperative and non-militant. They felt most strongly the need for government assistance."

The third group were identified by Spicer as "the resentful and reactionary." Made up of both Issei and Nisei, it included the "completely negative" and those who might, with some persuasion, take a more moderate ground. They were bitter about the treatment of the Japanese in America going back decades before the war; they were bitter at the War Relocation Authority and even more bitter over the decision to close the centers. All these feelings were combined, in Spicer's view, with "a strong feeling of Japanese nationalism." Those that Spicer called the "liberals," found exclusively in the first two groups, were confident that American public opinion would rally to their cause "if the facts could be presented to a sufficiently wide audience."

The conference lasted a week and devoted much of that time to discussions of the long-term problems facing the Japanese in the aftermath of the war.

The chairman of the conference in welcoming the delegates reviewed the events of the past three years. In that time, he declared, "a great many things have happened to us. We have found that there are many public and private organizations, and many people of good will who [are] interested in working toward a just solution to the difficult problems posed by evacuation.'' Referring proudly to the fact that ''thousands of our sons are now serving on all fronts of the world,'' the chairman noted that they had won praise from the President of the United States himself. ''America is a country of pioneers. We, too, wish to think of ourselves as pioneers. Most of us [aliens] came to this country 30 and 40 years ago. With the strength of our bodies we helped to build the West's railroads, to mine the ore and coal, we worked in forests and lumber mills, and we helped to turn desert and waste lands into fertile gardens. In terms of the vastness of America's millions, we are only a handful, but we would like to think that we too have contributed toward the building of this country.'' All that the delegates could ask of the government was that its policies should include ''in behalf of people of Japanese ancestry equal opportunities with all others for them to work out their destiny in proportion to their ability.''

Myer gave an eloquent and conciliatory speech to the conferees, promising that the War Relocation Authority would do all in its power to facilitate the return of relocatees to useful and productive lives outside the centers. He pledged that the authority would continue to fight prejudice and discrimination and pointed to the various civic groups that had labored to ease the lot of the evacuees.

To those delegates who continued to insist that they were still Japanese nationals (while demanding all kinds of special consideration from the U.S. government), the ''liberals pointed out that they had hopelessly compromised their Japanese 'nationalism' when they replied affirmatively to the question of their loyalty to the United States at the time of the initial registration.'' Since they had chosen then not to become segregants, apply for repatriation or expatriation, or move to Tule Lake with the other declared nationalists, they could not now claim to be Japanese nationals. Those ''remaining in the centers had by that fact committed themselves to seeking integration in American society.''

The delegates made twenty-one recommendations, preceded by a ''Statement of Facts'':

> (1) *Mental suffering has been caused by the forced mass evacuation.*
> (2) *There has been an almost complete destruction of financial foundations built during over half a century.*

(3) *Especially for the duration, the war has created fears of prejudices, persecution, etc., also fears of physical violence and fears of damage to property.*

(4) *Many Issei (average age is between 60 and 65) were depending upon their sons for assistance and support, but these sons are serving in the United States armed forces. Now these Issei are reluctant to consider relocation.*

(5) *Residents feel insecure and apprehensive towards the many changes and modifications of WRA policies.*

(6) *The residents have prepared to remain for the duration because of many statements made by the WRA that relocation centers will be maintained for the duration of the war.*

(7) *Many residents were forced to dispose of their personal and real properties, business and agricultural equipment, etc., at a mere trifle of their cost; also drew leases for the "duration," hence have nothing to return to.*

(8) *Practically every Buddhist priest is now excluded from the West Coast. Buddhism has a substantial following and the members obviously prefer to remain where the religion centers.*

(9) *There is an acute shortage of housing, which is obviously a basic need in resettlement. The residents fear that adequate housing is not available.*

(10) *Many persons of Japanese ancestry have difficulty in obtaining insurance coverage on life, against fire, on automobiles, on property, etc.*

We recommend:

(1) *That special governmental agencies or units be established solely for providing assistance to evacuees who might require funds in reestablishing themselves.*
   a. Resettlement aid (grants)
   b. Loans

(2)   *That the present relocation grant be increased. It should be given to every relocatee.*

      We further recommend that Federal aid be granted according to every individual's particular needs until such time as he is reestablished.

(3)   *That long term loans at a low rate of interest be made available, without security, to aid the residents in reestablishing themselves as near as possible to their former status in private enterprises, such as business, agriculture, fisheries, etc.*

(4)   *That the WRA use their good offices so that consideration may be given on priority by OPA [Office of Price Administration]. Because of evacuation, residents were forced to dispose of their equipment, trucks, cars, etc., many of which at present require the approval of an OPA board. These equipments are essential to many residents in order to reestablish themselves in former enterprises.*

(5)   *That the WRA make every effort to obtain a return of properties, for evacuees who, due to evacuation and consequent inability to maintain installment payments, have lost the same; further, in order to prevent loss of property, to obtain some definite arrangement for the granting of governmental aid, as may be necessary, to evacuees unable, as a result of evacuation, to maintain installment payments.*

(6)   *That the WRA give financial aid to residents with definite plans, for the purpose of defraying the expenses of investigating specific relocation possibilities.*

(7)   *That the WRA establish adequately staffed offices in important areas and employ persons of Japanese ancestry since they understand Japanese psychology; and also establish in these field offices, legal advisory and employment departments.*

(8)   *That the WRA continue the operation of evacuee property offices for the duration, to fulfill the needs of relocatees.*

(9)   *That the WRA accept for reinduction into centers those who relocate and who find themselves unable to make satisfactory adjustments.*

(10)   *That the WRA arrange for the establishing of hostels and other facilities in various areas; and furthermore, build new housing through the FHA [Federal Housing Administration], with WRA assistance.*

(11)   *That the WRA provide transportation of evacuee property door to door.*

(12)   *That the WRA negotiate for the establishing of old people's homes exclusively for persons of Japanese ancestry.*

(13)   *That the WRA make negotiations to arrange (1) so that evacuees formerly civil-service employees will be reinstated and (2) so that persons of Japanese ancestry will be able to secure business licenses as formerly.*

(14)   *That short term leave regulations be changed to permit an absence of two months with one month extension privileges. Also, that the evacuee investigating relocation possibilities be permitted to become employed, without change of status.*

(15)   *That when an evacuee relocates or returns to his former business or home, WRA should make every effort to release frozen assets (blocked accounts), both in cases of individuals or organizations.*

(16)   *That the WRA negotiate for the concluding of arrangements whereunder alien parents may be able to operate or manage properties with powers of attorney issued by their children, particularly by sons in the United States armed forces.*

(17)   *That the WRA arrange to secure outright releases for parolees who relocate.*

(18)   *That the WRA obtain the establishment of some avenue of governmental indemnities for relocatees who may become victims of anti-Japanese violence in terms of personal injuries or property damage.*

> *(19) That the WRA arrange for adequate Government
>   compensation against losses to evacuee property
>   by fire, theft, etc., while in Government or private
>   storage or while in transit.*
> *(20) That the WRA arrange to provide students of Jap-
>   anese ancestry with adequate protection in case of
>   need, and opportunities equal to those enjoyed by
>   Caucasian students.*
> *(21) That the WRA make every effort to secure work
>   opportunities for returnees and relocatees on
>   equal basis with Caucasian citizens, particularly
>   in reference to admittance into labor unions.*

In the eyes of the delegates: "It was believed to be a statement of the minimum government assistance needed to achieve just and decent reintegration of the evacuees into American community life."

In the aftermath of the conference, tempers cooled considerably in the centers. It had, after all, been a remarkable event. The evacuees had been listened to respectfully. The director himself had attended and spoken friendly and conciliatory words. In the assessment of Spicer: "From the all-center conference . . . came the first group expression of the hopes, needs, and aspirations of the thousands of people of Japanese ancestry who had been evacuated from the West Coast in 1942. It was more than a declaration by evacuees. It was in effect a definition of the position of Japanese Americans in America and was intended for consumption by the center residents, the American public, and the United States Government. . . . Before, during and after the conference, the National Director [Myer] visited the centers and addressed large meetings of the residents, taking a conciliatory tone and answering questions. For a people deeply respectful of authority to have the Director take the time and trouble to visit the centers made a deep impression on many of the evacuees and perhaps did more than anything else to both convince even the more obdurate that the centers would indeed be closed and to reconcile them to that inescapable fact." Myer's visit to Gila River had very positive results, according to the community analyst. A Nisei father commented that "the high school kids will become pressure groups [to reintegrate] inside their families."

Six weeks after the conference, the reply of the director to the twenty-one recommendations was received. Not surprisingly, there was considerable disappointment among the residents. While the recommendations, in toto, were politely but firmly rejected, the director reaffirmed his determination to see that all possible "economic and social" assistance be afforded to the relocatees, to do all in his power to fight terrorism and prejudice, and to assist in the reintegration of the evacuees into American life.

A letter drafted by the Topaz council on behalf of the conferees stated their dissatisfaction with the director's response. "We see no improvements or acquiescence to any of our recommendations," the letter declared, adding, "As we stated before, we need better understanding and cooperation from the WRA and the U.S. Government in order to go back to normal livelihood. Thus far, we see no special attempt made to make things easier for those relocated. Numbers of incidents have been occurring in which relocation has been discouraged even by the use of gun play and fire. No special policies or provisions have been advocated to right the wrong committed three years ago. To those of us still in these centers, such incidents and poor legal justice meted out do not enhance in any way our attempt to relocate."

The Federal Council of Churches of Christ, which included "25 Constituent Communions," entered the controversy over the closing of the centers with a resolution that "adequate provision" be made for the needs of all evacuees during the "return," and a delegation of five Japanese Protestant clergymen, John Yamazaki among them, traveled to Washington to urge Myer not to close the centers. Myer listened sympathetically but expressed his concern that if the centers remained open, the evacuees would simply become, like the Indians, permanent wards of the government.

A group at Rohwer, claiming that its views had not been reflected at the conference, held a three-day meeting of its own. At Granada, council members urged the residents to relocate in a cooperative spirit. At Poston, the chairman of the community council declared "the war is over," indicating that he no longer opposed relocation. At most of the centers, however, debate and discussion continued, but it was clear that resistance was weakening as the arguments of the more realistic began to prevail. But the conviction persisted that there would be a "residue" of evacuees who would not be able to reestablish themselves in the outside world and that the government must provide for these one way or another. The issue of closing the center schools at the end of the summer drew strong protests at several of the centers and the Minidoka community council began a lawsuit to prevent the closing. Parent-Teacher Association members took up the cause and made plans to continue the schools using their own resources. In Spicer's words: "The relocation centers had . . . become a fixed point of orientation in the thinking of evacuees. . . . They had become . . . the only security in a world that had made them completely insecure as a result of evacuation." Indeed, it could be said that the relocation centers had become, inadvertently, retirement communities. They were, in a sense, precursors of the "Sunset Villages" and "Twilight Manors" that would become such conspicuous features of the postwar landscape. There were security guards, in the form of kindly military police, assured incomes, numerous recreational activities, good hospital and nursing care, just about everything an older couple might desire.

While most Japanese nationalists clung stubbornly to their conviction that Japan would win the war, doubts clearly began to creep in. For a time those Issei who had come to suspect that Japan might actually lose the war did not dare say so aloud. An Issei who had relocated in Chicago and was convinced that Japan could not win the war tried to prevail on his fellow Issei to accept the fact that their future should be in the United States. He wrote a series of articles for the Japanese language newspaper *Rocky Shimpo,* published in Denver, urging such a course, but there was such a chorus of complaint that the paper discontinued publishing them, and when their author visited Heart Mountain and Granada in August to press his arguments, only a handful of Issei turned up to listen.

But there were a growing number of skeptics, even among the most ardent nationalists. An Issei woman (and Issei women increasingly spoke out for themselves and their own point of view) in one center wrote in May: "When Mr. X came back from Spokane, I was talking to him one day. I wanted to find out what he thought about the war. I had to go carefully because I didn't want to start an argument, and I knew how he used to think. So I just asked him if the people in the center had the right idea [that the war would end, at worst, in a negotiated treaty that would protect the interests of Japanese Americans]. 'They just don't know what is going on,' he said. 'In Spokane I was in just a little pin point of this country. But what I saw changed my mind. Trainloads of war material, week after week, all of it on the way to the Pacific. Then I realized what Japan was up against. The industrial power of this country is too great. If Japan is not beaten down, if peace comes in some way, we can be thankful. But we must expect the worst and act accordingly. We must go out and re-establish ourselves. Japan can never help us.' "

In response to the gloomy news of the course of the war, a senryu poet wrote:

> *The colors of the war maps*
> *Having lately changed,*
> *No longer can we smile.*

THE TIRELESS EFFORTS OF MYER TO ANSWER QUESTIONS AND QUIET ANX-ieties had, as Spicer notes, a salutary effect on the residents of the centers. Once again, Japanese fatalism kicked in. A well-to-do evacuee at Heart Mountain expressed the sentiments of a growing number of those remaining in the centers: "I guess I'll just have to go. . . . I don't want to go. I sort of like it here. My work is interesting. I have time for golf and fishing. I have lots of friends. I have no worries. . . . My wife likes it here all right and my daughter has her friends. . . . We're used to it. . . . Oh, I'll go. I have to. . . . But I don't want to."

In the words of an Issei woman: "When the WRA announced that the center would close, a lot of people said they didn't want to go out, some of them said they wouldn't. During the next two months, many of them changed their minds. They decided they did want to go out and they thought they could. They talked this way a little more before my husband left [in late March] than at any other time. Since then, what they have heard about the Coast has made them change their minds again. They still want to go, but they say they can't [this was in the period when rumors (and facts) circulated about hostile acts against returnees]. And . . . they don't just say this. It is true. They really can't. They want to go, but there is no place to live and jobs are hard to get. Employers are afraid to hire Japanese."

The center directors encouraged evacuees to go to the West Coast to scout out the lay of the land, to avail themselves of the various services of the War Relocation Authority offices, and especially to explore legal redress for recovering properties that had been in effect stolen in some instances by Caucasians in whose trust they had been left, and for recovering money owed on leases for farms or businesses. In Spicer's words, "the scouts went out for a week or two, looked over their old towns, interviewed many people, canvassed the possibilities for renewing their old lines of activity. They came back to the centers to add to the store of information that evacuees had been accumulating through correspondence with friends on the West Coast and through reading the home town newspapers.'' The reports of the scouts were often mixed. Two girls wrote that they were glad they had jobs as domestics so that they rarely needed to be on the street. ''They are uncomfortable and unhappy.'' They missed the center. It was reported that a large fertilizer company had refused to make deliveries to Japanese farmers. Some scouts returned to churches where furniture and belongings had been stored only to find that they had been broken into and their contents stolen, or even more un-nerving that their prized possessions had simply been vandalized. Others, though, found that Caucasian friends had been faithful trustees. This was usually the case with Christian churches that had undertaken to store Japanese possessions for the duration, although it is still a sore point with some Japanese American Baptists that a handsome church and auxiliary buildings that they had just completed in San Jose and that had been occupied by Caucasian Baptists at the time of evacuation remained in possession of a Caucasian congregation that refused to vacate.

On the other hand, each story of a farm reclaimed, a debt collected, or a business revived, circulated in the centers and moderated anxieties. It was especially reassuring to learn that lawyers, and even more important, the courts, were disposed to be helpful and that the principle of equality under the law seemed ready to reassert itself.

Many families that had stored belongings in government warehouses made inquiries about them and were reassured to learn that they had been, in most cases, well protected and that the cost of shipping them to an evacuee's new home would be borne by the War Relocation Authority. A number of cars and trucks were reclaimed.

Opinion was clearly shifting. Where relocatees had slipped away, fearful of arousing the ire of others in their block, they now openly discussed their plans to resettle. Where the Japanese language papers had the year before stressed hostile statements directed against Japanese Americans and reported in detail any incident of violence, they now reported on relocatees who had succeeded in establishing themselves in new lives. Success stories became more popular than accounts of preju-dice. All this, in Spicer's words, ''was working deeply against the vision of the outside world as an implacably hostile one on which much of the community sentiment had been built. It was being fostered by contacts with friendly and interested staff as well as with evacuees who had resettled.''

The War Relocation Authority commissioned Father John Yamazaki to visit the major cities on the West Coast to evaluate what community attitudes might be toward returning evacuees. Yamazaki found an ally in

Anne Patton, sister of the general, who was his hostess in Los Angeles and helped smooth the way for him in that city. Yamazaki returned to report that he had found people "generally . . . warm and welcoming and . . . foresaw no major attitudinal problems for returnees."

As early as July 1945 an assistant project director wrote: "They [the councilmen] were more relaxed, more at ease. Before, they seemed always on the defensive, sort of lined up against me. This morning a bunch of men sat down to talk things over. I was one of them."

Minidoka had had the largest number of evacuees who chose resettlement. Some 50 percent of the families in Minidoka had one or more members outside the center. When resettlers returned for visits they often appeared in snappy-looking new suits and dresses and often (although by no means invariably) with encouraging stories to tell of life outside. Even when their experiences were not entirely happy ones, the mere fact that they had gone and returned made the outside seem less formidable.

In June a staff member at Poston wrote: "There is a growing feeling in some Issei circles that there's just a little something wrong with a young person who is still in the center. . . . Prestige had once been attached to making a successful adjustment to center life. People in good, but not conspicuous center jobs were admired, as were those who had made great improvements in their apartments and yards. Community leaders universally advocated remaining in the center. . . . There have been more and more older men who were considered leaders—men who had advocated remaining in Poston—who have departed. Some of them were leaders of Issei cultural activities; they were most improbable candidates for relocation. Their departure may well make their admirers question the wisdom of staying."

"Yes," a married Issei wrote, "we're leaving the ninth [of October]. We don't have a home to go back to and will have to stay at the hostel or at a hotel until we can find something else. I want to go back to Tacoma where I lived for a long time. . . . We had a grocery store before but my wife sold it after I was interned. She sold it very cheaply but thought it was lucky that there was any buyer."

Now it was groups that began to plan to go back together to their old communities. In Topaz the Buddhist Church organizations worked with the center administration to encourage relocation. In May, a minister who had visited his hometown (the phrase was more frequently heard as the summer advanced) found a friendly, even rather embarrassed, welcome. There were still apprehensions evident but the best way to dispel them, he argued, was to go back in a good spirit and take up their lives. The

minister wrote eloquent letters on this theme and distributed them through
the centers. They helped to dissipate the mist of fear and anxiety created
by the closing. By the end of May, a relieved War Relocation Authority
was able to arrange for "whole carloads of returning people to go back
together." Railroad coaches were filled with returnees from Rohwer,
Granada, and Heart Mountain. With each new departure, the centers'
scheduled closing became more of a reality for those left behind. One
heard less of the "residue" and the "unrelocatables."

When a block population dropped below 125 people, the War Relocation Authority's policy was to close its mess hall and consolidate with
that of another block. At first this too was strongly resisted. It meant
getting used to new friends and, more disturbing, a new chef. At this
point the directors showed considerable tact and patience. A process of
bargaining went on—mutual concessions, postponements, the preparation of the favorite dishes of those "consolidating" by a chef whose food
was unfamiliar. But the dining halls contained something of the spiritual
as well as the material life of the blocks and losing a dining hall meant
losing the essence of block life. A bleakness enshrouded those blocks
whose dining halls had been closed. "People began to feel that the
substance of block life was disintegrating. . . . There was a feeling of
decay and decline in the air that weighed more and more on people
through the summer. . . . As the blocks crumbled, the relocation centers
began to disintegrate before people's eyes and under their feet," Spicer
wrote.

FAIR OR UNFAIR IT WAS CERTAINLY THE CASE THAT THE COURSE OF THE
war in the Pacific directly affected American attitudes toward the Japanese in America; conversely, as has been noted from time to time, the war
news or rather the version of the war news that the evacuees received on
the clandestine shortwave radios in the centers, affected the fears and
hopes of the evacuees themselves. The owners of shortwave radios listened to *Nippon Dai Honei-Hohkohu*, the official Japanese news station,
which, doggedly upbeat, glossed over Japanese defeats and reported
mythical victories. At the beginning of the marine invasion of Okinawa
the report came of a great (and illusory) Japanese victory marked by the
sinking of eleven Allied aircraft carriers and two battleships as well as a
number of destroyers and auxiliary vessels. The Tule Lake nationalists
held a noisy celebration.

Such reports were reinforced by the endless rumors that circulated through the centers. One such rumor was that Japanese planes had destroyed the Golden Gate Bridge. At Tule Lake the rumor spread that U.S. casualties had been so heavy that Tule Lake evacuees were going to be repatriated to Japan immediately in order to make room for the American wounded. The source of the rumor was traced to a shipment of laundry racks that had been identified as crutches.

From Midway (June 4–7, 1942) on, the toll of Allied victories mounted month by month. The marines landed on Guadalcanal in the Solomon Islands a month later and in November the attempt of the Japanese navy to retake the islands ended in a crushing defeat. In July 1943 the Marshall Islands were invaded by U.S. troops and Kwajalein and Eniwetok were captured. Guam followed, Palau, in the Carolines, a month later, then Leyte and the reconquest of the Philippines.

Still there were those evacuees who remained unshaken in their faith in Japanese victory or in a negotiated peace. Even American victories gave plausibility to the latter assumption. The battle for Iwo Jima lasted a month and cost 19,938 American casualties, including 4,198 dead. There was certainly a legitimate question as to how long the American people would be willing to sustain such horrendous casualties. In October 1944 the Japanese *kamikaze* pilots crashed their planes into three Allied aircraft carriers, the *Intrepid, Cabot,* and *Essex.* The three damaged carriers had to withdraw for repairs (the Japanese reported them sunk). The news of the achievements of the suicide pilots sent a thrill through Japan and gave new hope to those evacuees still convinced that the Japanese Imperial forces could never be defeated.

In the battle for Leyte Gulf the Allies suffered 2,260 killed and missing and thousands more wounded while the official count of enemy dead was 24,000. The latter was a fearful number because it represented the resolution of the Japanese to fight on until the last man had been killed or wounded. A few weeks later, on December 7, the third anniversary of Pearl Harbor, the destroyers *Mahan* and *Ward* were sunk by *kamikazes* and four days later *kamikaze* pilots crashed their planes into another destroyer, the *Reid,* sinking it, and badly damaged the *Caldwell,* which was struck by two *kamikazes.* This new tactic was profoundly demoralizing to the sailors and marines manning the Allied ships in the Pacific. It was as though the badly shattered Japanese air force had been revitalized. A Japanese pilot in exchange for an Allied war vessel was a calculus that the Allies could not long sustain. Japan now began an all-out program of training and psychological preparation for *kamikaze* pilots. The Emperor was persuaded to bless the venture. As the Allied fleet approached Luzon, a *kamikaze* crashed the cruiser *Nashville,* killing 133 officers and men and wounding 190. Two hours later another *kamikaze* plowed into the destroyer *Haraden,* which was put out of action.

Day after day the toll from *kamikaze* attacks mounted. The advantage for the Japanese was that older, often obsolete planes, planes unsuited for aerial combat or conventional missions, could be used. No great skill was required by the pilot. He had only to point his plane at an Allied ship. On January 4, 1945, a *kamikaze* crashed the escort carrier *Ommaney Bay* and sank her. The next day sixteen or more *kamikazes* hit the cruisers *Louisville,* HMAS *Australia,* another escort carrier, *Manila Bay,* and a destroyer. On and on the terrible toll went—the battleship *New Mexico,* the destroyer *Walke,* attacked simultaneously by four *kamikazes,* the minesweeper *Long,* two more destroyers, the battleship *California,* the light cruiser *Columbia.* On January 6, 1945, just when the Allies felt confident that the end of the Pacific war was in sight, they had suffered the heaviest losses of ships and lives since the Battle of Tassafaronga, more than two years earlier.

The Philippines campaign for the recapture of Manila proved far more costly than the Joint Chiefs had anticipated. The liberation of Luzon cost the Sixth Army 8,297 killed or missing and 29,557 wounded. Over 2,000 sailors and marines had been lost in the same period, most of them from *kamikaze* attacks.

The point to be emphasized here is that "objectively" there was much hard military reason for Japanese nationalists to anticipate in the winter and spring of 1945 if not victory, at least a peace that would protect their interests. The evacuees, no more than the Joint Chiefs of Staff, could guess what a desperate last-ditch effort the *kamikaze* tactic was and how seriously it diminished the Japanese air force. It has been estimated that over three thousand pilots died in *kamikaze* attacks; the great majority were intercepted by Allied planes or ship fire and never reached their targets. But the psychological effect was perhaps greater than the material damage they inflicted, great as that was. For the dedicated nationalists in the centers, the example of the *kamikazes* was an inspiration. It became increasingly clear that Japan, with no hope of winning the war, was bent on fighting a war of attrition so costly that the Allies would in time accept a negotiated peace. One of Asael Hansen's Issei friends at Heart Mountain confided his worries about the course of the war. "When American forces invaded Okinawa," he told Hansen, "and could not be repelled, I realized that the Empire was wounded, that it might bleed to death and suffer utter destruction. But I do not think that will happen. At some point the Emperor will say, *cease*. He will want to save the seed of the Japanese people.''

So it was that the constant flow of war news from the Pacific news, often open to conflicting interpretations, played on the hopes and fears of the evacuees.

The other military fact of importance to the fate of the evacuees (indeed, it is safe to say, of *far more importance*) took place in the European Theater of Operations. There the 100th (Hawaiian National Guard) Battalion covered itself with glory in its initial engagements in Italy. By the time the 442nd completed its training and joined the 100th, the 100th had been in combat for six months.

Shig Doi, who had volunteered for the 442nd, recalled the bitter fighting in the Vosges Mountains to try to reach the Lost Battalion. It was close range, hand-to-hand fighting in heavy forest. "My God," Doi exclaimed, "your enemy is ten or twenty feet away from you. The only reason I could fire at them is because the German has a white face compared with the Nihonjin. So when he peeks out at us between the bushes and the tree, I fired."

Later, in Italy, the 442nd joined with the elite 10th Mountain Division in an attack on Mt. Belvedere, the key mountain in the Apennines range. In a famous "night climb," elements of the 10th and the 442nd got behind the German lines. "I was mad," Doi told Tateishi, "because we had the 10th Mountain Division out there trained for mountain fighting. And we were climbing just like goats. If you fall you'll roll down, way down."

The 442nd got all the tough jobs in Doi's view. "We're always doing the flanking protection for somebody's division. . . . So you can't help but wonder, because we always seem to get the hard part. . . . Why was the 442nd so good? It's not that we had to prove anything. We were reckless because we were young you know. . . . I guess it's upbringing, the family, the closeness of family ties. When you're like that, you and your buddy are close."

The high casualties that the 442nd suffered inclined some cynics to suggest after the war that the commanding officers under whom the 442nd served, sharing the general prejudice against Japanese, deployed them in the most dangerous situations, as cannon-fodder, to use the common expression for soldiers ordered into difficult or hopeless assaults. There is even a hint of such a feeling in Shig Doi's account of his battle experiences. But the fact is, as every combat officer knows, it is the fate of units that fight exceptionally well to be used, time and again, in the most important (and perilous) engagements; the reward of excellence in combat is more combat.

Soldiers in the 442nd were often angry to hear of outbreaks of violence and riots in the centers. One soldier whose sister was in the relatively moderate center at Minidoka wrote: "I heard from Sis again. She tells me of more troubles at Hunt. Strikes and more strikes. People are discontented over nothing. I wish they would find out what hardships some of us go through at times. It seems to me the Issei are forever throwing monkey-wrenches into our machinery. . . . We try to build up some good reputation and it becomes overshadowed by some incident in Tule Lake or Hunt. I wish I could tell them off."

By a coincidence almost too pat to be credible, the Nisei 622nd Field Artillery Battalion, which had been assigned to the Seventh Army for its final drive into southern Germany, was among the units that came on the Nazi death camps, the notorious Dachau and its satellite camps. Ichiro Imanura recalled the encounter: "Two liaison scouts from the 622nd Field Artillery Battalion, 100th/442nd, were among the first Allied troops to release prisoners in the Dachau concentration camp. I watched as one of the scouts used his carbine to shoot off the chain that held the prison gates shut. He said he had just to open the gates when he saw a couple of the 50 or so prisoners sprawled on the snow-covered ground, moving weakly. They weren't dead as he had at first thought. . . . There were no prison guards. The prisoners struggled to their feet. . . . They were like skeletons—all skin and bones." Joseph Erbs, a Dachau prisoner, remembered "a big Oriental man" who "saved my life. . . . He picked me up from the ground." The eighteen-year-old Erbs weighed only seventy-six pounds and was barely alive. His rescuer was "a young Asian man. . . . Never before had I seen an Asian man or a black man." The soldier carried Erbs to a field hospital.

It was a strange coda to a strange story. A few days later Germany surrendered and Japan was left to fight on alone.

Those evacuees who had strong U.S. leanings followed the fortunes of the 442nd with special pride; they were "one of us," the "go-for-broke boys." Miyo Senzaki remembered running over to the camp center to see the latest list of casualties in the 442nd and often seeing the names of high school friends. She recalled a friend saying to her: "Miyo, how can you salute that flag?" Miyo looked at her friend and said, "I can't answer that, but I know how you feel. . . . From the time you're in first grade that's what you learn, and you're so proud when you do salute that flag, and then I remember going to ball games, the 'Star-Spangled Banner,' and there was a time when I couldn't even sing that, because I didn't feel it was right."

The memorial services held in the centers for Nisei killed in combat, at first resisted by the more militant, became increasingly an affirmation of solidarity, uniting factions in the centers as nothing else could.

The 442nd Combat Team became the most decorated unit in the U.S. Army, totaling up over a thousand citations, ranging from the Congressional Medal of Honor to 249 Silver Stars and 597 Bronze Stars. By the end of the war it had suffered a total of 4,430 casualties— 569 killed, 3,713 wounded. Tom Kawaguchi believed that the fighting qualities of the 442nd were due in large part to the fact that the education of most of the men in the unit was "above average—way above average. That was number one. Number two, they had a strong sense of pride, very strong. . . . I think the Japanese culture really came into play, all the things we were taught as kids—honesty, integrity, honor. And *haji,* 'not bringing shame on the family.' "

Almost forty years later, Haruko Niwa recalled the importance of the 442nd: "We have to be grateful no matter what kind of difficulty, what kind of bitterness and anger and all that, but when the Nisei decide to join the 442nd and do the righteousness, well, God gives us award of such effort by them."

The battle prowess of the 442nd was arguably the most newsworthy story of the winter of 1944–45. Its effect on public opinion is hard to overestimate. Story after story appeared in the national media. Its inherent drama was inescapable and the tales of heroism came just at the time when the centers were on the receiving end of the negative publicity generated by the Tule Lake episodes. A project that started off discouragingly in the sense that so few Nisei responded to the call for volunteers and that the accompanying registration proved the most divisive issue in the history of the centers, now ended gloriously, if we can say that in the face of the heavy casualties that the units suffered. But in the wartime atmosphere fighting qualities were honored, quite appropriately, above all else. The high casualties were the most eloquent testimony to the bravery with which the Nisei fought. One is tempted to appropriate Winston Churchill's praise of the RAF in the Battle of Britain, "Never have so many owed so much to so few." All Japanese Americans, of course, owed (and owe) an immeasurable debt to the Nisei fighters of the 442nd (and all other Japanese American soldiers). As the War Relocation Authority report put it: "Their performance had the effect, not instantaneously but gradually, of quieting the voices of all but the most rabid of the American racebaiters, and of enlarging materially the ranks of the forces of good will that were determined to see that the families of Nisei fighters were accepted as full Americans.'' In Dillon Myer's words: ''By the fall of 1944 it was no longer fashionable in most areas to bring irresponsible accusations against the Japanese.''

On the return of the 442nd to the United States in July 1946, the regiment paraded down Constitution Avenue to the Ellipse, where Harry Truman presented the regiment with the Distinguished Unit Citation. After reviewing the troops, Truman addressed the men of the 442nd. ''You fought for the free nations of the world with the rest of us. I congratulate you on that, and I can't tell you how very much the United States of America thinks of what you have done.

''You are now on your way home. You fought not only the enemy but you fought prejudice and you have won. Keep up that fight, and we will continue to win—to make this great republic stand for what the Constitution says it stands for: the welfare of all people all the time.''

The veterans, in turn, contributed $4,300 for a memorial to Franklin Roosevelt.

The War Relocation Authority took full advantage of the 442nd's combat record to try to create sentiment favorable for the resettlement of evacuees. A Caucasian officer, Captain George Grandstaff, a Californian from Arcadia, who had served with the 100th Battalion, requested a speaking assignment in his home state. ''As one of the few white officers who have served with the Japanese American 100th Battalion for some two and a half years, my main interest is to see that the splendid work they have done in combat is called to the attention of the people of the Pacific Coast in order that Japanese Americans who desire to return here may receive fair treatment,'' Grandstaff wrote. Three officers from the 442nd Regiment were also assigned to the War Relocation Authority ''as speakers in areas of most pronounced anti-evacuee sentiment.'' They talked, Myer noted, ''with key people such as local editors, mayors, chiefs of police, sheriffs and district attorneys.''

At Talbert, near Santa Ana in southern California, a young evacuee woman, Mary Masuda, who had recently returned from a relocation center, was visited by a deputation of local patriots who told her she was not welcome. Word of this incident reached the authority offices about the same time as the notice of a posthumous award to her brother for extreme heroism in a battle in Italy in which he lost his life. The Distinguished Service Cross, the nation's second highest military honor, was to be given to some member of his family. Mary Masuda was suggested.

General Joseph Stilwell, the hero of the China-Burma front, flew out from Washington to make the presentation on December 5, 1945. In Myer's words: "The incident was extremely widely featured in the nation's press and was covered by several of the newsreels. It virtually eliminated all the really significant vestiges of anti-evacuee feeling on the Pacific Coast."

On August 6, an atomic bomb was dropped on the city of Hiroshima, headquarters of the Japanese Second Army. Three days later a second bomb fell on Nagasaki and Russia declared war on Japan. Even in the face of those crushing events, the Imperial Conference, the highest authority in Japan, tried to avoid surrender. Admiral Soemu Toyoda, the Navy chief of staff, General S. Anami, the war minister, and General Y. Umezu, the army chief of staff, were as one in insisting that the Allies must give guarantees of "the Emperor's inviolability," that there be no occupation of Japan, no disarming of Japanese troops, and, finally, no trials of war criminals except in Japanese courts. At a second meeting of the conference, Emperor Hirohito, in whose name the war had been waged so fiercely, intervened. He insisted on accepting the Potsdam terms, which, in effect, were unconditional surrender; the decision was dispatched to the Allied governments and accepted by them. At a third Imperial Conference, the military lords, still unwilling to accept defeat, urged the Emperor to give his support to "one last battle" to save the national honor. The Emperor stood firm. He argued that the Allied reply to his message indicated the "peaceful and friendly intentions of the enemy." The Emperor then made a recording of an Imperial Rescript ordering all Japanese to lay down their arms. A plot to seize the Emperor, to destroy the recording of his rescript, and continue the war was narrowly averted. In the words of the premier historian of World War II, Samuel Eliot Morison: "Certainly the war would have gone on, and God knows for how long, if the bomb[s] had not been dropped. . . . If their Emperor had told them to fight to the last man, they would have fought to the last man, suffering far, far greater losses than those inflicted by the atomic bombs."

Of course, that leaves unanswered the question of whether the Allies would have had the stomach to fight on indefinitely under such conditions. Over five thousand young Japanese were in training for the feared *Kamikaze* Corps and 5,350 planes were still available for them to fly.

An old Issei woman recalled to Heihachiro Takarabe the tragedy of the day when it could no longer be doubted that Japan had been defeated. "Like my husband, for instance, he covered himself with *futon* and did not come out of it all day. Our son said, 'See, I told you. You said Japan was going to win, but they lost.' So it was doubly difficult for my husband to come out.'' The common emotion, a group of elderly Issei recalled, was *zannen*—profound chagrin. ''I cannot take joy in Japan's defeat at all,'' another old Issei declared, ''but that was *toki no nagare* (the way time flows).''

Haruko Niwa was riding a bus in Milwaukee on the way home from her office when she heard the church bells ringing, the pop of firecrackers and the shrill sound of whistles announcing the end of the war, ''and all the ladies in the seats in the bus kiss me and hug me. Oh, we were very happy that the war was ended. We just kept crying.''

One center resident, an Issei, wrote: ''It's hard to tell you how an Issei feels. I have a line that runs through me. On one side are my feelings for this country. It has done a lot for me. My kids are all-American and I want them to be. I have enjoyed my life here. On the other side are my feelings about Japan. Before the war, it was all right. I never thought of it. After Pearl Harbor I felt pulled apart inside. . . . Now I feel awfully sorry for Japan. If I am truthful, I must say I feel more for Japan than for this country. Not that I want or ever wanted Japan to win. . . . I didn't want nobody to win. I wanted the war to stop. I would feel terrible if this country was in danger of being crushed down. I guess I feel most for the country that is going to suffer most.''

When it was explained to an Issei woman that the war had ended, Mrs. Hirota's question was: ''Japan didn't lose, did she?'' When assured that it had, she shrugged resignedly. She was glad at least that it was over and that her sons, serving overseas, had survived. ''It was more important to her that her children were safe, she said, than how the war ended.''

At Tule Lake a pompous know-it-all urged an Issei couple to stay put because Japanese troops were only five miles from the center. He assured the couple that ''a special ship would come to pick up those who desired to return to Japan, and they would be given first class passage, plus a large sum of money. When they arrived in Japan the government would build them a beautiful house and give them a pension of 85 yen a month.'' Ridiculed by a Nisei who overheard this prognostication, Koshiyama replied that all stories of a Japanese surrender were lies. So was the story that Tojo, the prime minister, had committed suicide by shooting himself in the head. A person so eminent would never think of such a death. He would get his wife to bring him his sword and then commit *seppuku* in the classic fashion. ''If it's true that Japan surrendered unconditionally,'' Koshiyama replied, ''then it's pitiful there couldn't be any God or Buddha.''

With the news of Japan's surrender the last hope of the diehards for a negotiated peace that would compensate them for their sufferings vanished and a new degree of realism set in. In Spicer's words: "By some stroke of fate, the application of pressures to meet the deadline had been geared almost precisely to coincide with the disappearance of what was left of one of the old points of reference in the evacuee program to hold the centers."

By the end of September, evacuees were leaving the centers at the rate of two thousand a week, straining to the utmost the resources of the War Relocation Authority's relocation offices and the private agencies that were assisting them. At Granada, some of the older Issei refused to leave and were actually carried to the trains. A classic case of an evacuee refusing to leave was that of a man named Hirose. James Sakoda asked him his reasons. "My record is clear," he told Sakoda, "and they [the center administrators] should know where I stand. When I was once questioned before, I told them I would not go any place unless the war was over and settled. I haven't worked for a day since coming here. . . . You say that the war has ended, but I don't think so. If it has ended there should be some news of the settlement reached between Japan and America. Until that occurs I can't leave the project. I've made that clear to the people at the office. . . . Once, after that they asked me what I was going to do about my wife and children, I told them I wasn't able to take care of myself and wasn't going to be responsible for my children. . . . There should be some place they can send me until the war is over. I'll go any place they send me until the war is ended. . . . They can send me where they like—even to jail." When the center's internal police came to take Hirose to the railroad station, they found him hiding under his barracks. They thereupon locked his apartment and took him to the train, assuring him that they would pack his belongings and send them after him.

At Minidoka the Takagi familiy also refused to budge. James Sakoda recounted their final hours at the center. Surrounded by "shopping bags, carton boxes, and suitcases . . . randomly packed with the belongings of the family" they had to be forced into an authority car with their possessions following in the truck. Finally the Takagis and their two daughters were tugged aboard and the last evacuee train pulled out of Minidoka.

By December 1, 1945, the last relocation center (Tule Lake excepted) closed.

And so at last they left. They had endured an experience that had changed their lives, for better or worse, and often, be it said, for the better. Or ultimately for the better. The heritage, the memory, the life-shaping reality of the centers would be with the survivors all of their lives and, to a degree, with their children and grandchildren and, of course, with the Caucasians who had been players in this strange drama. It has often been said: "You can take the boy out of the town but you can't take the town out of the boy." One is reminded of the Nisei girl's cry, "You can't close a town!" The closing was, if possible, more traumatic for those who remained to the final days than the opening had been. Edward Spicer tells us that many women wept as they left. With all the excruciating episodes, all the traumas, the bitter rivalries, the betrayals, the conspiracies, the centers had become fortress-homes for the "stayers," those who had doggedly resisted leaving (or simply been unable to leave because, most commonly, of an inability to speak English and thus to make their way in the "white world"). They had experienced in the centers the classic rhythms of life—love and marriage, births and deaths. Gold Star mothers whose sons had died fighting for the United States had grieved in the centers and been comforted by the mothers of renunciants. The "evacuees" had become "residents"; they had participated in the small joys and graces that human beings create in the face of hardship and suffering. They had adorned their grim dwellings, made flowers grow where there had only been dust and sand and weeds. Yoshisadi Kawai reflected that when he had come to the "wilderness" of Minidoka it had been a rough and scarred landscape, "but now, because of our labor," he told Heihachiro Takarabe, "it had become a beautiful green field. We drew water from one of the tributaries of the Snake River. No matter where the Japanese people go, the place becomes green . . . think about West Coast farm land. It was the Japanese people who developed that land into green farm land." The words of the Twenty-third Psalm came to Kawai: "The Lord is my shepherd. . . . He makes me lie down in green pastures, and leads me beside the waters of peace; he renews life within me."

In their inhospitable environments the evacuees—the residents—had developed a remarkably rich and varied social and cultural life.

I have argued that history is best understood as a "tragic drama," so it was here; certainly one of history's most unique and dramatic events. It would be with the evacuees as an ever-present reality; they would lie down with it in the evening and rise in the morning in the vivid memory of those days strange beyond the telling of them. It was their secret. The other world, the white world, the *hakujin* world, the *keta* world, the world of the *haolies* would soon forget the whole event; it would come to exist only as a symbol of "racism," of a terrible injustice done to loyal Americans in the heat of wartime passion. That was all right with the *Nihonjin*, now irredeemably American in part at least because they had passed through the fiery furnace that had burned away the negative connotations in *Yamato Damashii*. They knew. It was their secret. If it had been a time of terrible testing for "persons of Japanese ancestry," it had also been a time of testing for America. And America had passed, too. Democracy, it turned out, had been capable of responding in enlightened ways to a tragedy of its own creating.

The "towns" the evacuees had created out of crude tar paper barracks and the infertile earth were abandoned to the elements or dismantled and borne away until only the memories remained. They went back, those reborn Americans, reborn out of suffering and loss, looking for an essential part of their past, *of them;* they would never cease in their returnings, in person or in memory.

The names of the centers became passwords, code words: "Where were you?" "Amache." "You?" "I was at Poston I." Or Topaz. Or Gila River. Each name had a weight and character. A history. A resonance. Minidoka summoned up a very different picture than Tule Lake or Manzanar; Jerome than Rowher, although both were in far-off Arkansas. Tule Lake was the "heaviest" name, the name most burdened with history. Stores and businesses were named after centers. If you were in the know you knew what the Topaz Pharmacy referred to and if you had been in Topaz you dropped in for a chat. Or if you had been at Amache, or Gila River. The Granada Restaurant sent a similar message to the initiated. Living in Cincinnati, thoughts of Topaz came back to Toyo Suyemoto Kawakami; she wrote a poem: "Topaz, Utah."

> *The desert must have claimed its own*
> *Now that the wayfarers are gone,*
> *And silence has replaced voices*
> *Except for intermittent noises,*
> *Like windy footsteps through the dust,*
> *Or gliding of a snake that must*
> *Escape the sun, or sage rustling,*
> *Or soft brush of a quickened wing*
> *Against the air—Stillness is change*
> *For this abandoned place, where strange*
> *And foreign tongues had routed peace*
> *Until the refugee's release*

Restore calm to the wilderness,
And prairie dogs no longer fear
When shadows shift and disappear.
The crows fly straight through settling dusk,
The desert like an empty husk
Holding the small swift sounds that run
To cover when the day is done.

Chapter 25

THE RETURN—*SHUSHOKU*

THE RESETTLEMENT THAT FOLLOWED THE LIFTING OF THE EXCLUSION-ary Ban may have been the most traumatic experience of all for the evacuees. The logistical problems were vast—transportation, habitation, jobs, were prominent among them. For those evacuees returning to urban areas, housing was the most urgent need.

The American Railway Association pitched in to facilitate the transportation of evacuees from the various centers and often the train trips took on the air of holiday ventures with flags and banners flying. A final trainload of 417 evacuees making the long journey from Rohwer in Arkansas, broke the trip in St. Louis, where a committee of Japanese Americans who had resettled there joined with the local resettlers' committee to meet the train and take the evacuees sightseeing. Movement by train in large groups turned out to be something of a lark and indeed became the common mode of departure in the last months of the centers. Manzanar, Gila River, and Poston depended primarily on chartered bus service.

George Wakatsuki, always flamboyant, left Manzanar in style. When it came time for what remained of the family to depart, he went to the nearest town and bought a flashy second-hand Nash to drive the family from Manzanar to Los Angeles, a four-hour drive. He had to make four round-trips, interrupted by numerous breakdowns, but it was a splendid gesture of bravado.

The concentration of defense industries in California had brought a great influx of workers into the state. Housing was thus at a premium. Individuals or families who had rented the dwellings of internees often had, literally, no place to go. Ironically, many of the farms owned or leased by evacuees had been taken over by refugees from the Dust Bowl, Okies and Arkies, who considered the vacated farms an opportunity, if not a gift sent from heaven. Many of them had prospered as farmers for the first time in their lives; not surprisingly, they considered themselves once again the victims of forces over which they had no control and of decisions in which they had no part.

In Los Angeles a section called Little Tokyo where Japanese had lived prior to evacuation had, in their absence, become a black neighborhood, Bronzeville. Now the Japanese gradually repossessed it. In the words of an Issei: "When I came back here in January last year, it was solid Negroes around here. I wondered if this would ever be Japanese town again. Nothing much happened for quite awhile. Even during the summer, there were just a few places opened by Japanese. I figured it would be at least three or four years before we could take over. Then during the summer and fall, they really started to come back. Soon there were more Japanese than Negroes, and Japanese businesses all up and down the streets. I was surprised."

Evacuees arriving at their destinations were met by representatives of the Authority who interviewed them as to their most immediate needs, including housing, employment, medical problems. In the San Francisco area some three thousand evacuees were interviewed and most of their problems worked out by relocation officers. "Relocation officers with agricultural backgrounds were assigned to help farm families, and specialists in urban and domestic employment were delegated to take care of the others." In virtually every community local committees of civic-minded citizens and church groups assisted in the difficult process of adjustment.

Hostels were set up in church parish halls or anywhere where space could be found to accommodate those who needed a roof over their heads. By November there were over two hundred hostels in twenty-five cities supported by groups like the Unitarian Service Committee, the American Baptist Home Missionary Society, the Japanese Methodist Church, Lutheran Church, Buddhist Brotherhood in America, and the Japanese American Citizens League. Where the churches and social organizations were unable to provide shelter, the War Relocation Authority took on itself the task of supplying cots, sheets and blankets, silverware and cooking utensils. In Pasadena, nine different Protestant churches joined in the Federated Mission of Pasadena to support the Japanese American church there and to help Japanese Christians get established. "A young man coming here" (to Pasadena), Nisuke Mitsumori recalled, "could stay at the church, get a job through the church's placement service and study English at their night school. There were quite a few people who received service and care from the church."

From Heart Mountain the Igarashi family returned to Sacramento to open their Christian Center and began operating it as a hostel for returnees, often putting up a hundred people a night. The average stay at the Christian Center hostel was about a month. Similarly, Isamu Nakamura turned his Sacramento church into a hostel that provided shelter and food for as many as thirty returnees at a time. Those who stayed were charged $1.25 a night for room and board. The hostel stayed open for two years before its services were no longer needed.

One of the ways that evacuees were resettled in their former communities was through a program of sponsorship. The Auernheimers, Mennonite sponsors of three Issei, remembered with anger a visit from a WRA official who brought with him an elderly Issei and introduced him with these words: "We need a sponsor for this man. If he doesn't get a sponsor he is going to have to be deported. And I would hate to see the little buzzard deported."

The National Housing Agency was enlisted and the Federal Public Housing Administration offered assistance. After VJ Day buildings vacated by the military began to be available. Temporary barracks were commandeered. At Fort Funston, San Francisco, sufficient space was found for five hundred families. The buildings on the Lomita Air Strip in Los Angeles had space for another five hundred. The Army Air Transport Command at Sacramento provided for all evacuees returning to the Sacramento area and in need of emergency housing. Trailers were pressed into service in many areas. The Wakatsuki family was relocated into former workers' housing—Cabrillo Homes—in Long Beach, and Jeanne's mother, Ko, went back to work in a fish packing plant.

Those returnees fortunate enough to find a house or an apartment often found themselves besieged by relatives and friends. June Toshiyuki had to take the responsibility for relocating with her parents and children. Her Issei husband, still confident of being rescued by the Japanese army, refused to leave the Gila Center. June went first to Cleveland, Ohio, and finding the climate too severe for her mother returned to Los Angeles. With the help of Father Pratt, an Episcopal minister, June, her uncle, mother, and three children were lodged in a hostel while she looked for more permanent quarters. When her husband finally left Gila River, he refused to participate in searching for a permanent home. When June finally found a two-bedroom house, her pregnant sister, Ruth, arrived from Utah with her husband, two brothers-in-law, her mother- and father-in-law, and the friend of an uncle. That brought the number in the house to twenty. It turned out, June recalled, to be "a hostile hostel because we were rubbing shoulders constantly." And June had to cook for everyone.

Some relocatees solved the housing problem by taking live-in jobs, housekeepers or gardeners, where rooms were furnished by the employer. Sam and Ruth Engel were delighted to welcome back their former gardener (whom they knew only as "Charles") and his wife, Hamato, who had worked for them as a maid before Pearl Harbor. The Engels had attended their elaborate Buddhist wedding. Now Hamato and Charlie returned with an infant and lived in the Engel house, happy to resume their former duties.

The problems in farming communities were very different, in the main, from those in the larger towns and cities. The principal one was the task of ousting Caucasians who had leased Japanese-owned farmland. Many of the "substitute operators" complained that they had been recruited on the grounds of assisting in the national defense effort. Having done their duty (and in some instances having profited materially) and having just begun to get the hang of unfamiliar farming practices, they were now to be evicted. Many farms were encumbered with loans and mortgages. In the words of a WRA report, "a substantial number of substitute operators showed the greatest disinclination to be dislodged." Many of their leases read that the property was leased to them "for the duration." It seemed plain enough to them that "duration" meant for the duration of the war, not, as the War Relocation Authority was now insisting, for the duration of the relocation camps.

Some returnees were able to move onto their former property but could not get into their houses until the wartime occupants had found other accommodations. In some such instances, they borrowed tents from the War Relocation Authority and camped out until they could reclaim their homes. One man recalled: "We had to pitch a tent, set up a kitchen area, buy and gather food. . . . Oh, yes, we had to make a toilet, too. For awhile it was very busy."

The Cortez Presbyterian Church was a hostel. "We all slept in the same hall," an elderly Issei recalled. "They say *zakone* in Japan, which means sleeping like many fish laid out on a board . . . at the same time there was no pride or shame. The only concern was to have a roof over our heads." One of the Japanese Issei who resettled at Cortez recalled that "sand buried the chickens when the wind blew."

In the immediate aftermath of evacuation, forays against abandoned Japanese farms were motivated primarily by simple hostility. Often there was random destruction; things smashed and broken for the pleasure of it. On farms that remained abandoned, many of those who had visited ruin on houses and barns, in Spicer's words, "now went with a view to appropriating anything which their own establishments might lack. Evacuee possessions of easily movable nature had long since been wrecked or stolen, but doors could be removed and carried away for use in the marauders' own houses, window frames were utilized, sinks were appropriated, toilets uprooted and carried away, and built-in shelves were taken apart and the boards taken away."

Shig Doi, it may be recalled, was a member of the 442nd Combat Team. When the Exclusionary Ban was lifted, Shig Doi's family was one of the first to leave Tule Lake. The senior Doi, having owned his land through his son, had leased it for the duration of the war and was eager to reclaim it. The land had passed through several hands before the raising of the ban and its present tenants were reluctant to give it up. A Caucasian friend told them of a plan to burn down the Dois' packing shed. Doi's sons were on the alert with a fire hose and quickly doused the flames. The following night a shotgun was fired at the farmhouse but the Dois stood fast, refusing to be frightened away and the attacks stopped. The fact that three of their sons were in the service (one of them— Shig—in the famous 442nd) doubtlessly played a part in the ending of the harassment.

The Florin area, the reader may recall, was an area of marginal land, of small, family-sized farms where the Japanese by heroic efforts raised Tokay grapes and strawberries. The farms in the Florin region had suffered severely from vandalism, in large part because no substitute operators could be found who were prepared to undertake the intensive labor required to produce even a modest return. Those farms that had found tenants, however indifferently maintained, were in far better condition than those that had remained unoccupied. When evacuees from the Florin area began to return, they encountered determined resistance. A War Relocation Authority official, visiting the district in March 1945, when evacuees were just starting to return, was appalled at the condition of many of the farms and dismayed at evidence that the Caucasian ranchers were trying to frighten off returnees. The official was confronted by the charred ruins of the Fumi Mukai Fujimoro ranch house and barn, consumed in a suspicious night fire during the owners' temporary absence. The Takeoka brothers owned a nearby ranch and had just returned to occupy it. The Fujimoro fire so alarmed them that they had decided to leave the area. As they were driving away they were intercepted by the official, who expostulated with them, urging them to remain, "pointing out that these cowardly acts were a desperate attempt to frighten away the first evacuees to return, and that courage to face these pioneering hazards until more of the evacuee farmers returned would be worth the effort." By staying they would demonstrate that they were determined to reclaim what was rightfully theirs and thereby encourage others. "When half a dozen adjoining farms were occupied by their owners, night terrorists would hesitate to attack. . . . The Takeokas turned around and resumed control of their property."

The WRA supervisor was right; the nighttime raids stopped. The owners had demonstrated their resilience. In the words of the supervisor: "They said that by rotation of other crops, by experimenting, by working a little harder, they could get along—it was good to be home again, even if they had to start out once again as they had years ago when they had taken over unimproved or hay land and made it productive." Perhaps the determinative phrase here was "home again." Many of the Japanese prior to Pearl Harbor had thought of Japan as home. The experience of being uprooted and carried off to the relocation camps had changed the meaning of the word.

It was soon evident that it was important to get a kind of critical mass of evacuees in communities around whom "local committees of fair-minded citizens who were concerned about racial prejudice and anxious to assist the returning evacuees in their problems of community adjustment" could rally. "Unless such a group was physically present in the evacuated area, it would be like battling racial intolerance in a vacuum." So you needed the combination—enough evacuees to constitute a kind of critical mass and the local organization or consortium of organizations ready and willing to help in whatever way they could.

The tactic developed by the War Relocation Authority was similar to that used by the Association of Southern Women to Prevent Lynching: the establishment of a network to make known any and every anti-Japanese incident and to immediately dispatch someone in authority to investigate the episode and call on local authorities for assistance in making clear that such actions would not be tolerated and, in the event that local law enforcement individuals or agencies were not responsive, an appeal to higher authorities, accompanied by copious publicity.

One of the most conspicuous obstacles was Dave Beck, head of the International Teamsters Union and associate of mobsters. Beck encouraged a Teamster boycott of Japanese farm products, whereupon the Authority sent a marketing specialist into the area to assist evacuees in finding other outlets for their produce. When Hood River Valley merchants posted signs in the windows of their stores saying "No Jap Trade Wanted," the authority encouraged the local Japanese to take their business to the neighboring community of the Dalles, which was glad to have it. The "No Jap Trade Wanted" signs in Hood River Valley soon disappeared. Often an inquiry from an Authority official or an interested Caucasian citizen would be enough to have an unfriendly sign removed. When Myer and the assistant director of the San Francisco office, Robert Cozzens, traveled up the San Joaquin Valley from Los Angeles to Sacramento to see for themselves what kind of reception returning evacuees were receiving, they found only one family, threatened by random rifle shots, which planned to move as a consequence.

Stopping at a fruit stand where the packing boxes from the Poston center were still in evidence, Myer and Cozzens visited with the family. When the mother appeared from the fields, Myer asked her if she was glad to be home. "No!" was the reply. When Myer asked her why she said: "Too much work!"

Peter Tsuchiyama had a poultry ranch at Downey, California, which he leased to a "Mr. J." (so identified in the War Relocation Authority's report). J., unable to make a go of the venture, leased it to "K. and L." With the rent five months in arrears, a new actor appeared, identified only as "N." He was leasing the farm from L. (K. had dropped out) and taking over its operation because of a large feed bill owed him (he represented himself as a feed dealer). In January 1945, when Tsuchiyama returned to his poultry ranch, there were neither chickens nor eggs and "a considerable quantity of equipment missing."

Vashon Island off the Washington coast was a center of Japanese settlement. When the Miyosha family was shipped off to Minidoka Relocation Center in Idaho they owned a "well-insured" home on the island in which they stored clothing, furniture, and agricultural equipment owned by them and the equipment of four other island evacuee families. With the premises empty, the insurance company canceled the Miyoshas' policy. Two of the Miyoshi sons, Masaru and Glenn, who as citizen children held title to the property, had volunteered for the 100th Infantry Battalion and were sent to Italy where Masaru was seriously wounded. On February 1, 1945, when the family was preparing to return to Vashon, their house was burned down by three boys "just for the thrill" as they testified. The two minor boys and their parents agreed to make restitution to the Miyoshas of $1,000 each.

Another victim with the fictitious name of Hideo Mori was living in the San Joaquin Valley when the war with Japan began. By his own account, he was an alien and owned a ranch in Yolo and Solano Counties that he had purchased prior to the Alien Land Law of 1913. Sent to the Gila River Relocation Center and going out early in 1944, Mori, "forewarned of the public sentiment" in Yolo and Solano Counties, found a temporary haven with friends in the San Joaquin Valley. From there he appealed to the War Relocation Authority for assistance. During his time in the Gila River camp, he had rented his land to "local Spaniards." In Mori's words, "They milked it for all it was worth, never bothering to keep it up or improve it, knowing that during the term of their lease no one would come to inspect their work." The consequence was that the value of the ranch decreased dramatically. When Mori reclaimed his land he found that the farm equipment that he had accumulated over some thirty years of farming was broken or stolen. Even water faucets had been carried off as well as household belongings and personal property stored in a locked closet of the farmhouse. Doors and windows had been broken and several doors removed from their hinges. "We were evacuated as a wartime measure," Mori wrote, "and as a result of this evacuation we suffered losses from negligence that borders on sabotage and looting such as can be associated with ransacking hordes of an invading army. Is it not only fair that restitution for such losses incurred as a result of this evacuation— proper restitution to put us back on the economic status from which we were forced—be treated by a measure as forceful as our evacuation?"

The letter was addressed to the director of the War Relocation Authority and the director replied to Mori that while "deeply disturbed to learn of this damage" the War Relocation Authority simply did not have funds to make up such losses. That could only be done by Congress.

Nobu Miyamoto had been a prosperous greenhouse and nursery operator in Seattle. He dealt in cut flowers and potted and bedding plants, owned a large, comfortable house, and had numerous smaller buildings and greenhouses. Ordered to evacuate, Miyamoto and his family collected their belongings, locked them in a sturdy building, and left the key and the authority with an old friend and family lawyer. The friend's health was so poor that he was unable to exercise any real supervision of the lessees and when the Miyamoto family returned in the spring of 1945 they found the place looted and the greenhouses with many smashed panes of glass. Miyamoto's inventory of missing possessions included carpenter and plumber tools, flower shop materials, a trunk containing Japanese silks to the value of $1,500, and a ring valued at the same price.

An especially offensive act to Japanese from the area was the vandalizing of the Nichiren Buddhist Church in Los Angeles, which was used as a storehouse for the belongings of its evacuated members. When a War Relocation Authority officer visited the church with a member, Mrs. Itano, they encountered in Mrs. Itano's words "a hopeless mass of deliberate destruction. . . . Nothing was untouched. Sewing machines were ruined, furniture broken, mirrors smashed to smithereens . . . household goods scattered helter-skelter, trunks broken open, albums, pictures . . . thrown to the four winds." In addition to the wanton destruction, everything of any possible value had been carried off—electric irons, sewing machines, refrigerators, washing machines, radios, Persian rugs, typewriters.

When Wilson Makabe, wounded in Italy, arrived in Florida, via a hospital ship in December 1944, he was given a free phone call. He called his brother George, still working in Idaho, and George told him that the family home in Loomis had been burned down just hours after the words had gone out on the radio that the Japanese in the relocation centers could return to the West Coast. "When he told me that," Makabe recalled, ". . . oh, you can't describe the feeling. I remember the pain and the hurt, the suffering in the hospitals in Italy—that was nothing compared to this. I cried for the first time. All that time in the hospital I don't remember shedding a tear, but I cried that night. . . . It was a big house where all of us grew up, and I remember a big dining room that fed all the help at one time, so that we would have as many as twenty or more people sitting around."

One episode from his return to Loomis stuck in Makabe's memory. When he stopped at the Loomis filling station for gas, the owner came out to help him and after the tank was filled he said to Makabe, "I'd like to talk to you." "Hop in." The two men traveled down the road a way and the station owner said, "Y'know, I was one bastard. I had signs on my service station saying 'No Jap trade wanted.' Now when I see you come back like that [referring to Makabe's amputated leg] I feel so small.' And he was crying."

There were, to be sure, many acts of kindness that helped to offset the random vandalism and threats of violence. Herman Neufeld, a Mennonite farmer, had purchased the land of the Takeuchi family at the time of the evacuation. When they returned, Neufeld tried to purchase nearby land in their name. When neighbors protested, Neufeld moved the family onto his farm, remodeled a chicken house for them, and let them stay for two years until they could "get their feet on the ground."

In Turlock, the *hakujin* Winton family opened their home to returnees and had, at one time, five families living on their ranch.

Isamu Nakamura recalled that on his way home from the relocation center in Colorado he was forced to spend the night in Turlock. When he could find no hotel that would provide a room, the friendly local sheriff, a retired Methodist minister, offered to put him up for the night in the women's cell at the jail.

Some convalescing *hakujin* veterans were enlisted by Josephine Duveneck to go to stores that displayed "No Japs Served Here" signs and suggest that they be taken down. When volunteers received word of particular families that were due to return to an area, they traveled to the town or section of a city where the returnees were headed to enlist leaders of the community in preventing any untoward incidents and, hopefully, to ensure welcomes.

THERE WAS A STRANGE CONTRAST BETWEEN THE EVACUATION AND THE return. The evacuation was from uncertainty to certainty; from weeks of rumors, of anxiety about their fate on the part of Issei and Nisei alike, of fear and uncertainty in the Japanese communities, to the certainty of the assembly centers and relocation. The return, conversely, was from the certainty and familiarity of the relocation centers to the uncertainty of a wholly new life. Of "starting over," as some of the evacuees put it. Evacuation meant pulling up roots; the return meant planting them once more. The painful and complicated process of resettlement, of picking up new lives, went on. A Nisei farmer, who had been a block manager in his center, told Edward Spicer: "In Santa Clara Valley very few owned their farms. Mostly they leased on a cash basis, but some sharecropped. A few of the Japanese were pretty big operators. More of them worked on a smaller scale and there were a lot of little places. The important thing to remember is that, big or small, almost everyone had a farm that he operated on his own account. I would say that no more than five percent worked for someone else as farm workers. Maybe not even that many. Except for those who owned their own places, now we are all farm laborers, working for somebody else for wages. A few have been able to buy land or get leases. But the prices are high. And if you sold your equipment at evacuation the way I did, you're stuck. So here I am.''

One relocatee in the Hood River Valley declared early in 1946: ''We are getting along. Some of the orchards are not in very good shape. They weren't taken care of right. Everybody is working hard to get them fixed up again. As long as prices stay the way they are, we'll be able to make money. We have trouble getting equipment, but so do all the other farmers I guess. It isn't the way it used to be though. The people of the Valley don't treat us the same as before evacuation. But it's a lot better than it was a year ago and is getting better all the time.'' He added: ''The wages I get are good and the people I work for treat me well. But I don't like it. I would sooner be on my own. But what else can I do? I have a family and we have to live.''

Another spoke to much the same effect: ''I am doing this kind of work I hadn't done for 15 to 20 years before evacuation. I used to hire other men to do it for me. But I'm not proud. I'll do anything that comes along. The only thing is that I want to be paid for it. I want all I can get. The whole family went out into the orchards and fields when we first came back. For five months, starting in July, we averaged a thousand dollars a month. Of course we couldn't keep on doing that well. That was the fruit-picking season. The girls kicked at doing farm work. I guess I spoiled them before evacuation. The relocation camp spoiled them too. They got ideas there about white-collar jobs. A girl can make more picking fruit and there is no question about her being hired even if she does have slant eyes.'' This Nisei was counting on a depression to bring down the price of land. ''That's why I want to get as much money as I can now. I want to have a little capital for when the chance comes.''

The Japanese who had money to invest seemed more interested in buying small hotels and apartment houses. It was a way to get both housing and income. The hotel indeed threatened to outdo the farm as a family business. Men who had sold their hotels for $1,000 to $1,500 at the time of evacuation now had to pay ten times as much to buy them back. In Los Angeles Japanese-owned hotels and restaurants catered to the new black population. Many Nisei who had been involved in the production and sale of fruits and vegetables, finding themselves often frozen out by Caucasian farmers, turned to other jobs in industries and businesses. ''A few,'' Edward Spicer noted, ''have obtained white-collar positions of a kind that were definitely closed to them before evacuation.'' And this movement accelerated with each passing decade. Spicer also noted in 1946 that the returning Issei and Nisei "are still largely outside of their two major pre-evacuation pursuits—farming on their own account and the marketing of vegetables. It follows that relatively few have arrived at what they would be willing to consider a permanent or fairly permanent adjustment. Not many, on the other hand, are still floundering around as far from adjustment as when they left the center. Most people have accepted some expedient which provides them a living and often permits them to save."

THE LIFTING OF THE EXCLUSIONARY BAN ON THE WEST COAST PRESENTED many evacuees who had resettled to the "East" with a dilemma—to return to the coast or not. A Kibei who had relocated to Boise, Idaho, and who had planned to return to Japan, wrote to James Sakoda: "I don't think I'm going to stay in Boise very long. I was working in Hollywood before, but I don't want to go back there until more people return. . . . A lot of people are leaving for Seattle. . . . I'm resigned to staying in this country now. Japan's lost the war and there's no use going back. . . . This winter people in Japan are going to suffer greatly."

When the centers closed, some 50,000 evacuees were in the east or, more accurately perhaps, "to the East." Some 57,000 had returned to the West Coast, a figure that included 5,600 from the east. The states to the east that had received more than 1,500 evacuees were Illinois, 11,200 (chiefly Chicago); Colorado, 5,300 (chiefly Denver); Utah, 3,900 (chiefly Salt Lake City); Michigan, 2,800 (chiefly Dearborn and Detroit); New York, 2,300; New Jersey, 2,200; and Minnesota, 1,700. Of California's pre-evacuation population of 93,717, by March 1946 there were 48,600.

It is also interesting to note where those returnees who returned to the coast settled; there was a marked shift away from small rural communities to the larger towns and cities. For example, of 5,167 living in Alameda County, California, in 1940, 2,703 returned, some 52 percent, 987 to Berkeley and 906 to Oakland. Contra Costa County got back 562 of 621, or 75 percent. Fresno County, which had 4,527 Japanese Americans in 1940, had 4,296 after the war and the city of Fresno experienced an actual increase in population so that the population of the county in 1946 was 95 percent of its prewar population. On the other hand, Imperial County, which had 1,585 in 1940, had only 142 six years later. And Los Angeles County, with 36,866 in 1940, declined to 17,172, or 46 percent of the prewar population (the city of Los Angeles actually grew by more than

1,000). Monterey fell from 2,460 to 616. Placer County, with 60 percent of its prewar population, was toward the upper end of the scale, as was Sacramento County with a prewar population of 6,764, contrasted with 4,304 after the war. The city itself grew by some 300, thereby reinforcing that impression that much of the decline was in farming communities and that the larger cities grew proportionately as Nisei switched from agricultural life to urban occupations.

Santa Clara County had 4,049 before the war and 3,418 afterward (84 percent), and as with other urban sites, the city of San Jose grew while the county's rural population declined. Santa Cruz County, which had 1,301 Japanese Americans in 1940, dropped to 434, almost all living in Watsonville. The county of Merced dropped from 715 to 432, 149 of whom were members of the cooperative Yamato Colony, an agricultural commune of Japanese American Methodists.

The state of Washington saw a decline from 13,889 to 4,039, less than 30 percent of the prewar population. Again, Seattle grew by some 400. One of the reasons so many relocatees settled in cities on their return was that branch offices of the War Relocation Authority were located in the major West Coast cities and were much better prepared to find homes and jobs in urban than in rural areas. In addition, returnees undoubtedly encountered far less resistance and hostility in the cities than in the small towns. City law enforcement agencies were, generally speaking, much better able to protect the lives and property of returnees than small-town sheriffs. In addition, the "helping services" of various organizations, including the churches, were much more readily available in the cities than in rural towns.

One of the interesting statistics concerns the towns in eastern Washington and Oregon that were on the edge of the exclusionary zone. Not surprisingly, these grew overall by some 300 percent. Oregon's Malheur County, for example, with a 1940 population of 137, grew to 1,254, and Washington's Spokane County comparably.

THE MOST IMPORTANT ELEMENT IN THE INTEGRATION OF JAPANESE Americans into the larger society after the war was, of course, the attitude of Caucasian Americans toward "persons of Japanese ancestry." Changing public attitudes were reflected in an editorial in a Los Angeles newspaper in January 1946. Under the headline "Restitution for Evacuee Citizens," it read, in part: "Secretary of the Interior Harold Ickes has come out pubicly with a declaration that American citizens of Japanese ancestry who were removed from their West Coast homes by the military 'are entitled to and should receive compensation for any damage inflicted on their property in California or elsewhere during their absence.' He referred only to stored goods damaged, and homes or other buildings burned. This would be most inadequate justice that can never satisfy a sensitive American conscience. From the standpoint of the individuals, goods may as well have been burned or stolen as to have been sold 'for anything you can get,' as advised by the bank representatives on evacuation boards. [This was not strictly true. As soon as the Federal Reserve Bank was involved, it did its best to ensure that evacuees got fair prices for their property.] These people are entitled to restitution for losses in business and in high earning power during the war period.'' The notion that the evacuees should be compensated for the ''high earning power'' that they might be presumed to have had in the course of the war if they had not been relocated went considerably further than anyone had yet proposed. The writer of the editorial did not suggest how such sums were to be calculated. The editorial concluded by declaring that the removal of the Japanese ''was the most un-American episode in American history. Those who think it was necessary should be the first to see to it that innocent citizens should not bear the whole burden of 'war necessity.' ''

There were numerous other indications of a kind of national bad conscience that seemed, with time, to be growing worse, and out of which came a general feeling of good will, a desire to make it up to our Japanese neighbors and demonstrate that we were not such bad types after all. Reflecting on the war, the Reverend Francis Hayashi noted: ''War is bad, but on account of war, people in America changed their attitude and treated the Japanese in a different way.''

Chapter 26

Loose Ends

Hᴉsᴛᴏʀʏ ɪs ɴᴏᴛᴏʀɪᴏᴜsʟʏ ғᴜʟʟ ᴏғ ʟᴏᴏsᴇ ᴇɴᴅs; ɪᴛ ɪs ᴛɪᴍᴇ ᴛᴏ ɢᴀᴛʜᴇʀ up some of them here. With all of the centers closed, the evacuees resettled (or in the process of being resettled), the War Relocation Authority busy going out of business, the principal loose end was Tule Lake. In the aftermath of the assassination of Takeo Noma, the co-op store manager, and the transfer of the center to War Department control, Frank Miymoto, the JERS contact at Tule Lake, wrote: "In the next three months, nine major rebellions, including six other strikes, shook the community. It was an exceedingly tense period." In a mood approaching a kind of hysteria, the pressures on Nisei to renounce their U.S. citizenship and apply for repatriation were enormous. The refrain "we are all Japanese together" was endlessly repeated. One consequence was that the number of Nisei renunciants, whose rejection of their American citizenship was approved by the attorney general, grew to 5,589 by April 18, 1946. Of these, 5,461 were at Tule Lake; 2,785 were released from interned status and relocated; 1,657 were placed in internment camps. Included in the renunciants were 2,764 single men and 754 single women; 1,174 married men and 928 married women. Of the 5,589, 1,868 had never been in Japan and 1,565 had lived in Japan for more than ten years.

Attitudes often seemed to change from week to week and even from day to day. A suit was brought against the U.S. government to block repatriation to Japan on the grounds that misguided government policies such as registration and the draft had driven many evacuees to apply for repatriation. The Justice Department was pleased to respond. It announced on December 10, 1945, that it would conduct hearings at Tule Lake for all renunciants who requested the opportunity to present the case for not being deported. A special unmarked office was set up so that evacuees could slip away, cancel their renunciation, and quietly make plans to relocate.

From the first of January until March 20, 1946, the hearings were held and the center was kept open essentially for that purpose. When the hearings started on January 1 a total of 3,161 applications had been received through the block managers. Of these, only 107 renunciants did not request hearings. Each evacuee appeared before a fifteen-member panel. He or she could bring witnesses and have an interpreter. The recommendations were either to hold for internment and possible deportation or release. These recommendations were forwarded to the office of the attorney general for final action. Of the 3,186 interviewed, 2,780 were given releases to relocate where they wished and 406 were sent to the Department of Justice internment camp at Crystal City, Texas. One of the renunciants, departing for the detention center at Crystal City, declared as he left: "Well, I'm paying for the great mistake of my life— listening to other people."

The arrival of release notices was usually occasion for celebration. One man was seen sitting on his doorstep in tears, waving his release and crying out, "This is the happiest moment of my life." In the week ending March 16, 1946, 1,085 individuals left the center.

Repatriation was another matter. The movement was, in the main, voluntary and anyone wishing to have his or her name removed was free to do so. In one family of seven, when the grandmother died prior to the departure, the family immediately withdrew their names.

Joe Kurihara, the World War I veteran who was so bitter over the evacuation, was among those who returned to Japan. Before he left, he wrote poignantly: "It is my sincere desire to get over there as soon as possible to help rebuild Japan politically and economically. The American Democracy with which I was infused in my childhood is still unshaken. My life is dedicated to Japan with Democracy as my goal."

A good many of the Issei seeking repatriation had property in Japan. Violet de Cristoforo's father-in-law had substantial land holdings in Japan and believed he and his wife could live comfortably on the rents but when they returned to Japan as repatriates they found Korean farmers living in their house. Moreover, the Occupation had broken up large land hold-ings, decreeing that individual farmers could only own as much land as they could cultivate themselves.

THE STORY OF THE WAR RELOCATION AUTHORITY ITSELF IS ANOTHER important loose end. Under Milton Eisenhower and his successor, Dillon Myer, the War Relocation Authority had developed into a classic New Deal bureaucracy. The Office of Relocation Planning grew from two to forty men and women and changed its mission to that of compiling statistics and maintaining files and records. Finance and Personnel changed its name to the Administrative Management Division and grew from seventeen persons in 1942 to 156 by the time the centers closed. Under its aegis fell a multitude of responsibilities, from property inven-tory and control to supply and the operation of all center mess halls.

The Community Management Division presided over health, educa-tion, community enterprises (stores, canteens, barber shops, and so forth), over community government itself, and over the Women's Affairs Section.

The Operations Division included the Engineering Section, Agricul-ture Section, Motor Transport Section, and Fire Protection Center.

The Office of Information had a Publication and Reports Section, a Press and Radio Section, and a Visual Information Section. Composed initially of eight persons, the Office of Information had grown to twenty-eight by the time the centers were closed. It could be said that, procure-ment aside, the Office of Information had the most critical assignment in the authority. It had to fend off a constant barrage of criticism directed against the agency itself, much of it along the line that it pampered the "Japs" when patriotic Americans were doing without. The principal offenders on the journalistic side were the Hearst papers, which never tired of sounding the "yellow peril" alarm in whatever form the occasion suggested, and the *Sacramento Bee* and *Fresno Bee,* equally tireless in trying to whip up popular resistance to the War Relocation Authority.

The *Sacramento Bee,* for example, announced that 20,000 to 25,000 Japanese automobiles were in storage in federal facilities. Not only were these vehicles of traitors unavailable to patriots to use in furtherance of the cause of freedom but they all had genuine rubber tires while patriotic Americans had to drive about on synthetic ones. When the war was over and the Japanese reclaimed their rubber-tired cars, patriots would still be driving on the synthetic ones. It seems hilarious that so much passion could have been generated over rubber, but gusts of tire passion swept the state. In the House of Representatives, Congressman Bertrand Gearhart from the Fresno district attacked Rubber Czar William Jeffers for failing to utilize "an estimated 100,000 tires on stored Japanese vehicles (25,000 vehicles x 4 tires equalled 100,000 tires unavailable for patriotic purposes, not, of course, to mention spares)." An investigation was launched but only a few hundred vehicles, most of them farm trucks, were located.

The Office of Information showed skill and resourcefulness in presenting a positive image of the centers and their residents to the general public. This was, as we have had ample occasion to observe, an unending (and often thankless) job. Needless to say, it was not aided in its task by the various crises, the riots, the refusal to register or to avow unconditional loyalty to the United States, the segregation of the irreconcilables at Tule Lake, the renunciation of citizenship by many Tuleans, and so forth. Widely publicized and hotly debated in Congress, these episodes kept the Office of Information working long hours to turn negatives into positives, to counter the more extreme charges, to explain and explain and explain. It was, in truth, a Sisyphian task.

One of the most laborious and time-consuming operations of the War Relocation Authority was the protection and restoration of the personal property to the evacuees. As noted, much had been stored by the evacuees themselves in churches, empty buildings, rented offices, or with Caucasian friends. Far more had been stored in warehouses under the supervision of the Federal Reserve Bank and in warehouses at the centers. Thousands of tons of such belongings had to be sorted out and sent to the returnees wherever they found permanent quarters.

It is clear that the WRA and its successor were extremely sensitive on the property issue. The WRA's report *Wartime Handling of Evacuee Property,* published in 1946, begins with the statement: "The right of a country at war to safeguard its interests by seizing the property of enemy nationals has never been open to question. Article I of the Constitution of the United States provides for the exercise of this right by Congress. Section 8 of that article, listing the powers of Congress, includes as the eleventh item the power of Congress 'To declare war, grant letters of marque and reprisal, and make rules concerning captures on land and water.' "

There was obviously a gray area here. While the Constitution gave the United States the right to confiscate the "property of enemy nationals" in time of war, that right clearly did not extend to the property of citizens.

Nor did the government ever make such a claim. While the bank accounts of the Issei—enemy aliens—were frozen, their real and personal property was not only not seized but, as we have seen, considerable pains were taken to protect it. At the same time there was no thought of appropriating the property of Nisei (or Kibei) citizens. A legal question did arise where Nisei renounced their U.S. citizenship and thereby could be said to have become by choice "alien enemies." Whatever the particular case was, the WRA went to considerable pains to ensure that all property was returned to its rightful owners. In 1943 it began an exhaustive survey of all property in the evacuation areas owned by Japanese, going through the records in every county in the evacuated area: "All parcels of evacuee-owned land were identified, classified, catalogued, and mapped." The whole process took almost three years. And while it was of considerable use to the War Relocation Authority, one of its basic purposes was to try to clarify ownership of such properties in anticipation of "postwar claims and damage suits." Thirty-nine counties in California recorded Japanese holdings; two in Oregon and three in Washington. California had 3,267 "urban holdings" and 1,715 "rural holdings."

In the words of the WRA report: "Verbal assurances of the Government's intention to help the destitute were made through the press, but substantial losses had been sustained before actual machinery for giving assistance was set up, and extraordinary hardships were experienced by the Japanese Americans because of the failure of the Government to make specific arrangements for shelter and care for the dispossessed who could not finance their removal and subsequently because of the failure of the Government to publicize adequately such arrangements as were made.

"Time and experience have demonstrated that padlocks and bolts on isolated farm buildings and deserted churches or stores afforded little protection to absentee owners against the lawless. Prejudice against the evacuated people ran high during the war throughout the evacuated area, and this prejudice was reflected in the indifference of many local law enforcement agencies toward the depredation of evacuees' property and their professed inability to find or identify vandals, arsonists and thieves.

"Although," the War Relocation Authority report continued, "it is a recognized fact that few tenants lavish such care of property as would the owner, the neglect and destruction of the evacuees' property by substitute operators during the period of the owners' exclusion from the West Coast far transcends the ordinary carelessness of tenants." The situation was greatly exacerbated by the prejudice against the "Japanese American minority." In consequence, the "public conscience was highly insensitive to pilfering and vandalism committed against the stored possessions or buildings of the exiled people." What followed was a record of especially egregious violations of the property of those now called "exiles."

The conclusion of the War Relocation Authority report was that "the evacuated people left behind them about $200,000,000 worth of real, personal and commercial property." Their losses had amounted to millions of dollars. Many evacuees who had leaseholds on farms had lost them "by transfer to operators of other races during the years of exclusion." It was estimated that 30 percent of the land farmed by the Japanese prior to the war was owned by those who farmed it. By sale and transfer of leases of Japanese-owned farms, their lease and ownership holdings were estimated to amount to less than a fourth of their prewar holdings of some sixty thousand acres.

Arrangements were made by the War Relocation Authority with "local agencies, organisations and firms" to take over War Relocation Authority duties in regard to evacuees' personal property at such time as the War Relocation Authority passed out of existence. Unclaimed property was to be auctioned off by April 30, 1946, but not until all bilingual newspapers, namely the *Rocky Shimpo* and *Colorado Times* (Denver), *Utah Nippon* and *Pacific Citizen* (Salt Lake City), had published notices of the auction and indicated that "the proceeds will be deposited in the U.S. Treasury where the rightful owners may make a claim for it."

In 1946, Congress passed the Evacuee Claims Bill. It authorized the Department of Justice to consider claims of persons of Japanese ancestry for damage or loss of real and personal property due to the exclusion program. The bill became law July 1948. Under its terms 26,552 claims were settled, totaling $36,874,240. "Which," Dillon Myer added dryly, "of course did not cover all the losses."

In the final issue of George Rundquist's *Resettlement Bulletin*, Rundquist included a letter from Myer thanking the Committee for Japanese American Resettlement for its "invaluable contribution" and "very courageous and tireless spirit in this work." Myer went on to urge the churches to lead the fight for "compensation for real and personal property losses directly resulting from evacuation," which, in fact, the churches did.

The determination of the War Relocation Authority to serve the interests of the evacuees was demonstrated by the fact that the initial guidelines, or "basic regulations," were "constantly reshaped, liberalized, embellished—or sometimes curtailed—according to the recognized needs of the evacuees.''

An indication of the light hand that the Authority laid on the centers might be found in the testimony of Ichiro Yamaguchi, who remembered the ease with which he and his companions came and went at Poston. "Some of us," he recalled, "got away with a lot of things, too, like we could always get out of camp when we wanted to. But there were no places to go to. The most popular place was down to the river about [four] miles from where we were. We fished and caught carp, crawfish, turtles.''

When the last relocation center (Tule Lake) closed on March 20, 1946, of the total of 120,313 persons who had passed through the centers only four had left a center permanently without authorization; they were a senile old man who wandered off into the desert from Poston, a thirty-five-year-old man under suspicion of murder from the same center, a fifty-six-year-old man in a state of deep depression who also disappeared, and a twenty-two-year-old girl with a history of mental problems who vanished from the Gila River center.

All this must redound to the credit of its two directors—the humane and intelligent Milton Eisenhower, who did his best to avoid setting up the centers at all, and, once the necessity of doing so was inescapable (in the sense that the evacuation had been ordered and places had to be found for people to go), made it the goal of the War Relocation Authority to get out of business as soon as possible by resettling, or "re-relocating," evacuees out of the centers.

Dillion Myer carried on in the same spirit. It seems to me hard to credit him too highly for his actions and his policies. He was the most vocal and eloquent defender of the evacuees. He expended himself without stint to testify before hostile Senate and House subcommittees. He visited the centers repeatedly to explain and defend his policies, often before challenging (and sometimes dangerous) audiences of evacuees, not to mention speaking before innumerable Chambers of Commerce, gatherings of World War I veterans, skeptical service club gatherings, and, indeed, to anyone who cared to listen. Most important, Myer's liberal spirit permeated the whole agency from its Washington headquarters down the line to the centers themselves. The best testimony to his accomplishments was the esteem in which most of the evacuees subsequently held the man who had presided over their destiny for some three and a half years. The Japanese American Citizens League was pleased to honor him and even the bitterest critics of the evacuation acknowledged that he was "a good man.''

At a dinner held in Myer's honor at the Roosevelt Hotel in New York City on May 22, 1946, by the Japanese American Citizens League, he was presented with a "testimonial scroll" commending him as a "champion of human rights and common decency whose courageous and inspired leadership as National Director of the War Relocation Authority . . . aided materially in restoring faith and conviction in the American way to . . . Americans of Japanese ancestry and their resident alien parents."

In Eleanor Roosevelt's introduction to Allen Eaton's *Beauty Behind Barbed Wire*, a kind of photographic inventory of the arts in the various centers, Mrs. Roosevelt wrote that the book not only showed "the character of the Japanese-Americans who took the sudden evacuation with such a remarkably fine spirit. It also shows how well the War Relocation Authority did its work, one of the achievements of government administration of which every American citizen can be proud."

For better or worse, the centers were "forcing grounds" of democratic principles. Whatever their differences, the evacuees learned, willy-nilly, the tactics of democratic politics and in this sense none of them were as they had been before.

Bill Hosokawa in his reflections on "The Uprooting of Seattle" in *Japanese Americans from Relocation to Redress* writes: "Today Nisei and an ever-increasing number of Sansei and Yonsei [third and fourth generation Japanese American] have achieved positions of respect, influence, and importance in the greater Seattle community. . . . This progress would have come about in time, but the trauma of evacuation for both the evacuees and for society at large helped speed the process." We need add only to the "the greater Seattle community" the words: "and indeed in all those communities where they live."

WHILE WE CAN MAKE ROUGH CALCULATIONS OF THE MATERIAL COSTS OF the evacuation, the personal costs are, quite naturally, far harder to assess. The reason is obvious. More than 110,000 individuals of both genders and different generations each had his or her own experience of the evacuation. What generalization could cover the experiences that ran from Issei bachelors "on vacation," to young Nisei who went out on college leave to Drake University or Smith College, to angry militants at Tule Lake who renounced their U.S. citizenship and were repatriated to Japan?

Interestingly enough, two of those in the best position to judge what we might call the moral or the psychological effect of the centers on the evacuees differed. It was Charles Kikuchi's observation that "on the whole the Nisei group didn't get too damaged by relocation." Then he added an arresting phrase: "Generally, we probably gained." That view was echoed by a number of other veterans of the evacuation. One of the important gains, in Kikuchi's view, was that the domination of the Japanese American community by the most tradition-bound Issei was broken. Kikuchi, who himself had gone to the Midwest, felt that those evacuees who had resettled in the nation's heartland had profited the most. For all the trauma, "the wide opportunities of working with Americans of different social stock was a completely new experience . . . and, on the whole, they adjusted in a positive manner to it."

To Edward Spicer, the Issei seemed less affected by the evacuation, since they were, to a much greater degree than the Nisei, spared the identity crisis issue; they were loyal subjects of the Emperor. Period. After the war, in Spicer's view, the Issei had "a new orientation toward the United States. For a time in the centers, the value that was Japan, their stake in this country, and the security and neutrality of the centers were balanced against each other. Even before the war was over, their stake in this country—presented by their children, their property, and their long experience here—had emerged as dominant. This dominance is now complete, so complete in fact that it is a change from the prewar situation. Before the war, the Issei weighed continued residence in the United States against eventual return to Japan. Anti-Japanese campaigns periodically made them wonder if they might be forced to go back. So the question was kept open.

"Today the question appears to be settled once and for all. The great majority of the Issei have concluded they are here to stay. From Seattle to Los Angeles, one can hear such statements as: 'Things are different now. People have made up their minds. They may think of taking a trip to Japan sometime to visit their relatives and to see how conditions are. But this is where they are going to live. They are more settled on this than they have ever been.' "

The one persistent hope that Spicer noted among the Issei to whom he talked was the desire to be compensated by the government for the material losses they had suffered and, perhaps more important, to be allowed to become citizens of the United States.

For Yoshisada Kawai, an Issei, the three years he and his wife spent in Minidoka became "one of the most significant periods in our lives. . . . There was no lack of food, clothing and shelter. There was no worry and we had lots of free time on our hands every day."

Nisuke Mitsumori was another Issei who welcomed the establishment of the centers. He thought they would be a means of "rescuing" the Japanese. "Our worries and uneasiness would be solved by this. A lot of people said that it was inhuman but I feel that war changes the psychology of people," he told Heihachiro Takarabe. "A lot of people say that it was inhuman, undemocratic, and un-Christian, not really understanding the circumstances under which we were then. . . . People were frantic then. So if you ask me what I think of the evacuation I still think it was good for the Japanese. At least it provided us stability for life." Mitsumori's positive view of the evacuation may well have been affected by the fact that he spent little time at Manzanar, getting a position not long after he arrived there as a Japanese language teacher at the University of Michigan. There he found that his fellow Japanese language teachers were strongly pro-Japanese. "Some school teachers were educated in Japan and some of them even had military training in Japan. Although they were educators, they still believed in Japan's victory in the war." They showed their irritation at Mitsumori's skepticism. It was, in their view, little short of treason.

It is clear that, generally speaking, the experience of the evacuation was quite different for the Christian evacuees. Yoshisada Kawai felt as if he had "gained some spiritual freedom by being confined physically in the barbed wires. . . . The American government did limit our activities in society, but it could not limit or confine our beliefs. When the government took control of all our bodily freedom, it had to feed us free. . . . We could not get outside without permission. But for that price the government had to give us food, clothing and shelter every day. . . . In this way for some Issei, like myself, these three years of life in a camp in the wilderness was a rare opportunity for life in 'paradise' and it was also the life of retreat. Actually ever since we had come to the United States, for the most part, Issei had to work continuously in the land of a different language, culture and under race discrimination, and never had time for rest."

"A" makes much the same point. For many older Issei the centers were not only a vacation from lives of unremitting toil but also "a vacation from assimilation." Before the war many Issei felt a constant pressure to assimilate into the dominant culture. They felt it from Caucasian neighbors and people that they did business with who often clearly resented their inability to speak English and their exotic ways. Most of all, perhaps, they felt it from their children and grandchildren, who were often embarrassed by their parents' or grandparents' foreignness. "There had always been the caution," "A" wrote, "the need to act and express oneself in ways that would not be misunderstood. . . . The relocation centers meant relaxation from this constant, however slight [and sometimes by no means slight] strain of being regarded as—and of feeling—a little different. In one's block there were Issei all around . . . they shunned discipline. . . . They took it easy." By the winter of 1944, "the older people who were still in the centers were taking, or trying to take, their vacations. . . . But there were always these persistent contradictions. Warring with the 'vacation mode' was the restlessness over the future of the centers and the rumors of their closing."

One of the most perceptive insights into the nature of the center experience was by Shugi Kimura, a Christian Nisei, who decided to go out. Kimura wrote in the *Tulean Dispatch,* the center newspaper: "Life within these camps is not in any sense a black hole of frustration as one might think, nor, on the other hand, a light-hearted round of depraved idle pleasures as some Congressmen seem to think. There is food enough to sustain life decently. If one is ambitious one can learn many skills, learn the English language if one be deficient in it; there is work enough for everyone, and to many college trained individuals, this is often the first opportunity to exercise their knowledge actively in the community's behalf.

"The evils lie in something more subtle than physical privations. It lies more in that something essential missing from our lives. No matter how insulated a person was psychologically, yet he walked the streets or the roads of the countryside and saw other human beings. Here the cutting off of self is complete. The barbed wire with its watch tower is a real and actual demarcation line between two real worlds. It cuts into the efforts toward real integration of life for which the Nisei has been so hungry, the successful balancing of our lives of all the elements of the three worlds of which he is a part. . . . The most devastating effect upon a human soul is not hatred but being considered not human."

Besides the bachelor Issei, the college Nisei felt that they had had the most positive experience of the evacuation. Kay Yamashita expressed such feelings. "As I look back on my 50 working years," she wrote in 1992, "I think the student relocation experience seems to me to be the most satisfying and meaningful. Almost everything I did after that grew from or hinged upon what I had learned. The Quaker ethic has left an

indelible mark on me.'' Many Nisei who had relocated (or resettled) in
the Midwest or East, but had taken jobs rather than going to college, had
similar reactions.

Certainly it would be a mistake to suggest that all was sweetness and
light even among the college Nisei. One angry Issei wrote of his sons: "I
sent both boys out to college as soon as possible. They have been outside
for three years now. The older one, the one who refused to be evacuated,
is in medical school. They are better but it seemed to me there is still a
little warping in them. Maybe they will get over it sometime.''

It was the Nisei, after all, who had suffered a kind of collective schizophrenia on the matter of dual citizenship. Clearly, those Nisei who were
Kibei, who had been educated in Japan, who were most conscious of dual
citizenship, suffered the most (and inflicted the most suffering on others
it might be said). We talk today quite glibly about identity crises. Who
are we? we seem to be continually asking ourselves. The condition of
evacuee schizophrenia is suggested by the indignant comment of a young
Nisei woman at Tule Lake who complained bitterly that some of the
residents there seemed to be loyal to both the United States *and* Japan.
She clearly had no patience with such types. Those evacuees who felt a
deep loyalty to the Emperor and yet were living in the United States had
perforce to ask themselves (or be asked) every day, "Am I an American
or am I Japanese?'' And many, plainly, came up with quite different
answers under different circumstances. So the wonder is (given our
present notions of human psychology) that the great mass of the evacuees
didn't end up psychologically damaged. The opposite was true. In the
main, they triumphed over adversity. Remarkably.

What impressed Spicer the most as he concluded his account of the
relocation experience was that so many of the evacuees "have come
through the experience with surprisingly undamaged personalities. Issei
especially seem to be the same kind of persons they used to be.'' They
had been the most prepared psychologically in that they had anticipated
a war between Japan and the United States and if they had not exactly
welcomed it (because again they assumed that it must have grave consequences in their own lives), most of them firmly believed in the triumph
of Japan. It was this state of mind that inclined them to think of the time
in the centers as a "vacation time,'' an interval before they were restored
to their homes and farms and compensated for the inconvenience they had
suffered. Things did not work out quite that way, of course, but the
conviction had armored the Issei to endure their hardships and inconveniences with considerable stoicism.

There were two other aspects of the Japanese psyche that served as buffers against the more corrosive aspects of evacuation. There was, first, the classic fatalism of the Japanese that considered adversity an inescapable part of life—the "five disaster syndrome" (fire, flood, tornado, earthquake, and father); and beyond that a disposition to see calamity as providing the ground of fortitude and, indeed, heroism. Andrew Markus, professor of Japanese language and literature at the University of Washington, has pointed out that the devastating fires that ravaged Edo in ancient times were considered opportunities for the performance of notable acts of bravery: "disaster might be a stepping stone to good fortune," and poets might compare the flames of the fires to blossoms and fall maple leaves.

Reliving her experience as a child at Manzanar, Jeanne Wakatsuki thought of the mysterious words of the Japanese national anthem:

> *May thy peaceful reign last long,*
> *May it last thousands of years,*
> *Until this tiny stone will grow*
> *Into a massive rock, and the moss*
> *Will cover it deep and thick.*

For Wakatsuki the meaning of the anthem was endurance.

I think it is important to stress what was perhaps the most profound characterological transformation forced on the evacuees by their experience and, at bottom, perhaps the most important reason for the reluctance of so many to leave the centers, to relocate or resettle. And that is that the Japanese were a people bound and sustained, to an almost unprecedented degree, by community, by associational ties and activities—family, *ken*, *kai*. Intimate, consoling, life-enhancing, and containing (and explaining) relationships. They had no notion of "autonomous individuals," the type that David Riesman described long ago as "inner-directed" men and women, ready to venture "out on their own." Individuals, those strange creatures invented by the Protestant Reformation; individuals, the founders of the modern industrial world. The consequence was that when the poor, benighted War Relocation Authority pleaded with the evacuees to leave the shelter of the centers, the "neutral havens," in Spicer's words, that had been promised them for the duration of the war, it was, in effect, asking them to be quite a different sort of human being—an individual. Nobody, of course, could quite articulate this point. Indeed, it was doubtful if Caucasian Americans could understand it at all (it had been so long since they had been anything but individuals); perhaps some immigrant groups could, folks from a farming village in Sicily or a Syrian town in the hills of Lebanon.

I suppose we could say with some confidence that one thing the relocation experience did for the evacuees as a whole was to force a not notably introspective people to consider the nature of their lives and their loyalties. They could no longer go on from year to year living on the margin of society, isolated, self-contained, discriminated against, leaving in abeyance the complex question of who, in fact, they were, Japanese *or* American.

I can only reiterate what I have said earlier. We cannot put the relocation episode into the proper perspective unless we rid ourselves of the standard notions of "loyal" and "disloyal." As General DeWitt's February 14, 1942, memorandum pointed out, we would expect Americans living in Japan to be loyal to the United States in the event of war with Japan; why, by the same logic, should we expect the largely "unassimilated" Japanese in the United States to be loyal to the country in which they happened to be living rather than to their homeland and their revered Emperor? We can only say once again: for the Japanese in the United States to be loyal to the Emperor of Japan was not wicked, evil, or morally reprehensible but natural, logical, and inevitable. What was notable was that a number were not. In the eyes of their countrymen, they were the disloyal ones.

I suspect that for Japanese Americans the real pain of the memory of the relocation was not so much in the loss of property, of treasured personal belongings, of material things (we recover quite quickly from such losses, especially if we prosper subsequently), but in the anguish of the Japanese soul where every day they were confronted by the most profound questions of where their loyalties and, in consequence, their futures, lay. In the bitter, bitter beyond the telling of it, divisions among the evacuees themselves lay the grimmest and most painful memories of all.

AT THIS POINT WE MUST REVIEW THE CIRCUMSTANCES THAT LED TO THE evacuation. Shortly after Pearl Harbor, General DeWitt told General Gullion that he was "very doubtful" about trying to intern 117,000 Japanese. "An American citizen, after all, is an American citizen. And while they all may not be loyal, I think we can weed the disloyal out of the loyal and lock them up if necessary." Some eight weeks later DeWitt declared: ''The Commanding General [DeWitt himself] found a tightly-knit, unassimilated racial group, substantial numbers of whom were engaged in pro-Japanese activities. . . . These considerations were weighed against the progress of the Emperor's Imperial Japanese forces in the Pacific.'' DeWitt added: ''To have suggested that the enemy would not exploit the fifth column technique to its fullest extent in the development of its expansive program would have been naive. To have ignored the potential dangers arising out of the presence of nearly 200,000 enemy aliens on the West Coast [a figure that included Italians and Germans] would have been indifference tantamount to military indiscretion. National security demanded that precautions be taken immediately.''

Our task is to account for such a dramatic change of heart. One of the most obvious factors was that DeWitt had access to intelligence information not generally known that he found highly alarming (the question here is not whether the information was false—some of it certainly was—but whether DeWitt sincerely believed it to be true). He reported to General Gullion that an FBI raid on Bainbridge Island had turned up ''guns, ammunition, explosives, radio, short-wave, and other contraband. . . . I wouldn't have you repeat that, but it shows the situation up here.'' That Japanese submarines were cruising off the coast was generally known but until recently we did not know of their fearsomeness. An Associated Press story, datelined December 22, 1993, tells of a book by Honolulu author Burl Burlingame who had unearthed Japanese records that reveal that nine Japanese supersubs were in U.S. coastal waters in the wake of Pearl Harbor. They carried small planes and midget submarines as well as torpedoes much more effective than their U.S. counterparts. According to Burlingame, submarine commanders had been instructed to surface on Christmas Eve and fire on San Francisco. At the last moment, the orders were countermanded, apparently out of concern that some Japanese Americans might be killed in the barrage.

Burlingame believes that the Japanese naval command made a major tactical error in instructing the submarines not to waste their torpedoes on merchant ships but to save them for attacks on U.S. naval vessels. The consequence was that only fourteen merchant ships were sunk by Japanese submarines off the West Coast while German submarines sank over two hundred such vessels off the Atlantic Coast. If DeWitt did not know the number or the armament of the Japanese submarines, he was certainly aware of their presence; it was part of the Japanese strategy to instill as much fear as possible in the inhabitants of the West Coast. The importance of the submarines was that they gave substance to DeWitt's anxiety

about radio communication between possible Japanese spies and the submarines and that anxiety spurred his determination to conduct "mass
raids" on areas suspected of harboring clandestine radio transmitters;
which, in turn, led to his standoff with Attorney General Biddle.

DeWitt's inclination was, quite naturally, to lean over backward in the
matter of the security of his forces. He had to be guided by the worst-case
scenario, the dreaded invasion, the threat of which had hung in the air for
some thirty years and which now seemed not only possible but imminent.
If the anticipated invasion had come and *if* some Japanese Americans had
taken an active role in supporting the invaders, the general, if he had
survived, might have had to explain to a court-martial board how it was
that in the face of considerable evidence of the capacity for and inclination to subversive action by some segments of the Japanese American
community, he had failed to urge the most prudent line. Those who
condemn the relocation as a "racist decision" have to climb over a
mountain of evidence that many Japanese living in California were ardent
Japanese nationalists. They might argue that this fact had no military
significance, no significance for the security of the United States, but they
cannot well maintain that such groups did not exist.

We noted before the alarming course of the war itself, with a succession of spectacular victories for the Imperial Army and Navy, which, it
was natural to assume, substantially increased the presumed danger of an
invasion or massive raid on the West Coast. Another factor that may well
have been significant (as DeWitt insisted it was) was a growing realization on DeWitt's part that he could not protect (and should not be asked
to) the Japanese themselves against the mounting public hostility against
them. In the words of the Wartime Civil Control Administration report:
"press and periodical reports of public attitudes along the West Coast
from December 7, 1941, to the indication of controlled evacuation clearly
reflected the intensity of feeling. Numerous incidents of violence involving Japanese and others occurred; many more were reported but were
subsequently either unverified or were [found] to be cumulative."

Mention must be made here of a series of remarkable reports, or
memoranda, by Lieutenant Commander Karl D. Ringle (a pseudonym),
head of Naval Intelligence, on loan to the War Relocation Authority.
Ringle was a friend of a number of leaders of the Japanese American
Citizens League, and his analysis of Japanese attitudes was the best
informed and most discerning document of its kind turned out in the
post–Pearl Harbor period. The reports undoubtedly exercised considerable influence on DeWitt and thereby merit our attention; indeed, they

merit our attention on their very considerable merit. The reports were headed: "The Japanese Question in the United States." In addition to "General Opinions" and "Backgrounds," Ringle made specific recommendations for "Procedure for Segregation" and offered some "Conclusions." He began by reminding his readers that he was, in effect, addressing "the primary present and future problem," that of "dealing with the American-born United States citizens of Japanese ancestry, of whom it is considered that at least 75 percent are loyal to the United States." It was Ringle's estimate that of the Japanese-born residents, "the large majority are at least passively loyal to the United States." The word "passively" was a key word here since it seems safe to assume that a number of those Issei "passively" loyal to the United States became increasingly disenchanted by evacuation and thus susceptible to the influence of the more militant nationalists. "That is," Ringle continued, "they would knowingly do nothing whatever to the injury of the United States, but at the same time they would not do anything to the injury of Japan. Most of the remainder would not engage in active sabotage or insurrection, but might well do surreptitious observation work for Japanese interests if given a convenient opportunity." There were, in Ringle's opinion, some 3,500 Issei and Nisei who had a "fanatical loyalty" to Japan and who would do whatever was required of them. Of those, Ringle noted, the "most dangerous" were "already in custodial detention" or were members of such organizations as Black Dragon Society or the Heimush Kai" (Military Servicemen's League). The membership of these groups was "fairly well known to the Naval Intelligence and the Federal Bureau of Investigation and should immediately be placed in custodial detention, irrespective of whether they are alien or citizen.

"As a basic policy tending toward the permanent solution of this problem, the American citizens of Japanese ancestry should be officially encouraged in their efforts toward loyalty and acceptance as bona fide citizens. They [should] be accorded a place in the national war effort through such agencies as the Red Cross, USO, civilian defense, and even such activities as ship and aircraft building or other defense production, even though subject to greater investigative checks as to background and loyalty, etc., than Caucasian Americans."

In Ringle's view the most dangerous Japanese Americans were the Kibei. "These people," he wrote, "are essentially and inherently Japanese and may have been deliberately sent back to the United States by the Japanese Government to act as agents. In spite of their legal citizenship and the protection afforded them by the Bill of Rights, they should be looked upon as enemy aliens, and many of them placed in custodial detention.''

Ringle's prescription was as sensible as his analysis. He recommended that the War Department proclaim ''openly and genuinely the fact that any person desiring to announce himself as a loyal citizen of Japan may do so without fear of prejudice, irrespective of whether or not he holds American citizenship. Such individuals should be solemnly assured upon the word of the government that they will be accorded the legal status of internees; and that if they so desire and opportunity presents, they will be exchanged during the period of hostilities for American citizens held by the Japanese Government. . . . I believe,'' Ringle added, ''it will be found that there are a number of people, both alien and citizen, who, if given the assurance that such an admission will not result in bodily harm, will frankly state their desire to be Japanese nationals.''

So far as I know, Ringle's report is the first official (or unofficial) document to face the reality of the situation and to try to de-demonize the fact of strong Japanese nationalist feeling among many Japanese Americans. Ringle did not attach any opprobrium to his statement of nationalist sentiment. He simply accepted it as a fact and suggested a sensible way of dealing with it.

Another category that Ringle identifies are the (usually) Issei parents who were ardent enough nationalists to go to the trouble and expense of sending their children to Japan for their education. It seemed reasonable to Ringle to assume that they, too, were wholly committed to the Japanese cause.

That Ringle's own assessment was free of racial bias was made clear by his concluding paragraphs. It was his view that there were two points ''which the writer feels should never be forgotten. The first is a racial one. Because these people have Oriental faces, it is natural to look for and possibly stress the *differences* between them and Caucasian Americans. This I believe is wrong; the point of *similarity* should be stressed. If this point of view is taken, I believe the intelligent observer will be amazed how little different basically these people are from their American contemporaries.''

Ringle ended by stressing the intergenerational problems of Issei and Nisei, which seemed to him greater than those between generations in other immigrant groups. ''Whether the younger and succeeding generations are truly American in thought, word, deed and sentiment will depend on the way in which they are treated now, and on how they are helped to meet the test of this war. In other words, I believe that whether or not we have a 'Japanese problem' in the United States for the next hundred and fifty years will be decided by the attitude of the United States as a whole to the Japanese Americans before 1950.''

It was argued by some of those individuals in the Department of Justice most involved in intelligence gathering (led by FBI Director Hoover) that the potentially subversive Japanese had already been identified and could simply be picked up and interned until the war was over and, as we have seen, this had already, in large part, been done. But there were clearly problems with such a piecemeal approach. The Japanese men apprehended by security agents were, in many instances, heads of families. They had wives and children who would be left destitute by the removal of the family breadwinner. The problem was complicated by the fact that traditional Japanese wives were hopelessly subordinate and dependent.

LOOKING BACK SOME YEARS LATER WITH THE WISDOM OF HINDSIGHT, two of the principal players, Biddle and Eisenhower, had somewhat different explanations of the forces (and people) behind the evacuation. Of the two men, Biddle, as attorney general, had firsthand knowledge of the events leading to the nondecision, as I have called it. Eisenhower, by his own admission, knew little of the circumstances leading to the evacuation. Looking back on the whole relocation episode, he declared it ''an inhuman mistake.'' Having brooded over the mistake—for some thirty years—he concluded that, like so many episodes in history, it was difficult, if not impossible, to fix blame with any confidence. Over the years various culprits had been proposed: the yellow press, the Hearst and McClatchy papers particularly, the rancorous congressmen, the Caucasian (predominantly Italian) farmers who coveted the Japanese farms, the labor unions who were tireless in their agitation against Japanese Americans, and on and on. Eisenhower was not even inclined to lay the blame on those tempting targets, Bendetsen, Gullion, and DeWitt. ''At the time,'' he wrote, ''many forces were at work—military, political, economic, emotional, and racial. The principal actors in the drama frequently acted independently of each other. Often they were unaware of what others were doing or thinking or how their decisions or actions related to other decisions or actions. I doubt that anyone saw the over-all pattern that was emerging or how his actions contributed to that pattern.

''Misunderstanding, rumor, fear, misinformation, prejudice, and ignorance were dark winds that blew across the land. An incident here, a rumor there, a political move, a military decision, an official memorandum—all fell like pieces into a mosaic that no single individual could perceive or had created."

The conspiracy theorists, Eisenhower suspected, would never rest until they had indicted an individual or a group of individuals, or Americans in general, as a "racist people." But to Eisenhower "such simplistic views" were easier than dealing with the "dense thicket of reality." "For the reality is that in such major movements the decision is not *made,* it happens."

There is certainly, in Eisenhower's analysis, a keen sense of the opaqueness and complexity of historical events and the rejection of any simplistic explanation. It makes an important counterpoint to Biddle's more specific account. To Biddle, the evacuation was a mistake (as, indeed, he had thought at the time) that might well have been avoided. "If Stimson had stood firm, had indeed insisted, as apparently he suspected, that this wholesale evacuation was needless, the President would have followed his advice. And, if, instead of dealing almost exclusively with McCloy and Bendetsen, I had urged the Secretary [Stimson] to resist the pressure of his subordinates, the result might have been different. But I was new to the Cabinet, and disinclined to insist on my own view to an elderly statesman whose wisdom and integrity I greatly respected."

And, Biddle might have added, if I hadn't so stubbornly and unrealistically resisted DeWitt's continued plea for mass raids. Certainly Biddle was well aware that DeWitt had moved reluctantly from the belief that while all the Nisei might not be loyal "we can weed the disloyal out of the loyal and lock them up, if necessary" to the conviction that such a discrimination was either impossible, or, given the urgency of the moment, impractical.

Biddle defended DeWitt, if that is the proper word, by making much of the public clamor for the removal of the Japanese, but he then took a good deal back by noting that a confidential report compiled by the Office of Facts and Figures on March 9, 1942, showed that outside of Southern California, less than half of those interviewed favored internment of Japanese aliens, and only 14 percent favored the internment of citizens of Japanese ancestry. The figures are striking in view of the fact that a standard argument in recent years has been that the evacuation was solely or primarily motivated by racial antagonism toward Japanese Americans. In addition to quoting the above figures, Biddle goes on to point out that the fear of violence *to* the Japanese was much exaggerated. Such acts as were committed were, according to Biddle, isolated events. Between December 8 and March 31, 1942, only thirty-six "racially motivated crimes'' (including seven murders) were reported against Japanese Americans; hardly a crime wave, although it is undoubtedly the case that many minor incidents went unreported.

In short, all those most directly concerned concurred that the decision was based exclusively on military considerations (however mistaken those considerations may have been) and that racial prejudice, while it indisputably existed, had no direct effect on the long slow slide into evacuation. As noted, Biddle himself never accepted the military necessity argument; he was much under the influence of the able young director of the FBI, J. Edgar Hoover. Hoover, in a memo to Biddle on February 9, ''denied the existence of any information showing that the attacks on ships leaving West Coast ports were associated with espionage activity ashore,'' and James Fly, chairman of the Federal Communications Commission, wrote on February 26, two weeks after the decision to evacuate had been made, criticizing the reports of radio transmission on the grounds not that such transmissions had not occurred but rather on the grounds that the army's communications equipment was too primitive and its personnel too poorly trained to intercept enemy transmissions. The soldiers, Fly wrote, ''know nothing about signal identification, wave propagation and other technical subjects, so essential to radio intelligence procedure. . . . It's pathetic to say the least.''

Biddle reported the results of FBI ''spot raids'' to the President in May 1942, well after evacuation had begun. ''We have not uncovered through these searches any dangerous persons that *we would not otherwise have known about* [italics added]. . . . We have not found among all the sticks of dynamite and gunpowder any evidence that any of it was to be used in a manner helpful to our enemies. We have not found a camera which we have reason to believe was for use in espionage.'' By this time, of course, the momentum for evacuation was irresistible. Hoover's reports to Biddle served no other purpose than to nourish Biddle's already considerable self-righteousness.

I suspect that another element that was part of the equation that led (one is tempted to say ''inevitably'') to the impasse between Francis Biddle and General DeWitt was what may be called ''East-Coastism.'' In addition to Biddle's unassailable rectitude, based, in part at least, on his class, his feeling of innate superiority over ''people like DeWitt,'' Biddle shared the patronizing attitude of East Coasters toward the inhabitants of the West Coast. To East Coasters, the West Coast, and more particularly California, was a refuge for a variety of nuts, eccentrics, and sun-worshippers, the land of oil wells and HOLLYWOOD, the land of the unbuttoned, softly self-indulgent who, not surprisingly, were inclined to panic in the face of some perceived danger. This attitude was summed up in the famous phrase of the comedian Fred Allen, who proclaimed Southern California an ideal place to live "if you were an orange." The New Deal officials with whom Biddle worked most closely were also quintessential East Coasters, Henry Stimson, upper class by ancient origin, McCloy by adoption.

In assessing the factors involved in the slide into evacuation, there is, finally, DeWitt's character or temperament or personality to consider. That, indeed, may have been the most decisive single element. We are often reluctant to assign much importance in the unfolding of historical events to something as difficult to define as the "character" of the principal actors. It seems too slippery, too chancy, too much an indication of the unpredictability and, even more disturbing, the uncontrollability of life and history. We have, I think, sufficient clues to credit DeWitt's actions (still being careful to avoid the word "decision") in large part to his temperament. The reader will recall the newspaper account of DeWitt's excited demeanor, bordering on hysteria, at the meeting he called in San Francisco to upbraid public officials and civic leaders for their failure to take seriously enough the dangers of an imminent invasion by Japanese forces. Apropos of another military matter, Lieutenant General Lesley J. McNair, deputy commander of the army ground forces and DeWitt's superior, told General Joseph Stilwell, "DeWitt is going crazy and requires ten refusals before he realizes it is 'No.' "

If another general with a more realistic notion of Japanese capabilities had been the commanding general of the West Coast Military Command, Mark Clark, for instance, the outcome would almost certainly have been a different one. By an odd conjunction of circumstances, the man in position to determine the course of events was a rigid, apprehensive, somewhat paranoid (at least about radio transmitters) type. He was a classic military man, somewhat beyond civilian control in the sense that for Stimson or, ultimately, the President, to have overruled him would have been to create a storm of public protest. In wartime, civilian authorities are disposed to take the advice of their generals until things have gone very wrong indeed. Vital as the matter seemed to the Japanese Americans and to their critics and detractors, the evacuation issue was a very small item in a global war that put the so-called free world at the risk of its life.

With DeWitt (and Bendetsen and Gullion) convinced beyond a shadow of a doubt that the security of California and indeed of the nation was at risk, it is small wonder that no one dared to gainsay them.

The piecemeal manner in which the process of evacuation began, and the plainly stated resistance of the civilian agencies and officials concerned, are the clearest evidence that the decision was neither hasty nor hostile, but was accepted, at least on the part of the nonmilitary, with great reluctance. Such officials were too well aware of the outcry that would arise from liberal and radical groups within and without the New Deal to have rushed into such a controversial decision. That the acceptance of mass evacuation was reluctant cannot be doubted. If only on practical grounds, grounds of self-interest, concern over the cost and the vast logistical problems involved, the disruption of agricultural production in a state (California) that produced much of the nation's food, the diversion of manpower from war-related construction projects, the diversion of much-needed troops to guard the centers and facilitate the movement of tens of thousands of people, for all these reasons and more, those involved in the evacuation were loath to take the last step. There were certainly humanitarian concerns as well. It was not so much that there was sympathy for the Japanese qua Japanese, but rather for distressed human beings torn from their homes and their communities and shipped off to an uncertain fate.

IN THE FINAL ANALYSIS THERE REMAINS THE ISSUE OF THE BIDDLE-DeWitt impasse. In the words of DeWitt's final report: "The Attorney General made the administration of such regulations a military problem by reason of the action of the Justice Department withdrawing from the administration of alien control." It is hard to avoid the thought that if Biddle had been less rigid, the decision for mass evacuation might have been avoided. All that DeWitt wanted to do, after all, was to have "mass raids" to search for the radio transmitters that so obsessed him. If Biddle had acquiesced or simply looked the other way, the mass raids would presumably have gone on, would have revealed few if any shortwave radio transmitters, hopefully appeased public opinion, and permitted a more rational approach to the whole problem. DeWitt's obsession with radio transmitters was matched by Biddle's obsession with habeas corpus. Mass raids, however dubious on constitutional grounds, were infinitely preferable to mass evacuations.

Because there was a thirty-plus-year-old record of hostility toward the

Japanese (as well as the Chinese, Koreans, Italians, Mexicans, and Filipinos), there was a natural disposition, especially among the Japanese Americans and their numerous Caucasian supporters, to attribute the relocation decision to racial prejudice. Even if it had been the case that the military commanders and government officials who participated in making the recommendation for relocation were overt or covert anti-Japanese (or anti-Italian) racists, they would have been recklessly irresponsible to have made a decision so costly in money and manpower on essentially racial grounds. It was obviously not the case that the decision to relocate was the result of racist attitudes. That these existed in the general public often in virulent form is undeniable. That such attitudes determined the outcome is, on the other hand, entirely deniable. All of this is not to say, of course, that the decision was right. Since the Japanese did not raid or invade the West Coast we cannot say that the decision to relocate was *right*. We can only say that it was based on military, not racial, considerations.

It is easy enough to say, in retrospect, that the relocation program was unnecessary. It was most clearly unnecessary *because* the Japanese army and navy did not in fact attack the West Coast of the United States. And if they had and the Japanese Americans had not been evacuated there is no way of telling what their role might have been. It seems safe to say that many would undoubtedly have done their best to defend their more or less adopted country against the invading forces. Others would probably have laid low and tried to be as inconspicuous as possible, and others, it seems entirely reasonable to assume, would have done their best to aid their Emperor. How many would have been in this latter group and how effective any action they might have taken would have been in the event of an invasion is, of course, impossible to say. We can also conjecture that as long as the war and the threat of invasion hung over the West Coast the more rabid Caucasian neighbors of the Japanese Americans would have subjected them to innumerable indignities and intermittent violence. Such, in fact, is human nature. But we would not wish to take the line that Japanese Americans were relocated *for their own safety*, an argument that was sometimes advanced. To press that point would be to assume that the law enforcement agencies of the United States were powerless to protect any particular segment of our society under threat from yahoos and, whether true or not, one would find it distasteful to believe it or argue it.

What I think we must admit is that responsible public officials, most of whom were publicly and privately extremely reluctant to take such a step, were persuaded by those "on the ground" and in command of the broadest range of evidence that the evacuation of the exclusionary zone was, if not essential, given the evidence, wise and prudent. And those officials involved, on the whole decent, intelligent and humane individuals, maintained until their dying day that the decision to relocate was, if not in retrospect necessary, at the least understandable and was based on what were genuinely believed to be security considerations and not, in any substantial degree, on race.

Perhaps the most important defection from the ranks of those who charged that the evacuation was the consequence of "racial prejudice" was that of Morton Grodzins. It was Grodzins, a member of the JERS staff, who wrote the first book that argued that the evacuation was racially motivated. He told Charles Kikuchi years later that much as he hated to admit it, "the accumulating evidence is beginning to indicate that it was not so much the pressure groups that forced the evacuation order, but the reverses in the Southwest Pacific." "The pressure groups" simply "spurred this fever on . . . and helped to mold the feeling along these lines."

In wartime it is difficult to argue with generals and colonels about what constitutes "military necessity." That, after all, is their business. Francis Biddle reported that Henry Stimson, a wise and humane man, referred to the evacuation as "a tragedy" that seemed to be a "military necessity."

Historians (and interested citizens) may debate until the millennium (and even during the millennium) the decision to relocate Japanese Americans, alien or citizen, out of Military Areas No. 1 and No. 2, the exclusionary zones. Since the Japanese Imperial forces did not attempt to land on the West Coast, and, it is evident in retrospect, did not have the capability of doing so, the question of how the Japanese Americans would have reacted is impossible to answer.

A Berkeley sociologist, Robert Spencer, who was one of the JERS contacts at Gila River, wrote many years later: "It [evacuation] cannot be justified but it is understandable as an exigency of war." It is probably hard to improve on that statement: wrong and indefensible but "understandable."

All of which may be said to bring us back necessarily to some further consideration of the dropping of the atomic bombs on Hiroshima and Nagasaki, the surrender of Japan to the Allied Forces, and the Allied occupation of Japan. There is an interesting story in connection with the selection of the Japanese cities to be the targets of the bombs. The story is told that Kyoto was initially one of the two cities chosen but Secretary of War Henry Stimson, who had visited Kyoto before the war and was aware of its status as perhaps the most beautiful and historic city of Japan, directed that it be crossed off the list of possible targets.

When the Japanese rejected the Allied demand for unconditional surrender on August 6, Truman ordered the bomb dropped on Hiroshima. As the reader will recall, the powers of the Japanese government were in the hands of the Supreme War Council. The council itself was sharply divided in its response to the bombing of Hiroshima. The prime minister and the foreign minister were unreservedly for peace if the Emperor's throne was preserved. The minister of the Japanese navy concurred; the war ministers, General Anami, and the chiefs of staff of the army and navy were resolutely opposed to surrender on any terms. They were the architects of the plan for final resistance. Emperor Hirohito himself wished for a peace that would preserve his people from further suffering. By tradition, all recommendations from the Supreme War Council to the Emperor must be consensus recommendations, having the appearance of unanimity.

When the response of the Supreme Council to the destruction of Hiroshima, sent through the neutral powers, was an offer of less-than-conditional surrender, Truman ordered the second bomb dropped on Nagasaki on August 9. This time, with the Supreme Council still hopelessly split, an extraordinary session was called in the presence of the Emperor deep in an underground bunker. It was the first time that the Emperor, his father or even his grandfather, going back to the beginning of the Meiji Restoration, had met with a divided cabinet. In fact, it was only the second time in five hundred years of Japanese history that an Emperor had met personally with his advisers.

The Emperor heard both sides out and then announced his decision to accept the Potsdam terms of unconditional surrender with the reservation of preserving the Imperial throne. Although no one dared oppose the Emperor directly, word of his decision brought about an immediate conspiracy to assassinate the members of the council who advocated peace and prevent the Emperor's voice—the Voice of the Crane as it was called—from reaching the Japanese people. It was known that the Emperor had recorded his peace message to the Japanese people, the only measure that could have brought universal compliance, and entrusted it to Baron Tokugawa Yoshihiro, a descendant of the Tokugawa shoguns who had been displaced by the Meiji Restoration. The baron found a particularly ingenious hiding place for the tape. The rebels assassinated the commander of the palace guard, forged an order that gave them access to the palace grounds, and ransacked the premises looking for the Emperor's speech to destroy it before it could be put on the air. But the coup was checked. Its leaders committed seppuku and the Emperor's speech was broadcast to the Japanese people, who listened with their heads respectfully bowed. So final was the Emperor's word that General MacArthur was able to go ashore without a military escort to receive the surrender of the armed forces of Japan.

It must also be said, parenthetically, that Truman's acceptance of the Japanese provision to preserve the Emperor's throne was a crucial element in avoiding a final bloodbath. Without the acceptance of that provision the Japanese would certainly have fought on at terrible cost to the United States and to Japan itself.

The dropping of the bombs, justified or not, marked a new era in world history and virtually destroyed two major Japanese cities. When my wife and I visited Japan in 1976, where, incidentally, the Bicentennial of the American Revolution was being almost as enthusiastically celebrated as in the United States, we were puzzled at the apparent lack of bitterness among Japanese people over the dropping of the bombs. When I asked our Japanese hosts why people did not seem to harbor resentment against Americans for the bombing of Hiroshima and Nagasaki, they offered two explanations. The first was that the Japanese people had no notion of the horrors committed in their name by the Japanese military in the period from 1931 to 1941, most especially in China, a nation the Japanese held in awe. When these facts came out in the war crimes trials conducted by the Allied occupation, the feeling of decent Japanese was one of great shame. Such Japanese, among whom were my friends, felt that fate had punished the Japanese people for the sins of their leaders, for having accepted or condoned military rule, even if they had not been aware of the crimes that had been committed in their name.

After further reflection, my friend, Mei Higashiura, amended the original explanation. The Japanese people had suffered extremely during the war. Everything in the civilian realm had been sacrificed to the military. Food and medicine were in desperately short supply. Old people and children had suffered especially. The casualties among soldiers and sailors instructed to fight to the death were staggering. Many of the Japanese people knew there was no hope of winning the war but the fanatical military men who ran the country were determined in the name of Japanese honor to force the country to commit a kind of collective seppuku. Thus, the bombs that concluded the war were bombs of deliverance that marked the end of a nightmare that otherwise promised to have no end.

To these two explanations, I add my own: a Freudian interpretation on an international scale. It seems to me that Japan stood in somewhat the same relationship to the United States as the son, in the Freudian system, to his father. The father is a powerful, dominating, if not domineering, figure who keeps the son in a state of dependence and, above all, subordination. The son, desperate to free himself from the dominating father, attacks and grievously injures the father to the point that his life seems for a time in danger. The son then lives in the fear of a recovered father who will surely punish him for his insubordination. The son nonetheless has freed himself from his subordination and though he will be punished severely, he will stand as an adult with his father. By the Smith Thesis, the Japanese subconsciously anticipated severe punishment for their rebellion against the domineering father. The atom bombs were the punishment. The brilliant initial success of the son's rebellion meant that the father could never again exercise unquestioned domination and the son, at the same time, was freed from the curse of his own furious, warlike psyche. His remarkable talents were channeled into peaceful pursuits.

Quite as important, it brought an end to the thralldom of the Japanese people to the code of *bushido,* the blind subordination to whatever was spoken in the name of the Emperor. The story of the Allied occupation lies beyond the scope of this work. It is a fascinating story in itself. Many members of the U.S. occupation group were idealistic New Dealers who could hardly wait to try their hands at making Japan into a "modern," "democratic" nation. Censorship was banished, freedom of the press instituted for the first time in Japanese history, abortion made legal, large land holdings were broken up, and land distributed to peasant farmers, and so on.

General MacArthur, who, like Theodore Roosevelt, was samurai enough to captivate the Japanese people and surprisingly liberal in his social and political leanings, suggested to the Emperor that it would facilitate things if he abjured divinity. The Emperor complied. He was not, he informed the Japanese people, divine. They seem to have revered him nonetheless for that. The symbolic importance was enormous, however. It should be noted that obedience to the Emperor had one final very important practical consequence. When Emperor Hirohito spoke on the Japanese national radio and declared the war at an end with the surrender of Japan and ordered all Japanese to cease fighting, it was as though God himself had spoken. It was the first time the Japanese had heard the Emperor's voice; all resistance ceased at once.

When Japan adopted a new constitution it contained most of the historic principles enunciated in the U.S. Bill of Rights. In addition, it did something that, so far as I know, no other constitution has done; it rejected warfare and militarism as an instrument of national policy. From the most militaristic nation in the world (Germany perhaps excepted) it became instantly the most pacific. The liberation of the Japanese people from the centuries-old yoke of the military was also a liberation of the Japanese in the United States. It was the perfect therapy for their schizophrenia. Suddenly it was possible for them to glory in the light of their splendid ancient culture *and* be loyal citizens of the United States.

A Postscript

W E ALL LIKE HAPPY ENDINGS (OR AT LEAST WE USED TO) AND THE story of the trials and tribulations of the Japanese people in America is certainly such a story, the story of their remarkable integration into the mainstream of American life to the great benefit of the nation. Note has already been taken of the dramatic turning of the tide of popular feeling. That tide continued to flow, washing away in time the last vestiges of racial prejudice.

Isamu Nakamura many years later remarked: "I believe in some respects the American people are quite tolerant. During the war, they might have had some ill feelings toward the Japanese here, but soon after the war they were very protective and helpful to us. Maybe they had the feeling of a victor helping the underdog, the conquered." Nakamura felt that the most noticeable change in *hakujin* attitudes toward the Japanese came in the early 1950s and was marked by the congressional legislation in 1952 permitting Issei to become naturalized citizens. Nakamura conducted night classes for some three months to prepare Issei friends for their naturalization. They were allowed to take the test in Japanese and Nakamura's students were, in his words, "very successful . . . most of the Issei became naturalized citizens."

Minoru Yasui's father, Masuo, who had spent the war in a series of detention camps as a suspected Japanese agent, also undertook to teach classes in citizenship to other Issei. His principal student was his wife, Shidzuyo. On July 16, 1953, Shidzuyo passed her test for citizenship (which involved, among other things, knowing the first ten amendments—the Bill of Rights—to the Constitution) and in September she took the oath of citizenship. Masuo himself appeared three months later before the same judge, Alger Fee, who some ten years earlier had upheld the curfew law applied to Japanese Americans when the edict had been challenged by Masuo's lawyer son, Minoru, and was sworn in as a citizen of the United States. He wrote to one of his daughters: "Thanks to God and America for the blessing we receive now! Now we of the Yasui family are at last 100 percent Americans." The oath of citizenship was "the greatest happiness and fortune we [Masuo and Shidzuyo] have ever received in our lifetime."

A symbol of the reconciliation of Japan and the United States might be found in the life of Masuo Akizuki. Before the war, and in the centers, Akizuki had been an ardent Japanese nationalist. In the 1930s he had organized baseball teams that traveled to Japan and he had taught the Japanese martial arts to the young Nisei of San Jose. In Heart Mountain he had been a block manager and built and operated a clandestine radio. After the war, living in San Jose, he established a mathematics prize to be awarded each year to a student of Japanese ancestry from San Jose in competition with a student from Okayama, San Jose's sister city in Japan.

The climax of Masuo Akizuki's life came with the visit from Emperor Hirohito, who gave Akizuki and other prominent Japanese Americans special awards for their contributions to Japanese and American friendship. History had come full circle and Akizuki could not help noting that while the Sansei were completely American, many fifth- or sixth-generation Chinese Americans in San Francisco still spoke and wrote Chinese and remained in their own "town."

Akizuki's pride was in the Sansei, who, he felt, had "a better attitude toward the old Japanese customs than the Nisei do. . . . As long as they have Japanese blood in them, I think the Sansei will retain Japanese customs."

Akizuki contacted some 250 families from *Fukuoka-Ken* living in San Jose to form a *kai*. Interestingly enough the families felt that since they had become American citizens they no longer needed such an organization. Moreover, one suspects that unhappy memories of conflicts at Heart Mountain were an impediment. A yearly get-together was settled on as a compromise.

*   *   *

THE EXPERIENCES OF THE RENUNCIANTS AND THOSE REPATRIATED TO
Japan make a strange and compelling story. They sailed back to a Japan
that existed only in their dreams, a nation devastated by war, a nation in
which, to their perplexity and confusion, they felt themselves aliens; they
had to return to discover that against any conscious intention, *against
their will,* they had become Americans; an "invisible molecular force,"
a kind of benign virus, had invaded their souls and bodies, their hearts.
They had gone to Japan with the avowed intention of becoming wholly
Japanese. Once there, they discovered that they were Americans after all.

In May 1959, U.S. Attorney General William Rogers reported that there
were "5,766 Nisei who renounced their citizenship and 5,409 have since
asked that it be returned. Only 357 failed to apply for a return of their
citizenship in the United States. So far 4,978 have recovered status as U.S.
citizens." Violet de Cristoforo was one of those who was repatriated with
her husband and found the experience profoundly disillusioning. "The war
devastated Japan, and we were not accepted in Japan either, first of all
because we were different." They were glad to return to the United States.
Much the same story was repeated thousands of times.

As time went on, Issei and Nisei both saw two challenges. The first
was to become, in Masuo Yasui's words, "100 percent Americans." The
other was to preserve (or in the case of many of the Nisei, recover) their
ancient Japanese heritage. In this connection it is agreeable to report that
Charles Kikuchi, our noble and endearing guide, settled in New York
after the war, married a Japanese American, Yuriko Amemiya, a modern
dancer from California, had a son and a daughter (also a dancer), got his
master's degree in social work from the New School, and worked as a
counselor and therapist for the Veterans Administration. And never lost
his zeal for good causes. Some thirty years later Kikuchi, in his Man-
hattan brownstone apartment, decorated his own "Japanese room," ta-
tami mats on the floor, no-shoes, everything. "Once there is no stigma,"
he told his friend and editor John Modell, "then why can't you have an
integrated society. . . . And if you want to have religion, food, so what?
. . . If my experience is closer to the majority culture, then that's the way
I ought to live. . . . [But] I wouldn't deny my own children some expo-
sure to the cultural background that they had." A little bit of the Japanesy
could only serve to evoke memories of that strange journey that Kikuchi
had made from the assembly center at the Tanforan racetrack to the
broader reaches of American life.

To Nisuke Mitsumori, looking back from the perspective of his eighty-four years, it seemed that the most important contribution of the Issei was that "they laid a foundation with their own efforts. Their efforts were fulfilled. Issei efforts and the hardships they went through are at the very basis of the prosperity the Japanese enjoy today and the fact that the Japanese-Americans have come a long way to the present situation. Their tears and sweat lie at the bottom."

While Isamu Nakamura's children all attended college and one earned a Ph.D. in microbiology, Nakamura worried that the Sansei were losing their sense of the value of their culture and tradition. The stories of the Issei and Nisei were "history" rather than vital elements of their own existence. Yet he took heart from the fact that "now they are accepted anywhere and everywhere" and among some of the Sansei there was "a movement of Japanese ethnic identity" and a renewed interest in the Issei. "I am strongly impressed," he told Heihachiro Takarabe, "by their thoughts and actions toward the Issei."

Within the Japanese American community itself there were deep wounds to heal. Time, as we know to our sorrow, does not heal all wounds. But it does give us the opportunity for second thoughts, for reconciliations. The occasions for redemption, for conversion if you will, are infinite, always there for the taking. Time does not heal all wounds, only justice and, beyond justice, compassion can heal wounds. And these the community discovered. Talking with Heihachiro Takarabe, Riici Satow recalled the blind Japanese evangelist who had preached at the Tanforan Assembly Center so many years ago, urging his listeners to keep their hopes alive and assuring them that when the war was over they would "have their day." "Gee, he is quite admirable to say such a thing. Here we are now," he told the Reverend Takarabe in 1974; "what he preached about at that meeting has come true. . . . It was when everybody was down and out in the camp that he told us that."

Yosishada Kawai told Heihachiro Takarabe: "Somehow the three years of suffering bore fruit. . . . After the war with the effort of the Nisei, we stood up with hope and courage, and we became not only the bridge between America and Japan, but also were to build the foundation for the future life of the Japanese people (*Yamato minzuku*) on this North American soil. I think the reason we were able to do this is because we were able to have such a good three years' retreat period.

"It has become our pride in that we were able to add to the building of the American nation, and have become a permanent page in its bright history."

Telling the great and moving story of his life to Takarabe, Kawai concluded: ''I do have such a background [as a Japanese] but also [I am] . . . very glad to feel honored as a good citizen of the United States. These glorious things I would like Nisei and Sansei and their children to keep permanently. This wish is not only that of the Japanese Christians but also the wishes of all Issei people.''

A Note on Sources

SOMETHING MUST BE SAID ABOUT THE MATERIALS AVAILABLE ON THE evacuation and relocation. The Wartime Civil Control Administration, an agency of the Western Defense Command, produced its *Final Report* some six months after it had turned the operation of the relocation centers over to the War Relocation Authority. Hastily cobbled together as it was, it contains a vast amount of essential material relating primarily to the establishment and operation of the assembly centers.

When the War Relocation Authority closed up shop in the fall of 1945, it was no less prompt in issuing a ten-volume series of reports on its custodianship of the relocation centers. The hero of this phase is Edward Holland Spicer, a professor of anthropology from the University of Arizona. As a community analyst, Spicer was an observer of much of what he wrote about in *Impounded People*. More important, the book and the series are imbued with the author's generous and humane spirit and his deep sympathy for the plight of the evacuees. I am pleased to acknowledge my debt to him in all aspects of this work dealing with life in the centers.

I have already taken note of the vast amount of material (over 450 filing cabinets) forwarded from the centers to the National Archives in the fall and winter of 1945–1946.

In addition, there was, of course, a large quantity of material, much of

it in the form of weekly reports from the community analyst, in the
Washington offices of the War Relocation Authority. There are also the
reports of the various Senate and House committees and subcommittees
under whose jurisdiction the centers fell.

Nine volumes of documents selected to buttress the case for redress
were published in 1989.

In addition, there are substantial quantities of material in the archives
of the Bancroft Library at the University of California, Berkeley, at the
Hoover Library at Stanford, at the University of California, Los Angeles,
Special Collections, and at the University of Arizona.

The JERS project was rather a flop. The first JERS volume, to appear
in 1946 entitled *The Spoilage,* was presented as a scientific study of ''the
ecology of 'disloyalty' '' and a ''point-by-point reproduction of stages in
the process of attitude formation.'' But people are not, after all, bugs or
amoebas to be examined under sociologists' or anthropologists' micro-
scopes. That is why the so-called social sciences are not ''sciences'' at
all. After the publication of *The Spoilage,* the JERS staff fell into one of
those unseemly academic brawls where the only thing at issue seems to
be the egos of professors. Morton Grodzins, a member of the JERS team,
broke ranks and wrote a polemical book, the burden of which was that the
evacuation was an example of American racism. He tried to get it published and Dorothy Thomas moved heaven and earth to prevent it. When
the University of Chicago Press agreed to print it, Robert Gordon Sproul,
president of the University of California, was prevailed upon to intervene
with the director of the University of Chicago Press to prevent its publication, presumably on the grounds that the material on which Grodzins's
book was based was the property of Dorothy Thomas and the University
of California. The book was published and Grodzins got tenure at the
University of Chicago.

Several years later (1952) another volume, much of it based on Charles
Kikuchi's interviews with evacuees who had gone out, was published
under the title *The Salvage.* Kikuchi's interviews are often enthralling
reading but the book itself never rises above the pedestrian and there is no
real effort to relate the multiplicity of experiences to one another in such
a way as to give the reader a sense of the reality of the whole experience
of evacuation and relocation. One senses that the major themes were too
vast and inchoate to be comprehensible, and the JERS staff too close to
them to have any real perspective. Flop or not, JERS did have the effect
of adding a vast amount of firsthand information to the material available
on the subject.

All in all, I think it safe to say that no event in history has been so thoroughly recorded. And that has clearly been a problem. Faced with a veritable mountain of documentary material that would take several lifetimes to master, historians (and "social scientists" of various denominations) have been limited to nibbling at the edges of the story, often more intent on confirming some a priori thesis than telling the full story.

The bibliography that follows is only a portion of published works dealing directly or indirectly with the evacuation.

Bibliography

American Baptist Quarterly. Vol. C, No. 2, June 1933. This issue is devoted to Jitsuo Morikawa, who was a Baptist minister in Poston.

American Concentration Camps. Vols. 1–9. These are documents relating to the evacuation of Japanese Americans, published at the direction of the Federal Commission on Wartime Relocation and Internment of Civilians, established in 1980.

Bailey, Paul. *City in the Sun: The Japanese Concentration Camp at Poston, Arizona*. Los Angeles, 1971.

Baker Lillian. *The Concentration Camp Conspiracy: A Second Pearl Harbor*. Glendale, CA: AFHA Publications, 1981.

Biddle, Francis. *In Brief Authority*. New York, 1962.

Chang, Thelma. *I Can Never Forget: Men of the 100th/442nd*. Honolulu, 1991.

Collins, Donald E. *Native American Aliens: Disloyalty and Renunciation of Citizenship by Japanese Americans During World War II*. Westport, CT, 1985.

Daniels, Roger. *Concentration Camps, North America: Japanese in the United States and Canada During World War II*. Melbourne, FL, 1981.

————. *Concentration Camps, USA: Japanese Americans and World War II.* New York.

Daniels, Roger, Sandra C. Taylor, and Harry H. L. Kitano. *Japanese Americans: From Relocation to Redress.* Salt Lake City: University of Utah Press, 1986.

Duveneck, Josephine Whitney. *Life on Two Levels: An Autobiography.* Los Altos, 1978.

Eaton, Allen. *Beauty Behind Barbed Wire.* New York, 1952.

Eisenhower, Milton. *The President Is Calling.* New York, 1974.

French, Fern. *Evacuated People: A Quantitative Description.*

Fukuzawa, Yukichi. *Autobiography.* Trans. Eechi Kiyooka. Columbia University Press, 1966.

Grodzins, Morton. *Americans Betrayed: Politics and the Japanese Evacuation.* Chicago, 1949.

Hosokawa, Bill, *JACL: In Search of Justice.* New York: William Morrow, 1982.

————. *Nisei: The Quiet Americans.* New York, 1969.

Houston, Jeanne Wakatsuki, and James Houston. *Farewell to Manzanar.* New York, 1966.

Ichioka, Yuji, ed. *Views from Within: The Japanese American Evacuation and Resettlement Study.* Los Angeles: Asian American Studies Center, UCLA, 1989. Papers from a two-day conference on JERS held at UC, Berkeley, 1987.

Department of the Interior. War Agency Liquidation Unit, Division of Budget and Administrative Management. *People in Motion: The Postwar Adjustment of Evacuated People.* (Prepared by Robert Cullum), 1947.

Issei Christians. Selected interviews from the Issei Oral History Project for the Centennial Celebration of the Japanese Christians of North America.

James, Thomas. *Exile Within: The Schooling of Japanese Americans, 1942–1945.* Cambridge: Harvard University Press, 1987.

Jansen, Marius B. *Japan and Its World: Two Centuries of Change.* Princeton: Princeton University Press, 1980.

————. *Sakamoto Ryoma and the Meiji Restoration.* Stanford University Press, 1971.

"Japanese American Internments: A Retrospective." *Friends Journal.* Vol. 38, No. 11, November 1992.

Kessler, Lauren. *Stubborn Twig.* New York, 1993.

Kikuchi, Charles. *The Kikuchi Diary: Chronicle From an American Con-centration Camp.* Edited by John Modell. University of Illinois Press, 1973.

Kitagawa, Diasuke. *Issei and Nisei: The Internment Years.* New York, 1967.

Koga, Sumio. *A Centennial Legacy: History of the Japanese Christian Missions in North America, 1877–1977.* Chicago, 1977.

Kutler, Stanley I. "At the Bar of History: Japanese Americans Versus the United States." *American Bar Foundation Research Journal* 2:361–73 (1985).

La Violette, Forrest E. *Americans of Japanese Ancestry: A Study of Assimilation in the American Community.* Canadian Institute of In-ternational Affairs, 1945.

Leighton, Alexander H. *The Governing of Men: General Principles and Recommendations Based on Experience at a Japanese Relocation Camp.* Princeton: Princeton University Press, 1945.

Lord, Charles R. "The Response of the Historic Peace Churches to the Internment of the Japanese Americans During World War II." The-sis submitted in partial fulfillment of the requirements for the Degree of Master of Arts in the Peace Studies Program, Associated Men-nonite Biblical Seminaries.

Masaoka, Mike, with Bill Hosokawa. *They Call Me Moses Masaoka: An American Saga.* New York, 1987.

Masaoka, Naoichi, ed. *Japan's Message to America: A Symposium by Representative Japanese on Japan and American-Japanese Rela-tions.* Tokyo, 1914.

McCloy, John J. "Repay U.S. Japanese?" *New York Times.* April 10, 1983.

Misawa, Steven, ed. *Beginnings: Japanese Americans in San Jose: 8 Oral Histories.* San Jose, CA, 1981.

Murphy, Thomas D. *Ambassadors in Arms.* Honolulu: University of Hawaii Press, 1946.

Myer, Dillon S. *Uprooted Americans.* University of Arizona Press, 1971.

McWilliams, Carey, *Prejudice: Japanese Americans, Symbol of Racial Intolerance.* Boston, 1944.

O'Brien, Robert W. *The College Nisei: Story of the National Japanese American Student Relocation Council.* Pacific Books, 1949.

Oda, James. *Heroic Struggles of Japanese Americans: Partisan Fighter from America's Concentration Camps.* North Hollywood: KNI, 1980.

Personal Justice Denied: Report of the Commission on Wartime Relocation and Internment of Civilians. Washington, 1982.

Rademaker, John Adrian. *These Are Americans: The Japanese Americans in Hawaii in World War II.* Palo Alto: Pacific Books, 1951.

Ringle, Kenneth D. [pseud., an intelligence officer]. "The Problem and Its Solution." *Harper's* 185:489–97 (1942).

Rostow, Eugene V. "The Japanese American Cases—A Disaster." *Yale Law Journal* 54:489–533 (1945).

Schilden, Robert. *Toyohiko Kagawa: Apostle of Love and Social Justice.* Berkeley, 1988.

Selective Service System. *Special Groups* (with bibliography) (by Campbell C. Johnson). Special Monograph 10, vol. 1; Appendices A–G, vol. 2, 1953. (Includes reports on the Japanese Americans and Selective service.)

Shirey, Orville C. *Americans: The Story of the 442nd Combat Team.* Washington, D.C.: The Infantry Journal, 1946.

Smith, Bradford. *Americans from Japan.* Philadelphia and New York: 1948.

Soyeshima, Yasoroku. *Essence of Bushido.* Tokyo: Herald Press, 1933.

Speir, Matthew Richard. *Japanese American Relocation Camp Colonization and Resistance to Resettlement: A Study in the Social Psychology of Ethnic Identity Under Stress.* University of California Press, 1965.

Spicer, Edward H., et al. *Impounded People: Japanese-Americans in the Relocation Centers.* Tucson: University of Arizona Press, 1969.

Sunada Sarasohn, Eileen, ed. *The Issei: Portrait of a Pioneer, An Oral History.* Pacific Books, 1983.

Suzuki, Lester. *Ministry in the Assembly and Relocation Centers of World War II.* Berkeley: Yardbird, 1979.

Tateishi, John. *And Justice for All: An Oral History of the Japanese American Detention Camps.* New York, 1984.

tenBroek, Jacobus, Edward N. Barnhart, and Floyd W. Matson. *Prejudice, War and the Constitution.* Berkeley and Los Angeles: University of California Press, 1954.

Thomas, Dorothy Swaine (and Richard Nishimoto) *The Spoilage: Japanese American Evacuation and Resettlement.* University of California Press, 1946.

Thomas, Dorothy Swaine (with the assistance of Charles Kikuchi and James Aadeda). *The Salvage.* University of California Press, 1952.

Department of War. *Japanese Evacuation from the West Coast, 1942* [General John DeWitt's final report], 1943.

Yoshima, Shizue, ed. *Nisei Christian Journey: Its Promise and Fulfillment*. Vols. 1 and 2. 1988. Published by Nisei Christian Oral History Project for the Japanese Presbyterian Conference and the Northern California Japanese Christian Church Foundation.

WAR RELOCATION AUTHORITY, U.S. DEPARTMENT OF INTERIOR, 1946 REPORTS:

Administrative Highlights of the WRA Program (prepared by Malcolm E. Pitts).

Community Government in the War Relocation Centers.

The Evacuated People: A Quantitative Description (prepared by Stauber and French).

Impounded People: Japanese Americans in the Relocation Centers (prepared by E. H. Spicer).

Legal and Constitutional Phases of the WRA Program (prepared by Glick and Ferguson).

The Relocation Program (prepared by H. Rex Lee).

Token Shipment: The Story of the War Refugee Shelter (prepared by Edward B. Marks, Jr.).

Wartime Exile: The Exclusion of Japanese Americans from the West Coast (prepared by Ruth McKee).

Wartime Handling of Evacuee Property.

WRA: The Story of Human Conservation (prepared by Morrill Tozier).

UNITED STATES CONGRESSIONAL HEARINGS AND REPORTS:

House of Representatives. Select Committee [Tolan] Investigating National Defense Migration. *Preliminary Report and Recommendations on Problem of Evacuation of Citizens and Aliens from Military Areas*. Report pursuant to H. Res. 113, 77th Cong., 2nd sess., March 10, 1942.

————. Special Committee [Costello] on Un-American Activities. *Military Views on Japanese War Relocation Centers*. Report and minority views [the minority views are those of Mr. Eberharter], H. Rep. 717, 78th Cong., 1st sess., Sept. 30, 1943.

————. Special Committee on Un-American Activities. *Investigations of Un-American Propaganda Activities in the United States*. Hearings on H. Res. 282 [77th Cong], 78th Cong., 1st sess. Appendix, Pt. S.,

Report on Axis Front Movement in U.S., 2nd sec., *Japanese Activities*, Nov. 1, 1943.

Senate. Military Affairs Committee, Subcommittee on Japanese War Relocation Centers. *Japanese War Relocation Centers*. Report on S. 444, and S. Res. 101 and 111, 78th Cong., 1st sess., May 7, 1943.

————. Military Affairs Committee. War Relocation Centers: Hearings before subcommittee on S. 444; 78th Cong., 1st sess, Nov. 24, 1943, 1944 [These hearings relate to events at Tule Lake center, Nov. 1–4, 1943].

————. Military Affairs Committee. War Relocation Centers: Hearings [January] before [Chandler] subcommittee on S. 444., 78th Cong., 2nd sess., March 6, 1943.

Index

About the Author

PAGE SMITH IS THE AWARD-WINNING AUTHOR OF NUMEROUS BOOKS on American history, including the eight-volume series *A People's History*.